ZAGAT.

World's Top
Restaurants
2008/09

Including 1,487 Restaurants in 58 Cities.
From the Diner's Point of View.

Published and distributed by
Zagat Survey, LLC
4 Columbus Circle
New York, NY 10019
T: 212.977.6000
E: world@zagat.com
www.zagat.com

D1497240

The reviews published in this guide
are based on public opinion
surveys. The numerical ratings
reflect the average scores given by
all survey participants who voted on
each establishment. The text is
based on direct quotes from, or fair
paraphrasings of, participants'
comments. Phone numbers,
addresses and other factual
information were correct to the best
of our knowledge when published
in this guide.

© 2008 Zagat Survey, LLC
ISBN-13: 978-1-57006-986-4
ISBN-10: 1-57006-986-7
Printed in the
United States of America

Contents

Ratings & Symbols

Zagat Top Spot	Name	Symbols		Cuisine		Zagat Ratings			
						FOOD	DECOR	SERVICE	COST

Area, Address & Contact

Z **Tim & Nina's** ◗ *Chinese*   ▽ 23 | 9 | 13 | I

W 50s | 4 Columbus Circle (8th Ave.) | 212-977-6000 | www.zagat.com

Review, surveyor comments in quotes

"You're the tapas" croon connoisseurs of the "cheap" cart-circulated Chinese-Castilian cuisine at this "cramped" concrete-clad Columbus Circle compound; to the contrary, critics claim Tim and Nina "push the concept too far" with dishes such as sweet-and-sour sardines, Sichuan ceviche and Beijing-Barcelona bouillabaisse, with service that comes from Spain in the '30s and China in the '60s.

Ratings

Food, Decor and **Service** are rated on the Zagat 0 to 30 scale.

0 – 9	poor to fair
10 – 15	fair to good
16 – 19	good to very good
20 – 25	very good to excellent
26 – 30	extraordinary to perfection
▽	low response	less reliable

Cost is estimated by the following symbols:

I	Inexpensive
M	Moderate
E	Expensive
VE	Very Expensive

A restaurant review listed without ratings is either a **newcomer** or survey **write-in**.

Symbols

Z	Zagat Top Spot (highest ratings, popularity and importance)
◗	serves after 11 PM
S	closed on Sunday
M	closed on Monday
⊄	no credit cards accepted

About This Survey

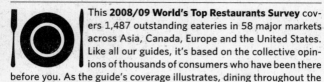

This **2008/09 World's Top Restaurants Survey** covers 1,487 outstanding eateries in 58 major markets across Asia, Canada, Europe and the United States. Like all our guides, it's based on the collective opinions of thousands of consumers who have been there before you. As the guide's coverage illustrates, dining throughout the world just keeps getting better and better.

WHO PARTICIPATED: Input from over 139,000 frequent diners forms the basis for the ratings and reviews in this guide (their comments are shown in quotation marks within the reviews). Of these surveyors, 45% are women, 55% men; the breakdown by age is 11% in their 20s; 28%, 30s; 22%, 40s; 22%, 50s; and 17%, 60s or above. Collectively they bring roughly 24 million annual meals worth of experience to this Survey. We sincerely thank each of these participants – in whatever language we put it, this book is really "theirs."

HELPFUL LISTS: While all the restaurants in this guide were chosen for their high quality, we have prepared two separate lists to facilitate your search: see Top Food Rankings by City (pages 7–10) and Most Popular by City (pages 11–14). We've also provided an Alphabetical Page Index (page 325).

ABOUT ZAGAT: This marks our 29th year reporting on the shared experiences of consumers like you. What started in 1979 as a hobby involving 200 of our friends has come a long way. Today we have well over 300,000 surveyors and now cover dining, entertaining, golf, hotels, movies, music, nightlife, resorts, shopping, spas, theater and tourist attractions worldwide.

SHARE YOUR OPINION: We invite you to join any of our upcoming surveys – just register at **ZAGAT.com,** where you can rate and review establishments year-round. Each participant will receive a free copy of the resulting guide when published.

AVAILABILITY: Zagat guides are available in all major bookstores, by subscription at **ZAGAT.com** and for use on web-enabled mobile devices via **ZAGAT TO GO** or **ZAGAT.mobi.** The latter two products allow you to contact your choice among many thousands of establishments by phone with just one click.

FEEDBACK: There is always room for improvement, thus we invite your comments and suggestions about any aspect of our performance. Is there something more you would like us to include in our guides? Did we get anything wrong? We really need your input! Just contact us at **world@zagat.com.**

New York, NY
April 16, 2008

Nina and Tim

Nina and Tim Zagat

What's New

This first-ever *World's Top Restaurants Survey* brings together the finest dining experiences across Asia, Canada, Europe and the United States. Designed to appeal to the upscale traveler as well as locals looking for their next culinary adventure, it covers the best and most popular places in 58 major cities.

QUALITY ON THE RISE: Wherever we look around the world the cooking just keeps getting better. Indeed, most commentators believe we are witnessing a "culinary revolution" supported by rising standards of living and the growth of service industries. That growth isn't surprising when you consider the nature of life in most cities today, where two-career couples are the norm and workplace demands keep rising, necessitating dining out several times a week. Fresh produce is now available year-round virtually anywhere, while the level of sophistication on the part of both chefs and restaurateurs is continually rising. The public's sophistication is growing as well, as diners travel more than ever before. And the level of innovation has never been greater. For example, Ferran Adrià of Spain's El Bulli restaurant.

OPTIONS ABOUND: As this guide illustrates, globalization has profoundly influenced the world's dining landscape. Virtually every city now has a robust mix of international cuisines. Consider that Osaka's No. 1 for Food is a French restaurant (Lumière), Toronto's is Japanese (Sushi Kaji) and in Moscow that honor goes to an Italian (Mario). Fortunately, most cities have managed to retain their unique culinary identities via restaurants and food that could exist nowhere but there. Take, for example, Moscow's Uzbekistan, featuring Uzbeki/Chinese cooking, and Honolulu's Hawaii Regional specialist, Alan Wong's. This expansion of cuisines in both global and local directions is good news for diners, since it adds to the diversity of options available.

GREEN CUISINE: It goes without saying that people around the world are increasingly concerned with issues such as global warming and sustainably raised food. In fact, a majority of our surveyors would like to see food that's better for them – and for the environment – coming out of restaurant kitchens. Sixty-five percent want trans fats abolished from restaurants, while 59% are actually willing to pay more for sustainably raised or procured produce. It seems restaurants are listening, since what is considered "modern food" is lighter, more health-conscious and more eco-friendly than ever before.

APPLES AND ORANGES: Finally, as much as we'd like to bestow the title World's Top Restaurant City, it's impossible to say that any one destination has the best food. While it's true that Hong Kong, London, New York, Paris and Tokyo are widely recognized for their outstanding dining, every one of the cities in this book is a winner in its own right in terms of quality, diversity and innovation.

New York, NY
April 16, 2008

Nina and Tim

Nina and Tim Zagat

Top Food Rankings by City

Based on a 30-pt. scale. Excludes places with low votes. See also listings at the start of each city section.

ASIA

BEIJING
- 27 Made in China
- 26 Taj Pavilion
- Alameda
- 25 Beijing Da Dong
- Danieli's

HONG KONG
- 28 Lung King Heen
- Sushi Hiro
- 27 Gaddi's
- Petrus
- L'Atelier de Joël Robuchon

OSAKA
- 29 Lumière
- 25 Agura

- Honkogetsu
- Arata
- La Baie

SHANGHAI
- 28 Hanagatami
- 26 Guyi Hunan
- Vedas
- Jean Georges
- Din Tai Fung

TOKYO
- 29 Jumbo
- 28 Rest. Hiramatsu
- Le Manoir d'Hastings
- Fregoli
- Araki

CANADA

MONTRÉAL
- 28 La Chronique
- 27 Milos
- Toqué!
- Le Club Chasse
- Ferreira

TORONTO
- 29 Sushi Kaji
- 28 Scaramouche

- Chiado/Antonio
- 27 North 44°
- Hiro Sushi

VANCOUVER
- 29 West
- 28 Lumière
- Bishop's
- Vij's
- Pear Tree

EUROPE

AMSTERDAM
- 28 Ron Blaauw
- 27 Yamazato
- Van Vlaanderen
- La Rive
- 26 Bordewijk

ATHENS
- 29 Spondi
- 26 48
- Varoulko
- 24 Sale e Pepe
- Pil Poul et Jérôme Serres

BARCELONA
- 28 Passadis del Pep
- Drolma
- Àbac
- 27 Gaig
- Alkimia

BERLIN
- 26 VAU
- 24 Lorenz Adlon
- Maxwell
- 23 Alt Luxemburg
- Die Quadriga*

---

* Indicates a tie with restaurant above

BRUSSELS

28	Comme Chez Soi
	Bruneau
27	La Truffe Noire
	Sea Grill
26	La Maison du Cygne

BUDAPEST

28	Baraka
	Vadrózsa
27	Páva
25	Lou-Lou
	Kacsa

COPENHAGEN

27	Era Ora
	Restaurationen
26	Søllerød Kro
	Kong Hans Kælder
25	Krogs Fiskerestaurant

DUBLIN

27	Thornton's
	Patrick Guilbaud
26	Seasons
25	L'Ecrivain
	One Pico

FLORENCE

27	Enoteca Pinchiorri
	La Giostra
26	Alle Murate
	Fuor d'Acqua
	Cibrèo

FRANKFURT

25	Gargantua
	Osteria Enoteca
24	Restaurant Français
23	Aubergine
	Sushimoto

GENEVA

29	Dom./Châteauvieux
26	Auberge du Lion d'Or
25	Patara
24	La Vendée
	Chez Jacky

HAMBURG

25	Haerlin
23	Jacobs
	Landhaus Scherrer
	Le Canard Nouveau
	Doc Cheng's

ISTANBUL

26	Borsa
25	Körfez
	Develi
	Seasons
	Tugra

LISBON

27	Varanda
	Ristorante Hotel Cipriani
	Sua Excelência
24	Gambrinus
	Casa da Comida

LONDON

28	Chez Bruce
	G. Ramsay/68 Royal
	Hunan
	Square, The
	Pétrus

MADRID

28	Santceloni
27	Zalacaín
	Goizeko
26	Príncipe de Viana
	Combarro

MILAN

29	Il Luogo/Aimo e Nadia
28	Sadler
27	Ristorante Cracco
25	Da Giacomo
	Boeucc

MOSCOW

25	Mario
24	Palazzo Ducale
23	Café Pushkin
	Cantinetta Antinori
22	Vogue Café

MUNICH

27	Tantris
25	Vue Maximilian
	Schuhbeck's
	Boettner's
24	Königshof

PARIS

28	Taillevent
	Le Cinq
	Guy Savoy
	L'Astrance
	Pierre Gagnaire

PRAGUE

- 26 Allegro
- 25 Aquarius
- David
- V Zátiší
- Essensia

ROME

- 26 Vivendo
- La Pergola
- Alberto Ciarla
- La Rosetta*
- Agata e Romeo

STOCKHOLM

- 28 Paul & Norbert
- Wedholms Fisk
- 27 F12
- 26 Lux Stockholm
- Ulriksdals Wärdshus

VENICE

- 27 Vini da Gigio
- 26 Da Ivo
- Osteria Da Fiore
- Corte Sconta
- 25 Fortuny

VIENNA

- 28 Steirereck
- 26 Imperial
- 25 Coburg
- 24 Demel
- Walter Bauer

WARSAW

- 25 Rest. Polska Tradycja
- Dom Polski
- 23 U Kucharzy
- Parmizzano's
- 22 Malinowa

ZURICH

- 27 Petermann's
- 26 Rest. Français
- Lindenhofkeller
- 24 Ginger
- Casa Aurelio

UNITED STATES

ATLANTA

- 29 Bacchanalia
- 28 Quinones Room
- Rathbun's
- Ritz/Buckhead Din. Rm.
- 27 Aria

BALTIMORE

- 28 Sushi Sono
- 27 Charleston
- Samos
- Peter's Inn
- Prime Rib

BOSTON

- 28 L'Espalier
- Oishii
- Clio/Uni
- 27 No. 9 Park
- Aujourd'hui

CHICAGO

- 29 Carlos'
- 28 Les Nomades
- Tru
- Alinea
- Tallgrass

DALLAS/FT. WORTH

- 28 French Room
- Tei Tei Robata
- Local
- Teppo Yakitori
- Abacus

DENVER/MTN. RESORTS

- 28 Mizuna
- Frasca
- Fruition
- Sushi Den
- 27 Sushi Sasa

HONOLULU

- 28 Alan Wong's
- 27 La Mer
- 26 Hoku's
- Roy's
- Chef Mavro

HOUSTON

- 28 Mark's American
- Da Marco
- 27 Tony's
- Kanomwan
- China View

KANSAS CITY

27 Bluestem
26 Oklahoma Joe's
Le Fou Frog
Tatsu's
40 Sardines

LAS VEGAS

28 L'Atelier de Joël Robuchon
Joël Robuchon
Rosemary's
Nobu
Todd's Unique Dining

LOS ANGELES

28 Mélisse
Nobu Malibu
Asanebo
27 Matsuhisa
Brandywine

MIAMI

28 Michy's
27 Palme d'Or
Nobu Miami Beach
Romeo's Cafe
Prime One Twelve

NEW ORLEANS

28 August
Brigtsen's
Bayona
Stella!
Cuvée

NEW YORK CITY

28 Daniel
Sushi Yasuda
Le Bernardin
Per Se
Peter Luger

ORLANDO

27 Le Coq au Vin
Victoria & Albert's
Chatham's Place
Del Frisco's
Taquitos Jalisco

PALM BEACH

27 Chez Jean-Pierre
Marcello's La Sirena
L'Escalier

Four Seasons
Little Moirs Food Shack

PHILADELPHIA

28 Fountain
Le Bar Lyonnais
Birchrunville Store
Le Bec-Fin
Vetri

PHOENIX/SCOTTSDALE

28 Pizzeria Bianco
Sea Saw
27 Binkley's
Barrio Cafe
T. Cook's

SAN DIEGO

28 Sushi Ota
WineSellar & Brasserie
27 El Bizcocho
Karen Krasne's
Pamplemousse Grille

SAN FRANCISCO BAY AREA

29 Gary Danko
French Laundry
28 Cyrus
Erna's Elderberry
Fleur de Lys

SEATTLE

29 Herbfarm, The
28 Mistral
Rover's
Cafe Juanita
Sitka & Spruce

ST. LOUIS

28 Sidney St. Cafe
Paul Manno's
27 Tony's
Trattoria Marcella
Niche

WASHINGTON, DC

29 Inn at Little Washington
28 Makoto
Citronelle
Marcel's
27 Eve

Most Popular by City

ASIA

BEIJING
1. Alameda
2. Din Tai Fung
3. Made in China
4. Beijing Da Dong
5. Courtyard, The

HONG KONG
1. Felix
2. Yung Kee
3. Gaddi's
4. Nobu
5. Spoon by Alain Ducasse

OSAKA
1. La Baie
2. Hagakure

3. Indian Curry
4. Calendrier
5. Ginpei

SHANGHAI
1. M on the Bund
2. Jean Georges
3. T8
4. Din Tai Fung
5. Laris

TOKYO
1. L'osier
2. Shotai-En
3. Ukai-tei
4. Kyubey
5. Sushi No Midori

CANADA

MONTRÉAL
1. Toqué!
2. Ferreira
3. Gibbys
4. L'Express
5. Chez L'Épicier

TORONTO
1. Canoe
2. North 44°

3. Scaramouche
4. Susur
5. Jamie Kennedy/Wine Bar

VANCOUVER
1. Lumière
2. C Restaurant
3. West
4. Bishop's
5. Vij's

EUROPE

AMSTERDAM
1. D'Vijff Vlieghen
2. Dylan, The
3. La Rive
4. Christophe'
5. De Kas

ATHENS
1. Spondi
2. Daphne's
3. GB Corner*
4. 48
5. Milos Athens*

BARCELONA
1. 7 Portes
2. Botafumeiro
3. Barceloneta
4. La Dama

5. Ca l'Isidre
6. Los Caracoles*

BERLIN
1. VAU
2. Borchardt
3. Lorenz Adlon
4. Margaux
5. Bacco/Bocca

BRUSSELS
1. Comme Chez Soi
2. Aux Armes/Bruxelles
3. Belga Queen
4. La Maison du Cygne
5. L'Ecailler/Palais Royal
6. L'Ogenblik*
7. Sea Grill*

BUDAPEST

1. Gundel
2. Páva
3. Kacsa
4. Café Kör
5. Centrál Kávéház
6. Spoon Café*

COPENHAGEN

1. Krogs Fiskerestaurant
2. Café Ketchup
3. Era Ora
4. Le Sommelier
5. Café Victor
6. Restaurationen*

DUBLIN

1. Patrick Guilbaud
2. Shanahan's
3. Seasons
4. Tea Room
5. Eden

FLORENCE

1. Enoteca Pinchiorri
2. Cibrèo
3. Il Latini
4. Villa San Michele
5. Cantinetta Antinori

FRANKFURT

1. Apfelwein Wagner
2. Holbein's
3. Edelweiss
4. Gargantua*
5. Aubergine

GENEVA

1. Auberge du Lion d'Or
2. Le Relais/l'Entrecôte*
3. Brasserie Lipp
4. Dom./Châteauvieux
5. Les Armures

HAMBURG

1. Jacobs
2. Doc Cheng's
3. Haerlin
4. Rive
5. Cox

ISTANBUL

1. Seasons
2. Tugra
3. Laledan
4. Körfez
5. Ulus 29

LISBON

1. Gambrinus
2. Bica do Sapato
3. Alcântara Café
4. Varanda
5. A Travessa

LONDON

1. Nobu London
2. G. Ramsay/68 Royal
3. J. Sheekey
4. G. Ramsay/Claridge's
5. Le Gavroche

MADRID

1. Botín
2. Zalacaín
3. Viridiana
4. Balzac
5. La Trainera*

MILAN

1. Bice
2. Ristorante Cracco
3. Armani/Nobu
4. Tratt. Bagutta
5. Il Teatro

MOSCOW

1. Café Pushkin
2. Galereya
3. Shinok
4. Scandinavia
5. Cantinetta Antinori

MUNICH

1. Tantris
2. Dallmayr
3. Königshof
4. Käfer-Schänke
5. Chinesischen Turm

PARIS

1. Taillevent
2. L'Atelier de Joël Robuchon
3. Le Grand Véfour
4. Alain Ducasse
5. La Tour d'Argent

PRAGUE

1. Kampa Park
2. Allegro
3. Bellevue
4. Pravda
5. U Modré Kachnicky

subscribe to ZAGAT.com

ROME

1. La Pergola
2. Imàgo
3. Harry's Bar
4. La Terrazza
5. Dal Bolognese

STOCKHOLM

1. Operakällaren
2. F12
3. Wedholms Fisk
4. Berns Asian
5. Sturehof*

VENICE

1. Harry's Bar
2. Fortuny
3. Osteria Da Fiore
4. La Terrazza
5. Al Covo

VIENNA

1. Demel
2. Steirereck
3. Imperial
4. Korso bei der Oper
5. Drei Husaren

WARSAW

1. Rest. Polska Tradycja
2. Belvedere
3. Blue Cactus
4. Dom Polski*
5. Malinowa

ZURICH

1. Kronenhalle
2. Petermann's
3. Widder
4. Brasserie Lipp
5. Rest. Français

UNITED STATES

ATLANTA

1. Bacchanalia
2. Rathbun's
3. Bone's
4. Chops/Lobster Bar
5. Aria

BALTIMORE

1. Clyde's
2. Ruth's Chris
3. Prime Rib
4. Charleston
5. McCormick & Schmick's

BOSTON

1. Legal Sea Foods
2. Blue Ginger
3. Hamersley's Bistro
4. L'Espalier
5. No. 9 Park

CHICAGO

1. Charlie Trotter's
2. Tru
3. Frontera Grill
4. Wildfire
5. Morton's

DALLAS/FT. WORTH

1. Abacus
2. Mi Cocina
3. French Room
4. Stephan Pyles*
5. Del Frisco's

DENVER/MTN. RESORTS

1. Frasca
2. Sweet Basil
3. Mizuna
4. rioja
5. Barolo Grill

HONOLULU

1. Alan Wong's
2. Roy's
3. Hoku's
4. La Mer
5. Duke's Canoe Club

HOUSTON

1. Mark's American
2. Carrabba's
3. Cafe Annie
4. Perry's Steak
5. Da Marco

KANSAS CITY

1. Fiorella's Jack Stack
2. Plaza III
3. Lidia's
4. McCormick & Schmick's
5. 40 Sardines

LAS VEGAS

1. Picasso
2. Bouchon
3. Delmonico Steak
4. Bellagio Buffet
5. Aureole

LOS ANGELES

1. Spago
2. A.O.C.
3. Café Bizou
4. Water Grill
5. Mélisse

MIAMI

1. Joe's Stone Crab
2. Prime One Twelve
3. Nobu Miami Beach
4. Blue Door
5. Barton G.

NEW ORLEANS

1. Galatoire's
2. Bayona
3. NOLA
4. Emeril's
5. Brennan's

NEW YORK CITY

1. Union Square Cafe
2. Gramercy Tavern
3. Le Bernardin
4. Babbo
5. Jean Georges

ORLANDO

1. California Grill
2. Emeril's Orlando
3. Seasons 52
4. Victoria & Albert's
5. Wolfgang Puck Café

PALM BEACH

1. Kee Grill
2. Abe & Louie's
3. Café Boulud
4. Chez Jean-Pierre
5. New York Prime

PHILADELPHIA

1. Buddakan
2. Le Bec-Fin
3. Fountain
4. Lacroix/Rittenhouse
5. Brasserie Perrier

PHOENIX/SCOTTSDALE

1. T. Cook's
2. Roy's
3. P.F. Chang's
4. Mary Elaine's
5. Mastro's Steak

SAN DIEGO

1. George's Ocean Terrace
2. Pamplemousse Grille
3. Prado at Balboa Park
4. Sammy's Woodfired Pizza
5. Roppongi

SAN FRANCISCO BAY AREA

1. Gary Danko
2. Boulevard
3. Slanted Door
4. French Laundry
5. Michael Mina

SEATTLE

1. Wild Ginger
2. Dahlia Lounge
3. Metropolitan Grill
4. Canlis
5. Restaurant Zoë

ST. LOUIS

1. Sidney St. Cafe
2. Annie Gunn's
3. 1111 Mississippi
4. Trattoria Marcella
5. Tony's

WASHINGTON, DC

1. Kinkead's
2. Citronelle
3. Jaleo
4. Zaytinya
5. TenPenh

ASIA
RESTAURANT
DIRECTORY

Beijing

TOP FOOD RANKING

	Restaurant	Cuisine
27	Made in China	Chinese
26	Taj Pavilion	Indian
	Alameda	Brazilian
25	Beijing Da Dong	Chinese
	Danieli's	Italian
	Din Tai Fung	Chinese
	Hatsune	Japanese
	Comptoirs de France	French
	Feiteng Yuxiang	Chinese
24	Pure Lotus	Vegetarian
	Liqun Roast Duck	Chinese
	Sichuan Provincial	Chinese
23	Courtyard, The	Eclectic
	Olive, The	European/Mediterranean
	Morel's	Belgian/French
	Haiku by Hatsune	Japanese
	Cafe Sambal	Malaysian
	South Beauty*	Chinese
	Crystal Jade Palace	Chinese
	Vineyard Cafe	European
	Yuxiang Renjia*	Chinese
22	Ba Guo Bu Yi	Chinese
	Orchard, The	Continental

Ⓩ Alameda *Brazilian*   **26 | 20 | 22 | M**

Chaoyang | Sanlitun Beijie (bet. Sanlitun Xiwujie & Sanlitun Xiliujie) | (86-10) 6417-8084

Trendy twenty- and thirtysomethings generate a "buzz" at Beijing's Most Popular restaurant, a "bustling" Brazilian whose "delicious-looking" crowd syncs up with the "chic", glass-walled Chaoyang setting and "consistently excellent" fare; overall, it's "hard to find better", especially factoring in the "gracious" service and "steal" of a lunch at 60 yuan.

Ba Guo Bu Yi *Chinese*   **22 | 20 | 20 | M**

Chaoyang | 10 Dongsanhuan Zhonglu (Jianguomenwai Dajie) | (86-10) 6567-2188
Dongcheng | 89-3 Di'anmen Dongdajie (Jiaodaokou Nandajie) | (86-10) 6400-8888
Haidian | Xinzhi Plaza | 28 Fucheng Lu (bet. Landianchang Nanlu & Xisanhuan Beilu) | (86-10) 8819-0088
Xicheng | 68 Nanxiaojie (Xizhimen Dajie) | (86-10) 6615-2230
www.baguobuyi.com

The tourists and locals who frequent this Chinese chain like its "great" variety of "excellent", "authentic" Sichuan dishes; an "attentive" staff and traditional 'face-changing' shows sweeten the deal.

---

* Indicates a tie with restaurant above

	FOOD	DECOR	SERVICE	COST

⚡ Beijing Da Dong *Chinese*

| 25 | 17 | 18 | M |

Chaoyang | Bldg. 3, Tuanjiehu Beikou, Dongsanhuan Lu (southeast corner of Changhong Qiao) | (86-10) 6582-2892
Dongcheng | Nanxincang Int'l Tower | 22 Dongsishitiao (bet. Chaoyangmen Beidajie & Chaoyangmen Beixiaojie) | (86-10) 5169-0329

"Spectacular Peking duck" that fans call "the best, hands down" is what this popular duo is prized for (they accept reservations only for the 6:30 PM seating – otherwise, expect a wait); the other Chinese fare is "thoroughly satisfying" too, so it's no wonder backers say they're "worth the trip from wherever you are"; P.S. the Dongcheng location features a glassed-in kitchen, and the Chaoyang setting is just as "modern."

Cafe Sambal ❂ *Malaysian*

| 23 | 20 | 21 | M |

Xicheng | 43 Doufuchi Hutong (Jiugulou Dajie) | (86-10) 6400-4875
Deemed the "perfect neighborhood hangout", this hip, rustic, "mellow" Malaysian in Xicheng dishes up "excellent", spicy fare paired with "warm" service; added attractions are the nearby Rear Lakes, around which pre- or post-dinner strolls are not uncommon.

Comptoirs de France ⊟ *French*

| 25 | 22 | 24 | I |

NEW **Chaoyang** | East Lake Villas | 35 Dongzhimenwai Dajie (Xindong Lu) | (86-10) 6461-1525
Chaoyang | Central Park Place, Bldg. 15 | 89 Jianguo Lu (Zhenzhi Lu) | (86-10) 6530-5480
www.comptoirsdefrance.com

"So hard to choose" say surveyors of all the "decadently tasty", "visually appealing" breads, croissants and sandwiches at these "oases of deliciousness" opened by the son of a French bread-baking family whose prices make it Beijing's No. 1 Bang for the Buck; the East Lake location offers more space than the *mignardise*-size Central Park outlet.

⚡ Courtyard, The *Eclectic*

| 23 | 26 | 24 | VE |

Dongcheng | 95 Donghuamen Dajie (bet. Beichizi Dajie & Nanchizi Dajie) | (86-10) 6526-8883 | www.courtyardbeijing.com

"As good as any top NYC restaurant", this "magical" "remodeled courtyard house" in Dongcheng boasts "spectacular" panoramas of "the Forbidden City and its surrounding moat" from a "cool" interior with high ceilings, "bright white" curtains, track lighting and "modern Chinese art"; the Eclectic cuisine, laying "Asian riffs on mostly Western food", is "expensive" but "worth it"; P.S. "don't miss" the upstairs cigar bar for the "best views."

Crystal Jade Palace *Chinese*

| 23 | 22 | 20 | M |

Dongcheng | Malls at Oriental Plaza | 1 Dong Chang'an Jie (bet. Dongdan Beidajie & Wangfujing Dajie) | (86-10) 8515-0238
Fans applaud the "fantastic variety" served up at this Dongcheng Chinese filled with "lovely" antiques; not only is it "well run", but the dim sum is "the best", so "what more could you ask for?"

⚡ Danieli's *Italian*

| 25 | 23 | 26 | VE |

Chaoyang | St. Regis | 21 Jianguomenwai Dajie (Ritan Lu) | (86-10) 6460-6688, ext. 2441 | www.stregis.com/beijing
"Superb" service (voted Beijing's No. 1), a "lavish" selection of "high-quality" (and "expensive") Italian cuisine and a "tremendous wine

	FOOD	DECOR	SERVICE	COST

list" make this a "perfect special-occasion destination" in Chaoyang; at press time, the restaurant and its home, the St. Regis, were closed for refurbishment (which may affect the Decor score) – look for a May 2008 reopening.

☒ Din Tai Fung *Chinese*

| 25 | 18 | 20 | M |

Chaoyang | 24 Xinyuan Xili Zhong Jie (bet. Xindong Lu & Zuojiazhuang Xijie) | (86-10) 6462-4502
NEW **Chaoyang** | Shin Kong Place | 87 Jianguo Lu, 6th fl. (bet. Dongsanhuan Zhonglu & Jintai Lu) | (86-10) 6533-1536
www.dintaifung.com

The "outstanding", "perfectly light" soup dumplings are "little pieces of heaven" say allies of this "bright, airy" Chaoyang Chinese pair hosting "huge" crowds; "quick", "attentive" service only increases the "good-value" factor; P.S. the upstairs kids' room (at Xinyuan Xili Zhong) is "a plus."

Feiteng Yuxiang ⇎ *Chinese*

| 25 | 17 | 15 | I |

Chaoyang | Chunxiu Lu (bet. Gongti Beilu & Xingfucun Zhonglu) | (86-10) 6415-3764 | www.ftyx.com

It's the "famed" shui zhu yu ('water-cooked fish', a misnomer since the fish is actually cooked in a lot of oil) that brings accolades to this Chaoyang site that, aside from its signature dish, cooks up other "consistently good", reasonably priced Sichuan-style fare for a hip, young clientele; snaring one of the sunken booths is a challenge – the place is "popular" and no reservations are taken.

Haiku by Hatsune *Japanese*

| 23 | 24 | 21 | E |

Chaoyang | Block 8 | 8 Chaoyang Gongyuan Xilu (bet. Liangmaqiao Lu & Nongzhanguan Nanlu) | (86-10) 6508-8585 | www.block8.cn

Located in the nightlife district near Chaoyang Park's west gate, this Japanese venture from Alan Wong (of Hatsune) is home to "amazing" cocktails, "flawless" sushi and "wonderful" cooked fare; the sparse space, set off in white and oak tones, draws local and foreign patrons, just about all of them ultrafashionable.

Hatsune *Japanese*

| 25 | 22 | 21 | M |

Chaoyang | Heqiao Bldg. C | Jia 8 Guanghua Lu, 2nd fl. (bet. Jintai Lu & Zhenzhi Lu) | (86-10) 6581-3939

Marrying a "slick" setting with "unique" fare, this second-floor address in Chaoyang is acclaimed for its "fresh", "addictive" "American-style" sushi ("throw authenticity to the wind, and you'll love it"); it's a "lunchtime favorite" too, thanks to the "great" deals.

Liqun Roast Duck *Chinese*

| 24 | 9 | 13 | M |

Dongcheng | 11 Beixiangfeng Hutong (Qianmen Dongdajie) | (86-10) 6705-5578

As the pictures in the corridors attest, everyone from Anthony Bourdain to Al Gore has sampled the famously "fabulous" duck roasted at this taste of the "real China" located in "what's left of" a "historic hutong" in Dongcheng (it's also known for "silky", "translucent" pancakes and "unhelpful service"); the "grease on the walls", "makeshift tables" and general "dilapidation" may prove "too authentic" for a few, but "for the adventuresome", it's "quite the experience."

	FOOD	DECOR	SERVICE	COST

☑ Made in China *Chinese*   27 | 26 | 24 | E

Dongcheng | Grand Hyatt | 1 Dong Chang'an Jie
(bet. Dongdan Beidajie & Wangfujing Dajie) |
(86-10) 6510-9608 | www.beijing.grand.hyatt.com
"Popular with tourists", but "far from a trap", this "elite" eatery in Dongcheng's Grand Hyatt serves the "best Peking duck in the whole wide world" – or so say surveyors who've voted all of the "outstanding" "fancified" Northern Chinese fare the No. 1 Food in Beijing; a dash of "fun" is added to the "stylish", "stunning setting" with multiple "glass-walled" kitchens to view (which you won't be able to enjoy unless you "reserve well ahead"); P.S. your local "friends will be shocked by the price tag."

Morel's ☑ *Belgian/French*   23 | 14 | 18 | M

Chaoyang | 27 Liangmaqiao Lu (Lucky St.) | (86-10) 6437-3939
Chaoyang | 5 Xinzhong Jie (Gongti Beilu, opposite Workers' Indoor Arena north gate) | (86-10) 6416-8802 ◗
www.morelsgroup.com
Cross the street from Workers' Indoor Arena in Chaoyang and, voilà, "you're in a small Brussels bistro" where "authentic Belgian" and French tastes abound in dishes like "succulent mussels", "juicy steak" and "awesome waffles", all "well worth the money" (and they're "not even that expensive!"); the decor strikes some as "corny" and space is "cramped", but the "fabulous beer selection" obliterates protests; N.B. the Liangmaqiao sibling has bigger tables better for large groups.

Olive, The *European/Mediterranean*   23 | 17 | 18 | M

Chaoyang | 17 Gongti Beilu (opposite Workers' Stadium north gate) |
(86-10) 6417-9669
Offering "healthier than average dining options" in Beijing, this "quaint eatery" across from Workers' Stadium in Chaoyang presents "fresh", "refreshing and flavorful" European and Mediterranean fare "cooked just right"; the "friendly" venue comprises several small rooms festooned with contemporary art, an open kitchen and a "relaxing" patio (the "perfect spot for brunch").

Orchard, The ☑ *Continental*   22 | 24 | 20 | M

Chaoyang | Shun Bai Lu (Hegezhuang Village) | (86-10) 6433-6270
About 45 minutes from the city center, this Continental "oasis for expats" in a Chaoyang suburb has the feel of a "countryside" home in which "fabulously decorated" rooms with antique furniture, black-and-white photographs and vaulted ceilings sprout from a central covered patio; much of the organic food is grown in the "perfectly pleasant" garden, and while all dishes are "prepared and presented with meticulous detail", the Sunday brunch buffet is "the best part."

Pure Lotus Vegetarian *Vegetarian*   24 | 23 | 22 | M

Chaoyang | 10 Nongzhanguan Nanlu (bet. Chaoyang Gongyuan Lu & Dongsanhuan Beilu) | (86-10) 6592-3627
Chaoyang | Holiday Inn Lido | 6 Jiangtai Lu (Fangyuan Xilu) |
(86-10) 6437-6688, ext. 3812
"How can this not be meat?" ask "amazed" carnivores when they taste what these monk-run Chaoyang veggie venues "accomplish": "intriguing", "inventive" dishes served in "stimulating artistic preparations";

FOOD | DECOR | SERVICE | COST

with stone statues, prayer wheels and incense, the "temple"-like Holiday Inn Lido locale is the more ornate, but both are completely "serene" and blessed with servers who "genuinely care."

Sichuan Provincial Government Restaurant ⊅ *Chinese*

24 | 11 | 12 | I

Dongcheng | 5 Gongyuan Toutiao (Jianguomennei Dajie) | (86-10) 6512-2277

"Have your last meal in Beijing" at this "real slice" of Sichuan life in Dongcheng, because "you won't get anything this authentic until your next trip" (the "fresh chile oil makes all the difference" in the "zingingly tasty" dishes); you'll have to "wait for ages" to get into the "chaotic", pink-plastic-tablecloth-bedecked "government building", but it's "worth" it for "some of the best", "cheapest" fare to be found.

South Beauty *Chinese*

23 | 20 | 19 | M

Chaoyang | Kerry Centre Mall | 1 Guanghua Lu (Dongsanhuan Zhonglu) | (86-10) 8529-9458

Chaoyang | China World Mall | 1 Jianguomenwai Dajie (Dongsanhuan Zhonglu) | (86-10) 6505-0809

Chaoyang | Henderson Ctr. | 18 Jianguomenwai Dajie (Beijingzhan Jie) | (86-10) 6518-7603 ❷

Chaoyang | Sunshine Plaza | 68 Anli Lu (Zhi Zhonglu) | (86-10) 6495-1201

Chaoyang | Pacific Century Place | Jia 2 Gongti Beilu (bet. Dongsanhuan Beilu & Sanlitun Nanlu) | (86-10) 6539-3502 www.qiaojiangnan.com

"With branches all over" China, this "popular", "dependable" chain's specialty is "spicy", "top-class Sichuan cuisine" with "bold, bright flavors"; "each one has different decor" – from "highly stylish" baroque to "innovative" "modern" minimalism – but all have plenty of private rooms that "work for large" business groups (and "professional service" to match); P.S. for fans who plead "please open some in Europe", plans are afoot, and in the U.S. to boot.

❷ Taj Pavilion, The *Indian*

26 | 21 | 25 | M

Chaoyang | China World Mall | 1 Jianguomenwai Dajie (Dongsanhuan Zhonglu) | (86-10) 6505-5866

Chaoyang | Holiday Inn Lido | 6 Jiangtai Lu, 3rd fl. (Fangyuan Xilu) | (86-10) 6436-7678 www.thetajpavilion.com

"Absolutely the best Indian food" in Beijing can be found at these "ideally located" Chaoyang destinations whose "gracious" owner not only ensures the "consistency" of the "high-quality" fare, but "adds warmth" to the already "fantastic" service; the China World Mall branch feels "authentic" with candlelight illuminating the intricate wood carvings on the wall, while the Holiday Inn Lido iteration is "nice and bright."

Vineyard Cafe Ⓜ *European*

23 | 18 | 17 | M

Dongcheng | 31 Wudaoying Hutong (Yonghegong Dajie) | (86-10) 6402-7961 | www.vineyardcafe.cn

"While away a lazy Sunday afternoon" (or anytime) at this "great getaway" "in a converted courtyard house" "nestled in the shadow of the Lama Temple" in Dongcheng – but "go early to secure a seat" (especially on the patio), because its "simple yet tasty", "generously portioned" European eats are "famous"; as its name suggests, wine is key, and the list is "always changing" and "affordable."

Yuxiang Renjia *Chinese*   23 | 15 | 15 | I

Chaoyang | Union Plaza | 20 Chaoyangmenwai Dajie, 5th fl. (east of Chaoyangmen Qiao) | (86-10) 6588-3841
Chaoyang | 5-2 Hepingli Dongjie (Sanhuan Lu) | (86-10) 8422-0807 ⊄
Chaoyang | Holiday Inn Lido | 6 Jiangtai Lu (Fangyuan Xilu) | (86-10) 6437-6688, ext. 1558
Dongcheng | New Dong'an Plaza | 138 Wangfujing Dajie (bet. Dong Chang'an Jie & Donghuamen Dajie) | (86-10) 6528-0668
Haidian | Zuo'an Gongshe (Haidian Qiao) | (86-10) 8267-6898
Xicheng | Parkson | 101 Fuxingmennei Dajie, 6th fl. (Jinrong Jie) | (86-10) 6602-3706 ⊄
www.yuxiangrenjia.com

"Order plenty of beer" (or "herbal tea") to "tame the fire" of the "hot, hot, hot" Sichuan fare "freshly prepared" at this "reliable chain" that draws "as many Chinese as Westerners" to its "kitschy" dining rooms; there's "usually a line" to get into some of the more popular locations (like Union Plaza), but it's "definitely worth it", considering how "inexpensive" it is.

Hong Kong

TOP FOOD RANKING

	Restaurant	Cuisine
28	Lung King Heen	Chinese
	Sushi Hiro	Japanese
27	Gaddi's	French
	Petrus	French
	L'Atelier de Joël Robuchon	French
26	Fook Lam Moon	Chinese
	Morton's	Steak
	Nadaman	Japanese
	Da Domenico	Italian
	Yan Toh Heen	Chinese
	Man Wah	Chinese
	Spring Moon*	Chinese
25	Mandarin Grill & Bar	Eclectic
	Caprice	French
	One Harbour Road	Chinese
	Nobu	Japanese
	Steak House	Steak
	Gaia Ristorante	Italian
	Dim Sum	Chinese
	Inagiku	Japanese
24	M at the Fringe	French/Mediterranean

Caprice *French*   25 | 27 | 26 | VE

Central | Four Seasons | 8 Finance St. (Connaught Rd.) | (852) 3196-8888 | www.fourseasons.com/hongkong

"One of the most beautiful" restaurants in all of Hong Kong is the Four Seasons' French establishment in Central, where you "enter through carved doors" onto a "glass walkway lit from below", and continue into an "elegant" room with "glorious views" of Victoria Harbour; when you factor in the "impeccable" service from an "attentive" staff, chef Vincent Thierry's (ex Le Cinq in Paris) "exquisite" Gallic cuisine and an "epic" wine selection, the result is a "wonderful", albeit "expensive", destination for celebrating any "special occasion."

Da Domenico *Italian*   26 | 14 | 15 | VE

Causeway Bay | Sunning Plaza | 8 Hoi Ping Rd. (Hysan Ave.) | (852) 2882-8013

"Simple but top-notch" Italian cooking and a "cult"-like following heavy on "tycoons and celebrities" are the claim to fame of this Causeway Bay scenester; everything down to the salt is "freshly flown in" from Italy – a mark of "authenticity" that's reflected in its "astronomical" prices – and while the "small" quarters are decidedly "down-to-earth" and the service "limited", nothing seems to stifle its "snob appeal."

---

* Indicates a tie with restaurant above

	FOOD	DECOR	SERVICE	COST

Dim Sum The Art Of Chinese Tidbits *Chinese* `25` `15` `20` `M`

Happy Valley | 63 Sing Woo Rd. (Shing Ping St.) | (852) 2834-8893
"Dim sum elevated to an art form" is the deal at this "tiny", no-frills Happy Valley standout that's a rare "24-hour" source for "fantastic", "quality" tidbits the likes of dumplings with shark fin or shu mai with gold leaf; it's *"gweilo*-friendly" (i.e. "English menu with pictures") and "has been discovered by everyone", so "come at off times to avoid long waits."

☑ Felix *Continental* `21` `27` `23` `VE`

Tsim Sha Tsui | The Peninsula | Salisbury Rd., 28th fl. (Nathan Rd.) | (852) 2315-3188 | www.hongkong.peninsula.com
Philippe Starck makes his way to Hong Kong via this "lavish" "hipster" atop Tsim Sha Tsui's Peninsula Hotel, where "jaw-dropping" 360-degree vistas of the harbor and city skyline meet "sexy" modern design with "stunning" results (and prices to match); maybe it's mostly about the "over-the-top atmosphere" and "beautiful-people" crowd here, but those who can focus on the Continental cuisine say it's "delicious"; N.B. "don't forget to check out" the "spectacular" men's WC, as well as the "must-visit" upstairs bar.

Fook Lam Moon Restaurant *Chinese* `26` `16` `21` `VE`

Wan Chai | Newman House | 35-46 Johnston Rd. (Luard Rd.) | (852) 2866-0633 | www.fooklammoon-grp.com
"Some of the best Cantonese food you can find in Hong Kong" comes out of the kitchen of this "old-school" Wan Chai institution known for its "to-die-for dim sum" and luxury specialties ("shark's fin soup, abalone", etc.); "upscale" prices and a "tycoon and *tai tai*"-heavy clientele have earned it the nickname the "millionaire's canteen", where "you must go with a regular" or service "can be lacking", but still to most it "doesn't get much better than this."

☑ Gaddi's *French* `27` `26` `29` `VE`

Tsim Sha Tsui | The Peninsula | Salisbury Rd. (Nathan Rd.) | (852) 2315-3171 | www.hongkong.peninsula.com
"Time stands still" (in a good way) at this "old-world", chandelier-bedecked "jewel box" in Tsim Sha Tsui's Peninsula Hotel, a "European palatial"–style "landmark" that's "as fancy and classically French as can be found in Hong Kong"; the "world-class" fare and decor are surpassed only by the near-"perfect" "formal" service (Hong Kong's No. 1), and while such "not-to-be-missed" experiences come at a "stiff price", the "rich-and-famous" types who dine here swear it's "worth every cent"; P.S. for "extraordinarily special occasions", book the chef's table in the kitchen.

Gaia Ristorante *Italian* `25` `23` `23` `VE`

Sheung Wan | Grand Millennium Plaza | 181 Queen's Rd. Central (Wing Wo St.) | (852) 2167-8200 | www.gaiaristorante.com
This "romantic" Italian "sanctuary" in a "quiet" corner of Sheung Wan is beloved for its "verdant" "outdoor terrace" complete with gurgling fountain, a fitting backdrop for its "simple" yet "divine" (and "expensive") dishes paired with "well-selected" wines; inside, its "dramatic" quarters are ruby-plush and offer a plethora of semi-private rooms, making it ideal for first dates as well as "special occasions and business dinners."

	FOOD	DECOR	SERVICE	COST

Inagiku *Japanese* ⎹ 25 ⎹ 24 ⎹ 23 ⎹ VE ⎹

Central | Four Seasons | 8 Finance St., 4th fl. (Connaught Rd.) |
(852) 2805-0600 | www.fourseasons.com/hongkong
Tsim Sha Tsui | Royal Garden Hotel | 69 Mody Rd., 1st fl. (Mody Ln.) |
(852) 2733-2933 | www.rghk.com.hk

Considered an all-around "class" act, this upscale hotel Japanese duo
in Central's Four Seasons and Tsim Sha Tsui's Royal Garden Hotel specializes in teppanyaki dishes and "lighter-than-air" tempura, but it
also boasts a sushi bar offering "fresh, varied" takes on the genre; it's
admired nearly as much for its "cool" decor and "wonderful" staff as
for its "excellent" cuisine, and though the experience will cost you,
most maintain "you get what you pay for."

Z NEW L'Atelier de Joël Robuchon *French* ⎹ 27 ⎹ 27 ⎹ 26 ⎹ VE ⎹

Central | The Landmark | 11 Pedder St., 4th fl. (Queen's Rd. Central) |
(852) 2166-9000 | www.joel-robuchon.com

"Spend your children's inheritance" for a "fabulous experience" at this
Joël Robuchon production in Central, where you "sit at the counter and
watch the show" unfold in the open kitchen producing a tasting menu of
"superbly executed", "modern" French cuisine in "small portions",
paired with one of the "best wine lists in town"; "beautiful, yet subdued"
decor graces the "impressive" space, and the service is "excellent."

Z Lung King Heen *Chinese* ⎹ 28 ⎹ 24 ⎹ 24 ⎹ E ⎹

Central | Four Seasons | 8 Finance St. (Connaught Rd.) | (852) 3196-8888 |
www.fourseasons.com/hongkong

"Everything from the menu is well executed" at this Chinese in the
Four Seasons in Central (rated Hong Kong's No. 1 for Food), where
"innovative", "top-notch" Cantonese cuisine and an "excellent
selection" of "scrumptious" dim sum are paired with an eclectic,
China-centric wine list, while "amazing views of the harbor" serve as
a backdrop to the "pretty", contemporary room accented with silver
and glass; it's "expensive", but most agree it's "worth it."

Mandarin Grill & Bar *Eclectic* ⎹ 25 ⎹ 24 ⎹ 27 ⎹ VE ⎹

Central | Mandarin Oriental | 5 Connaught Rd. (Ice House St.) |
(852) 2522-0111 | www.mandarinoriental.com/hongkong

A "sure winner every time", this "newly renovated", "expense-
account" Eclectic in Central's Mandarin Oriental is a "class act",
where the "attentive" staff has "everything down pat" and the kitchen
turns out "excellent" fare, including the "freshest sashimi and oysters"; the "addition of windows was a tremendous improvement" to
the "classic", "elegant" dining room, although a few prefer the old
"formal club" setting to the present "glass, chrome and marble" look.

Man Wah *Chinese* ⎹ 26 ⎹ 24 ⎹ 26 ⎹ VE ⎹

Central | Mandarin Oriental | 5 Connaught Rd. (Ice House St.) |
(852) 2522-0111 | www.mandarinoriental.com/hongkong

"Still worth a visit" after more than 40 years ("if you have the money"),
this "old standby" in the Mandarin Oriental in Central delivers "superb" "traditional" Cantonese cuisine and "excellent" service in an "elegant" room with a "spectacular view of the harbor"; while a few fault
the chef for "unimaginative" cooking, it's the "favorite" "upmarket
Chinese" of many others.

	FOOD	DECOR	SERVICE	COST

M at the Fringe *French/Mediterranean*   24 | 23 | 24 | VE

Central | 2 Lower Albert Rd. (Wyndham St.) | (852) 2877-4000 |
www.m-atthefringe.com

Fans "go out of their way" to this long-standing "gem" located above
the Fringe club, an art and performance space in Central, for a "romantic
meal with a special someone (or someone else)"; with "wonderful",
"imaginative" French/Med cuisine, including "superb" sucking pig, a
"fabulous" wine list, "subtle, refined" service and a "*très* stylish" space, it
"always lives up to expectations" and, no surprise, is "always quite full."

Morton's of Chicago *Steak*   26 | 22 | 25 | VE

Tsim Sha Tsui | Sheraton | 20 Nathan Rd. (Salisbury Rd.) | (852) 2732-2343 |
www.mortons.com

For a "taste of America" in Tsim Sha Tsui, carnivores commend this outpost of the chophouse chain in the Sheraton that cronies contend is a
"step above most locations in the U.S.", thanks to "excellent" steaks, a
"well-balanced wine list" and "prompt", "professional" service; the
"clubby, sophisticated" setting and "first-class view of the skyline" are
"icing on the cake", and though tabs are "hefty", many feel it's "worth it."

Nadaman *Japanese*   26 | 20 | 25 | VE

Admiralty | Island Shangri-La | Pacific Pl., 7th fl. (Supreme Court Rd.) |
(852) 2820-8570 | www.shangri-la.com/island

A crowd of mostly "old-money" and "business clientele" gravitates to
this "fabulous", "pricey" outpost of a venerable Tokyo-based Japanese
chain in Admiralty's Island Shangri-La hotel for "amazing", "masterful" kaiseki courses, including "excellent" Wagyu beef, and "impeccable" service; the space, a modern take on "traditional" decor from Japan,
includes sushi and teppanyaki counters and a private tatami room.

☑ Nobu *Japanese*   25 | 24 | 23 | VE

Tsim Sha Tsui | Intercontinental | 18 Salisbury Rd. (Ave. of Stars) |
(852) 2721-1211 | www.hongkong-ic.intercontinental.com

A "solid" addition to Nobu Matsuhisa's global "empire", this Tsim Sha
Tsui outpost offers "outstanding" "non-traditional" Japanese cuisine,
including a chef's menu that "always has something special" and
"fresh", "super" sushi; a "stellar" harbor view serves as a backdrop to
the Rockwell Group–designed space, which features an undulating
ceiling and bamboo-embedded terrazzo walls, while the service is
"quick and efficient."

One Harbour Road *Chinese*   25 | 24 | 26 | VE

Wan Chai | Grand Hyatt | 1 Harbour Rd. (Convention Ave.) |
(852) 2588-1234 | www.hongkong.grand.hyatt.com

"Impeccable" service, "high-quality" Cantonese fare (including "excellent" dim sum) and a "wonderful" space with a "spectacular view of
the harbor" win raves for this Chinese in the Grand Hyatt in Wan Chai;
it's "expensive", but that's "the price you pay" for "one of the best fine-
dining places on Hong Kong Island."

☑ Petrus *French*   27 | 26 | 27 | VE

Admiralty | Island Shangri-La | Pacific Pl., 56th fl. (Supreme Court Rd.) |
(852) 2820-8590 | www.shangri-la.com/island

"Expensive, but worth it" according to *amis*, this *haute* French in the
Island Shangri-La in Admiralty showcases "top-notch" toque Frederic

FOOD | DECOR | SERVICE | COST

Chabbert's "excellent", "inventive" cuisine, paired with an "amazing" wine selection; the "helpful staff" provides "impeccable" service, while "jaw-dropping views" of Victoria Harbour complement the "romantic", chandelier-lit room that some find a bit "gaudy"; while the tabs might approach the "Chinese GDP", most agree it's the "right place" to "impress a date or client."

☑ Spoon by Alain Ducasse *French*
23 | 25 | 25 | VE

Tsim Sha Tsui | Intercontinental | 18 Salisbury Rd. (Ave. of Stars) | (852) 2313-2256 | www.hongkong-ic.intercontinental.com

"Superb" food, "impeccable" service and a "breathtaking view of the harbor" make this "chic" French export in Tsim Sha Tsui's Intercontinental Hotel "a must for the total experience"; although some call the "eclectic" menu a bit "odd" (with "small portions") and wish that star chef "Alain would visit more often", most appreciate the "attention to detail and quality", recommending it for "impressing clients" on your "expense account" or for a "very special date"; P.S. "take a seat before 8 PM to enjoy the light show on the harbor."

Spring Moon *Chinese*
26 | 25 | 27 | VE

Tsim Sha Tsui | The Peninsula | Salisbury Rd. (Nathan Rd.) | (852) 2315-3160 | www.hongkong.peninsula.com

"Sublime" is the word on this "traditional" Cantonese in Tsim Sha Tsui that diners say "sets the standard for Chinese cuisine" across the country, with favorites including "fabulous dim sum" and "heavenly" Peking duck; its "exceptional Peninsula service", "classic art deco design" and "fine tea menu" further elevate the experience, making it well worth the "expensive" tab; N.B. jacket suggested.

Steak House *Steak*
25 | 24 | 26 | VE

Tsim Sha Tsui | Intercontinental | 18 Salisbury Rd. (Ave. of Stars) | (852) 2313-2405 | www.hongkong-ic.intercontinental.com

Fans tout this "expense-account" hotel chophouse in Tsim Sha Tsui the "coolest yet hottest steakhouse in Hong Kong", which offers patrons "multiple choices" of steak knives, mustards and salts to complement the "unbelievable" cuts from the Americas, Australia and Japan (including "Kobe beef to die for") and "fabulous salad bar"; oenophiles "love" the wine bar serving some 270 labels, and "proper" service enhances the "warm" ambiance in the otherwise "masculine" setting.

☑ Sushi Hiro *Japanese*
28 | 18 | 21 | VE

Causeway Bay | Henry House | 40-42 Yun Ping Rd., 10th fl. (Pak Sha Rd.) | (852) 2882-8752

It's "definitely one of the best sushi restaurants in town" declare diners about this find inside a Causeway Bay office building, serving "ultra-fresh fish" that keeps it "popular among a Japanese clientele"; the minimally decorated room is relaxed but formal enough for a business meal, and most agree the "expensive" tab is "reasonable" considering the "excellent" quality – plus "lunch is a great deal"; P.S. be sure to "book ahead."

Yan Toh Heen *Chinese*
26 | 26 | 28 | VE

Tsim Sha Tsui | Intercontinental | 18 Salisbury Rd. (Ave. of Stars) | (852) 2721-1211 | www.hongkong-ic.intercontinental.com

"Magnificent in every way", this Chinese set in Tsim Sha Tsui's Intercontinental Hotel is "true decadence", offering "top-notch" service, "splendid" Cantonese cuisine, including some of the "best dim sum in the world", and an "elegant, beautiful" space featuring "jade place settings" and "amazing" views of the harbor; not surprisingly, "you'll pay through the nose", but "oh, is it worth it."

Z Yung Kee *Chinese*   23 | 14 | 17 | M

Central | 32-40 Wellington St. (D'Aguilar St.) | (852) 2522-1624 | www.yungkee.com.hk

A "classic Hong Kong establishment", this "famous" Central landmark (circa 1942) is a "must-try for visitors", serving "generous" portions of "wonderful" "traditional" Cantonese cuisine, including "out-of-this-world" roast goose and "perfectly done" preserved eggs, that "packs in the crowds"; the scene gets "hectic" in the "large", "bright" space that can accommodate "families and large groups", but you "don't come here for the ambiance or service."

Osaka

Ζ Agura ●Ⓜ *Japanese*   **25 | 15 | 13 | M**

Honmachi | 4-8-7 Honmachi (Honmachi) | Chuo-ku | (81-6) 6253-1129 Ⓢ
Sakaisuji Honmachi | Excel 6 Bldg., 1st fl. | 2-4-9 Tokiwa-machi (Sakaisuji-Honmachi) | Chuo-ku | (81-6) 6943-0029

The staff at this pair of yakiniku specialists is "so confident" in the quality of their "first-rate", "delectable" meats that they recommend BBQ seasoned with nothing more than salt, and regulars agree, rating it a "cut above the competition" and a "terrific value for the money"; the "bright", "unpretentious" interiors and "pleasant" service round out the "satisfying" experience.

Ζ Arata ●ⓈⓂ⇆ *Japanese*   **25 | 7 | 13 | M**

Nishi-Nakajima | 4-2-8 Nishi-Nakajima (Nishinakajima-Minamigata) | Yodogawa-ku | (81-6) 6304-5250 | fsic.net/arata

The daily lineup of raw giblets is "awesome" and the hotpot "superb" at this Nishi-Nakajima Japanese organ-meat specialist, one of the "city's jewels", where there's often a line outside the no-frills digs because it doesn't take reservations; since the veteran proprietor is "not so young anymore", some concerned loyalists wish he would "limit his customers" and "take it easy."

Ζ Calendrier Ⓜ *French*   **24 | 21 | 23 | VE**

Honmachi | Ohara 3 Bldg., 1st fl. | 3-2-15 Honmachi (Honmachi) | Chuo-ku | (81-6) 6252-5010

This traditional French in Honmachi is the showcase for chef Ryozo Kadoguchi's "brilliantly crafted, yet unpretentious" cuisine that's "always reliable"; the disciplined, yet "casual" service is "in a word, lovely", and the atmosphere is "relaxed" in the "chic", if somewhat "narrow" room, leaving many feeling "fortunate" for the experience.

Chambord *French*

23 | 24 | 24 | VE

Nakanoshima | The Rihga Royal Hotel, 28th & 29th fls. | 5-3-68 Nakanoshima (Fukushima) | Kita-ku | (81-6) 6448-1121 | www.rihga.co.jp

"Everything is grand" at this "special-occasion" establishment in Nakanoshima's Rihga Royal Hotel – the "surprising" Gallic cuisine, "refined" interior and "impressive, yet low-key" service; aficionados attest the experience will show novices "what fine French dining is all about", and while it's "expensive", most agree it's "worth the cost."

Essence et Goût Ⓜ⇗ *French*

24 | 16 | 18 | M

Takatsuki | Forest Court, 1st fl. | 1-3-19 Tenjinmachi (Takatsuki) | Takatsuki-shi | (81-72) 685-0313

Carnivores "go out of their way" for some of the "region's best meats" served at this French located in a residential section of Takatsuki, where you "get a lot for your money", which is why landing a reservation "can be tricky"; the "warm" husband-and-wife team delivers "unpretentious" yet "surprisingly formal" service in the "tiny, casual" surroundings.

☑ Ginpei ⓏⓂ *Japanese*

21 | 13 | 13 | M

Doutonbori | RITZ Building, 1st fl. | 2-2-20 Doutonbori (Nanba) | Chuo-ku | (81-6) 6211-9825 ⇗
Shinsaibashi | 2 Bangai Building, 1st fl. | 2-1-10 Shinsaibashi (Shinsaibashi) | Chuo-ku | (81-6) 6214-0519
Dojima | Hatsune Building, 1st fl. | 1-5-4 Dojima (Umeda) | Kita-ku | (81-6) 6341-6000
www.ginpei.com

The "only spots in this part of town" you can get such "marvelous" seafood "at such prices", this Japanese chain based in the city of Wakayama serves fin fare as "fresh as you can get in a fishing port", including "wonderful" sashimi, "superb" boiled fish and the "masterpiece" *taimeshi* (sea bream and rice); prices are reduced after 8 PM, but if you come too late most items will be sold out; P.S. the Doutonbori branch's private rooms are "ideal for entertaining clients."

☑ Hagakure ⓈⓂ⇗ *Japanese*

21 | 7 | 11 | I

Umeda | Osaka Ekimae 3 Bldg., fl. B2 | 1-1-1 Umeda (Kitashinchi) | Kita-ku | (81-6) 6341-1409 | www.hagakure.cc

Devotees of Sanuki-style udon flock to this Umeda "mecca" for its "awesome" signature dish of "shiny, lovely" noodles in a "pure" soy sauce broth, and the "seconds on the house" also ensure "long lines all the time", but fortunately the "tables turn quickly" in the "cramped" space that's "not conducive to lingering"; the staff is "famous" for giving "lessons on how to eat" the pasta properly, but while some deem it "entertaining", critics find it "bothersome."

Honkitcho *Japanese*

23 | 22 | 22 | VE

Kitakyuhojimachi | 2-1-14 Kitakyuhojimachi (Sakaisuji Line Honmachi) | Chuo-ku | (81-6) 6261-8181 ⇗

(continued)

(continued)

Honkitcho

Koraibashi | 2-6-7 Koraibashi (Midosuji Line Yodoyabashi) | Chuo-ku | (81-6) 6231-1937 🄢🍴

Nishi-Shinsaibashi | Shinsaibashi OPA. 10th fl. | 1-4-3 Nishi-Shinsaibashi (Midosuji Line Shinsaibashi) | Chuo-ku | (81-6) 6258-3700

Chayamachi | Hotel Hankyu International, 25th fl. | 19-19 Chayamachi (Midosuji Line Nakatsu) | Kita-ku | (81-6) 6377-0888

Nakanoshima | Rihga Royal Hotel, fl. B1 | 5-3-68 Nakanoshima (Hanshin Line Fukushima) | Kita-ku | (81-6) 6448-3168

Tenmabashi | Imperial Hotel Osaka, 24th fl. | 1-8-50 Tenmabashi (JR Osaka Loop Line Sakuranomiya) | Kita-ku | (81-6) 6881-2900

Umeda | Daimaru Umeda, 14th fl. | 3-1-1 Umeda (JR Line Osaka) | Kita-ku | (81-6) 6347-0380

www.kitcho.com

One of the originators of the art of kaiseki, this venerable high-end Japanese chain combines "tradition and innovation" in its "impressive", "memorable" cuisine in settings that are "stylish", from the "tableware" to the "wall art", and "ideal for entertaining guests and clients"; in short, "everything is wonderful, even the prices"; N.B. the original Koraibashi and the Kitakyuhojimachi locations don't take plastic.

🄩 Honkogetsu 🄢 *Japanese*

| 25 | 22 | 17 | VE |

Doutonbori | Hozenji-Yokocho | 1-7-11 Doutonbori (Nanba) | Chuo-ku | (81-6) 6211-0201

Located in a "lovely" area of Doutonbori, this Japanese serves "artistic" presentations of "subtle" fare on "impressive" fine china; a few find the atmosphere a bit "tense" in the upscale room, but regulars advise sitting at the counter, where you can "chat with the chef."

🄩 Indian Curry 🄜🍴 *Indian/Japanese*

| 18 | 8 | 9 | I |

Kitahama | Kitahama Chuo Bldg., fl. B2 | 2-2-22 Kitahama (Kitahama) | Chuo-ku | (81-6) 6203-0370 🄢

Namba | 1-5-20 Namba (Namba) | Chuo-ku | (81-6) 6211-7630

Dojima | Dojima Abansa Bldg., fl. B | 1-6-20 Dojima (Kitashinchi) | Kita-ku | (81-6) 6345-5616 🄢

Nakanoshima | Asahi Shinbun Bldg. | 3-2-4 Nakanoshima (Higobashi) | Kita-ku | (81-6) 6202-5213 🄢

Sonezaki-Shinchi | Dojima Underground | 1 Sonezaki-Shinchi (Kitashinchi) | Kita-ku | (81-6) 6344-3941 🄢

Minami-Senba | Nagahori Underground, 2-8 | 2 Minami-Senba (Sakaisuji-Honmachi) | Chuo-ku | (81-6) 6282-2040

Shibata | Hankyu 3 Bangai | 1-3 Shibata (Umeda) | Kita-ku | (81-6) 6372-8813

www.indiancurry.jp

"Osaka soul food" is what surveyors call the Japanese-style curry at this 60-year-old Namba-based Eclectic destination that has earned a loyal following with its "addictive" signature cuisine that is "spicy, with a hint of sweetness"; according to some people, the staff is "insolent" and the "wretched" counter-only spaces "need improvement", but since the "food comes as soon as you sit down", it's "good for a quick bite", and "women can dine alone comfortably" here.

	FOOD	DECOR	SERVICE	COST

Ippo *Japanese* | 23 | 20 | 20 | VE |

Chayamachi | Hotel Hankyu International, 2nd fl. | 19-19 Chayamachi (Midosuji Line Nakatsu) | Kita-ku | (81-6) 6377-5540
Edobori | Higobashi IP Bldg. 1, 2nd fl. | 1-18-35 Edobori (Yotsubashi Line Higobashi) | Nishi-ku | (81-6) 6443-9135 🗷 🅼
www.ippoh.com

The tempura that's "prepared in front of you" "surpasses most others", even the complimentary souvenir of *tenkasu* (a garnish made from the coating), at this venerable institution (circa 1850) near Higobashi Station (with a somewhat more casual hotel branch in Chayamachi), and though the "prices are high, so is the quality"; the refined, VIP-suitable setting, with an interior boasting precious woods, is like "another world", and the private rooms are the "ultimate in comfort."

Iwansui 🗷 🅼 ⇷ *Chinese* | 24 | 12 | 8 | M |

Sakaisuji Honmachi | Osaka Honmachi Bldg., 1st fl. | 1-4-5 Azuchi-machi (Sakaisuji-honmachi) | Chuo-ku | (81-6) 6263-5190

An "exceptionally tough table" is this Chinese in Sakaisuji-Honmachi, where the "creative" and "flawless" cuisine comes complete with "lots of surprises"; though the tiny counter-only seating can accommodate no more than a dozen diners at a time, since the chef-owner is running a "one-man operation", service can still occasionally be "slow" and "inadequate."

Kahara 🗷 🅼 *Eclectic/French* | 24 | 18 | 18 | VE |

Sonezaki-Shinchi | Kishimoto Bldg., 2nd fl. | 1-9-2 Sonezaki-Shinchi (Kitashinchi) | Kita-ku | (81-6) 6345-6778

One of the "best in the Shinchi area", this popular, unassuming eight-seat counter outpost elicits "sighs" of appreciation from cognoscenti for all aspects of its innovative French-accented Eclectic fare, from the "high-quality ingredients to the preparations to the intriguing presentations" in attractive tableware; as an added bonus, the "edgy" proprietor "adds some flair" to the menu with his explanations.

Kashiwa-ya 🗷 *Japanese* | 24 | 23 | 20 | VE |

Senriyama-Nishi | 2-5-18 Senriyama-Nishi (Senriyama) | Suita-shi | (81-6) 6386-2234

While many surveyors report it's "hard to find" in a residential section of Senriyama-Nishi, as soon as you enter this veteran Japanese you find it as "relaxing as a country inn"; adding to the comfort level is the "authentic", "impressive" kaiseki menu that appeals to the "eyes as well as the palate", thanks to the "meticulous", "flawless" presentations.

Kuramata 🅼 *Chinese* | 24 | 25 | 23 | VE |

Daito | 6-4-17 Haizuka (Kounoike-Shinden) | Daito-shi | (81-72) 874-4323

Housed in a "splendid" traditional Japanese building in a residential section of Daito city, this Chinese venue (a sibling of Tokyo's Opus One) is "pricey" but "well worth the expense" for its original, seafood-centric cuisine and "corresponding" service; regulars would just as soon "keep it a secret" from the rest of the world.

	FOOD	DECOR	SERVICE	COST

Kyubey ⓜ *Japanese* — 23 | 19 | 19 | VE

Tenmabashi | Imperial Hotel Osaka, 24th fl. | 1-8-50 Tenmabashi (Sakuranomiya) | Kita-ku | (81-6) 6357-1388 | www.kyubey.jp

The "genuine" Edomae-style sushi at this outpost of the famous Ginza-based sushi chain housed in Tenmabashi's stately Imperial Hotel comes as a "shock" to vocal local Tokyo-bashers who grudgingly concede they've "never had anything that compares"; although the tabs can be "frightening", the "addictive" rolls and "fresh seasonal" offerings keep fans coming back.

🄴 La Baie *French* — 25 | 26 | 25 | VE

Umeda | The Ritz-Carlton Osaka, 5th fl. | 2-5-25 Umeda (Umeda) | Kita-ku | (81-6) 6343-7020 | www.ritz-carlton.co.jp

"Everything's superb" at the "Kansai region's exemplary high-end French", housed in the Ritz-Carlton Osaka, where the "delicate, inventive" cuisine is "memorable" and the atmosphere is "exceptional" in the "chic", "gorgeous" space; "no complaints" about the "warm, thoroughly attentive" service or the "abundant" wine list, which makes it a popular site for people "celebrating anniversaries."

La Becasse 🅂 *French* — 24 | 23 | 20 | VE

Koraibashi | Ginsenyokobori Bldg. | 4-2-6 Koraibashi (Yodoyabashi) | Chuo-ku | (81-6) 4707-0070

The "genuine article", this Koraibashi French near Yodoyabashi Station showcases chef Yoshinori Shibuya's "artistic", "refined" creations that are "impressive" for their "innovation" and "impeccable executions"; the "splendid" space is "dignified" yet "relaxing", the "thoughtful" service "unforgettable", and "for such a high-end" establishment, it's surprisingly "unpretentious."

La Tortuga 🅂ⓜ *French* — 24 | 13 | 14 | E

Koraibashi | 1-5-22 Koraibashi (Kitahama) | Chuo-ku | (81-6) 4706-7524

At this popular Koraibashi French near Kitahama Station, chef Hirokazu Mantani's cooking is the "pride of all Kansai bistros" according to fans, who are "astonished" by the "volume" of his menu offerings, at such "reasonable" prices, and "impressed" by his "rustic" cuisine (including game in season) that features "accents of Asia and Africa" in its presentations; less impressive, however, are the "cramped" quarters and "slow" service.

L'heure Bleue 🅂ⓜ *French* — 24 | 17 | 18 | E

Edobori | Line Bldg., 1st fl. | 1-19-2 Edobori (Higobashi) | Nishi-ku | (81-6) 6445-3233

"Everything's top-notch", from the "flavorful" vegetable dishes to the "magnificent" seafood, at this French spot near Edobori's Higobashi Station serving up "generous portions" of Gallic fare that make it an "excellent value"; in an open kitchen the chef "prepares meals in front of" customers while "entertaining" them with his "banter", adding to the comfort level in the "compact", "cozy" space.

🄴 Lumière 🅂ⓜ *French* — 29 | 29 | 29 | E

Higashi-Shinsaibashi | Unagidani-Block, 3rd fl. | 1-19-15 Higashi-Shinsaibashi (Shinsaibashi) | Chuo-ku | (81-6) 6251-4006 | www.k-coeur.com

This "shining new star" of the city's French dining scene, which opened at the end of 2006 in Higashi-Shinsaibashi, is Osaka's No. 1

	FOOD	DECOR	SERVICE	COST

for Food, Decor and Service; the "surprises keep coming" in chef Yasushi Karato's "bold, yet delicate use of produce" and "flamboyant", "complex" flavors, while the "high-end, yet comfortable" interior and "considerate" service are "consistent" with the stellar cuisine.

Ristorante Matsumura ⓜ⇄ *Italian*

24	13	15	E

Fukushima | Royal Heights Tango, 1st fl. | 1-2-1 Fukushima (Umeda) | Fukushima-ku | (81-6) 6455-7977

"Spot-on" northern Italian cuisine is showcased at this Fukushima *cucina*, including "can't-miss" meat dishes and "exceptional" pastas, all of which "reflect the chef's passion" for his craft; critics, though, are full of complaints about "haughty, overbearing" service and warn of cramped conditions in the tiny, eight-seat space.

Saisai ⓜ⇄ *Chinese*

23	14	16	M

Toyonaka | 195 Street Bldg. | 6-1-3 Honmachi (Toyonaka) | Toyonaka-shi | (81-6) 6852-2338

A "reliable" purveyor of Chinese fare, this spot near Inariyama Park in Toyonaka attracts fans with its "wonderfully seasoned", "outstanding" ma po tofu, which is "best paired" with *kogane chahan* (egg over fried rice), and a lunch set menu that's an "excellent value"; the atmosphere is mellow in the simple, no-frills digs.

Shanghai

TOP FOOD RANKING

	Restaurant	Cuisine
28	Hanagatami	Japanese
26	Guyi Hunan	Chinese
	Vedas	Indian
	Jean Georges	French
	Din Tai Fung	Chinese
25	Kitchen Salvatore Cuomo	Italian
	Palladio	Italian
	T8	Asian/Mediterranean
	Crystal Jade	Chinese
	Danieli's	Italian
	South Beauty 881	Chinese
	Yi Café	Eclectic
	Bukhara Grill	Indian
	Vegetarian Lifestyle*	Chinese/Vegetarian
24	Sens & Bund	French
	Di Shui Dong	Chinese
	Jade on 36	Eclectic/French
	Maneo	Eclectic
	Laris	Eclectic
	Nan Xiang	Chinese
	South Beauty	Chinese
23	1221	Chinese

Bukhara Grill *Indian*   25 | 20 | 23 | M

Gubei/Hongqiao | 3729 Hongmei Lu (Yan'an Xi Lu) | (86-21) 6446-8800
Granted, it's "a bit far" from the center of town, in the expat enclave of
Gubei, but this "consistently excellent", "family"-friendly Indian is
"worth the trip" for its "delicious, authentic" dishes and "professional,
friendly" staff; a pleasant bar/lounge on the ground floor broadcasts
sporting events on a giant flatscreen.

Crystal Jade *Chinese*   25 | 19 | 19 | M

Huaihai/Xintiandi | South Block Xintiandi | House 6-7, Ln. 123 Xingye Lu
(Madang Lu) | (86-21) 6385-8752
"Popular" is the word for this "always packed" Singapore import in
Xintiandi, where the Cantonese-Shanghainese offerings are "excellent" and "affordable", despite the "upscale" neighborhood; "don't be
put off by the shopping mall setting" – it's beside the point once they
roll out their "delicious" dim sum and "sublime" dumplings.

Danieli's *Italian*   25 | 24 | 25 | E

Pudong | St. Regis | 889 Dongfang Lu, 39th fl. (Weifang Lu) |
(86-21) 5050-4567 | www.stregis.com/shanghai
Although "a little out of the way", this "elegant" Italian in the St. Regis
Hotel is worth seeking out for an "impressive business dinner" owing

---

* Indicates a tie with restaurant above

to its "sublime" cooking and "fabulous view" of the Pudong from its 39th-floor perch; sure, "you'll definitely pay for it", but economizers tout the "reasonable" set-menu lunch and Sunday brunch, a "well-kept secret" featuring free-flowing champagne.

☑ Din Tai Fung Chinese
26 | 17 | 21 | M

Gubei/Hongqiao | Peace Sq. | 18 Shuicheng Lu (Hongqiao Lu) | (86-21) 6208-4188
Huaihai/Xintiandi | South Block Xintiandi | Unit 11, House 6, Ln. 123 Xingye Lu (Huangpi Lu) | (86-21) 6385-8378
www.dintaifung.com.tw

"Some of the best dumplings in the Far East" turn up at this "all-time favorite" Taiwanese chain serving "street food in restaurant settings", notably that "addictive" *xiaolongbao* that will "keep your mouth watering"; add in "quality service" and "modern" if "simple" decor, and it's no surprise that many say dining here is "mandatory for Shanghai newcomers."

Di Shui Dong ⌦ Chinese
24 | 11 | 13 | I

Xuhui | 5 Dongping Lu (Hengshan Lu) | (86-21) 6415-9448
Xuhui | 56 Maoming Nan Lu (Changle Lu) | (86-21) 6253-2689

"Cheap and tasty", this "popular" Xuhui duo serves "excellent" Hunan cuisine (in "spicy and not-too-spicy" versions) to a crowd of "locals and expats"; for some, the "alarmingly casual" settings may be too "downscale" and the acoustics too "boisterous", but a "big menu" brimming with "delicious" options and a "smiling if harried" staff help distract.

☑ Guyi Hunan Chinese
26 | 12 | 15 | M

Jing An | 87 Fumin Lu (Julu Lu) | (86-21) 6249-5628

"If you like it spicy", check out this "fiery hot" Hunan in Jing An that's "popular with locals", who "keep a few bottles of beer handy" to "cool their throats"; it's a "bustling, noisy" scene with "prices that are a throwback to the '50s", so naturally, "ridiculous lines" and "long waits" come with the territory.

☑ Hanagatami Japanese
28 | 21 | 26 | VE

Jing An | Portman Ritz-Carlton | 1376 Nanjing Xi Lu (Xikang Lu) | (86-21) 6279-8888 | www.ritzcarlton.com

What could be Shanghai's "best sushi bar" lies in this Japanese "marvel" in Jing An's Portman Ritz-Carlton that also offers kaiseki, teppanyaki and a variety of sakes in a "comfortable" yet sophisticated space done up with plenty of light wood and screen dividers; maybe you'll wind up paying "higher-than-Japan" prices, but this "excellent" place does take Top Food (and Top Service) honors in our Shanghai Survey.

Jade on 36 Eclectic/French
24 | 26 | 24 | VE

Pudong | Pudong Shangri-La | 33 Fucheng Lu, 36th fl. (Huayuanshiqiao Lu) | (86-21) 6882-3636 | www.jadeon36.com

The "food is as spectacular" as the "stunning", picture-postcard views of the Bund from this glamorous 36th-floor aerie in the Pudong Shangri-La hotel, where chef Paul Pairet concocts "unique" French-Eclectic dishes that are truly "out of the ordinary" (think foams, infusions, etc.) and served in pricey, prix-fixe-only menus; "impeccable service" and "inspirational" decor via Adam Tihany enhance the "crème de la crème" mood, leading many to swoon "does it get any better than this?"

	FOOD	DECOR	SERVICE	COST

☑ Jean Georges *French*   26 | 27 | 26 | VE

Huangpu | Three on the Bund | 3 Zhongshan Dong Yi Lu (Guangdong Lu) |
(86-21) 6321-7733 | www.jean-georges.com

"Impress the boss or the wife (or both)" at Jean-Georges
Vongerichten's "wow"-inducing French "splurge", a "world-class dining experience" set in Huangpu's "sophisticated" Three on the Bund
complex; look for "exceptional" New French cooking, "super-attentive
service", a "must-see" Michael Graves setting that includes a "million-
dollar view" of the river and the "new Shanghai", and "money-is-no-
object" pricing, of course.

Kitchen Salvatore Cuomo *Italian*   25 | 23 | 21 | E

Pudong | 2967 Lujiazui Xi Lu (Fenghu Lu) | (86-21) 5054-1265

The eponymous Naples-born chef brings his Japanese franchise to
Shanghai via this "authentic Italian" set along the river in Pudong with
an "absolutely spectacular view of the Bund"; the "modern" menu (including some of the "best pizza" in the city) lives up to the "exceptional" setting, as does the "attentive staff."

☑ Laris *Eclectic*   24 | 25 | 24 | VE

Huangpu | Three on the Bund | 3 Zhongshan Dong Yi Lu (Guangdong Lu) |
(86-21) 6321-9922 | www.threeonthebund.com

Australian chef David Laris is the brains behind this "elegant" Eclectic
with "stunning" river views parked in the swell Three on the Bund complex; given the "incredibly imaginative" seafood-centric menu, "attentive" service and "ultramodern", "white-on-white" decor courtesy of
Michael Graves, it's no surprise that all this "high class comes with high
tabs", but that doesn't seem to faze its "international" following one bit.

Maneo *Eclectic*   24 | 23 | 21 | E

Jing An | 333 Tongren Lu (Beijing Xi Lu) | (86-21) 6247-9666 |
www.maneo.com.cn

Parked under Mint nightclub on Jing An's Tongren Road, this "quality"
Eclectic features the "California-inspired", "down-to-earth" cooking
of San Francisco chef Brad Turley; the minimalist, "stark white" space
set in an old art deco mansion is "great for entertaining", with a well-
stocked champagne bar as part of the package.

☑ M on the Bund *Continental/Eclectic*   21 | 25 | 23 | VE

Huangpu | 5 Zhongshan Dong Yi Lu, 7th fl. (Guangdong Lu) |
(86-21) 6350-9988 | www.m-onthebund.com

Swells seeking the "chic side of Shanghai" tout this circa-1999 Bund
"trailblazer" that's still a "place to be seen" thanks to a "delicious"
Continental-Eclectic menu, "knock-your-socks-off" river views from
its outdoor terrace and the newly revamped Glamour Bar downstairs
that some call an even "better scene"; sure, a few critics carp "you're
paying for the address" not the "unspectacular" food, but then again,
this "institution" was voted Most Popular in our Shanghai Survey.

Nan Xiang ⊅ *Chinese*   24 | 13 | 14 | I

Old Town | Yu Gdn. | 85 Yuyuan Lu (adjacent to the Bridge of Nine Turnings) |
(86-21) 6355-4206

"Be prepared to push and shove" for a taste of the "heavenly" soup
dumplings (*xiaolongbao*) at this "tourist"-heavy Shanghainese triplex
opposite Yu Gardens; while the crowds can be "unbearable" at the

	FOOD	DECOR	SERVICE	COST

ground-floor take-out counter, the more comfortable upper floors offer sit-down dining with "better service" but "higher prices."

Palladio *Italian*

| 25 | 23 | 25 | VE |

Jing An | Portman Ritz-Carlton | 1376 Nanjing Xi Lu (Xikang Lu) | (86-21) 6279-8888 | www.ritzcarlton.com

"Exactly what you would expect from a restaurant in the Ritz-Carlton", this Jing An "special-occasion" Italian offers "flawless food" (from a wood-burning oven–equipped kitchen), "great service" and, "of course, high prices"; swanky decor incorporating Palladian arches and columns and an "exceptional wine list" make it a natural for everything from power lunches to romantic suppers.

Sens & Bund *French*

| 24 | 24 | 25 | VE |

Huangpu | Bund 18 | 18 Zhongshan Dong Yi Lu, 6th fl. (Nanjing Dong Lu) | (86-21) 6323-9898 | www.sensandbund.com

Situated "directly on the Bund", this "world-class" restaurant from Jacques and Laurent Pourcel (of Le Jardin des Sens in Montpellier, France) lives up to its "first-rate" billing with "classy", avant-garde French food served in a "posh", "jet set"–ready setting; add in "terrific service" and "fantastic" terrace views of the "futuristic Pudong skyline", and the "costly" tabs don't sting so much; P.S. the prix fixe lunch menu is a "good deal."

South Beauty *Chinese*

| 24 | 23 | 18 | M |

Gubei/Hongqiao | 100 Zunyi Lu (Tianshan Lu) | (86-21) 6237-2891
Luwan | Times Sq. | 99 Huaihai Zhong Lu, 5th fl. (Pu'an Lu) | (86-21) 6391-0890
Pudong | Super Brand Mall | 168 Lujiazui Xi Lu (Fucheng Lu) | (86-21) 5047-1817
Xuhui | 28-1 Taojiang Lu (Hengshan Lu) | (86-21) 6445-2581
www.qiaojiangnan.com

"Not for the timid", this Beijing-based chain specializes in "fiery hot" "modern Szechuan" cooking ("leave your tongue at home") hailing from Southwest China; the staff "really tries", and thanks to the "rich flavors", "hip settings" and "classy" vibes, these are naturals for "showing off to foreign guests."

South Beauty 881 *Chinese*

| 25 | 27 | 17 | E |

Jing An | 881 Yan'an Zhong Lu (Shanxi Nan Lu) | (86-21) 3222-0118 | www.qiaojiangnan.com

This "splashy" Jing An branch of the fast-growing chain offers "terrific" Szechuan dishes in a "beautiful" setting incorporating two buildings: a "elegantly renovated" period mansion and an ultramodern glass-lined garden house; the menu's heavy on seafood – and very spicy and rather pricey – but it's the glamorous old Shanghai vibe that draws in the movers, the shakers and the deep-pocketed "out-of-towners."

⚡ T8 ◑ *Asian/Mediterranean*

| 25 | 27 | 23 | VE |

Huaihai/Xintiandi | North Block Xintiandi | House 8, Ln. 181 Taicang Lu (Huangpi Nan Lu) | (86-21) 6355-8999 | www.t8shanghai.com

"High style" is alive and well at this "magical" Xintiandi "class act", one of the "most decorated" places in town, where the "elegant" setting complete with a "fun" open-fronted glass kitchen is matched by a "fancy" fusion menu of Asian and Mediterranean dishes, an "interest-

	FOOD	DECOR	SERVICE	COST

ing wine list" and service that runs as "smoothly as a Swiss clock"; ok, it's "definitely not cheap", but that doesn't seem to faze patrons of this "expat heaven" one bit.

1221 *Chinese*

| 23 | 17 | 21 | M |

Changning | 1221 Yan'an Xi Lu (Panyu Lu) | (86-21) 6213-6585

"Targeted to foreigners", this chic Changning Shanghainese is a "popular expatriate hangout" where the homestyle offerings may be "slightly tailored to non-Chinese palates" but are still plenty "authentic"; hidden "at the end of an alley", it's "not so easy to find" but worth seeking out for its "friendly service" and overall "good value."

☒ Vedas *Indian*

| 26 | 22 | 21 | M |

Luwan | 550 Jianguo Xi Lu (Wulumuqi Lu) | (86-39) 6445-8100 | www.vedascuisine.com

The unbeatable recipe of "great food" and "good prices" keeps the trade brisk at this much admired French Concession Indian that seals the deal with a spacious, classy setting that avoids the usual curryhouse decor clichés; a moodily lit bar area is ideal for pre-dinner drinks, while those hoping for entertainment with their meal can peer through a glass partition into the kitchen to see the chefs in action.

Vegetarian Lifestyle *Chinese/Vegetarian*

| 25 | 16 | 17 | I |

Gubei/Hongqiao | 77 Songshan Lu, 1st fl. (Huaihai Zhong Lu) | (86-21) 6384-8000
Gubei/Hongqiao | 848 Huangjincheng Dao (Shuicheng Nan Lu) | (86-21) 6275-1798
Jing An | 258 Fengxian Lu (Nanjing Xi Lu) | (86-21) 6215-7566 | www.jujubetree.com

"Traditional" Chinese dishes "prepared only with vegetables" fill out the menu of this "pleasant" mini-chain where they do a good enough job to "fool the most discernable carnivore" while supplying real "value for your money"; P.S. in keeping with the overall "healthy" mindset, the "no-smoking rules are strictly enforced" here.

Yi Café *Eclectic*

| 25 | 22 | 21 | E |

Pudong | Pudong Shangri-La | 33 Fucheng Lu (Huayuanshiqiao Lu) | (86-21) 6882-8888, ext. 210 | www.shangri-la.com

"Eat yourself silly" at this "something-for-everyone" Eclectic buffet in the Pudong Shangri-La Hotel, where the walk-through layout is designed to replicate a public market equipped with "multiple food stations" from around the globe; there's also an "impressive array of desserts" and a candy counter geared toward small fry.

Tokyo

TOP FOOD RANKING

	Restaurant	Cuisine
29	Jumbo	Japanese
28	Rest. Hiramatsu	French
	Le Manoir d'Hastings	European
	Fregoli	Eclectic
	Araki	Japanese
	K.u.K	Austrian
	Shofuku-ro*	Japanese
	La Bouef	Japanese
	La Tourelle	French
27	Casa Vinitalia	Italian
	Kiraku-tei	Korean
	Shotai-En	Japanese
	Uguisudani-En	Japanese
	Stamina-En	Japanese
	Kinoshita	French
	Obana	Japanese
	La Table De Com,ma	French/Seafood
	Les Saisons	French
	Trattoria della Lanterna Magica*	Italian

☑ Araki Ⓜ⇄ Japanese   28 | 25 | 26 | VE

Nakamachi | Kaminoge Little Town 102 | 4-27-1 Nakamachi (Yoga) | Setagaya-ku | (81-3) 3705-2256

The owner of this Nakamachi sushi spot near Yoga Station is a "dead-eye at selecting the best fish", and every handmade morsel will "show you how good" the "real thing" can be; it's strictly omakase, and while some are put off by "not being given any choices", the "entertaining" service is "top-notch", with everyone getting "equal treatment"; the space holds only 12 seats at a counter, so it's "tough to get a reservation."

Casa Vinitalia ◑Ⓜ Italian   27 | 26 | 25 | VE

Minami-Azabu | M Tower | 1-7-31 Minami-Azabu, 2nd fl. (Azabu-Juban) | Minato-ku | (81-3) 5439-4110 | www.vinitalia.jp

Though you'll have to reserve "three months in advance", this Minami-Azabu Italian near Azabu-Juban Station is a "worthwhile experience", with chef Shinji Harada creating "masterpieces" with "seasonal ingredients" that'll "tempt you to overindulge"; oenophiles salute the "knowledgeable" sommelier, while "spacious" seating and "impeccable" service from a staff that's "attentive without being overbearing" also win praise.

☑ Fregoli ◑☒Ⓜ Eclectic   28 | 16 | 19 | E

Ebisu | 2-8-9 Ebisu (Ebisu) | Shibuya-ku | (81-3) 5423-1225

"Dynamic", creative Euro-accented Eclectic fare appeals to "hearty appetites" at this Ebisu establishment, which features "wonderful"

---

* Indicates a tie with restaurant above

dishes including horsemeat, and whets a "thirst for sake" among many; the owner, a native of Kyushu, and his assistant "run the show by themselves", "maintaining a proper distance" from diners and creating a "comfortable" vibe.

⚡ Jumbo ⇔ *Japanese*   29 | 12 | 19 | E

Shirokane | Dai-ichi Azabu Bldg. | 3-1-1 Shirokane (Shirokane-Takanawa) | Minato-ku | 03-5795-4129 | www.y-jumbo.com
Shinozakimachi | 4-13-19 Shinozakimachi (Shinozaki) | Edogawa-ku | (81-3) 3679-8929 | www.yakiniku-jambo.com ● Ⓜ

Voted No. 1 for Food in Tokyo, this yakiniku duo has the "best selection" of beef "in town", including unusual shoulder and top loin cuts, but whatever you order, "you can't go wrong"; the owner at the Shinozaki original wins props for his "tutorials on grilling", even if some find him "obnoxious", and while the branch location may be more "attractive" than its elder sibling, many find its "Shirokane price tags" a bit "presumptuous."

Kinoshita Ⓜ⇔ *French*   27 | 17 | 22 | E

Yoyogi | Yoyogi Estate Bldg. | 3-37-1 Yoyogi, 1st fl. (Sangubashi) | Shibuya-ku | (81-3) 3376-5336

"Charming" chef-owner Kazuhiko Kinoshita creates "rich, hearty" French cuisine at his eponymous spot in Yoyogi, and while his "reliable" dishes reflect his "dedication" to his craft, the "user-friendly" prices make some regulars "wonder how he stays in business"; his "thoughtful hospitality" is another reason for the restaurant's "steady popularity", as well as the constant "difficulty in getting a reservation."

Kiraku-tei ● Ⓜ *Korean*   27 | 17 | 17 | E

Minami-Azabu | Minami-Azabu Bldg. | 4-11-26 Minami-Azabu, fl. B1 (Hiroo) | Minato-ku

"Even the middling cuts" of Kuroge *wagyu* beef are "terrific" at this "laid-back" yakiniku spot in Minami-Azabu near Hiroo Station that resembles an "underground lair", where waiters resembling "teen idols" provide "lively" and "prompt" service; "reasonable" prices "for what you get" also make it a "standout."

K.u.K ⊠Ⓜ *Austrian*   28 | 27 | 27 | VE

Akasaka | 1-4-6 Akasaka (Tameike-Sanno) | Minato-ku | (81-3) 3582-6622

"Without peer – even in Vienna" gush groupies of this "first-rate" Austrian located near Akasaka's Tameike-Sanno Station, serving that country's wines and dishes, including a "perfectly seasoned" ham that's "sliced at your table"; the chandelier-lit space has a "luxuriousness" that "adults" will appreciate, and the "relaxed", "friendly" service also wins praise.

⚡ Kyubey Ⓜ *Japanese*   27 | 22 | 23 | VE

Kioicho | Hotel New Otani, Garden Tower, lobby | 4-1 Kioicho (Akasaka-Mitsuke) | Chiyoda-ku | (81-3) 3221-4144
Kioicho | Hotel New Otani, main floor lobby | 4-1 Kioicho (Yotsuya) | Chiyoda-ku | (81-3) 3221-4145
Ginza | 8-7-6 Ginza (Shinbashi) | Chuo-ku | (81-3) 3571-6523 ⊠
Toranomon | Hotel Okura Tokyo, Main Bldg. | 2-10-4 Toranomon. 5th fl. (Toranomon) | Minato-ku | (81-3) 3505-6067

(continued)

Kyubey

Nishi-Shinjuku | Keio Plaza Hotel Main Tower | 2-2-1 Nishi-Shinjuku. 7th fl.
(Tochou-mae) | Shinjuku-ku | (81-3) 3344-0315
www.kyubey.jp

"Always excellent", this sushi chain serves "insanely fresh" seafood that makes "other places' pale in comparison", while the Ginza mother ship has "amazing" atmosphere and fans "tip their caps" to the service there and at the luxe hotel branches; still, "everything comes at a price", but for those "nervous" about the tabs, regulars recommend "lunch" or the "good-value omakase" menu.

La Bouef Ⓜ *Japanese*   28 | 13 | 18 | E

Nakamachi | 5-21-8 Nakamachi (Yoga) | Setagaya-ku | (81-3) 5707-0291 |
www.la-bouef.com

The beef at this yakiniku spot in Nakamachi is some of the "best in the city" according to carnivores who find the "thick slabs" "more like steaks than BBQ meat" and the beef liver sashimi "incomparable"; despite the "inconvenient" location, the "line never ends", but thanks to the "thoughtful" staff, you "never feel neglected", even during peak times.

La Table De Com,ma Ⓜ *French/Seafood*   27 | 23 | 20 | VE

Komazawa | Nakamura Bldg., 1st fl. | 1-16-7 Komazawa
(Komazawa Daigaku) | Setagaya-ku | (81-3) 3418-1011 | www.comma.co.jp

"Farm-fresh" organic produce from a contract grower are emphasized in the "carefully prepared" French cuisine at this Komazawa stand-alone spot where "ladies who lunch" like to "gaze at the Japanese garden" in the courtyard; oenophiles praise the "superb" wine list, while teetotalers tout the herbal tea as a "revelation."

La Tourelle Ⓜ *French*   28 | 18 | 25 | VE

Kagurazaka | 6-8 Kagurazaka (Kagurazaka) | Shinjuku-ku |
(81-3) 3267-2120 | www.tourelle.jp

At this "refined" stand-alone French in Kagurazaka, you almost "feel like Marie Antoinette" (pre-Revolution, we assume) thanks to the chef's "first-class" cuisine and nearly "perfect" service from a "witty" staff; regulars report "no drop-off" since the departure of original owner Tadaaki Shimizu, and oenophiles give "high marks" to the helpful sommelier.

Ⓩ Le Manoir d'Hastings Ⓜ *European*   28 | 21 | 22 | VE

Ginza | 8-12-15 Ginza (Shinbashi) | Chuo-ku | (81-3) 3248-6776

This Ginza French close to Shinbashi Station is "shockingly good every time", according to fans especially enamored with the "flawless, novel" variety meats and "first-rate" game in season, which are presented, along with other dishes, "like artwork on the plate"; as you depart the "warm", rouge-based room, the "dedicated" staff will "see you off long after you're out of sight."

Les Saisons Ⓜ *French*   27 | 23 | 27 | VE

Uchisaiwaicho | Imperial Hotel, Main Building Mezzanine |
1-1-1 Uchisaiwaicho (Hibiya) | Chiyoda-ku | (81-3) 3539-8087 |
www.imperialhotel.co.jp

At the Imperial Hotel's haute French establishment, chef Thierry Voisin's "innovative" yet "authentic" Gallic cuisine is "creative and intoxicating", including dishes such as the "must-try" duck and "excep-

	FOOD	DECOR	SERVICE	COST

tional" *poisson*, while the desserts also "pack a punch"; the sleek "contemporary" interior and "meticulous" service are what many have "come to expect" from this "venerable" Uchisaiwaicho landmark.

☑ L'osier ☒Ⓜ *French*   `26` `26` `27` `VE`

Ginza | 7-5-5 Ginza (Gizna, Shinbashi) | Chuo-ku | (81-3) 3571-6050 | www.shiseido.co.jp/losier

"Always superb" cuisine and "highly gratifying" atmosphere and service make this Ginza French one of the "best in the country" and Tokyo's Most Popular; the service is "top-notch" and "flawless", and "friendly" for such a "luxe" establishment, while chef Bruno Menard's "delectable", "visually pleasing" fare is at once "classic" and "innovative"; from the "moment you enter" the sumptuous digs, you "feel like a VIP."

Obana Ⓜ⇄ *Japanese*   `27` `16` `14` `M`

Minami-Senju | 5-33-1 Minami-Senju (Minami-Senju) | Arakawa-ku | (81-3) 3801-4670

"Expect to wait two hours" or "even three on the Day of the Ox" (the first day of summer in the lunar calendar) at this "out-of-the-way" Minami-Senju unagi institution that "refuses to take reservations"; eel enthusiasts brave lines for "impressive", "tender" fish that'll make you "wonder what you've been eating all your life", served on "tiny" *chabudai* tables in a "time-warp" space that "doesn't encourage lingering."

☑ Restaurant Hiramatsu Ⓜ *French*   `28` `28` `28` `VE`

Minami-Azabu | 5-15-13 Minami-Azabu (Hiroo) | Minato-ku | (81-3) 3444-3967 | www.hiramatsu.co.jp

"Everything is grand" at this haute French in Minami-Azabu near Hiroo Station thanks to "diligent, magnificent" hospitality, "artistic" dishes that are "beautiful" as well as "delicious" and the sommelier's pairing recommendations, which are "right on the money"; the "superb furnishings and paintings" add to the "luxurious" atmosphere.

Shofuku-ro Ⓜ *Japanese*   `28` `21` `22` `VE`

Marunouchi | Maru Bldg. | 2-4-1 Marunouchi, 36th fl. (Tokyo) | Chiyoda-ku | (81-3) 3240-0003 | www.shofukuro.jp

Located on the top floor of Marunouchi's Maru Building, Tokyo's top-rated Japanese serves "simple but beautiful", "first-class" dishes made with the "best ingredients", all of them offering the most "elegant flavors"; the "traditional" decor is "so relaxing, you forget you're in a high-rise", although the private rooms are divided only with partitions, which could be a "problem if you have a loud neighbor"; more gregarious types "recommend sitting at the counter."

☑ Shotai-En Ⓜ *Japanese*   `27` `17` `17` `E`

Machiya | AN Machiya 102 | 1-20-9 Machiya (Machiya) | Arakawa-ku | (81-3) 5901-2929 ●
Machiya | 8-7-6 Machiya (Machiya) | Arakawa-ku | (81-3) 3895-2423
Ginza | Cheers Ginza | 5-9-5 Ginza, 9th fl. (Ginza) | Chuo-ku | (81-3) 6274-5003 ●

Carnivores call this Machiya-based yakiniku chain a "top-notch value", serving up cuts such as the top loin that you "must reserve in advance" and the "melt-in-your-mouth" kalbi, all of them "so fresh" you "can eat them raw"; while the original Machiya location looks a bit "run-down", the branches are "stylish" and "clean", and "suitable for dates."

	FOOD	DECOR	SERVICE	COST

Stamina-En Ⓜ�'''➑ *Japanese* | 27 | 6 | 13 | E

Shikahama | 3-13-4 Shikahama (Ouji) | Adachi-ku | (81-3) 3897-0416 |
www.mode-web.jp/sutamina

Despite a Shikahama address so "out of the way" "you won't believe
you're still in Tokyo" and waits that "rival the lines at Disneyland", fans
insist this yakiniku spot is "well worth it" for "tender, delicious" BBQ beef
and "melt-in-your-mouth" organ meats; devotees are so smitten that
even the "beach house"–like digs and "lousy" service seem "charming."

ⓩ Sushi No Midori Sohonten Ⓜ *Japanese* | 21 | 12 | 13 | M

Ginza | Ginza Corridor Gai, 1st fl. | 7-108 Ginza (Shinbashi) | Chuo-ku |
(81-3) 5568-1212
Tamagawa | Tamagawa Takashimaya Main Bldg. | 3-17-1 Tamagawa, 6th fl.
(Futagotamagawa) | Setagaya-ku | (81-3) 3708-8282
Umegaoka | 1-20-7 Umegaoka (Umegaoka) | Setagaya-ku |
(81-3) 3429-0066
Umegaoka | 1-25-6 Umegaoka (Umegaoka) | Setagaya-ku |
(81-3) 3425-1122
Dogenzaka | Shibuya Mark City East | 1-12-3 Dogenzaka, 4th fl. (Shibuya) |
Shibuya-ku | (81-3) 5458-0002
www.sushi-no-midori.jp

With its original location in Umegaoka, this sushi chain offers a "great
deal" with prices that are "affordable for all", "generous" portions and
"fresh" ingredients, evident in dishes such as the popular glazed
anago; though "long lines" are to be expected at all branches, devotees keep coming back for the "bargain" fare.

Trattoria della Lanterna Magica ●ⓍⓂ *Italian* | 27 | 20 | 22 | E

Kami-Ozaki | T&H Memory | 2-9-26 Kami-Ozaki, 1st fl. (Meguro) |
Shinagawa-ku | (81-3) 6408-1488

A "hideaway" in a residential section of Kami-Ozaki, just minutes from
Meguro Station, this "authentic" Italian offers "outstanding value"
along with a "lively" atmosphere and "cheerful" service; regulars who
fear that it'll soon "be impossible to get a table" here would just as
soon "keep mum about this place."

Uguisudani-En ●Ⓜ➑ *Japanese* | 27 | 8 | 12 | M

Negishi | 1-5-15 Negishi (Uguisudani) | Taito-ku | (81-3) 3874-8717
Acclaimed Maezawa beef at "rock-bottom prices" is served at this
yakinikuist near Uguisudani Station in Negishi, where the "thick" signature filet "blows your mind", and the "cheaper cuts hit the spot" as
well, including the skirt steak that often "sells out early"; the BBQ'd
meat makes up for the "tiny" digs and "poor" service.

ⓩ Ukai-tei *Japanese* | 25 | 24 | 24 | VE

Ginza | Jijitsushin Bldg. | 5-15-8 Ginza, 1st fl. (Higashi-Ginza) | Chuo-ku |
(81-3) 3544-5252 Ⓜ
Akatsukicho | 2-14-6 Akatsukicho (Hachioji) | Hachioji-Shi |
(011-81) 426-26-1166
www.ukai.co.jp

It's easy to "order too much" from the "generous" à la carte menu at
these teppanyaki "kings" serving "outstanding" grilled surf 'n' turf; set
in a renovated "merchant's house", the Hachioji location is like a
"work of art" with "verdant" views, while the Ginza sibling is "wonderful" as an "after-work" stop, thanks largely to "impeccable" service.

CANADA
RESTAURANT
DIRECTORY

Montréal

TOP FOOD RANKING

	Restaurant	Cuisine
28	La Chronique	Eclectic/Québécois
27	Milos	Greek
	Toqué!	Québécois
	Le Club Chasse	Eclectic/Québécois
	Ferreira	Portuguese
26	Joe Beef	French/Seafood
	Moishe's Steak	Steak
	La Colombe	French
	Laloux	French
25	Au Pied de Cochon	French/Québécois
	Ginger	Pan-Asian
	Le Jolifou	French/Mexican
	Chez L'Épicier	Eclectic
	Mikado	Japanese
	Nuances	French
	Les Chenêts	French
	Chao Phraya	Thai
24	Queue de Cheval	Seafood/Steak
	L'Express	French
	Leméac	French

Au Pied de Cochon ●Ⓜ *French/Québécois* 25 | 18 | 22 | E

Plateau Mont-Royal | 536, ave. Duluth Est (rue St-Hubert) | 514-281-1114 | www.restaurantaupieddecochon.ca

A "cult" of "little piggies" (the name means 'at the pig's foot') promotes the "heavy but oh-so-delicious" dishes of *enfant terrible* chef-owner Martin Picard at his Plateau French brasserie–"meets–rural Québec" "temple to excess"; the menu stars foie gras in "more ways than you can imagine", plus such theatrical presentations as "superb duck in a can" and "delicious risotto in a wheel of Parmesan" (offered in the fall); "enthusiastic waiters" and an open kitchen add to the "party atmosphere."

Chao Phraya *Thai* 25 | 19 | 20 | M

Mile End | 50, ave. Laurier Ouest (rue St-Urbain) | 514-272-5339 | www.chao-phraya.com

The "flavors actually do explode in your mouth" agree acolytes who come to this "neighborhood favorite" on a "pretty" Mile End street for the "best Thai food in Montréal"; after nearly 20 years it's "still a pacesetter", offering "upscale, quality" dishes, including a signature crispy spinach, "spiced as requested" and served by a "thoughtful, attentive staff"; all this, in a sleek setting, is especially "nice to visit with a group."

Ⓩ Chez L'Épicier *Eclectic* 25 | 22 | 23 | E

Old Montréal | 311, rue St-Paul Est (rue St-Claude) | 514-878-2232 | www.chezlepicier.com

You know a place is "haute" "when the chef-owner comes out of the kitchen to a standing ovation" – a not-uncommon occurrence at

Laurent Godbout's "quaint renovated storefront" in Old Montréal; locals love "to take out-of-towners" here for "fanciful, fresh-market,
French-influenced" Eclectic fare (say, a chocolate club sandwich and
pineapple fries) and "quirky presentations" (e.g. appetizers served in
"tiny wooden boxes with drawers"); it "has a store too, where you can
buy wonderful", "obscure ingredients."

🔢 Ferreira Café 🗷 *Portuguese* **27 | 24 | 23 | VE**
Downtown | 1446, rue Peel (rue Ste-Catherine O.) | 514-848-0988 |
www.ferreiracafe.com

"Flawless" "fresh fish grilled simply" and "a festive atmosphere" will
"transport you to the Azores" at this "ritzy", high-priced "Portuguese
wonder" Downtown; the "hopping" "power scene" can get "clamor-
ous" when "the music is cranked up", but the "nice staff" and sunny-
hued "smart setting" also "exude warmth", so even "if you're alone,
you won't feel out of place eating at the bar" or sampling some of
the "interesting ports."

🔢 Gibbys *Seafood/Steak* **23 | 22 | 23 | E**
Old Montréal | Youville Stables | 298, pl. d'Youville (rue du Port) |
514-282-1837 | www.gibbys.com

"Dependable" "super-sized" "steakhouse standards" and "fresh seafood" served with a smile in a "weathered stone edifice" ensure this
18th-century "converted stable" "never disappoints"; "it's a little senior citizen/tourist-y" and, like its former equine occupants, gotten
"long in the tooth" foes fume, but worshipers whinny with pleasure at
this "ode to Old Montréal."

Ginger *Pan-Asian* **25 | 21 | 21 | E**
Plateau Mont-Royal | 16, ave. des Pins Est (boul. St-Laurent) | 514-844-2121

Some of "the best damn sushi in Montréal", plus Pan-Asian dishes
with a "modern edge", is sliced up at this "small" specialist whose
quarters "close to the St-Laurent action" means it's "always full of
beautiful people, but without the chichiness"; partiers proclaim the
"staff is a riot", especially after a "great lychee martini" or two.

Joe Beef 🗷Ⓜ *French/Seafood* **26 | 19 | 23 | VE**
St-Henri | 2491, rue Notre-Dame Ouest (bet. rues Charlevoix & Vinet) |
514-935-6504 | www.joebeef.ca

"With that name, you'd never expect seafood, but that's what they specialize in" at this St-Henri "hot spot" opened by "chef-owner *célèbres*"
Frederic Morin and David McMillan "of Globe and Rosalie fame"; admirers have "no beef" with the "wonderful creations" of "retro-chic French
comfort food", the "convivial" oyster bar or the "famous duo" "dab-
bling as waiters", but even they call the "prices a little high" and warn
"getting in might be a challenge, as it only has 25 seats" indoors.

🆕 La Brasserie Brunoise ●🗷 *French* **- | - | - | E**
Downtown | 1012, rue de la Montagne (bet. rue de la Gauchetière O. &
boul. René-Lévesque O.) | 514-933-3885 | www.brunoise.ca

The duo behind the former Brunoise goes casual with this Downtown
brasserie that matches no-nonsense, moderately pricey French classics such as calf's liver, duck confit and chocolate beignets with a
smart wine list split into *beau* (pricey), *bon* (great value) and *pas cher*
(bargain bottles); TVs, wireless connection and a bar cater to the

business and 5-à-7 crowd, and to pre-game diners en route to the Bell Centre next door.

☑ La Chronique 🅂🅼 *Eclectic/Québécois* | 28 | 23 | 25 | VE |

Mile End | 99, ave. Laurier Ouest (rue St-Urbain) | 514-271-3095 | www.lachronique.qc.ca

Fans "float" in a "foodie heaven" at chef-owner Marc de Canck's Mile End Eclectic-Québécois, aka "one of the most consistently satisfying tables in town"; "plan for a long, sensual meal" of "market-fresh", "creative and classic" fare, enriched by wine pairings that are "second-to-none" and "warm waiters who are all passionate" about their work; small wonder that, though it's *très cher*, the "intimate" "setting with black-and-white photos on the walls" is "alive with the sound of people enjoying their food."

La Colombe ●🅂🅼 *French* | 26 | 20 | 23 | E |

Plateau Mont-Royal | 554, ave. Duluth Est (rue St-Hubert) | 514-849-8844

"Bring your best wine" to this "intimate", pale-hued Plateau place that's perpetually "packed for a good reason" – it's BYO, which makes it an "incredible deal", considering the "enticing, eclectic" Classic French fare and "friendly, on-point" staff; the two nightly seatings (on Tuesdays, Fridays and Saturdays) are always "booked well in advance", but you can reserve at any hour on other days.

Laloux *French* | 26 | 22 | 24 | E |

Plateau Mont-Royal | 250, ave. des Pins Est (ave. Laval) | 514-287-9127 | www.laloux.com

You "cannot go wrong" with the "refined French cuisine with Classic roots" at this veteran (with new savory and pastry chefs) that has the "secret feel" of "your own little Left Bank bistro", since it's "off the beaten" Plateau path; "the environment is upscale, but not uptight" – the "attentive" staff "accommodates requests" and "treats children well."

La Porte *French* | - | - | - | VE |

Plateau Mont-Royal | 3627, boul. St-Laurent (rue Prince Arthur O.) | 514-282-4996

The beautiful carved door (imported from Marrakech) is meant to symbolize openness, hence the welcoming vibe at this Plateau Mont-Royal eatery that bucks the bistro trend with haute, and undeniably pricey, exotic New French fare; echoing the sophisticated cuisine is the posh decor that's accented with pillows and slick black-leather chairs.

☑ Le Club Chasse et Pêche 🅂🅼 *Eclectic/Québécois* | 27 | 22 | 25 | VE |

Old Montréal | 423, rue St-Claude (rue Notre-Dame) | 514-861-1112 | www.leclubchasseetpeche.com

This expensive Eclectic-Québécois is "among the best", thanks to chef Claude Pelletier's "fresh-market cuisine" featuring wild game and fish that "will creep into your dreams" because of the way it "combines the crazy and the classic" – e.g. suckling pig risotto – and is "supported by" "informative service"; some say the atmosphere reminiscent of "an old, country hunt club" "is not my style", but to romantics it's a "cozy" "place to bring one's mistress" – especially as it's "on a tiny Old Montréal street."

	FOOD	DECOR	SERVICE	COST

Le Jolifou *French/Mexican*

| 25 | 21 | 25 | E |

Little Italy/Petite-Patrie | 1840, rue Beaubien Est (rue Cartier) | 514-722-2175 | www.jolifou.com

"New French food with a Mexican touch" – so "unique" and "excellent" "you have to pinch" yourself to believe it – wins plaudits for this "truly charming", highly "reasonable" Petite Patrie site, a "labor of love" for the "congenial", enthusiastic husband-and-wife chef-owners who see to it that "things work right"; on the tables are "cute" replicas of antique toys "for you to fiddle around with while you wait"; just be sure to "leave room for dessert (more pinching)."

Leméac ● *French*

| 24 | 22 | 22 | E |

Outremont | 1045, ave. Laurier Ouest (ave. Durocher) | 514-270-0999 | www.restaurantlemeac.com

Sure, "French bistros are a dime a dozen in Montréal, but this one outdoes them all" claim converts of this "chic Outremont" specimen; the "competently served" dishes "never disappoint" and if they're a bit rich, "face it – everything tastes better with butter", anyway; some regulars recommend you "go during the day to enjoy the light flooding through the spectacular windows", but late-nighters love the "amazing after–10 PM" prix fixe (two courses for $22).

Les Chenêts *French*

| 25 | 20 | 22 | VE |

Downtown | 2075, rue Bishop (rue Sherbrooke O.) | 514-844-1842 | www.leschenets.com

It's "a little on the stuffy side", but "old-world charm still reigns" at this 30-year-old Downtowner, serving "superb Classic French cooking" in a room where "a fortune in copper pots hangs on the walls"; while modernists may mock the menu as "a heavy reminder of why nouvelle cuisine was invented", most opine this "pricey" veteran's "an oldie but a goodie"; P.S. "ask to visit the wine cellar, one of the best in Montréal."

☑ L'Express ● *French*

| 24 | 21 | 21 | E |

Plateau Mont-Royal | 3927, rue St-Denis (rue Roy E.) | 514-845-5333

On one of the "poshest streets" in the Plateau, its "sign cheekily embedded in floor tiles in front of the door", sits this "very Left Bank" bistro that's "Parisian to the core", from the "*extraordinaire*" classics ("marrow bones to die for") to the "traditional zinc bar" to the "black-and-white-attired" staff, who are "attentive despite the hectic pace" of the "pulsating, jam-packed scene."

Mikado *Japanese*

| 25 | 19 | 19 | E |

Notre-Dame-de-Grâce | 5515, ave. Monkland (ave. Girouard) | 514-369-3659

Outremont | 368, ave. Laurier Ouest (ave. du Parc) | 514-279-4809

Plateau Mont-Royal | 1731, rue St-Denis (bet. boul. de Maisonneuve E. & rue Ontario E.) | 514-844-5705

www.mikadomontreal.com

Those not "afraid to try" "innovative" sushi will "be hooked" by such goodies as the Relax Maki at this trio with "lablike, minimalist decor" that rates among the "best Japanese in town"; just "ask the servers to explain the specials" – both raw and cooked – then "finish your meal" with an "artist's palette of sorbets and ice creams."

FOOD | DECOR | SERVICE | COST

⏟ Milos *Greek*
27 | 23 | 25 | VE

Mile End | 5357, ave. du Parc (bet. ave. Fairmont O. & rue St-Viateur O.) | 514-272-3522 | www.milos.ca

Be transported from Mile End to a "Greek island taverna" by the "undisputed best seafood" – as "fresh" "as if caught hours ago" – that's "perfectly served" amid "boisterous atmospherics" at this "rustic-chic" "landmark of the rich and famous"; those awed by "outrageous prices" (you "pay by the pound") call "the fabulous $20 lunch special" "a steal."

Moishe's Steak House *Steak*
26 | 18 | 23 | VE

Plateau Mont-Royal | 3961, boul. St-Laurent (bet. aves. Duluth E. & des Pins E.) | 514-845-3509 | www.moishes.ca

"Serious steak in a Jewish restaurant in French Canadian Québec? yes, it's true" – and "red meat freaks" can rejoice in this "schmaltzy" Main "original" that "deserves its reputation" for "perfectly done" beef in portions "large enough to feed the Canadian army" – plus "classic appetizers" and sides like chopped liver and twice-baked potatoes; a "who's who" clientele dines amid a "frayed" "Catskills hotel–like" grandeur; now, if only the waiters who "have been there forever" wouldn't "clear the table before you're done" ("most expensive fast food ever!").

Nuances *French*
25 | 25 | 26 | VE

Île Notre-Dame | Casino de Montréal | 1, ave. du Casino, 5th fl. | 514-392-2708 | www.casino-de-montreal.com

Classic and New French fare that's "beyond reproach", a "superb" wine list and "classy" service (No. 1 in Montréal) will make you feel like a "winner" at this "beautiful hideaway", all mahogany wood and white tones, perched "atop the Expo 67 French Pavilion, now the Casino de Montréal", with its "amazing sunset" views; happily, it's "away from the casino noise, though close enough to be entertaining"; just bear in mind you may have to join the high rollers to handle the tab.

Queue de Cheval Steak House *Seafood/Steak*
24 | 24 | 23 | VE

Downtown | 1221, boul. René-Lévesque Ouest (rue Drummond) | 514-390-0090 | www.queuedecheval.com

Totally "OTT (over the top)", this "solid contender" among surf 'n' turfers "spares no effort" to "pamper" celebs and expense-accounters with "gargantuesque" portions "you could cut with a butter knife" and served "with the seriousness of a science presentation"; some scoff that it's "overpriced" – "had I known the lobster cost $300, I'd have kept it as a pet" – but most say go on and "spoil yourself" in the "hypermacho" space fittingly located opposite Bell Centre.

⏟ Toqué! ⬛Ⓜ *Québécois*
27 | 24 | 25 | VE

Old Montréal | Place Jean-Paul-Riopelle (bet. rues De Bleury & St-Antoine) | 514-499-2084 | www.restaurant-toque.com

"The inventor of Québec fusion cuisine", chef-owner Normand Laprise, has "influenced a generation", using regional ingredients – his treatment of "foie gras alone is worth the significant damage to the wallet" – in "minimal" "masterpieces" that trigger "a taste bud orgasm" (don't worry, the "professional" staff is "discreet"); many "miss the old digs" on St-Denis – this Old Montréal venue, while "elegant", can be "cold" – but this is a minority gripe for a mainstay that's "often called the city's finest", not to mention, Montréal's Most Popular as well.

Toronto

TOP FOOD RANKING

	Restaurant	Cuisine
29	Sushi Kaji	Japanese
28	Scaramouche	Continental
	Chiado/Antonio	Portuguese/Seafood
27	North 44°	Continental
	Hiro Sushi	Japanese
	Susur	Asian Fusion/French
	Lai Wah Heen	Chinese
	Lee	Asian Fusion/Mediterranean
	Splendido	Mediterranean
	Oro	Mediterranean
	Bistro & Bakery Thuet	French
	Perigee	French/Mediterranean
	Célestin	French
	Scaramouche Pasta	Italian
26	George	Canadian
	Truffles	French
	Canoe	Canadian
	Starfish Oyster	Seafood

Bistro & Bakery Thuet Ⓜ *French*   27 | 23 | 23 | VE

King West | 609 King St. W. (Bathurst St.) | 416-603-2777 |
www.thuet.ca

"Outstanding and original culinary delights" await at this Alsatian bistro in King West where "daring" chef-owner Marc Thuet dreams up "seasonal", loftily priced dishes to be paired with "aspirational" wines from an "extensive" list; diners can "focus on the flavor" thanks to an unobtrusively "comfortable" dining room and the "discreet" attentions of a "right-on" staff; N.B. they've recently added a glassed-in bakery area as well as a 35-seat private room beneath the kitchen.

Ⓩ Canoe Ⓢ *Canadian*   26 | 26 | 25 | VE

Financial District | Toronto Dominion Bank Tower | 66 Wellington St. W., 54th fl. (Bay St.) | 416-364-0054 | www.canoerestaurant.com

Voted the city's No. 1 for both Decor and Popularity, this literally "top-tier" "destination" on the 54th floor of the Toronto Dominion Bank Tower lives up to its "stunning location" with "exquisitely flavored" Canadian cuisine that's "presented with class" by a "first-rate" staff; prices that are "as lofty as the setting" don't deter those devotees who say the view alone justifies "the cost of your meal"; P.S. it's "worth waiting or bribing" to snag the large table "in the southwest corner, overlooking [the skyline] and lake."

Cava *Spanish*   - | - | - | E

Midtown | 1560 Yonge St. (Heath St.) | 416-979-9918 |
www.cavarestaurant.ca

Veteran chef-owner Chris McDonald (of the now-shuttered Avalon) shows off his range at this Midtown tapas and wine bar that offers traditional Spanish treats as well as dishes delivering French, Italian and Mexican flair, from sardines done two ways to chipotle-caramel popcorn; the Basque-centric wine selection is as extensive as the food menu, and it's all served up in a simple, rustic setting.

Célestin ⊠Ⓜ *French* | 27 | 22 | 22 | VE |

Midtown | 623 Mt. Pleasant Rd. (Manor Rd. E.) | 416-544-9035
Best "savored one plate at a time", chef-owner Pascal Ribreau's "refined", "creative" New French cuisine makes this Midtown "haute bistro" one of "the top spots in town"; "everything is above par here", including "knowledgeable" personnel and a renovated 1920s bank building interior that's "upscale", "clean" and "calm"; P.S. fans of the "to-die-for handmade bread" can stop by the "exquisite bakery next door" and get some to go.

☑ Chiado/Senhor Antonio *Portuguese/Seafood* | 28 | 21 | 25 | VE |

Little Italy | 864 College St. (Concord Ave.) | 416-538-1910 | www.chiadorestaurant.com
"Melt-in-your-mouth" seafood lures pescavores to this "top-notch" Little Italy Portuguese where "simple preparations emphasize" "superb" ingredients and the cellar contains what may be the "best Portuguese wine list in Canada"; staffers work so smoothly as to be "almost invisible" within the "intimate" old-world dining room and the minimalist tapas bar next door; yes, tabs are "steep" – but then "you've got to be terrific to charge these prices in this part of town."

🆕 Colborne Lane ●⊠Ⓜ *Eclectic* | – | – | – | VE |

Downtown Core | 45 Colborne St. (Leader Ln.) | 416-368-9009 | www.colbornelane.com
At this edgy Downtown Core eatery, chef-owner Claudio Aprile (ex Senses) whips up sophisticated, pricey Eclectic creations that won't be pigeonholed – think Peking duck with licorice sauce – plus a $149 15-course tasting menu that truly displays the toque's range; it's all set in a historic building amid modern decor and rock 'n' roll background music; N.B. open Tuesday–Saturday for dinner only.

George ⊠ *Canadian* | 26 | 24 | 24 | VE |

Downtown Core | Queen Richmond Ctr. | 111C Queen St. E. (bet. Church & Jarvis Sts.) | 416-863-6006 | www.georgeonqueen.com
By George, it's "amazing" assert admirers of this onetime chocolate factory in the Downtown Core's Queen Richmond Centre; "master chef" Lorenzo Loseto's "flavorful", seasonal Canadian cuisine comes on "small plates [that] allow for maximum sampling" and can be paired with three- or six-oz. pours; the antique "industrial" open-plan setting manages to be both "stylish" and "soothing", helped along by "smooth, accommodating service."

☑ Hiro Sushi ⊠Ⓜ *Japanese* | 27 | 15 | 21 | VE |

St. Lawrence | 171 King St. E. (Jarvis St.) | 416-304-0550
Hiro worshipers say "sitting at the sushi bar is the only way to experience" this small, traditional St. Lawrence Japanese; they adore the "genius" chef-owner's "amazing" omakase (a culinary "walk on the wild side") but caution that since "you'll eat at the master's pace", you may spend "a few hours" here.

	FOOD	DECOR	SERVICE	COST

Z Jamie Kennedy
Wine Bar & Restaurant *Canadian/French*

| 25 | 21 | 21 | VE |

St. Lawrence | 9 Church St. (south of Front St.) | 416-362-1957 |
www.jamiekennedy.ca

"Superstar" chef Jamie Kennedy's "legions of fans" laud his "fabulous" conjoined Canadian-French eateries in St. Lawrence; the open-kitchen wine bar "churns out" "explosively flavorful" small plates for pairing with "outstanding" vintages "often unavailable elsewhere", while the "small", minimalist restaurant also offers "superb bistro fare" served by a "knowledgeable" crew with a touch of "attitude"; not surprisingly, this "finger food [comes] at full-torso prices."

kaiseki-SAKURA *Japanese*

| - | - | - | VE |

Downtown Core | 556 Church St. (Wellesley St.) | 416-923-1010 |
www.kaisekisakura.com

Those who love Japanese cuisine will appreciate this Downtown Core temple to *kaiseki*-style small plates, where chef Daisuke Izutsu offers monthly changing tasting menus that range from five to eight courses ($60–$100); a relative secret, this dinner-only destination also serves intricate, artfully presented à la carte choices in a quiet setting that's ideal for relaxed conversation; N.B. closed on Tuesdays.

Kultura Social Dining *Eclectic*

| - | - | - | E |

Downtown Core | 169 King St. E. (bet. George & Jarvis Sts.) | 416-363-9000 |
www.kulturarestaurant.com

Delivering small plates that are big on taste and creativity, this ultra-romantic Downtown Core restaurant offers an Eclectic menu from chef/co-owner Roger Mooking that reveals his Caribbean and Japanese roots in dishes like jerk chicken with a lemon and coconut risotto; it's already attracting a business and celebrity clientele that's likely to appreciate the deft wine list (with 50 selections by the glass) from noted Canadian sommelier Kim Cyr.

Lai Wah Heen *Chinese*

| 27 | 22 | 25 | VE |

Downtown Core | Metropolitan Hotel | 108 Chestnut St.
(bet. Bay St. & University Ave.) | 416-977-9899 |
www.metropolitan.com/lwh

Renowned for "divine" dim sum "made with tremendous care" and served similarly by a "top-notch" staff, this "superior" Sino in the Downtown Core's Metropolitan Hotel is likely to "make visitors from Hong Kong feel right at home"; dining in this "serene" "white-tablecloth" setting may be "expensive by Chinese standards", but it's "a bargain" for such "a wonderful experience."

Lee Z *Asian Fusion/Mediterranean*

| 27 | 23 | 22 | VE |

King West | 603 King St. W. (Portland St.) | 416-504-7867 |
www.susur.com

The comparatively "affordable little sister" to next door's Susur, this King West "favorite" allows followers of "the master" to "get a taste" of Susur Lee's "sensational", "surprising" Asian-Mediterranean "fusion food" ("tapas meets dim sum") "without breaking the bank"; the "stylish" loftlike space with pink Lucite tables is a "hip" and "hopping" (if "chaotic") scene that's "good for groups", as is the new outdoor patio.

	FOOD	DECOR	SERVICE	COST

☑ North 44° ⑤ *Continental* | 27 | 25 | 25 | VE

North Toronto | 2537 Yonge St. (Eglinton Ave.) | 416-487-4897 |
www.north44restaurant.com

"Sophisticated" and "serene", Mark McEwan's North Toronto "show-piece" guarantees a "memorable" "special occasion" rave respondents, reporting the chef-owner's "magnificent" Continental cuisine evinces "superb quality and craftsmanship" while service is simply "state-of-the-art"; it's undoubtedly "pricey" and may be a "hassle to get to", but foodies urge their fellows to "walk, crawl, hitchhike . . . do whatever is necessary."

Oro ⑤ *Mediterranean* | 27 | 22 | 26 | VE

Downtown Core | 45 Elm St. (bet. Bay & Yonge Sts.) | 416-597-0155 |
www.ororestaurant.com

"Somehow seeming out of the way while right in the middle of town", this "quiet" Downtown Core Med delivers with "exceptional", "innovative" cuisine ("melt-in-your-mouth calamari", "delectable desserts") as "attentive" owners circulate and "make everyone feel like family"; interiors are a "pleasantly odd mix" of "upscale" and retro, with three fireplaces adding both atmosphere and warmth ("first-class for a first date").

Perigee ⑤Ⓜ *French/Mediterranean* | 27 | 23 | 25 | VE

Distillery District | Cannery Bldg. | 55 Mill St. (Trinity St.) | 416-364-1397 |
www.perigeerestaurant.com

For "pure theater", "adventurous" gastronomes gather at this "fantastic" French-Med in the historic Distillery District and settle into "arena-side seats" by the open kitchen to be served a "blissful" blind tasting menu; "social", "creative and charming" chef Pat Riley "explains each course to you" amid converted industrial environs with thick wooden beams and exposed brick; N.B. early-birds and night-owls can try pre-theater and dessert menus, respectively.

☑ Scaramouche ⑤ *Continental* | 28 | 26 | 27 | VE

Forest Hill | 1 Benvenuto Pl. (bet. Avenue Rd. & Edmund St.) | 416-961-8011 |
www.scaramoucherestaurant.com

Devotees of this "consistently" "top-notch" Forest Hill Continental declare its staff is "second to none" – indeed, surveyors voted this veteran Toronto's No. 1 for Service, citing "expert", "exquisite" ministrations that make you "feel like a millionaire" while chef/co-owner Keith Froggett feeds you his "delectable", "trustworthy, superb" cuisine; the "quiet, elegant" room is also renowned for "magnificent views of Downtown" ("without the Downtown traffic"), so "movers and shakers" recommend "lingering over a wonderful meal" to "savor" the "magic."

Scaramouche Pasta Bar & Grill ●⑤ *Italian* | 27 | 25 | 27 | VE

Forest Hill | 1 Benvenuto Pl. (bet. Avenue Rd. & Edmund St.) | 416-961-8011 |
www.scaramoucherestaurant.com

Sharing its Forest Hill building and "gorgeous views of Downtown", this "sophisticated sibling to Scaramouche" "continues to excel" as well, offering "lighter meals" of "marvelous" Italian *cucina* ("not just pasta") and "exceptional" service for a comparatively "reasonable price"; overall, it's a "more casual yet no less worthy" experience; N.B. the kitchen closes at midnight.

	FOOD	DECOR	SERVICE	COST

Splendido 🅼 *Mediterranean* — 27 | 24 | 25 | VE

South Annex | 88 Harbord St. (Spadina Ave.) | 416-929-7788 |
www.splendidoonline.com

"Splendido indeed" rhapsodize respondents about this South Annex Med where chef David Lee's "sublime", "celestial" cuisine ("one of the city's best tasting menus") is complemented by an "impressive wine cellar" and served in a "classy", "modern", "clean"-lined dining room by a staff that offers a "perfect combination of professional and friendly" ministrations; "for a special occasion, you can't go wrong" here.

Starfish Oyster Bed & Grill 🆉 *Seafood* — 26 | 19 | 22 | VE

St. Lawrence | 100 Adelaide St. E. (bet. Church & Jarvis Sts.) | 416-366-7827 | www.starfishoysterbed.com

Everyone knows "great things come in small packages", and that goes for the "exceptional" bivalves at this St. Lawrence seafooder (owned by World Oyster Opening Champion Patrick McMurray) as well as the "memorable" pleasures to be found within its "cozy", "understated" confines; for a "lesson" in freshness, "sit at the bar" and chat with "knowledgeable" shuckers over a mug of microbrewed stout.

🆉 Sushi Kaji 🅼 *Japanese* — 29 | 19 | 25 | VE

Mimico | 860 The Queensway (Islington Ave.) | 416-252-2166 | www.sushikaji.com

"Don't let your first impressions cloud your judgment" – this "unassuming" 30-seat Mimico Japanese, voted Toronto's No. 1 for Food, is a "hidden treasure"; with "talent and a wry sense of humour", "artist" Mitsuhiro Kaji creates "sumptuous sashimi and sublime sushi" from sea creatures who "move from packing crate to dinner plate in seconds" ("fish so fresh it really does flop around"), while his "intriguing and expertly presented" omakase incorporates "exquisite hot dishes" as well; N.B. prix fixe only.

🆉 Susur 🆉🅼 *Asian Fusion/French* — 27 | 24 | 24 | VE

King West | 601 King St. W. (Bathurst St.) | 416-603-2205 | www.susur.com

"Adventurous foodies" make their way to King West for Susur Lee's "cutting-edge", "complex", "diverse yet cohesive" French-inflected Asian fusion fare (especially "brilliant" tasting menus in which "mains come first"); "gracious" staffers are "informative" and "minimalist decor" with "spaceship lighting" is "ultrahip" to boot – but be sure to "call your financial planner" and set aside "at least four hours" for dinner; still, a vocal minority is "not too sure about Susur", deeming its "shock-therapy approach" to cuisine "highly overrated."

Truffles 🆉 *French* — 26 | 26 | 26 | VE

Bloor Yorkville | Four Seasons Hotel | 21 Avenue Rd. (Bloor St. W.) | 416-928-7331 | www.fourseasons.com/toronto

"They don't trifle" at this "exceptional" New French, a "gourmand's delight" in Bloor Yorkville's Four Seasons, where the "delectable", almost "flawless" dishes are "adeptly paired with appropriate wines" from a "superb" list; what with the staff's "courtesy" and "attention to detail", diners love to "linger for hours" in the "intimate" room.

Vancouver

TOP FOOD RANKING

	Restaurant	Cuisine
29	West	Pacific NW
28	Lumière	French
	Bishop's	Pacific NW
	Vij's	Indian
	Pear Tree	Continental
27	ToJo's	Japanese
	Le Crocodile	French
	La Régalade	French
26	Cioppino's	Mediterranean
	Il Giardino/Umberto	Italian
	Villa del Lupo	Italian/Pacific NW
	Vij's Rangoli	Indian
	Diva at the Met	Pacific NW
	Cru	Pacific NW
	Gotham Steak	Steak
	C Restaurant	Seafood
25	Caffe de Medici	Italian
	Raincity Grill	Pacific NW
	Parkside	European

Z Bishop's M *Pacific NW*   28 | 23 | 27 | VE

West Side | 2183 W. 4th Ave. (bet. Arbutus & Yew Sts.) | 604-738-2025 | www.bishopsonline.com

Thanks to the "sincerity and warmth" of "unsurpassed host" John Bishop and his "amazing" team of professionals, this "intimate" West Side "classic" ranks No. 1 for Service in the Vancouver Survey; the kitchen, too, is "brilliant", using mostly "organic ingredients" to prepare "top-of-the-line" fare that reflects the "Pacific Northwest at its best"; "save your pennies for a splurge" at this "perennial favorite."

NEW Bistrot Bistro ● M *French*   - | - | - | M

West Side | 1961 West Fourth Ave. (bet. Cypress & Maple Sts.) | 604-732-0004 | www.bistrotbistro.com

Its colorful, contempo decor of unadorned tables and slate floors breathes cool, but the welcome is warm at Valérie and Laurent Devin's new apple green–trimmed Kits bistro; the classic menu offers a fervently French salute to the flavors of their homeland, with robust but polished plates of richly lardoned boeuf bourguignon or Pernod-laced fisherman's stew in its own stainless-steel bucket; each is matched with a smart wine pick from a sensible cellar.

Caffe de Medici *Italian*   25 | 23 | 27 | E

Downtown | 109-1025 Robson St. (bet. Burrard & Thurlow Sts.) | 604-669-9322 | www.caffedemedici.com

Known for "memorable" plates of "hearty", "traditional" fare, paired with "spectacular" wines, this "stylish", "little secret" in a "cozy nook on bustling Robson" has been "dependable" for "high-quality Italian dining"

	FOOD	DECOR	SERVICE	COST

since 1979; "fabulous service" from a "knowledgeable staff" helps create "a delightful evening" for regulars and "European guests" alike.

Cioppino's
Mediterranean Grill ⊠ *Mediterranean* | 26 | 23 | 25 | VE |

Yaletown | 1133 Hamilton St. (bet. Davie & Helmcken Sts.) | 604-688-7466 | www.cioppinosyaletown.com

"Brilliant" chef-owner Pino Posteraro "turns out amazing" Mediterranean dishes from the "open kitchen" of his "outstanding" Yaletowner, run by a "helpful staff"; it's a "fine destination for wine weenies" – the "serious list" includes 1,200 labels – and while it's "not inexpensive", *amici* aver that this "epitome of sublime cuisine and service" is "one of the town's best."

☑ C Restaurant *Seafood* | 26 | 24 | 26 | VE |

Downtown | 2-1600 Howe St. (Beach Ave.) | 604-681-1164 | www.crestaurant.com

"The passion shows" affirm fin-atics of "wildly innovative" chef Robert Clark's "superlative seafood", "superbly presented" and "expertly served" in a "stylish", "stunning" "waterfront setting" Downtown overlooking False Creek; environmentalists applaud the spot's "eco-friendly" support for "sustainable fishing practices", and everyone agrees that, while you'll "C your wallet shrink" ("the prices are unbelievably high"), it's a "must-visit."

Cru *Pacific NW* | 26 | 21 | 24 | E |

West Side | 1459 W. Broadway (bet. Granville & Hemlock Sts.) | 604-677-4111 | www.cru.ca

Oenophiles appreciate the "unique, color-coded" list of "scrumptious wines" that match with "fantastic" Pacific Northwest "plates to share" or one of the "best prix fixes in the city" at this "intimate" West Side bistro; though the storefront is "small" and "minimalist", a grape-savvy staff that encourages you to "try something new" "without a bit of snobbery" at "relatively affordable prices" "allows you to be a regular."

Diva at the Met *Pacific NW* | 26 | 23 | 25 | VE |

Downtown | Metropolitan Hotel | 645 Howe St. (bet. Dunsmuir & W. Georgia Sts.) | 604-602-7788 | www.metropolitan.com

At lunch when "deals are made", "prior to the opera" or "for a splurge night", this Downtown "delectable diva" draws ovations for "beautifully plated" Pacific Northwest dishes and "orgasmic desserts" by chocolatier Thomas Haas; "prepare to be impressed" by the "witty staff" in this "airy" space, particularly if you sit near "the open kitchen that shows the chefs working their magic."

Flying Tiger, The *Asian* | - | - | - | M |

West Side | 2958 W. Fourth Ave. (Bayswater St.) | 604-737-7529 | www.theflyingtiger.ca

Ex–Bin 942 chef Tina Fineza has returned from her world travels to re-create her take on Pan-Asian street food at this casual black-and-gold West Sider, which doubles as a laid-back lounge and dining destination; well-conceived small plates rule, from duck confit crêpes to curried Salt Spring Island mussels to exuberantly spiced chick pea and potato samosas, all served up with smart wine picks and edgy cocktails.

	FOOD	DECOR	SERVICE	COST

Fuel Restaurant ⓜ *Pacific NW*

| - | - | - | E |

West Side | 1944 W. 4th Ave. (bet. Cypress & Maple Sts.) | 604-288-7905 | www.fuelrestaurant.ca

Sit at the kitchenside bar up front or hide away in back at this hot Kits newcomer, a partnership between wine guy Tom Doughty and chef Robert Belcham, both well honed by C Restaurant; seasonally changing Pacific NW plates range from crispy-skinned trout with almond butter to an organic pork loin and belly duo; but many opt to try one of the wine-paired tasting menus to reap the joys of the surprisingly deep cellar.

Gastropod ⓜ *European*

| - | - | - | E |

West Side | 1938 W. Fourth Ave. (bet. Cypress & Maple Sts.) | 604-730-5579 | www.gastropod.ca

Drawing on skills and influences gained through stints at NY's Jean Georges, London's The Ledbury and Berkshire's Fat Duck, chef-owner Angus An has created this contemporary, minimalist West Sider where his updated takes on Continental classics (often using the sous-vide process) can shine; his trademark tastes – from foie gras bonbons to frogs' leg beignets – aren't cheap, but there's a well-priced prix fixe.

Gotham Steakhouse *Steak*

| 26 | 25 | 24 | VE |

Downtown | 615 Seymour St. (bet. Dunsmuir & W. Georgia Sts.) | 604-605-8282 | www.gothamsteakhouse.com

"Wear a power suit" and "impress your carnivore friends" with "the best steak in the city" at this "top-notch" Downtown chophouse boasting the "gorgeous vaulted ceilings" and "dark-leather" interior "you'd expect" from "old-school" "fine dining"; the "knowledgeable" servers treat you like you "belong to a private club", but with the à la carte pricing ("which means 'no potato' in French"), you might hope that "someone else is picking up the tab."

Il Giardino di Umberto ⓢ *Italian*

| 26 | 24 | 25 | E |

Downtown | 1382 Hornby St. (Pacific St.) | 604-669-2422 | www.umberto.com

Some of "the best Italian fare" is served in this "rustic yet regal" Tuscan-style "period house" Downtown that's "romantic" enough "for any intimate celebration"; owner Umberto Menghi ("Vancouver's Wolfgang Puck") presides over a "power patio" that makes for "good beautiful-people viewing" at a "little gem" that's all about "consistent" "fine dining" and "warm hospitality."

La Régalade ⓢⓜ *French*

| 27 | 19 | 25 | E |

West Vancouver | 102-2232 Marine Dr. (bet. 22nd & 23rd Sts.) | 604-921-2228 | www.laregalade.com

"*C'est magnifique*" rave regulars who "adore *la cuisine française*" at this "mighty authentic" West Vancouver bistro that's "worth the trip over a bridge – any bridge" – to tuck into "ample portions" of "heartwarming" "French country" fare "meticulously prepared" by chef-owner Alain Rayé; the "quarters are close", but it's "like finding yourself in France."

Le Crocodile ⓢ *French*

| 27 | 23 | 26 | VE |

Downtown | 100-909 Burrard St. (Smithe St.) | 604-669-4298 | www.lecrocodilerestaurant.com

"Are we in France?" clientele query chef-owner Michel Jacob, an "Alsatian prince" whose "sublime" cuisine bears the "Gallic consistency of a master"; there are "no crocodile tears" shed in this "stylish" Downtown "oasis" where the "discreet" staff "spoils" you (and the diners, *bien sûr*, are "expected to behave"), so whether "for a civilized lunch or a romantic evening", it is "worth every penny."

❷ Lumière Ⓜ *French* 28 | 24 | 26 | VE
West Side | 2551 W. Broadway (bet. Larch & Trafalgar Sts.) | 604-739-8185 | www.lumiere.ca

"Breathtaking in its simplicity", with "fabulous tasting menus" "show-casing local purveyors", chef Rob Feenie's "awesome" French fare is a "serious gourmand experience" that rates as the Vancouver Survey's Most Popular; "special-occasion" pilgrims to this candlelit West Side room revere the "decadent parade" of "well-planned courses" brought by a "superb" (if slightly "pretentious") staff; those who "love every bite" but flinch at a meal "on par with a mortgage" dine in the adjacent Tasting Bar for "a steal."

Parkside *European* 25 | 23 | 25 | E
West End | 1906 Haro St. (Gilford St.) | 604-683-6912 | www.parksiderestaurant.ca

"Mouth orgasms" – that's what smitten surveyors call chef-owner Andrey Durbach's "seasonally changing" Modern European inventions, made with "the freshest ingredients" and served on a prix fixe for "one of the best deals in town"; the staff is "attentive but not hovering" at this "intimate" West End "hideaway" where, from "succulent cocktails" to "delicious desserts", a "brilliant" meal leaves you "feeling happy-happy."

❷ Pear Tree, The Ⓢ Ⓜ *Continental* 28 | 22 | 27 | E
Burnaby | 4120 E. Hastings St. (bet. Carleton & Gilmore Aves.) | 604-299-2772

At this "sophisticated", "welcome find in the culinary desert of Burnaby", "one of the country's top talents", chef-owner Scott Jaeger, puts out "fabulous", "imaginative" Continental plates; Stephanie Jaeger heads up a "stellar front-of-house" team, and "recent renovations have added a high-end touch" to the "small" but "charming" room.

Raincity Grill *Pacific NW* 25 | 19 | 24 | E
West End | 1193 Denman St. (Morton Ave.) | 604-685-7337 | www.raincitygrill.com

"For a true taste of Vancouver", regionalists rave about this "Pacific Northwest winner" with its "commitment to local suppli-ers", "seasonal" "menu variations that keep it interesting" and an "incredible" BC wine list; add "terrific" service and a "fabulous" West End setting "with an English Bay view", and this spot "defines West Coast" dining.

ToJo's Ⓢ *Japanese* 27 | - | 23 | VE
West Side | 1133 W. Broadway (bet. Heather & Willow Sts.) | 604-872-8050 | www.tojos.com

For some of "the best sushi in North America", "put yourself in the hands" of chef-owner Tojo Hidekazu and order the "mind-blowing omakase", then "taste pure decadence" in an array of "inventive" "nouvelle" creations; always an "undisputed winner" gastronomically, it recently moved to new West Side digs, so that it now offers a com-plete experience of "Japanese food heaven – in credit-card-limit hell."

	FOOD	DECOR	SERVICE	COST

☑ Vij's *Indian*

28	22	25	E

West Side | 1480 W. 11th Ave. (bet. Granville & Hemlock Sts.) | 604-736-6664 | www.vijs.ca

"Every meal is a sensual experience" at "consummate host" Vikram Vij's West Sider, known equally for the "genial" chef-owner's "personal touches" and for the "world-class", "inventive interpretations" of Indian cuisine; while "the single detractor is a no-reservations policy" that can lead to "hour-plus line-ups", the "back lounge is the best cocktail party in town", with "complimentary tasty treats" to "soothe the wait."

Vij's Rangoli *Indian*

26	19	20	M

West Side | 1488 W. 11th Ave. (bet. Granville & Hemlock Sts.) | 604-736-5711 | www.vijs.ca

"If you don't want to face the wait next door", or if you're looking for the "best bet for lunch" on the West Side, this "poor-man's Vij's" is "a cheaper, quicker alternative", offering a "limited selection" of "succulent" Indian fusion dishes; with the option to bring these "big flavors" home in the frozen "take-out boil-in bags", the "time-stressed" wonder "who cooks anymore."

Villa del Lupo *Italian/Pacific NW*

26	23	26	E

Downtown | 869 Hamilton St. (bet. Robson & Smithe Sts.) | 604-688-7436 | www.villadellupo.com

"Take a date" (or "your trophy wife") "for a romantic rendezvous" at this "intimate", "elegant" Downtown heritage house where the "superb service" "makes you feel like royalty" and the "high-end" Italian-Pacific Northwest fare is "outstanding"; the "artfully presented plates" are matched with an "excellent wine list" for a meal that is "*delizioso* in any language."

☑ West *Pacific NW*

29	26	27	VE

West Side | 2881 Granville St. (W. 13th Ave.) | 604-738-8938 | www.westrestaurant.com

Ranked No. 1 for Food in the Vancouver Survey, this "jewel in the city's culinary crown" is "exquisite in every way"; chef David Hawksworth creates "extraordinary" Pacific Northwest "dishes with divine flavors" that are paired with "superb" wines "graciously served" by an "exemplary" staff in a "stunning" West Side room; "it'll cost you a pretty penny", but for a "superlative" experience that will have "you floating home in a state of perfect serenity", "go West as quickly as possible."

EUROPE
RESTAURANT
DIRECTORY

Amsterdam

Beddington's ⊠Ⓜ *French/Asian* | 24 | 18 | 18 | E |

Frederiksplein | Utrechtsedwarsstraat 141 | (31-20) 620-7393 | www.beddington.nl

"Long live Jean!" exclaim fans of this "nice place" in the Frederiksplein area that's "run by female chef" Jean Beddington, who always cooks "excellent", "inventive" French-Asian fare; still, some find the "sober" space with "only a few tables" a bit "cold" and feel the "informal (but correct) service" "could use some work", saying it all "just misses being superior."

Blauw aan de Wal ⊠Ⓜ *French/Mediterranean* | 26 | 22 | 23 | E |

Centrum | Oudezijds Achterburgwal 99 | (31-20) 330-2257

"Hidden away" at the end of "a small alley" in the Centrum, this "smallish", "serene spot" with its own "private dining terrace" offers a "great respite from the Red Light District" "just around the corner"; its "cozy, peaceful setting" is home to "sweet" staffers who "are happy to explain in great detail" their "terrific" French-Med "fare made from the best ingredients" and accompanied by a "well-selected", "solid wine list"; no wonder so many consider it an "absolutely wonderful", "special place."

Blue Pepper *Indonesian* | 23 | 20 | 22 | M |

Centrum | Nassaukade 366 | (31-20) 489-7039 | www.restaurantbluepepper.com

If you "want something other than" "the standard rijsttafel", "go straight to this top-notch" Centrum "treat" where a "creative" "nouveau Indonesian" kitchen delivers "dazzling", "delicious dishes" that are "full of flavor" and definitely "out of the ordinary"; the "friendly, accommodating staff" provides equally "sizzling service" and will happily "inform you about the details of the menu", but insiders insist that "the tasting menu is a must."

☒ Bordewijk ◪ *French/Mediterranean*   26 | 18 | 23 | E

Jordaan | Noordermarkt 7 | (31-20) 624-3899 | www.bordewijk.nl
The "chef visits" "your table" and "takes your order" at this "terrific place" "in a charming Jordaan location", a "favorite" of many for its "incredible" French-Med "haute cuisine", "comprehensive wine list" and "fantastic" service; still, some sigh it's "too bad" the "noisy room" "doesn't do justice to the rest of the experience", adding that "the restaurant is less inviting" to tourists, since the staff is not as welcoming "if you are not a native."

Chez Georges ☒ *French*   24 | 21 | 23 | E

Jordaan | Herenstraat 3 | (31-20) 626-3332
"It's always full" at this tiny Jordaan French in the nicest part of Amsterdam, because the "beautifully classic" cuisine is "superb", particularly the "fine" five-course tasting menu, which is a "great value"; a "staff that takes such pride in what it serves" and a "charming", "cozy" and "civilized" interior are other pluses.

☒ Christophe' ☒◪ *French*   26 | 22 | 24 | VE

Jordaan | Leliegracht 46 | (31-20) 625-0807 | www.restaurantchristophe.nl
"Brilliantly inventive" and "beautifully presented" "dishes that combine upscale French cuisine" with "Mediterranean ingredients" and "African influences" "delight the eye and palate" at this "perfectly located" "canal-side" Jordaan "jewel" manned by an "eager-to-please staff"; those who think the "atmosphere is rather dull" quip that the "lovely" interior is "as quiet and peaceful as the floral arrangements, and about as lively", but most report "a special night out"; N.B. post-Survey, Jean-Christophe Royer turned over the chef-ownership reins to his long-standing protégé, Jean-Joël Bonsens.

Ciel Bleu *French*   22 | 21 | 21 | E

Pijp | Hotel Okura | Ferdinand Bolstraat 333, 23rd fl. | (31-20) 678-7450 | www.okura.nl
"Go on a clear night" to this "peaceful" establishment on the 23rd floor of the Hotel Okura in the Pijp to enjoy "marvelous views" (perhaps the "best in the city") along with "exquisite", "original and delicate" New French dishes that are delivered by a "helpful staff"; all agree that the "food is up to the level of the location", though some feel "the boring decor needs an upgrade" – still, it's "definitely a place for a repeat visit."

☒ De Kas ☒ *Dutch/Mediterranean*   23 | 26 | 21 | E

Oost | Frankendael Park | Kamerlingh Onneslaan 3 | (31-20) 462-4562 | www.restaurantdekas.nl
Set in an "impressively large" and "beautiful greenhouse" "situated in the Park" Frankendael in Oost, "this sparkling glass temple to food" takes its "sensitivity and passion for local", mostly "organic ingredients" "to a whole new level", creating "a daily prix fixe menu" of "stellar" Dutch-Mediterranean fare "based upon the day's harvest"; whether seated in

"the stunning dining room" or on the "lovely terrace", expect an "absolutely enchanting" experience as you "inhale the heady fragrances" of "fresh vegetables and herbs" growing all around you.

De Silveren Spiegel ⑤ *Dutch*   24 | 22 | 22 | VE

Centrum | Kattengat 4-6 | (31-20) 624-6589 | www.desilverenspiegel.com
This "beautiful little historic" Centrum treat "tucked away" "near Centraal Station" may be so "old" (circa 1614) that it "looks as though it's falling over", but its kitchen actually "impresses" with an "interesting" array of "well-executed dishes" that are some "of the best" examples of "nouvelle Dutch" cuisine; the "quaint" setting with "lead-glass windows and candles" is an "old-world delight" whose "warm", "intimate atmosphere" is abetted by "gracious service" from a "staff with exceptional knowledge" of the "great wine list."

☑ D'Vijff Vlieghen *Dutch*   21 | 23 | 20 | E

Centrum | Spuistraat 294-302 | (31-20) 530-4060 | www.thefiveflies.com
"Small rooms connected by narrow winding corridors" spanning "five charming old houses" in the Centrum are the "marvelous setting" of this "Amsterdam institution" that's "still going strong", serving up a "great variety" of "flavorful" Dutch dishes that are more "contemporary" than you'd expect; still, some say it's "living on its reputation" and complain that it's "chronically overfilled" with "tons of tourists" and "complacent", "slow" servers – so "be prepared" for a "long (though memorable) evening"; P.S. "the name means 'The Five Flies.'"

☑ Dylan, The ⑤ *French/African*   24 | 26 | 23 | VE

Jordaan | Dylan Hotel | Keizersgracht 384 | (31-20) 530-2010 |
www.dylanamsterdam.com
Though the "name has changed", this "don't-miss place" "within the hip, tasteful" Dylan Hotel in the Jordaan remains "trendy", in part because its "sleek, cool interior" continues to "wow" the city's "handsome people", but also because the kitchen creates "beautifully presented" French–Northern African cuisine; in fact, it's so "tremendous across the board" most overlook that the "stuck-up staffers" still "take themselves too seriously.

Excelsior *French/Mediterranean*   25 | 24 | 25 | VE

Centrum | Hotel de L'Europe | Nieuwe Doelenstraat 2-8 | (31-20) 531-1705 |
www.leurope.nl
"Fine dining in Amsterdam" is found at this "luxurious" venue "within the Hotel de L'Europe", a "beautiful" Centrum establishment "with old European charm", where chef Jean-Jacques Menanteau creates "delicious" "traditional French-Med dishes" that are "worth the splurge"; fans feel the "excellent service" and "elegant" interior "recall the graciousness of times past", but even "bored" sorts who say the "stuffy decor" "could use an upgrade" are "simply delighted" by the "lovely" terrace with its "romantic view" of the Amstel River.

French Café, The ⑤Ⓜ *French*   22 | 19 | 20 | E

Pijp | Gerard Doustraat 98 | (31-20) 470-0301 | www.thefrenchcafe.nl
The straightforward name sums up this French cafe in Pijp, where patrons are "pleased" with "delicious" classic dishes served in a "chilled-out atmosphere"; the intimate interior includes an open kitchen, and in summer a handful of tables spill outside.

	FOOD	DECOR	SERVICE	COST

Gala ⓜ *Catalan* | 22 | 20 | 20 | E |

Leidseplein | Reguliersdwarsstraat 38 | (31-20) 623-6303 |
www.restaurantgala.com

This "hip" and "trendy" new "place to be seen" in the Leidseplein area
offers a narrow, sexy and stylish setting with a moodily lit bar that
makes for a "romantic evening"; influenced by contemporary Catalan
cooking, the kitchen turns out "excellent Spanish tapas" that are indeed a gala "celebration of good eating."

ⓩ La Rive *French/Mediterranean* | 27 | 26 | 26 | VE |

Oost | InterContinental Amstel | Professor Tulpplein 1 | (31-20) 520-3264 |
www.restaurantlarive.nl

"You know you've a-Rived when you" visit "this breathtaking waterfront restaurant" "right on the river" "in the city's premier hotel", the
"elegant" InterContinental Amstel in Oost, where the "fabulous
views" are actually trumped by the "phenomenal", "magical" French-
Med creations of "master chef Edwin Kats"; furthermore, "you'd be
hard-pressed to find a grander dining room" or more "wonderful" staff
to "wait on you hand and foot", so it's no surprise "sated" surveyors
swear the experience produces "ecstasy"; P.S. "in summer, dine waterside" on the "beautiful terrace."

ⓩ Ron Blaauw ⓩ ⓜ *French/International* | 28 | 21 | 24 | VE |

Ouderkerk aan de Amstel | Kerkstraat 56 | (31-20) 496-1943 |
www.ronblaauw.nl

Expect "a real feast" at this "wonderful" winner, rated No. 1 for Food
in Amsterdam, that "can be counted on" for "consistently high-
quality" French-International cuisine offered in "surprising" multicourse menus of "gorgeous, creative tapaslike dishes that go on and
on"; servers who ensure "you're really pampered" and "great" decor
also make it "worth" "the journey" to the "out-of-the-way" location in
Ouderkerk aan de Amstel; P.S. "on a hot summer evening, head for a
seat on the terrace."

Sichuan Food *Chinese* | 23 | 16 | 18 | M |

Centrum | Reguliersdwarsstraat 35 | (31-20) 626-9327

"Extraordinary Peking duck" and "great oysters from the wok" are the
stars of the show at this "classic" Chinese in the Centrum that fans call a
"wonderful place" for its "high-quality" cuisine, including "some dishes
that are actually authentic"; still, heat-seekers say there's "not much
spice" in the Westernized fare, while others insist that "service can be
slow when it's busy" and the "outdated decor" is "slightly gaudy."

Tempo Doeloe *Indonesian* | 23 | 15 | 19 | M |

Rembrandtplein | Utrechtsestraat 75 | (31-20) 625-6718 |
www.tempodoeloerestaurant.nl

"Fantastic fare" "keeps patrons coming back" to this "classic Indonesian
rijsttafel restaurant", a "moderately priced" and "always crowded"
"Amsterdam favorite" "on a beautiful block" in the Rembrandtplein
area, where the "attentive owner" and his "friendly", "patient servers
will explain the entire menu" ("let them guide you"); some "critics
claim the decor", "stuffy atmosphere" and "tight quarters" "take away
from the experience", "but real foodies would travel far for cooking
this authentic"; P.S. "ring the bell and the door opens."

	FOOD	DECOR	SERVICE	COST

Tomo Sushi *Japanese*

22 | 16 | 20 | M

Centrum | Reguliersdwarsstraat 131 | (31-20) 528-5208

"Don't tell too many people" plead patrons panicked that this "small" Japanese place "hidden away" "near the Rembrandtplein" "will become overcrowded" with customers clamoring for its "excellent sushi" "cut well and served imaginatively" ("awesome" yakitori too); other pluses include "good", "friendly service", "hip decor" with a "clean", "modern design" and relatively "low prices" that make it "a good value."

⊠ Van Vlaanderen ⊠Ⓜ *French/Mediterranean*

27 | 20 | 24 | E

Leidseplein | Weteringschans 175 | (31-20) 622-8292

"An antidote to overly trendy places" is this "lovely, low-key" spot in the Leidseplein area featuring "fantastic" French-Mediterranean fare that "always pleasantly surprises"; perhaps the "informal", "quite-small" interior "with not much space between the tables" doesn't fully do justice to "the caliber of cuisine", but it's nevertheless "a quiet" refuge from "the heart of the action", and the "nice", "capable waiters do their utmost to make your dinner a success."

Vermeer ⊠ *French/International*

24 | 23 | 24 | VE

Centrum | NH Barbizon Palace Hotel | Prins Hendrikkade 59-72 | (31-20) 556-4885 | www.restaurantvermeer.nl

"Outstanding cuisine" is a hallmark of this "top-class" "favorite" in the Centrum's NH Barbizon Palace Hotel, where the French-International "food is amazing" and the "wine list elaborate"; some find "the majorly elegant dining room" "pretty", others "a bit stiff", but all agree the "friendly yet professional staff" provides "impeccable service", leading most to insist that you "couldn't have a more enjoyable evening."

Visaandeschelde *International/Seafood*

26 | 20 | 21 | E

Rivierenbuurt | Scheldeplein 4 | (31-20) 675-1583 | www.visaandeschelde.nl

"Visitors to Holland" in search of "wonderful" International cuisine "with a focus on seafood" should follow the hordes of locals who crowd this "very hip place" that's "a little out of the way" in the Rivierenbuurt; after all, "you come here for really great fish" dishes, which incorporate Japanese, French and Mediterranean influences, and are "nicely served" at "well-situated tables" by a "stellar" staff; P.S. "don't forget the excellent wines."

⊠ Yamazato *Japanese*

27 | 19 | 25 | VE

Pijp | Hotel Okura | Ferdinand Bolstraat 333 | (31-20) 678-8351 | www.okura.nl

"For real Japanese food, this is the place to be in the Netherlands" say fans of this "absolute treat" in the Pijp's Hotel Okura that serves "fresh", "fabulous presentations" of "some of the best sushi in Europe" along with other "outstanding" offerings, all backed up by an "extensive sake list"; "alas", some say, it's a "shame the decor doesn't quite reach the same level", but "excellent service" from the "trilingual staff" more than compensates – "be prepared" for the bill, though, as it's definitely "costly."

Athens

TOP FOOD RANKING

	Restaurant	Cuisine
29	Spondi	French/Mediterranean
26	48, The Restaurant	Greek
	Varoulko	Mediterranean/Seafood
24	Sale e Pepe	Italian
	Pil Poul et Jérôme Serres	French/Mediterranean
	Thalassinos	Seafood
23	Parea	Greek
	Kiku	Japanese
	Vassilenas	Greek
	Daphne's	Greek/International
22	Papadakis	Greek
	Milos Athens	Greek/Seafood
	7 Thalasses	Greek/Seafood
21	GB Corner	Mediterranean
20	Kafeneio	Greek
	Balthazar	Mediterranean
	Boschetto	Mediterranean
	Premiere*	Greek/Mediterranean
19	Mamacas	Greek
18	Orizontes	Mediterranean

Balthazar ❷ *Mediterranean*   **20** | **24** | **18** | **E**

Ampelokipi | Tsoha 27 & Bournazou | (30-210) 641-2300 | www.balthazar.gr
"Dangerously trendy", this Mediterranean in the "hip" Ampelokipi neighborhood is "great in the summer", when diners forgo an "amazing" modern art–filled interior for the century-old mansion's "superb" garden; the fare is "up to par" though "not exquisite", but that doesn't bother the "beautiful"-"people watchers" at the bar.

Boschetto ❷🅂 *Mediterranean*   **20** | **19** | **21** | **VE**

Kolonaki | Evangelismos Park | Gennadiou St. & Vassilissis Sofias Ave. | (30-210) 721-0893 | www.boschetto.gr
A "favorite of foreigners, businessmen" and affluent Athenians, this sophisticated "old reliable" in Kolonaki combines "good" "Italian-inspired" Med cuisine with "friendly" service; an elegant glass-conservatory interior looks onto the National Gallery, while terrace tables in "lovely" Evangelismos Park make it an oasis amid "magnificent" greenery.

🅉 Daphne's *Greek/International*   **23** | **23** | **21** | **E**

Plaka | Lysikratous 4 | (30-210) 322-7971 | www.daphnesrestaurant.gr
Set in a restored 19th-century townhouse, this "wonderful" Greek-International in the Plaka is "a find", starting with its "beautiful", enclosed courtyard and continuing on to its "superb" old-world decor replete with "lovely" Pompeii-esque frescoes painted by the owner; the interior's "warmth and charm" extend to an "attentive staff"

---

* Indicates a tie with restaurant above

and a menu of "traditional" favorites – "by all means, don't miss the rabbit *stifado* (stew)."

☑ 48, The Restaurant ●☒ *Greek* | 26 | 26 | 25 | VE |

Ampelokipi | Armatolon & Klefton 48 | (30-210) 641-1082 | www.48therestaurant.com

"Easily the coolest place I've ever been to" say fans of this "beautiful", "modern" Ampelokipi Greek with dramatic lighting and a "magical" courtyard where diners eat literally "over the water" via a see-through platform; chef Christoforos Peskias caters to a "hip", "pretty" clientele with pricey, "innovative takes" on traditional fare, while "friendly service" and an extensive French *vin* list complete a "wonderful experience."

☑ GB Corner ● *Mediterranean* | 21 | 22 | 22 | VE |

Syntagma | Hotel Grande Bretagne | Syntagma Sq. | (30-210) 333-0000 | www.grandebretagne.gr

Situated in the lobby of the stately Hotel Grande Bretagne, this "bit of old Europe" in a "beautiful space" attracts power-lunchers with its "good", "very expensive" Mediterranean cuisine, "attentive but not intrusive" staff and "excellent wine list, including Greek vintages"; P.S. for a more "serene" experience, romantics recommend the GB Roof Garden upstairs, with its "incredible, magical views of the Acropolis to your left and Parliament to your right."

Kafeneio ●☒ *Greek* | 20 | 14 | 19 | M |

Kolonaki | Loukianou 26 | (30-210) 722-9056

"For a true Kolonaki dining experience", try this trendy but "traditional" "treat" serving "quite original" takes on "affordable" Greek favorites; the simple, nondescript interior boasts "little atmosphere", so a mostly local clientele advises "eat outside" at one of the sidewalk tables that are "great for people-watching" in this "hot" section of Athens.

Kiku ●☒ *Japanese* | 23 | 16 | 21 | VE |

Kolonaki | Dimokritou 12 | (30-210) 364-7033

Considered "the best sushi restaurant in town", this Japanese located on a busy side street in Kolonaki is an "excellent" choice "for a business meal" of "good" raw fish, albeit at "expensive – prices; the minimalist setting – think blond wood and hanging scrolls – strikes some as "boring", but its "nearly authentic" cooked dishes make it a "favorite of Japanese tourists" as well as those "living in Athens."

Mamacas ● *Greek* | 19 | 19 | 16 | M |

Gazi | Persephone 41 | (30-210) 346-4984 | www.mamacas.gr

'*Mamaca*' is Greek for 'mommy', and this pioneer of the modern, "fashionable" taverna contrasts its contemporary clean lines and whitewashed walls with "great, homestyle", like-mom-used-to-make cooking that's so "traditional" some snipe it "doesn't even pretend to be imaginative"; while critics claim it's "overrated", it's a "Gazi favorite" that's "packed" with a hip, late-night crowd and "great for people-watching."

☑ Milos Athens ● *Greek/Seafood* | 22 | 22 | 23 | VE |

Kolonaki | Hilton Athens | Vassilissis Sofias 46 | (30-210) 724-4400 | www.hilton.com

With long-standing restaurants in New York City and Montréal, chef-owner Costas Spiliades came home to open this "starkly modern"

Greek seafooder with a "convenient" location in the landmark Hilton Athens; an "elegant" dining room (complete with open kitchen and marble display cases) and outdoor terrace set the stage for "superb" seasonal specialties and grilled fish "so fresh, you'll have to wash the salt spray off of your face" – much as you'll do with your smile once the über-"expensive" check arrives.

Orizontes ● *Mediterranean*   18 | 22 | 19 | VE

Kolonaki | Lycabettus Hill | (30-210) 722-7065 | www.kastelorizo.com.gr
There's no other way to get there, so "take the funicular up Lycabettus Hill and get ready" for a "spectacular view" – the name means 'horizons' – overlooking the Acropolis and all of Athens from this "memorable", upmarket Mediterranean; several terraces make summer dining "a treat" for tourists and the city's see-and-be-seen elite, although some say the "good", globally influenced fare doesn't live up to the setting or "justify the cost."

Papadakis ✉ *Greek*   22 | 19 | 21 | E

Kolonaki | Voukourestiou 47 & Fokilidou | (30-210) 360-8621
On a citrus-tree-lined street in the heart of Kolonaki lies this "popular" Greek import "straight from Paros Island" that specializes in "excellent", "imaginative" fish dishes, along with "ample alternatives for carnivores and vegetarians", all at "fairly reasonable" prices; a "welcoming staff" presides over a small but "beautiful" setting that evokes "a seaside taverna."

Parea ●Ⓜ *Greek*   23 | 22 | 22 | E

Kerameikos | Eridanus Hotel | Pireos 78 | (30-210) 520-0630 | www.eridanus.gr
Top toque Lefteris Lazarou of the highly rated Varoulko is producing "excellent food" at this new Hellenic in the basement of the Eridanus Hotel; come summer it moves up to the rooftop terrace to take advantage of views of the Acropolis, the ancient cemetery of Keramikos and Philoppapou Hill; whatever season, it all adds up to "a wonderful evening and great memories" – "everything anyone could ask for the full Greek experience."

Ⓩ Pil Poul et   24 | 25 | 22 | E
Jérôme Serres ●✉ *French/Mediterranean*

Thisio | Apostolou Pavlou 51 & Poulopoulou | (30-210) 342-3665 | www.pilpoul.gr
Star chef Jérôme Serres (ex his own namesake spot and Spondi) has just joined forces with this establishment in a beautiful restored mansion in Thisio, and the result is "great" "creative" French-Mediterranean cuisine served by an "excellent" staff; the "incredible" setting includes "a dreamlike" terrace with "one of the most magnificent views of the Acropolis."

Premiere ●✉ *Greek/Mediterranean*   20 | 19 | 18 | E

Neos Kosmos | Athenaeum InterContinental | Syngrou Ave. 89-93 | (30-210) 920-6981 | www.interconti.com
The Greek-Med food at this venue on the rooftop of the Athenaeum InterContinental is "good", but it's the all-white outdoor terrace and its "amazing", "under-the-stars" view of the Acropolis and Lycabetus Hill that gets the most applause; sculptures and paintings from re-

nowned contemporary collector Dakis Ioanou and an "attractive" clientele stand out against a minimalist backdrop.

☑ Sale e Pepe ●☒ *Italian*   24 | 18 | 22 | E

Kolonaki | Aristippou 34 | (30-210) 723-4102

A "lovely dining experience", this "high-class Italian" "aims to please" with simple, "well-executed" dishes and a "pleasant", antiques-filled setting; "great service" and a chef who "adds a personal touch" draw a chic crowd from surrounding Kolonaki, although most visit this "gem" for "one of the best wine lists in Athens", an "exquisite" selection of over 5,000 bottles.

7 Thalasses ●☒ *Greek/Seafood*   22 | 20 | 22 | E

Kolonaki | Omirou 11 & Vissarionos | (30-210) 362-4825

The name of this Kolonaki establishment means 'seven seas', so the fact that this Greek specializes in "excellent" fish should come as no surprise; the nautically decorated setting "could use an update", but "good value for the money" keeps luring locals back.

☑ Spondi ● *French/Mediterranean*   29 | 24 | 26 | VE

Pangrati | Varnavas Sq. | Pyrronos 5 | (30-210) 752-0658 | www.spondi.gr

At this elegant Pangrati restaurant rated No. 1 for Food in Athens, travelers and the city's well-to-do are "totally blown away" by chef Arnaud Bignon's "excellent", "creative" French-Mediterranean fare that's praised for its "outstanding taste and presentation"; set on three "beautiful" floors with a "spectacular" courtyard and terrace, this pricey 'offering to the gods' (the meaning of its name) rounds out the experience with "wonderfully attentive" service and a "superb wine list", including a "nice selection of Greek" labels.

Thalassinos ●Ⓜ *Seafood*   24 | 17 | 23 | M

Tzitzifies | Irakleous & Lysikratous 32 | (30-210) 940-4518

Seafood lovers from around the city descend on this "Athens treasure", a "quality" Tzitzifies taverna that's a good choice for "exquisite fish" and a "great variety" of other "delicious" dishes; some deem the rustic, tchotchke-filled interior "dull", but moderate prices help this local favorite "stay busy."

☑ Varoulko ●☒ *Mediterranean/Seafood*   26 | 20 | 23 | VE

Kerameikos | Pireos 80 | (30-210) 411-2043 | www.varoulko.gr

This "can't-miss" Med seafooder in historic Karameikos from acclaimed chef-owner Lefteris Lazarou "continues to surprise" a host of regulars who appreciate a "uniquely executed", ever-changing menu that exhibits the wealth of "Poseidon's bounty"; a simple, elegant interior dotted with modern sculpture lets the "fresh" fish shine, although wallet-watchers warn the fin fare also "really bites – once you get the check."

Vassilenas ●Ⓜ *Greek*   23 | 20 | 23 | M

Pireas | Aitolikou 72 | (30-210) 461-2457 | www.vassilenas.gr

"One of the best" tavernas in Athens, this stalwart "has modernized its cuisine while maintaining some original" Greek dishes, with an emphasis on fish; moderate prices lead locals to the simple basement space near Piraeus, but in summer the action moves to the flower-bedecked rooftop.

Barcelona

TOP FOOD RANKING

	Restaurant	Cuisine
28	Passadis del Pep	Mediterranean/Seafood
	Drolma	Catalan
	Àbac	Catalan
27	Gaig	Catalan
	Alkimia	Catalan
26	Jean Luc Figueras	French/Catalan
	Cinc Sentits	Catalan/Mediterranean
	Hofmann	Mediterranean
25	Caelis	Catalan/French
	Comerç 24	Spanish/International
	Ca l'Isidre	Catalan/Mediterranean
	Lasarte	Basque
	La Dama	Catalan/Mediterranean
	Botafumeiro	Seafood/Galician
24	Els Pescadors	International/Seafood
	Neichel	French/Mediterranean
	Gorría	Basque/Navarraise
	Arola	Catalan
	Tapaç 24	Catalan

Z Àbac ⧄Ⓜ *Catalan* 28 | - | 26 | VE

Sarrià-Sant Gervasi | Avenida Tibidabo 1357 | (34-93) 319-6600 |
www.restaurantabac.com

Foodies and the fashionable flock to this "exciting" modern Catalan for top toque Xavier Pellicer's "original" "cutting-edge" cuisine with an "amazing combination of flavors" and textures, "especially the tasting menu"; the staff works the room with "choreographed gracefulness", leading gastronomic groupies to conclude it's "top-notch in every way"; N.B. post-Survey the restaurant moved from the Born district to this new locale in Sant Gervasi.

Z Alkimia ⧄ *Catalan* 27 | 21 | 22 | E

Eixample | Indústria 79 | (34-93) 207-6115

"Currently one of the best restaurants in Barcelona" state supporters of star chef Jordi Vilà's new-wave Catalan in the Eixample, with its "excellent" and "unusual amalgam of explosive flavors"; the "white minimalist" setting evokes a "sense of purity that is carried over into the food", while alchemy symbols on the wall stylishly suggest the restaurant's name.

Arola Ⓜ *Catalan* 24 | 25 | 24 | VE

Port Olímpic | Hotel Arts | Marina 19-21 | (34-93) 483-8090 |
www.arola-arts.com

Chef Sergi Arola, a Ferran Adrià disciple who also runs Madrid's groundbreaking La Broche, heads up this "trendy" modern Catalan in the "fantastic" Hotel Arts; a "beautiful"-looking staff serves "creative", "attractive small plates" in a "perfect location" with "wonderful views" of the Olímpic Harbor and the sea.

	FOOD	DECOR	SERVICE	COST

☒ Barceloneta ● *Mediterranean/Seafood*   21 | 18 | 18 | M

Barceloneta | Moll dels Pescadors | L'Escar 22 | (34-93) 221-2111 | www.rte-barceloneta.com

This big, "boisterous", "fairly priced" Med with "top-quality fish" and a "cordial" staff has an "excellent location on the water" in Barceloneta; the "dining room doesn't need a lot of decoration because the view is enough", and in summer "a table on the terrace" is even more ideal.

☒ Botafumeiro ● *Seafood/Galician*   25 | 18 | 23 | VE

Gràcia | Gran de Gràcia 81 | (34-93) 218-4230 | www.botafumeiro.es

For the "freshest seafood", particularly the "pristine cold shellfish platter", many head to this 31-year-old "emblematic" Galician in Gràcia with a "good" regional wine list, "warm" setting and popular bar; the sprawling, "hustle-bustle" space can be "noisy", and it's "expensive", but that doesn't keep loyal crowds from coming back.

Caelis ☒Ⓜ *Catalan/French*   25 | 23 | 26 | VE

Eixample | Hotel Palace | Gran Via de les Corts Catalanes 668 | (34-93) 510-1205 | www.caelis.com

The former "grande dame" that was called Diana got a new name and a redo and the result is this handsome contemporary space in the Eixample that's a suitable backdrop for "superior service" and chef Romain Fornell's "excellent" Catalan-French cuisine; it ain't "cheap", but what do you expect, "it's the Palace."

☒ Ca l'Isidre ☒ *Catalan/Mediterranean*   25 | 18 | 23 | VE

El Raval | Les Flors 12 | (34-93) 441-1139 | www.calisidre.com

"Creative but not froufrou" describes the "culinary delights" found at this family-run Catalan-Med in El Raval, where chef Núria Gironés, the daughter of the owner and former noted chef, especially excels at "superb" desserts like the "best chocolate soufflé"; a "most accommodating and helpful staff" presides over a quietly "elegant" room with original art – Picasso, Miró – on the walls; "it's expensive, but you leave with the sense that you invested your money very well."

Cinc Sentits ●☒ *Catalan/Mediterranean*   26 | 22 | 24 | E

Eixample | Aribau 58 | (34-93) 323-9490 | www.cincsentits.com

"Barcelona is the new capital of world dining", and this family-run Catalan-Med in the Eixample showcasing Jordi Artal's "creative but intelligible cuisine" is "one of its heads of state"; surveyors single out the tasting menus paired with "surprising but always exquisite wines" as providing not only "a great meal but a great foodie deal"; "service is a rare blend of refinement and genuine hospitality", and the setting is sleek contemporary chic.

Comerç 24 ●☒Ⓜ *Spanish/International*   25 | 23 | 22 | E

El Born | Comerç 24 | (34-93) 319-2102 | www.comerc24.com

"Exciting, unpredictable" and "adventurous" sums up this avant-garde Spanish-International in the Born district run by "dynamic" chef-owner Carles Abellán, a disciple of legendary Ferran Adrià of El Bulli; "inventive", "unforgettable" tapas are "taken to a sexy new level" and served by a "charming staff" in a cooler than cool, colorful minimalist setting, making this a "must-eat-at in Barcelona."

	FOOD	DECOR	SERVICE	COST

⚡ Drolma 🔲 *Catalan* — 28 | 25 | 27 | VE

Eixample | Hotel Majestic | Passeig de Gràcia 68 | (34-93) 496-7710 |
www.hotelmajestic.es

Chef Fermí Puig's "outstanding" modern Catalan in the Hotel Majestic
features "out-of-this-world", cutting-edge cuisine (glazed baby goat is
his signature) and a small but "stylish" setting with views of the Paseo
de Gràcia; it's "exceptionally expensive", but that hasn't kept it from
becoming a "bastion for Barcelona's rich and powerful."

El Bulli 🔲 *Eclectic/Spanish* — - | - | - | VE

Roses | Cala Montjoi, Ap. 30 | (34-97) 215-0457 | www.elbulli.com

On the Costa Brava coastline near Roses, this deceptively rustic-
looking lair of molecular gastronomy originator Ferran Adrià draws
epicureans from around the world for extravagant 33-course modern
Spanish tasting menus featuring the surrealist likes of freeze-fried
eggs and caviar made from olive oil (the dishes change annually); a
polished staff, quaint bulldog-themed dining room and terrace overlooking an Arcadian inlet complete the picture; N.B. if you score a
reservation – it's open April-September only and books up a year in
advance – bring your sense of humor and a fat wallet.

Els Pescadors ❶ *International/Seafood* — 24 | 19 | 21 | E

Poblenou | Plaça Prim 1 | (34-93) 225-2018 | www.elspescadors.com

This large International stalwart with "great seafood" ("amazing salt-
baked fish") and a strong Spanish wine list is "worth the trip to
Poblenou" (about a mile down the waterfront north of the Olympic
Port); there's a trio of dining rooms to choose from, and in summer
terrace tables are a cool alternative.

⚡ Gaig 🔲 *Catalan* — 27 | 21 | 24 | VE

Eixample | Cram Hotel | Aragó 214 | (34-93) 429-1017 |
www.restaurantgaig.com

Though this family-owned establishment in the Eixample dates back
to 1869, its current chef, Carles Gaig, produces "creative" modern
Catalan cuisine that's "among the best in Barcelona", with the
"emphasis on elegant dishes made with the best ingredients"; an "intimate", "quiet" setting and "superb service" add to the "fine-all-
around", "very expensive" experience.

Gorría 🔲 *Basque/Navarraise* — 24 | 16 | 20 | E

Eixample | Diputació 421 | (34-93) 245-1164 | www.restaurantegorria.com

Long-standing, family-run Basque-Navarraise in the Eixample featuring "classic" dishes like suckling pig and "meat as good as Peter
Luger's in Brooklyn"; a timeless "rustic" setting with wood, brick walls
and stained glass, an "excellent wine list" and "doable" prices add to
the laid-back vibe.

Hofmann 🔲 *Mediterranean* — 26 | 19 | 21 | E

La Ribera | Argentería 74-78 | (34-93) 319-5889 | www.hofmann-bcn.com

"They aim high in the kitchen and succeed most of the time" at this
restaurant/culinary school in La Ribera run by chef/owner/teacher
Mey Hofmann; "fantastic" Mediterranean dishes and "work-of-art"
desserts are served in a series of "charming" dining rooms housed in
a 19th-century building; N.B. closed Saturday and Sunday.

	FOOD	DECOR	SERVICE	COST

Jean Luc Figueras ⊠ *French/Catalan* — 26 | 24 | 28 | VE

Gràcia | Santa Teresa 10 | (34-93) 415-2877

If you feel like French-Catalan while you're in Spain, try Jean Luc Figueras' "top-notch", "inventive" cuisine, which is served in "the refined" and "elegant" setting of legendary couturier "Balenciaga's former studio" in a 19th-century Gràcia palace; "superb service" and a "wonderful wine list" add to a "memorable evening" that's "worth every euro."

☑ La Dama *Catalan/Mediterranean* — 25 | 26 | 25 | VE

Eixample | Avinguda Diagonal 423 | (34-93) 202-0686 | www.ladama-restaurant.com

"Absolutely elegant", this "grand, old" dame excels with a "gorgeous", "romantic" art nouveau setting in a 1918 Eixample building; "very good" creative Catalan-Mediterranean food, an exceptional wine list and "immaculate", "not stuffy", service also lead devotees to declare "it's a gem that could hold its own anywhere."

Lasarte ⊠ *Basque* — 25 | 23 | 23 | E

Eixample | Hotel Condes de Barcelona | Mallorca 259 | (34-93) 445-3242 | www.restaurantlasarte.com

This modern Spanish Basque "masterpiece" owned by star chef Martín Berasategui and located in the Hotel Condes de Barcelona was one of the city's most anticipated openings; "outstanding food and attention to detail" and a "beautiful" split-level contemporary space make it a "must-stop" hot spot for foodies and fashionistas alike.

☑ Los Caracoles ● *Spanish* — 20 | 18 | 17 | M

Barri Gòtic | Escudellers 14 | (34-93) 302-3185

The name of this "cavernous", "rustic" 1835 "landmark" Spanish in Barri Gòtic translates as 'snails' and that's the specialty here, along with "wonderful, spit-roasted chicken" and "paella served in skillets the size of flying saucers"; sure, it's "touristy", "campy" and "service is slap-dash", but most maintain it's a "must for first-time" visitors and for its "reasonable prices."

Neichel ⊠Ⓜ *French/Mediterranean* — 24 | 21 | 22 | VE

Pedralbes | Beltrán i Rózpide 1-5 | (34-93) 203-8408 | www.neichel.es

"Everything is great" enthuse admirers of this 26-year-old French-Med where chef-owner Jean-Louis Neichel's "fantastic food" and a "superb wine list" are served by an "impeccable" staff in a room overlooking a garden in residential Pedralbes; but the less-impressed assess the experience as "old-fashioned" and "very expensive."

☑ Passadis del Pep ⊠ *Mediterranean/Seafood* — 28 | 21 | 25 | E

El Born | Plaça de Palau 2 | (34-93) 310-1021 | www.passadis.com

"Don't expect a written menu or a choice" at this "difficult-to-find gem", a Mediterranean seafooder in El Born that's voted No. 1 for Food in the city; the second you sit down, you'll be served sparkling *cava* and an "extravaganza" of "plate-after-plate" of appetizers that "just keep coming" ("don't forget to say stop"), followed by a main course ("if you can still fit it in") that's "the best fish in the world"; it all adds up to a down-to-earth "awesome experience."

	FOOD	DECOR	SERVICE	COST

☒ 7 Portes ◐ *Catalan* | 21 | 21 | 20 | E |

Ciutat Vella | Passeig Isabel II 14 | (34-93) 319-3033 | www.7portes.com
"An old standard that's still going strong", this sprawling 1836 Catalan "institution" and "paella palace" in Port Vell is "one of the oldest continuously operating restaurants in the world"; although "touristy" and "hectic", most maintain that the "good value for the money" and "festive" atmosphere that "reeks of old-world charm" "make up for it."

Tapaç 24 ◐ *Catalan* | 24 | 20 | 21 | E |

Eixample | Diputació 269 | (34-93) 488-0977 | www.tapac24.com
Supporters say "*olé!*" to star chef Carles Abellán, of the city's highly rated and experimental Comerç 24, and his new Catalan in the Eixample, where "sublimely simple" traditional tapas "full of flavor" like ham croquettes are complemented by an "excellent wine list"; open from 8 AM to midnight, the place draws a continuous crowd that clusters at the bar, tables and small dining terrace.

Berlin

TOP FOOD RANKING

	Restaurant	Cuisine
26	VAU	International
24	Lorenz Adlon	French
	Maxwell	French/International
23	Alt Luxemburg	French/Mediterranean
	Die Quadriga*	French/Mediterranean
	44	French/International
	Vox	Asian/French
	Ana e Bruno	Italian/Mediterranean
22	Hartmanns	German/Mediterranean
	Margaux	French
21	Aigner	Viennese
	Guy	French/Mediterranean
	Balthazar	Mediterranean
	San Nicci	Italian
	Grill Royal	Seafood/Steak
	Altes Zollhaus	German
	Borchardt	French/German
	Bacco/Bocca di Bacco	Tuscan
	Diekmann	German/International
20	MaoThai	Thai
	Paris-Moskau	French/Mediterranean
19	Fellini	Italian
16	Paris Bar	French

Aigner ◐ *Viennese*   21 | 19 | 19 | E

Mitte | Französische Str. 25 | (49-30) 203-751-850 |
www.aigner-gendarmenmarkt.de

"Pretty, fashionable people" flock to this "popular" "place in Mitte",
"on the Gendarmenmarkt", where you'll "want to order seconds" of
the "excellent Viennese cooking" that's "well-rounded" with German
influences – the signature roast "duck is spectacular" – and served by
a "friendly, fast" staff; though located within a typical GDR-style
'Plattenbau' (concrete slab building), its "wonderful" 19th-century
bistro setting comes from transplanting "beautiful decor" from the
former Café Aigner in Vienna.

Altes Zollhaus Ⓢ Ⓜ *German*   21 | 17 | 20 | E

Kreuzberg | Carl-Herz-Ufer 30 | (49-30) 692-3300 |
www.altes-zollhaus-berlin.de

Located within an "old customs office" in a "picturesque setting beside" the Landwehrkanal in Kreuzberg, this "standby" boasts "rustic"
yet "dignified decor" that complements its "appealing", "extensive
menu" of "excellent" traditional *Deutsch* dishes, which are served by
an "accommodating" staff; some say it's "a bit touristic", but more
maintain it "successfully straddles the line between historical kitsch

---

* Indicates a tie with restaurant above

and authentic old-style German eating"; N.B. its Smugglers Barn space is perfect for parties.

Z Alt Luxemburg *French/Mediterranean*   23 | 21 | 25 | E

Charlottenburg | Windscheidstr. 31 | (49-30) 323-8730 | www.altluxemburg.de

"One expects the old Kaiser to walk in" to this "wonderful place", a "Berlin standard" not far from the Charlottenburg Castle, where the "fast service" provided by Ingrid Wannemacher's "nice" staff always "satisfies", as does her husband Karl's "comprehensive menu" of "delicious" New French–Med cuisine ("no schnitzel here") offered amid "quiet" surroundings; no wonder so many regulars are "happy" to call it a "favorite."

Ana e Bruno *Italian/Mediterranean*   23 | 17 | 22 | E

Charlottenburg | Sophie-Charlotten-Str. 101 | (49-30) 325-7110 | www.ana-e-bruno.de

"Made for a lovely, quiet evening", this "cozy" Charlottenburg spot is home to "accommodating chef" Bruno Pellegrini, whose "ambitious" menu offers a taste of "*bella Italia*" via "excellent, inventive" Italian-Mediterranean cuisine at prices that may be "high" but are "appropriate for the quality of the food"; some call the decor "less than striking", but at least "you know you're in good hands" with the "polite staff"; P.S. "be sure to make reservations, as tables are limited."

Z Bacco *Tuscan*   21 | 19 | 19 | E

Charlottenburg | Marburger Str. 5 | (49-30) 211-8687 | www.bacco.de

Z Bocca di Bacco ● *Tuscan*

Mitte | Friedrichstr. 167/168 | (49-30) 2067-2828 | www.boccadibacco.de

The Mannozzi family oversees this Tuscan pair, the original an old-fashioned trattoria "with history" that's been serving "good, traditional cuisine with no surprises" in Charlottenburg since the late-'60s, and its 'mouth of Bacchus' offshoot in Mitte a more "sophisticated", "upmarket" eatery offering "nouvelle" fare and a "good selection of wines" in a "modern, stylish" setting; both, however, are often "star-studded" and feature "fresh ingredients" and "charming, attentive" staffers, making either one "worth a try."

Balthazar *Mediterranean*   21 | 20 | 20 | E

Wilmersdorf | Kurfürstendamm 160 | (49-30) 8940-8477 | www.restaurant-balthazar.de

Tucked into a classical Berlin townhouse in Wilmersdorf, at the "less-fashionable end of Kurfürstendamm", is this urbane-looking Mediterranean with Asian accents that offers "enjoyable", "high-class cuisine", a "great wine list" and a "warm staff"; moreover, the practical point out there's a bargain 10 euros business lunch and at dinner "you can walk away without emptying your wallet."

Z Borchardt ● *French/German*   21 | 20 | 19 | E

Mitte | Französische Str. 47 | (49-30) 8188-6262

"Popular" with "politicians, movie stars" and other "celebrity patrons", "this Gendarmenmarkt classic" in Mitte is known for a "wonderful menu" of French-German fare – including "delicious fish" dishes and some of "the best Wiener schnitzel in Berlin" – "hospitably" presented in a "large", "beautiful" "brasserie" setting with "pre-war flair";

still, those with "unfulfilled expectations" posit that "one pays for the stargazing" and "glam" scene, adding that certain "snooty" staffers are "less accommodating when serving Mr. and Ms. Average."

Diekmann *German/International*   21 | 18 | 21 | M

Charlottenburg | Meinekestr. 7 | (49-30) 883-3321
Dahlem | Châlet Suisse | Clayallee 99 | (49-30) 832-6362 ◑
Mitte | Weinhaus Huth | Alte Potsdamer Str. 5 |
(49-30) 2529-7524 ◑
Mitte | Hauptbahnhof | Europlatz 1 | (49-30) 209-1929 ◑
www.j-diekmann.de

Of this "fantastic"quartet serving "German food with a nouveau twist", "the original", a brasserie on the ground floor of a townhouse in a "beautiful Charlottenburg spot", "offers a genteel experience", while the "always-bustling Potsdamer Platz" branch in Mitte provides a "reliable dinner before the Philharmonie"; unlike its French-inflected siblings, the one in Dahlem has a Swiss flavor and the newest locale on Europlatz boasts an oyster bar, but each is "a safe bet" for a "good selection" of "tasty", "well-prepared food" served by "friendly people" in "pleasant" digs.

Z Die Quadriga ⧆ *French/Mediterranean*   23 | 25 | 23 | E

Wilmersdorf | Brandenburger Hof | Eislebener Str. 14 | (49-30) 2140-5650 |
www.brandenburger-hof.com

"A memorable meal" awaits at this "nice hotel dining" venue whose two rooms flank a "beautiful [Japanese] garden" in Wilmersdorf's Brandenburger Hof; chef Bobby Bräuer creates a "varied menu" of "exquisite" New French–Mediterranean cuisine, which is accompanied by an extensive all-German wine list and "incredible service" from a "helpful, charming" staff; sure, it's "somewhat expensive", but it's definitely a "first-class" experience; N.B. there's live jazz on Tuesdays.

Fellini ◑ *Italian*   19 | 20 | 22 | E

Mitte | Hilton Berlin | Mohrenstr. 30 | (49-30) 20230 |
www.hilton.com

"Wonderful service" from "attentive" staffers who "always have a smile on their faces" sets the mood at this Italian "in the basement" of the Hilton Berlin, at the Gendarmenmarkt in Mitte; admirers advise "spoil yourself with something good" from the "delicious" menu and enjoy the "eye-catching decor" of the "beautiful" "cellar vault"; some say there's "nothing spectacular" going on in the kitchen, but more appreciate the "pleasing food" and "surprisingly" "appropriate" prices.

44 *French/International*   23 | 18 | 21 | VE

Wilmersdorf | Swissôtel | Augsburger Str. 44 | (49-30) 220-100 |
www.restaurant44.de

Fans of chef "Tim Raue, one of the '*junge wilde*' (young wilds)", credit him for translating his "good ideas" into "excellent", "inventive" New French–International cooking that "never fails to excite", making "multiple" visits to this "quiet, romantic" venue on the top floor of Wilmersdorf's modern Swissôtel "a joy"; critics, though, claim the menu "tries very hard to be interesting" but "overwhelms the taste buds with competing flavors"; N.B. ask for a table on the small terrace overlooking the famous Kurfürstendamm.

	FOOD	DECOR	SERVICE	COST

Grill Royal ●Ⓜ⇶ Seafood/Steak
21 | 20 | 20 | E

Mitte | Friedrichstr. 105B | (49-30) 2887-9288 | www.grillroyal.com
This "great" new steakhouse and seafooder in trendy Mitte (the "best location in Berlin") offers "delicious" food and is "often packed" with a chic crowd that doesn't complain about the "expensive" tabs; the spacious wood and marble setting boasts a vintage motor boat, a "spectacular" terrace and a view of the Spree River.

Guy Ⓩ French/Mediterranean
21 | 19 | 19 | E

Mitte | Jägerstr. 59-60 | (49-30) 2094-2600 | www.guy-restaurant.de
Ensconced "in a courtyard" in Mitte between the Gendarmenmarkt and the Friedrichstrasse shopping area, this French-Med is a "favorite regular stop in town", "satisfying" surveyors with "delicious" fare that's "hard to beat", not to mention "tasteful decor" and "excellent service" from a "well-trained staff"; "it isn't cheap, but the bill isn't irritating" – especially if you "go on someone else's tab"; P.S. though the "dining area is beautiful", "the terrace is an oasis."

Hartmanns ●Ⓩ German/Mediterranean
22 | 20 | 19 | E

Kreuzberg | Fichtestr. 31 | (49-30) 6120-1003 | www.hartmanns-restaurant.de
Chef-owner Stefan Hartmann's intimate and "enjoyable" new spot combines German and Mediterranean influences, and the result is a "delicious" and "very creative" combination; set in the basement of a classical turn-of-the-century Kreuzberg townhouse, the serene minimalist space gets a kick of color from modern art and strikingly spare floral arrangements.

Ⓩ Lorenz Adlon ⓈⓂ French
24 | 24 | 22 | VE

Mitte | Hotel Adlon Kempinski | Unter den Linden 77 | (49-30) 22610 | www.hotel-adlon.de
"Indulge yourself" at this "romantic" "gourmet restaurant" in Mitte's Hotel Adlon Kempinski, "just steps from the Brandenburg Gate"; it features classic French cuisine, a "comprehensive list" of "exquisite wines", a "stylish" setting and "refined staff" that gives one a "feeling of being pampered"; yes, it's "very expensive", but most are prepared "to pay a little more" for such a "luxe" experience – after all, "you have to spoil yourself sometime."

MaoThai am Fasanenplatz Thai
20 | 16 | 20 | M

Wilmersdorf | Meierottostr. 1 | (49-30) 883-2823
MaoThai Stammhaus Thai
Prenzlauer Berg | Wörther Str. 30 | (49-30) 441-9261
"Tasty, tempting" Thai fare made from "fresh" ingredients and prepared at "all levels of spiciness" ensures that patrons "eat well" at this Wilmersdorf Siamese set in a "pleasantly" restored townhouse; the "friendly, quick" staffers decked out in "nice costumes" are "accommodating" and "always able to cope with large groups"; N.B. its Stammhaus sibling opened post-Survey.

Ⓩ Margaux Ⓩ French
22 | 23 | 20 | VE

Mitte | Unter den Linden 78 | (49-30) 2265-2611 | www.margaux-berlin.de
With its "impressive decor", this "fine-dining" venue in Mitte is a "chic", "cosmopolitan" showcase for the "world-class" creations of

chef-owner Michael Hoffmann, whose "high-end" "classic French fare" is "prepared with amazing care" (and some avant-garde touches) then offered with "generous pours" from "an extraordinary wine list"; many are also "wowed" by the "excellent staff", though a few feel they "could do better"; P.S. the desserts are "unbelievable."

☒ **Maxwell** ❂ *French/International*   24 | 21 | 16 | E

Mitte | Bergstr. 22 | (49-30) 280-7121 | www.restaurant-maxwell.de
For "some of the coolest dining" around, experience an "enjoyable meal" at this "trendy" spot set in a "former brewery" "tucked away in a courtyard" in Mitte, where an "inventive" French-International menu of "excellent" cuisine (incorporating Asian, Italian and German influences) is offered in a "beautiful high-ceilinged" space with "modern but not chilly furnishings"; sure, "the service could be more efficient", but at least "the friendly staff" "will smile at you – which in Berlin is like striking gold."

Paris Bar ❂ *French*   16 | 18 | 14 | E

Charlottenburg | Kantstr. 152 | (49-30) 313-8052 | www.parisbar.de
Offering a "great getaway from the Teutonic vibe of Berlin", this "happening" Charlottenburg "landmark" with a "classic French" brasserie feel "has been here forever" and is "always crowded" with fans who "love" "sitting beside" "celebrities and captains of industry" in "homey" digs; still, those who find the "food unremarkable" and the "staff arrogant" insist this "institution" is "now well past its prime", adding "you'll have to dig deep into your pockets" when the bill comes.

Paris-Moskau ⊘ *French/Mediterranean*   20 | 18 | 20 | E

Tiergarten | Alt-Moabit 141 | (49-30) 394-2081 | www.paris-moskau.de
A "special place" to many, this French-Med brasserie in Tiergarten, "near the Reichstag" and "on the old rail tracks" between Paris and Moscow, features a "varied" menu of "imaginative creations" with "great flavor combinations"; the "friendly" staffers "know their jobs extremely well" and the "cozy" setting – a half-timbered tavern dating from 1898 – has "great ambiance", so even if the cash-only experience "could be cheaper", most come away "satisfied."

San Nicci ❂ *Italian*   21 | 19 | 21 | E

Mitte | Friedrichstr. 101 | (49-30) 3064-54980 | www.san-nicci.de
"Who knew Italian in Germany translates well?" but that's what supporters say about this Mitte sibling of Berlin's very popular Borchardt that's being touted as the "new place to go" for breakfast, lunch and dinner; it boasts a "great location" a stone's throw from the Admiralspalast theater, and the "cosmopolitan" brasserie setting includes dramatic columns and an expansive courtyard.

☒ **VAU** ☒ *International*   26 | 23 | 25 | VE

Mitte | Jägerstr. 54-55 | (49-30) 202-9730 | www.vau-berlin.de
"You can't miss" this Mitte "must", an "exquisite-in-every-way" "oasis" "next to the famous Gendarmenmarkt" that's rated No. 1 in Berlin for Food; chef and TV personality Kolja Kleeberg's "heavenly menu" of "excellent", "extremely creative" International cuisine, a "quality wine list", "wonderful service" from a "thoughtful, unintrusive" staff and "cool", "crisp, modern" decor add up to a "superb dining experience"

	FOOD	DECOR	SERVICE	COST

that most insist is "worth the splurge", even if your "wallet still hurts" long after (at least the "lunch prices are more reasonable").

Vox ◐ *Asian/French* | 23 | 23 | 24 | E |

Tiergarten | Grand Hyatt | Marlene-Dietrich-Platz 2 | (49-30) 2553-1234 | www.berlin.grand.hyatt.com

"Everything is top-notch" at this hotel restaurant overlooking the Potsdamer Platz shopping area in Tiergarten's Grand Hyatt, where the service from the "well-trained staff" is "discreet and attentive", the "unconventional decor" is "posh and stylish" and the "great open kitchen's" "fantastic" food – ranging from "excellent sushi" to "interesting" New French–Asian dishes – "is a pleasure for the palate"; no wonder some foreigners insist they "would fly to Berlin just to have dinner here again."

Brussels

TOP FOOD RANKING

	Restaurant	Cuisine
28	Comme Chez Soi	Belgian
	Bruneau	French
27	La Truffe Noire	French/Italian
	Sea Grill	International/Seafood
26	La Maison du Cygne	French
25	Chez Marie	French
24	L'Ecailler du Palais	Seafood
	Villa Lorraine*	Belgian/French
	L'Ogenblik	French
	Café des Spores	European
	Bon-Bon	Belgian/French
23	Blue Elephant	Thai
	Le Fourneau	French/Tapas
	La Maison du Boeuf	French
	Scheltema	French
	L'Idiot du Village	Belgian/French
	La Manufacture	French
22	Lola	French/Italian
	La Porte des Indes	Indian
	Friture René	Belgian
21	Le Marmiton	Belgian/French
	Aux Armes de Bruxelles	Belgian

Z Aux Armes de Bruxelles Ⓜ *Belgian* | 21 | 19 | 19 | E |
Ilôt Sacré | Rue des Bouchers 13 | (32-2) 511-5550 |
www.armesdebruxelles.be

It's "a jewel in the pedestrian" Rue des Bouchers say fans of this Belgian "favorite" since 1921; "few things are better than mussels in Brussels", so those here are a "must", along with "wonderful *waterzooi*" from the "classic menu"; it's a "prototypical brasserie" for "eating like the locals."

Z Belga Queen ◑ *Belgian* | 18 | 27 | 17 | E |
Lower Town | Rue du Fossé aux Loups 32 | (32-2) 217-2187 |
www.belgaqueen.be

"Sexy" describes the "fab" setting – an "ornate", stained-glass ceiling, moody lighting and cool unisex loos – of this Belgian brasserie housed in what was a former belle epoque bank in the Lower Town; gourmands call the food "nothing to write home about" and say "stick to the seafood platter" and raw bar, but scenesters simply go for the "beautiful people."

Blue Elephant *Thai* | 23 | 22 | 21 | E |
Uccle | Chaussée de Waterloo 1120 | (32-2) 374-4962 |
www.blueelephant.com

For 27 years, this Thai in Uccle (with other outposts from London to Dubai) has been leading loyalists on a "wonderful culinary journey"

---

* Indicates a tie with restaurant above

with "fine", "wonderfully spiced" fare; a "beautiful" setting "complete with coconuts and flowers" leads to thoughts of "lush" lands and away from the realities of "Belgian weather."

Bon-Bon ⧄Ⓜ *Belgian/French* | 24 | 19 | 19 | E |

Uccle | Rue des Carmélites 93 | (32-2) 346-6615 | www.bon-bon.be
Chef Christophe Hardiquest's market-driven "modern, refined" Belgian-French cuisine is improvisational, "excellent" and earns him "rising star" status; in a quiet residential street in Uccle, his intimate bistro relies on claret-colored walls and gray banquettes for its unpretentious appeal.

☑ Bruneau *French* | 28 | 25 | 28 | VE |

Ganshoren | Avenue Broustin 73-75 | (32-2) 421-7070 | www.bruneau.be
"Exquisite" exclaim admirers of this 31-year-old Classic French in an elegant double townhouse in residential Ganshoren, about a 15-minute taxi ride from the City Center; chef-owner Jean-Pierre Bruneau's "outstanding" cuisine is complemented by equally "excellent service", a "tremendous" wine list, handsome dining rooms and a summer garden terrace; in all, it's a very "costly" but "outstanding" experience.

Café des Spores ●⧄ *European* | 24 | 20 | 23 | E |

Saint-Gilles | Chaussée D'Alsemberg 103 | (32-2) 534-1303 | www.cafedesspores.be
Fungi fans sprout up at this small, simple European cafe in Saint-Gilles for the namesake spores – namely, "delicious" and "varied fresh mushroom dishes" that are market-driven; oenophiles can also be accommodated by "a fine array of wines" to complement the earthy ingredients.

Chez Marie ⧄Ⓜ *French* | 25 | 21 | 22 | E |

Ixelles | Rue Alphonse de Witte 40 | (32-2) 644-3031
A firm favorite with EU professionals, this Classic French in Ixelles features chef Lilian Devaux's "delicious" cuisine, including a great "value" prix fixe lunch at 17 euros; "tiny", "warm" and "cozy" with "low lights", mirrors and candles, it's also "romantic."

☑ Comme Chez Soi ⧄Ⓜ *Belgian* | 28 | 24 | 27 | VE |

Lower Town | Place Rouppe 23 | (32-2) 512-2921 | www.commechezsoi.be
Pierre Wynants and his son-in-law Lionel Rigolet's "sublime" Belgian in the Lower Town is voted No. 1 for Food in Brussels; a "very attentive but unobtrusive" staff presides over a "fantastic" art nouveau setting with stained-glass flower motifs, although the chef's table in the kitchen is also a coveted spot; it's "extremely expensive", but it's a "gem that's a joy to visit" and "one of the world's great restaurants."

Friture René *Belgian* | 22 | 17 | 19 | M |

Anderlecht | Place de la Résistance 14 | (32-2) 523-2876
Locals love this unpretentious (a red neon sign marks the spot) but "renowned" 1932 Anderlecht Belgian specializing in some of the "best moules and frites in Brussels"; "come hungry", knowing that the "portions are quite large" and the price is right.

La Maison du Boeuf *French* | 23 | 18 | 22 | E |

Upper Town | Hilton Brussels | Boulevard de Waterloo 38 | (32-2) 504-1334 | www.hilton.com
"When you miss USA prime ribs, this is the place to go" urge enthusiasts of this Classic French with a focus on beef in the Upper Town

that's "fantastic for a Hilton"; a "tremendous wine list", "attentive" service and a warm setting with views of palatial gardens make for an "enjoyable experience even if dining alone."

Z La Maison du Cygne 🛱 *French* | 26 | 27 | 24 | VE |

Grand' Place | Rue Charles Buls 2 | (32-2) 511-8244 | www.lamaisonducygne.be

"Beautifully decorated" and in a "stunning location" "overlooking the historic Grand' Place" is this long-standing Classic French in a former 17th-century guildhall; velvet banquettes and paintings by Belgian masters are the "magnificent" backdrop for "excellent" cuisine, "exceptional service" and an "extensive wine list"; given the stratospheric prices, it's ironic that Karl Marx once worked on his Communist Manifesto here.

La Manufacture 🛱 *French* | 23 | 24 | 20 | E |

Ste-Catherine | Rue Notre Dame du Sommeil 12-20 | (32-2) 502-2525 | www.manufacture.be

Housed in a "famous old" former handbag factory – hence the name – this "innovative", "delicious" and fashionable French in the up-and-coming Ste-Catherine district is "not expensive if you compare the price with the quality of the meals"; the "great atmosphere" comes from an expansive, dramatic industrial space with leather banquettes, stone tables and a "sexy staff."

La Porte des Indes *Indian* | 22 | 21 | 19 | E |

Ixelles | Avenue Louise 455 | (32-2) 647-8651 | www.blueelephant.com/pi

"The best Indian food in Brussels by far" brag believers in this "expensive" subcontinental in Ixelles, the brainchild of Karl Steppe, a Belgian antiques dealer, who also owns the global Blue Elephant chain; a traditionally clad staff and vibrant red-and-mauve "setting that's unapologetically colonial" – wooden carvings, tropical flowers and potted palms – add to the authentic experience.

Z La Truffe Noire 🛱 *French/Italian* | 27 | 22 | 25 | VE |

Ixelles | Boulevard de la Cambre 12 | (32-2) 640-4422 | www.truffenoire.com

A "must for truffle lovers", this "excellent" French-Italian in Ixelles features the unearthed fungus from start (with carpaccio) to finish (substituting its sweet chocolate namesake at dessert); "perfect service" and a "sophisticated" room with modern paintings round out the extravagant experience; of course, you'll be digging deep too when it comes time to pay the big bill.

Z L'Ecailler du Palais Royal 🛱 *Seafood* | 24 | 21 | 22 | VE |

Grand Sablon | Rue Bodenbroek 18 | (32-2) 512-8751 | www.lecaillerdupalaisroyal.be

Since 1967, not a morsel of meat has passed through the portals of this "top-quality" seafooder featuring "fish, just fish, but the best" of the catch in the Grand Sablon; "excellent service" and a "wonderful" two-story setting (one room with soothing traditional plaid decor, the other a scarlet salon) make it "great for business lunches", but the exuberant bar with "turquoise fish-scale tiles" is "good for single diners too."

	FOOD	DECOR	SERVICE	COST

Le Fourneau 🖼️Ⓜ️ *French/Tapas* | 23 | 20 | 21 | E |
Ste-Catherine | Place Sainte-Catherine 8 | (32-2) 513-1002
A "must-visit" is what supporters say about this "excellent" new French small-plates specialist whose "sophisticated" "handling of ingredients on a continuously changing menu" "makes it a place to return to whenever the season changes"; you'll "love the location" on medieval Sainte Catherine square, and inside, a handful of tables, long bar and open kitchen are set against a spare but stylish black-and-white room punctuated with snappy red lights.

Le Marmiton ⏺️ *Belgian/French* | 21 | 19 | 20 | E |
Ilôt Sacré | Rue des Bouchers 43A | (32-2) 511-7910 | www.lemarmiton.be
At this long-standing "gem in the Rue des Bouchers", the city's packed restaurant district, the emphasis of the "good-quality" classic Belgian-French fare is on fish dishes like bouillabaisse; it's a "favorite" haunt for many because the "unpretentious" but pretty bistro setting – brick walls, brass lamps and a view of the beautiful arcade, Les Galleries Royales St. Hubert – makes for "a cozy night out."

L'Idiot du Village 🖼️ *Belgian/French* | 23 | 21 | 21 | E |
Marolles | Rue Notre-Seigneur 19 | (32-2) 502-5582
You'd be the idiot if you didn't book way ahead at this popular tiny boîte tucked away in a 17th-century house in Marolles; "inventive" Belgian-French cuisine that "soars with flavor" and a "quirky" "bohemian-chic" atmosphere with "whimsical" flea-market decor attract "Eurocrats wanting to get in touch with their inner hippie."

🆉 L'Ogenblik ⏺️🖼️ *French* | 24 | 18 | 20 | E |
Ilôt Sacré | Galerie des Princes 1 | (32-2) 511-6151 | www.ogenblik.be
"What a bistro should be" declare devotees of this French that's in part of the "beautiful" glassed-in Galeries Saint-Hubert, the "oldest shopping arcade in Europe"; there's "delicious food", an "excellent wine list", "attentive service" and a homey setting, so although it's been a "favorite Brussels haunt" since 1969, it still attracts a cosmopolitan crowd.

Lola *French/Italian* | 22 | 20 | 19 | E |
Grand Sablon | Place du Grand Sablon 33 | (32-2) 514-2460 | www.restolola.be
This French-Italian establishment is in a "great location" for "people-watching" on the "beautiful" Place du Grand Sablon; "tasty" food, "charming" service and "cool" "modern" decor with bright primary colors add to its appeal.

Scheltema 🖼️ *French* | 23 | 19 | 19 | E |
Ilôt Sacré | Rue des Dominicains 7 | (32-2) 512-2084 | www.scheltema.be
Named for a Dutch poet, this huge, "bustling" Classic French brasserie in the Ilôt Sacré features "excellent seafood and desserts" and a warm burnished wood setting; "friendly waiters" and an "Old Europe without the stiff upper lip atmosphere" add to the "wonderful experience."

🆉 Sea Grill 🖼️ *International/Seafood* | 27 | 23 | 27 | VE |
Lower Town | Radisson SAS Royal Hotel | Rue du Fossé aux Loups 47 | (32-2) 217-9225 | www.seagrill.be
"Embedded in the Radisson SAS Royal Hotel" in the Lower Town is this "top-class" International seafooder with "superb" cuisine, "an excel-

lent wine list" and "incomparable service"; still, some carp about the corporate atmosphere and sky-high prices – it's so "expensive" that even "expense accounts will get strained here."

Villa Lorraine ⊠ *Belgian/French*   24 | 25 | 25 | VE
Uccle | Chaussée de la Hulpe 28 | (32-2) 374-3163 | www.villalorraine.be
Nestled on the fringes of the "beautiful" Bois de la Cambre in Uccle, about a 20-minute taxi ride from the City Center, is this "landmark" "temple of Belgian-French haute cuisine" in a 19th-century villa; a "posh" setting, "fine food", sterling service and a "stellar wine cellar" lead to long, lovely lunches or "romantic evenings", particularly out on the summer garden terrace; N.B. jacket required.

Budapest

TOP FOOD RANKING

	Restaurant	Cuisine
28	Baraka	International/Mediterranean
	Vadrózsa	Hungarian/International
27	Páva	Italian
25	Lou-Lou	French
	Kacsa	Hungarian/International
24	Gundel	Hungarian/International
	Fausto's	Tuscan
23	Café Kör	Hungarian/International
	Rézkakas	Hungarian
	Segal*	International
	Bistro Jardin	Hungarian/International
	Papageno*	International
	Kisbuda Gyöngye	Hungarian/International
21	Cyrano	Hungarian/International
	Kárpátia*	Hungarian
	Chez Daniel	French
20	Alabárdos	Hungarian
	Belcanto	Hungarian/International
	Remiz*	Hungarian/International
	Bagolyvár	Hungarian
	Múzeum	Hungarian/International

Alabárdos Ⓢ *Hungarian* — 20 | 21 | 21 | E

Várnegyed | Országház utca 2 | (36-1) 356-0851 | www.alabardos.hu
The "original decor" of weaponry on display recalls "the age of chivalry" at this "top-flight" Várnegyed spot with a "hospitable" staff and an "excellent menu" that offers both "gourmet and traditional" Hungarian "favorites"; if some feel tabs are "a bit higher than they should be", at least "big portions" come with the "big prices."

Bagolyvár *Hungarian* — 20 | 18 | 20 | M

Városliget | Állatkerti út 2 | (36-1) 468-3110 | www.bagolyvar.com
A "woman's" touch defines this "charming" Városliget "spot adjacent to the Budapest Zoo" that's "entirely staffed by ladies", from the "quick, precise" servers to the female "chefs who do a fine job" with the "wonderful traditional Hungarian cuisine"; a few feel its "restrained" "antique decor" "could be better", but all appreciate its "especially nice garden", and "compared with Gundel", its far pricier sibling next door, "it is indeed a better value."

Ⓩ Baraka *International/Mediterranean* — 28 | - | 27 | E

Andrássy út | Andrássy Hotel | Andrássy út 111 | (36-1) 462-2189 | www.andrassyhotel.com
"Truly one of Budapest's great finds", this "outstanding" International-Med ranking No. 1 for Food in the city moved Uptown from Belváros

---

* Indicates a tie with restaurant above

to a glam silver-and-black art deco–style space in the Andrássy Hotel; "running the show" is the "husband-and-wife team" of David and Leora Seboek, whose "regularly changing menu" of "inventive" "world cuisine" is "complemented by" an "expensive wine list" and "excellent service"; P.S. you'll also stand "a good chance of seeing local celebrities."

Belcanto ❶ *Hungarian/International*　　20 | 18 | 24 | E

Terézváros | Dalszínház utca 8 | (36-1) 269-2786 | www.belcanto.hu
Set in Terézváros, this "friendly" Hungarian-International is applauded by "music lovers" in part because it's "located near the [State] Opera" House but also because its "informal, relaxed staff" is composed of "smooth", "attentive" waiters who not only provide "impeccable service" "but are great singers too"; folks are further "impressed" with its "endless menu" of "proper food" – perhaps it's "a trifle expensive" and "not gourmet, but it's very good" and there's "plenty of it."

Bistro Jardin *Hungarian/International*　　23 | 22 | 21 | E

Belváros | Kempinski Hotel Corvinus | Erzsébet tér 7-8 | (36-1) 429-3777 | www.kempinski-budapest.com
You "can bring the most fastidious of guests" to this "favorite" in the Kempinski Hotel Corvinus in Belváros since you "can always rely on" chef Rudolf van Nunen's "high standards", as evidenced by his "delicious" Hungarian-International fare; the "pleasant atmosphere", "elegant" setting (including a "nice outside" terrace) and "first-class service" further "justify" the "expense"; meals here are accompanied by live jazz on Sundays, which adds to "the grand experience."

Ƶ Café Kör ⊠🗗 *Hungarian/International*　　23 | 18 | 23 | M

Lipótváros | Sas utca 17 | (36-1) 311-0053 | www.cafekor.com
Anyone "looking for delicious food at reasonable prices" – from "intellectuals" to "tourists" to "expats" – should check out this "charming", "classic" "hot spot near St. Stephen's" Basilica in Lipótváros, where a "wide choice" of "excellent" "traditional Hungarian fare" and "International dishes" is offered in "generous portions" by "friendly, upbeat" staffers who make you "feel as if you were surrounded by friends"; P.S. "don't skip dessert", as "you won't believe the variety of cakes and pastries!"

Ƶ Centrál Kávéház *Hungarian/International*　　17 | 19 | 16 | M

Belváros | Károlyi Mihály utca 9 | (36-1) 266-2110 | www.centralkavehaz.hu
There's "always an interesting crowd" at this coffeehouse, "an island of peace and quiet" in bustling Belváros with an "authentic" 19th-century "period feeling" and a "welcoming atmosphere"; true, "there are better choices" for Hungarian-International food, and "service can be a bit perfunctory", but the staffers are "friendly" (save for "one or two grumpy ones") and "they don't rush you", which makes it a "great place to hang out, have strong coffee and chat with friends."

Chez Daniel *French*　　21 | 16 | 16 | E

Terézváros | Szív utca 32 | (36-1) 302-4039
"Indulge" in "good-sized portions" of "fine French food" featuring "quite outstanding flavors" at this "pleasant spot" in Terézváros, where regulars know to "ask the chef to choose" for them, ensuring a

FOOD | DECOR | SERVICE | COST

"memorable meal"; still, some are "stung [by] the price" (especially considering the "nothing-special decor"), while others cite "repeated requests" as evidence that the "service is acceptable but could be better"; P.S. wags wager it's fortunate that "Daniel's dog", who has the run of the restaurant, "is very well behaved."

Cyrano ● Hungarian/International
21 | 22 | 19 | E
Terézváros | Kristóf tér 6 | (36-1) 266-3096
"Trendy and posh", this "recently remodeled" spot boasts an "elegant" yet "relaxing ambiance" (and an unusual chandelier shaped like an inverted Christmas tree); the "consistently creative" kitchen is "always experimenting" with the "very good" Hungarian-International menu, and the "attentive, polite" staff is "well trained and helpful"; in short, it's "one of the better places for a stylish lunch or dinner off of Váci utca" – especially on the "outside terrace."

Fausto's ⊠ Tuscan
24 | 18 | 24 | E
Erzsébetvaros | Székely Mihály utca 2 | (36-1) 877-6210 | www.fausto.hu
"A great evening" of "chic eating" awaits at this "excellent Italian" "in the old Jewish quarter" in Erzsébetvaros, where "top-notch service" from an "attentive" but "not constantly hovering" staff is matched by chef Fausto Di Vora's "outstanding" Tuscan fare; perhaps the food's "expensive", but fans insist there's "value" for the money, saying you'll "pay more for less in many other restaurants – on either side of the river."

⊡ Gundel Hungarian/International
24 | 26 | 25 | VE
Városliget | Állatkerti út 2 | (36-1) 468-4040 | www.gundel.hu
"Memories are made" at this "venerable" Hungarian "legend" "near Hero's Square", a "palatial", "elaborately decorated", ultra-expensive "salon" with "turn-of-the-century grandeur" and "beautiful views" of Városliget; within its "elegant setting", a "cultured" staff "indulges" "lucky" patrons with "the epitome" of "quality service" and a "delicious menu" of "national and International cuisine"; factor in "marvelous strolling musicians" playing "wonderful" "live gypsy music" and you can expect a "magical evening in a magical city"; N.B. jacket required.

⊡ Kacsa ● Hungarian/International
25 | 19 | 23 | E
Viziváros | Fö utca 75 | (36-1) 201-9992 | www.kacsavendeglo.hu
Its "name means 'duck'", and "as you'd expect" you'll find "excellent" examples of that fowl's flesh on the "wide-ranging and delicious menu" of "magnificent" Hungarian-International fare at this "stellar" spot in Viziváros, where the "amazing meals" are heightened by "wonderful service" from a "lovely staff"; it's "pricey but not outrageous", and while the "not particularly captivating" "decor could be improved", at least the "atmosphere is romantic", making it "a must when you're in Budapest."

Kárpátia Hungarian
21 | 23 | 19 | E
Belváros | Ferenciek tere 7-8 | (36-1) 317-3596 | www.karpatia.hu
"The historic past makes its mark" on the present at this "fairly pricey" venue set in a circa-1877 Belváros building in which there's "not an unadorned inch" in the "over-the-top" yet mostly "tasteful" interior; the "varied" menu of "excellent" cuisine – including a "great Sunday smorgasbord" in winter – is "authentically Hungarian", the service is a "plea-

sure" (even if a few fault certain "indifferent" staffers) and a "nice gypsy violin ensemble" helps cement its status as a true "taste of Budapest."

Kisbuda Gyöngye 🗷 *Hungarian/International*   23 | 19 | 23 | E

Óbuda | Kenyeres utca 34 | (36-1) 368-9246 | www.remiz.hu

A 'pearl' in Óbuda, this "favorite" is peopled by "observant" staffers with "high standards" who serve "exceptionally well-prepared" Hungarian-International fare featuring "all the good flavors of home cooking"; a few find the flea-market ambiance of its "intimate" setting "a little contrived", but most are won over by its old-world atmosphere and live piano, "wondering what else do you need?"

🖪 Lou-Lou 🗷 *French*   25 | 18 | 20 | E

Belváros | Vigyázó Ferenc utca 4 | (36-1) 312-4505 |
www.loulourestaurant.com

"Always a treat", this French bistro in Belváros brings a "modern" approach to its "delicious" fare, while its "excellent" staff provides "quick, attentive service", making for an "overall good dining experience"; as for the setting, perhaps the "tables are too close together for intimate conversation", but "the food is so scrumptious you don't mind the slightly cramped dining room"; N.B. a chic, post-Survey major renovation may outdate the above Decor score.

Múzeum 🗷 *Hungarian/International*   20 | 18 | 19 | M

Belváros | Múzeum Körút 12 | (36-1) 267-0375 | www.muzeumkavehaz.hu

"Satisfied" surveyors salute this "classic" venue "quite close to the National Museum" in Belváros for Hungarian-International fare that's "well executed" "in a modern style", resulting in "attractive, delicious" dishes that are lighter yet still "traditional"; those who "fancy a bit of romance" also appreciate the "high standards" of the "courteous staff", as well as the "elegant dining room" whose "atmosphere, heavy with fin de siècle nostalgia", "recalls the old days of Hungary."

Papageno ●🗷 *International*   23 | 19 | 22 | E

Belváros | Semmelweis utca 19 | (36-1) 485-0161

This "smart little" International bistro a "bit off the beaten path" on a quiet Belváros side street offers a "small but well-thought-out menu" and "innovative" cuisine; "wonderful service from a hip proprietor" and a "cozy" but chic atmosphere also make it "perfect for a romantic dinner."

🖪 Páva 🗷 *Italian*   27 | 26 | 25 | VE

Belváros | Four Seasons Gresham Palace | Roosevelt tér 5-6 |
(36-1) 268-6000 | www.fourseasons.com/budapest

"First-rate Italian food on the banks of the Danube" is found at this "winner" (whose name means 'Peacock') within the "gorgeous" "art nouveau" Four Seasons Gresham Palace hotel "across from the Chain Bridge"; its "cutting-edge" cuisine is complemented by "a perfect Hungarian wine list", decor of "classical elegance (radiant but not ostentatious)", "lovely views" and "excellent service" from a "considerate" staff; in short, it's "one of the city's best" "for the real connoisseur."

Remiz *Hungarian/International*   20 | 17 | 20 | M

Zugliget | Budakeszi út 5 | (36-1) 394-1896 | www.remiz.hu

A "likable staff" of "well-trained waiters" who are "precise, polite and not pushy" will "patiently" help you choose from the "great range of

	FOOD	DECOR	SERVICE	COST

outstanding dishes on the menu" at this Zugliget Hungarian-International whose "ingenious decor" pays homage to the same-named tram depot next door; regulars report that "the grilled meat dishes are wonderful", but all "the cooking's great" – and "the prices are not sky-high"; P.S. don't miss "the especially beautiful garden area."

Rézkakas ◐ *Hungarian*

23	22	25	E

Belváros | Veres Pálné utca 3 | (36-1) 267-0349 | www.rezkakasrestaurant.com

An "excellent attitude toward customers" distinguishes the "professional" staff's "unusually" "top-notch service" at this "truly captivating" Belváros venue, a "lovely", "romantic" wood-paneled dining room where "terrific traditional Hungarian cuisine is complemented by a wonderful musical ensemble" playing "live gypsy music"; for such a "magical" (albeit "somewhat touristy") experience, most say "never mind the cost – what's important is that you enjoy yourself."

NEW Segal ◐ *International*

23	-	22	E

Terézváros | Ó utca 43-49 | (36-1) 354-7888 | www.segal.hu

"Superstar" chef Viktor Segal (ex top-rated Baraka) has opened his own new namesake establishment and the result is "innovative" and "excellent" International cuisine that "advances the Budapest palate to the next level" and is complemented by "attentive service"; N.B. a post-Survey move from Belváros to these new larger digs in Terézváros also comes with a garden.

Z Spoon Café & Lounge ◐ *Mediterranean/International*

17	22	18	E

Belváros | Vigadó tér 3 Kikötö | (36-1) 411-0934 | www.spooncafe.hu

Set "on a boat" "docked on the Danube" by the Chain Bridge in Belváros, this "stylish" tri-level "floating restaurant" and "fashionable lounge" attracts a "cooler-than-thou crowd" of "trendy and chic" "hipsters" with its "novel concept"; some find "the wide-ranging menu" of Med-International fare to be "not particularly enticing", but most are content to "sit back and enjoy" "the spectacular view of Castle Hill across the river"; P.S. "visiting the restrooms is a must" experience!

Z Vadrózsa ◐ *Hungarian/International*

28	24	24	E

Rózsadomb | Pentelei Molnár utca 15 | (36-1) 326-5817 | www.vadrozsa.hu

"Come hungry" to this "outstanding" "off-the-beaten-path" Rózsadomb 'Wild Rose' whose "fresh" Hungarian-International fare is "lovingly prepared" "with the finest ingredients" and full of "interesting flavors"; its "classic, elegant" setting (complete with a "charming private garden terrace") is "lovely, romantic and a little magical" thanks in part to "polite" staffers who provide "wonderful old-world service" and "a pianist who plays requests" – so "if you can't live in a mansion", at least "you can dine in one."

Copenhagen

TOP FOOD RANKING

	Restaurant	Cuisine
27	Era Ora	Italian
	Restaurationen	Danish/French
26	Søllerød Kro	French
	Kong Hans Kælder	French/International
25	Krogs Fiskerestaurant	French/Seafood
	Alberto K at The Royal	Italian/Scandinavian
24	Pierre André	French
	Paul, The	International
	Koriander	Indian
23	Slotskælderen hos Gitte Kik	Danish
	Kanalen	Provençal
	Le Sommelier	French
22	D'Angleterre	French
	Den Sorte Ravn*	French
	Leonore Christine	Danish/French
	Fifty Fifty	Asian
21	Kiin Kiin	Thai
	Søren K	French
	Salt	European
20	Sticks'n'Sushi	Japanese

Alberto K at The Royal Ⓢ *Italian/Scandinavian*   25 | 24 | 23 | E |

Vesterbro | Radisson SAS Royal | Hammerichsgade 1, 20th fl. |
(45-33) 42-61-61 | www.alberto-k.dk

Chef Betina Repstock's "superb" Italian-inspired Scandinavian cuisine "melts in your mouth" at this "fantastic location" on the 20th floor of the Radisson SAS Royal in Vesterbro; in addition to "to-die-for views" outside, it's "a treat for the eye" within, as well, thanks to a "so-cool interior" that's overseen by a staff that will "treat you like dignitaries"; the cost is as "high" as the altitude, but most maintain it's "worth the krona."

☑ Café Ketchup Ⓢ *International*   17 | 18 | 15 | E |

Indre By | Pilestræde 23 | (45-33) 32-30-30
Tivoli | Tivoli Gardens | Vesterbrogade 3 | (45-33) 75-07-55
www.cafeketchup.dk

"Night after night, young beauties pack" into this "large" "place to be seen" "in Tivoli" to "enjoy the view of the gardens" (as well as one another) "while dining on good food from" a "modern" International menu; foes, though, find a few factors "going against it", including "pricey" fare that's "nicely presented" "but nothing extraordinary", "dull decor" "lacking intimacy", "lagging service" and too many "tourists"; P.S. insiders assert that "its more sophisticated sibling across town" in Indre By "is better" – plus it's open all year-round.

---

* Indicates a tie with restaurant above

	FOOD	DECOR	SERVICE	COST

☒ Café Victor *French/Danish* | 17 | 17 | 14 | E |

Kongens Nytorv | Ny Østergade 8 | (45-33) 13-36-13 | www.cafevictor.dk
"Sharpen your elbows to get past" the "pretty people" "packed into" this "classic but hip" Kongens Nytorv "fixture" that's "still hot" with "the well-heeled crowd" that "loves" "to be seen" "on either side" of its divided space – the cafe, with its "limited menu", or the restaurant, which has more choices" of "good French" cuisine (at lunch the dishes are Danish); some suggest it's too "snobbish", with "slack service" from a "pretentious staff", but few fault the "fun atmosphere."

D'Angleterre *French* | 22 | 25 | 22 | VE |

Kongens Nytorv | Hotel D'Angleterre | Kongens Nytorv 34 | (45-33) 37-06-45 | www.remmen.dk
"Passersby must envy diners" at this "don't-miss" destination (formerly known as Wiinblad) in the "charming old-world" Hotel D'Angleterre that's graced with a "spectacular setting overlooking Kongens Nytorv" and a burnished brown-and-gold formal dining room; the kitchen produces "wonderful" New French creations with an Asian accent that are served by a staff that is "attentive without being overbearing."

Den Sorte Ravn *French* | 22 | 20 | 21 | E |

Nyhavn | Nyhavn 14 | (45-33) 13-12-33 | www.sorteravn.dk
Occupying a "great location on the canal", "on the main street of the Nyhavn neighborhood", this "small cellar" spot (whose name means 'The Black Raven') is one of the area's more "high-class" venues, where "delicious" French fare is "pleasantly" served by a "friendly, attentive" staff; some dub the decor "a bit worn", quipping that "the shiny black feathers are molting a bit", but most find the "simple" interior "inviting" – and if it's "expensive", at least the "quality matches the price."

☒ Era Ora ☒ *Italian* | 27 | 21 | 24 | VE |

Christianshavn | Overgaden Neden Vandet 33B | (45-32) 54-06-93 | www.era-ora.dk
For "a meal you'll remember", "you just have to go" to this "always-crowded" Northern Italian along the canal in Christianshavn, whose "authentic" Tuscan and Umbrian fare "bursting with natural flavors" (and "accompanied by delicious wines") earns it the ranking of No. 1 for Food in Copenhagen; "excellent in every way", it's manned by a "warm, extremely efficient" staff providing "impeccable service" "from start to finish" and features a "gorgeous atmosphere to match the gorgeous food"; "bring a really fat wallet", though, as it's "wildly expensive."

Fifty Fifty ☒ *Asian* | 22 | 20 | 21 | E |

Vesterbro | Vesterbrogade 42 | (45-33) 22-47-57 | www.fiftyfiftyfood.dk
There's far more than a 50/50 chance both carnivores and finatics will "love" this "cool" Asian newcomer in Vesterbro, since it offers grilled meats and raw fish; "good value and high standards" also have made it a "fast favorite of the hungry 'beautiful people.'"

Kanalen ☒ *Provençal* | 23 | 20 | 22 | E |

Christianshavn | Wilders Plads 2 | (45-32) 95-13-30 | www.restaurant-kanalen.dk
"Good-size portions" of "delicious", "basic French fare" "will make you smile" at this "charming", "upmarket" Provençal in a "superb location"

in "beautiful" Christianshavn, providing it with a "lovely canal view"; the "simple" space is "a bit tight", but most find its "intimate atmosphere" "delightfully" "cozy" and "romantic", and the "excellent wine list" is another reason it's considered "a true pleasure."

Kiin Kiin ☒ Thai
21 | 21 | 20 | E

Nørrebro | Guldbergsgade 21 | (45-35) 35-75-55 | www.kiin.dk

This "hip" and "ambitious newcomer" "takes Thai to another level" with the chef-owner's "modern and untraditional interpretation of that cuisine"; throw in "spacious seating", futuristic decor interspersed with big golden Buddhas and a "trendy" bohemian neighborhood locale in Nørrebro and no wonder fans feel it "deserves praise."

☒ Kong Hans Kælder ☒ French/International
26 | 25 | 24 | VE

Kongens Nytorv | Vingaardsstræde 6 | (45-33) 11-68-68 | www.konghans.dk

"One of the best culinary experiences" in Copenhagen can be found at "this historic, vaulted-ceiling wine cellar" "situated in King Hans'" 16th-century royal mint (the city's "oldest" building) in the Kongens Nytorv area; "out-of-this-world" French-International cuisine – with an emphasis on "top-notch" fish dishes – is offered in a "lovely" setting with "nicely spaced tables" by a "personable" staff that "looks after you really well"; yes, you'll "pay through the nose", but "you should visit at least once in your lifetime."

Koriander ☒ Indian
24 | 23 | 21 | E

Kongens Nytorv | Store Kongensgade 34 | (45-33) 15-03-15 | www.restaurantkoriander.dk

This trendy, "excellent" Indian set in a glittering ultramodern space in Kongens Nytorv takes its name from coriander, a key ingredient in that cuisine, and is graced by an expansive wine list leaning toward German whites; on the downside, it's "expensive" and service can be "slow."

☒ Krogs Fiskerestaurant ☒ French/Seafood
25 | 20 | 22 | VE

Indre By | Gammel Strand 38 | (45-33) 15-89-15 | www.krogs.dk

The "fabulous" fish is "fit for a king" at this "old-fashioned", "high-class" French seafooder in Indre By; though the "sublime food" (with "wonderful wine pairings") is certainly "the center of attention", "everything is elegant" – from "superb service" to the "lovely setting" – which may be why faithful fans forgive that the fare is "ferociously expensive", the room can be "stuffy" and some servers are "a bit pretentious."

Leonore Christine Danish/French
22 | 19 | 22 | E

Nyhavn | Nyhavn 9 | (45-33) 13-50-40 | www.leonore-christine.dk

"Pleasant without being intrusive", the "very competent staff" of this "crowded and popular" Nyhavn spot, "in the sailor part of town", performs a "table ballet" nightly while delivering "gorgeous" plates of "super" Danish-French fare, accompanied by a "good wine selection"; perhaps the interior of its circa-1681 building with low ceilings and crooked floors "feels a bit faded", but a recent redo may have remedied that, and there's "lovely alfresco dining" as an alternative.

☒ Le Sommelier French
23 | 18 | 23 | E

Kongens Nytorv | Bredgade 63-65 | (45-33) 11-45-15 | www.lesommelier.dk

"As the name indicates", the "fantastic wine list" at "this friendly restaurant" in the Kongens Nytorv area "is in a class of its own", but rest assured that the "excellent French cuisine" is also "outstanding" ("well prepared" and "quite flavorful") – as is the "warm welcome" from the "professional" staff; a few feel the decor of its "large, open" and "very white" interior "could be better", but more are put "at ease" by the "peaceful", "relaxed" and "well-laid-out" space.

Paul, The ⓈⒾ International   24 | 21 | 21 | VE

Tivoli | Tivoli Gardens | Vesterbrogade 3 | (45-33) 75-07-75 | www.thepaul.dk
"Small dishes with gigantic flavors" are featured on chef-owner Paul Cunningham's "very expensive" International menu at this "impeccable" venue whose "modern" setting – a light-drenched, white-on-white glass pavilion – is an "enjoyable refuge from the masses in Tivoli Gardens"; "yes, you do pay the usual premium" for the area, but affluent "gourmets" insist it's "worth the money", while clever folks of lesser means advise "this is your pick when somebody else is paying"; N.B. open mid-April to late September and most of November and December.

Pierre André ⓈⓂ French   24 | 18 | 23 | E

Indre By | Ny Østergade 21 | (45-33) 16-17-19 | www.pierreandre.dk
Named for the proprietors' two sons, this "classic French" in Indre By features chef-owner Philippe Houdet's "exciting, well-prepared", "elegant" dishes, which are offered by an "observant" staff overseen by his wife, Sussie; some see a "romantic edge" to the "traditional" decor, while others sigh that it's "not the most exciting in the city", but all agree the "choice of prix fixe menus to fit both mid and high budgets" adds up to "great value for the money."

ⓏⓈ Restaurationen ⓈⓂ Danish/French   27 | 21 | 27 | VE

Indre By | Møntergade 19 | (45-33) 14-94-95 | www.restaurationen.com
"Run by people who truly love good food", this "just amazing" Danish-French in Indre By offers a "well-rounded" five-course prix fixe menu nightly – "no à la carte!" – of "innovative, gorgeous dishes" made from "the best ingredients", accompanied by an "excellent wine" list and "presented by owner Bo Jacobsen" and his wife, Lisbeth, or by their "attentive" staff; a few find "nothing to cheer about" in the "nice-but-nothing-special" decor, but most maintain the overall "experience is absolutely superb."

Salt European   21 | 21 | 18 | E

Indre By | Copenhagen Admiral Hotel | Toldbodgade 24-28 | (45-33) 74-14-44 | www.saltrestaurant.dk
Sir Terence Conran's "stylish adaptation of a waterfront warehouse" with "huge timbers" is the "well-designed setting" of this "thoroughly enjoyable" venue in Indre By's Copenhagen Admiral Hotel; the "innovative" menu of "delicious" modern European cuisine is backed up by an "unexpectedly good wine list", but some suggest the "competent" staff "could be warmer"; N.B. the inspiration for the restaurant name comes in part from having each table topped with three kinds of sea salt.

Slotskælderen hos Gitte Kik ⓈⓂ Danish   23 | 21 | 21 | E

Indre By | Fortunstræde 4 | (45-33) 11-15-37
"One of the outstanding purveyors" of "good, old-fashioned Danish open sandwiches" is this lunch-only Indre By "classic" *smørrebrød* specialist dating back to 1910; choose from the likes of herring or tiny

| | FOOD | DECOR | SERVICE | COST |

shrimp, beer or schnapps and join the crowd of MP's from the nearby parliament building that frequents this popular place.

🗹 Søllerød Kro Ⓜ French   26 | 24 | 25 | VE

Hellerup | Søllerødvej 35 | (45-45) 80-25-05 | www.soelleroed-kro.dk
For French "food at its best", a "to-die-for wine list" and "an evening to remember", "this is it" say supporters of this 1677 "charmer" in Hellerup, about a 15-minute cab ride from the city center; housed in an "authentic Danish cottage" surrounded by a garden and pond, it comes with an "impossibly romantic atmosphere" and a very "expensive" price tag.

Søren K 🗷 French   21 | 20 | 18 | E

Indre By | Søren Kierkegaards Plads 1 | (45-33) 47-49-49 | www.soerenk.dk
"Start your trip off on the right foot" at this "modern" spot (named for famed philosopher Søren Kierkegaard) in Indre By, where the "delicious, light, experimental New French" cuisine is "well prepared" using as little cream and butter as possible and the "incredible building" – a shiny, black-granite extension of the Royal Danish Library – offers "fine minimalist" decor and "amazing" vistas "of the Copenhagen harbor"; nevertheless, some detractors declare that "divine food, clean lines and sexy views don't make up for lackluster service."

Sticks'n'Sushi Japanese   20 | 16 | 16 | E

Frederiksberg | gl.Kongevej 120 | (45-33) 29-00-10
Hellerup | Strandvejen 199 | (45-39) 40-15-40
Indre By | Nansensgade 59 | (45-33) 11-14-07
Østerbro | Oster Farimagsgade 16 | (45-35) 38-34-63
Vesterbro | Istedgade 62 | (45-33) 23-73-04
www.sushi.dk

A pioneer "of sushi and yakitori in Copenhagen", this Indre By Japanese "original" is "still going strong", remaining "an 'in' place" for more than a decade and spawning a slew of siblings, each serving up its trademark brand of "fine, festive", "freshly made" raw-fish creations along with "high-quality sticks" of skewered, grilled chicken in "minimalist" digs; sure, they're on "the expensive end", but "not more so than" some competitors.

TyvenKokkenHansKoneOgHendesElsker 🗷   - | - | - | VE
French/Danish

Indre By | Magstræde 16 | (45-33) 16-12-92 | www.tyven.dk
When the highly rated Kommandanten lost its space in the Kongens Nytorv area, its chef, Kasper Rune Sørenson, brought his staff and took over ownership of this equally notable and "beautiful restaurant" "in a historic building" in Indre By; the French menu has also acquired a Danish emphasis now, but they've kept the mind-boggling name, which was borrowed from the 1989 film *The Thief, The Cook, His Wife & Her Lover.*

Dublin

TOP FOOD RANKING

	Restaurant	Cuisine
27	Thornton's Restaurant	Irish/French
	Patrick Guilbaud	French
26	Seasons	Irish/European
25	L'Ecrivain	Irish/French
	One Pico	French/Irish
	Shanahan's on the Green	American/Steak
24	Mint Restaurant	French
	Tea Room	Irish/International
23	Balzac	French/Irish
	Chapter One Restaurant	French/International
	O'Connells	Irish
	Poulot's	French/Irish
22	Lobster Pot	Seafood
	Jaipur	Indian
	Eden	Irish
	Jacob's Ladder	Irish/International
21	Mermaid Café	French/American
	Winding Stair	Irish
	Halo	Irish/International
	Roly's Bistro	Irish/French
	Alexis Bar & Grill	French
20	Peploe's	European/Irish
	Brownes	Irish/International

NEW **Alexis Bar & Grill** Ⓜ *French*   21 | 18 | 18 | M

Dun Laoghaire | 17-18 Patrick St. | (353-1) 280-8872 | www.alexis.ie
"Very enjoyable" is the verdict on this "delicious" French bistro and "worthwhile new addition" to Dun Laoghaire; throw in a "relaxing" setting with red banquettes, a "charming and friendly staff that treats you like family" and "moderate prices" and "what else could you wish for?"

NEW **Balzac** *French/Irish*   23 | 23 | 21 | E

St. Stephen's Green | La Stampa Hotel & Spa | 35 Dawson St. | (353-1) 677-4444 | www.balzac.ie
"One of the loveliest rooms in Dublin" and "the new 'it' spot" is this French-Irish brasserie "in a neat hotel" "on trendy Dawson Street" that serves "proper grown-up food" "worthy of its surroundings"; "vaulted ceilings, tall mirrors" and a Victorian cocktail bar are an "elegant" backdrop for chef Paul Flynn's "excellent" albeit "expensive" cuisine.

Brownes *Irish/International*   20 | 23 | 23 | E

St. Stephen's Green | Brownes Townhouse Hotel | 22 St. Stephen's Green | (353-1) 638-3939 | www.brownesdublin.com
Set in a stunning listed Georgian townhouse in a "great locale on St. Stephen's Green" is this "elegant" Irish-International with a fireplace and chandeliers; "excellent" dishes and "warm service" make it "popular" with a posh crowd.

	FOOD	DECOR	SERVICE	COST

Chapter One
Restaurant 🗷 🅼 *French/International*   23 | 23 | 24 | E

Parnell Square | Dublin Writers Museum | 18-19 Parnell Sq. |
(353-1) 873-2266 | www.chapteronerestaurant.com

"You can almost hear Joyce and Yeats reading their work while you're dining on delicious food" at this French-International in the Dublin Writers Museum; considered one of the city's "finest" spots, with a "good value pre-theater menu" from Tuesday–Saturday, it's a "must" for literate libation-lovers who like to salute the "inspirational" setting with the establishment's infamous Irish Coffee.

🗷 Eden *Irish*   22 | 21 | 22 | E

Temple Bar | Meeting House Sq. | (353-1) 670-5372 |
www.edenrestaurant.ie

"Located in throbbing Temple Bar", this "buzzy" Irish "staple" boasts "sophisticated food", a "modern" setting and "friendly" service; "lots of locals" descend to dine on the legendary 'smokies' (smoked haddock with crème fraîche and cheddar cheese), and in summer the gas-lamp-lit terrace is a "great scene" and place to watch films and shows.

Halo *Irish/International*   21 | 23 | 23 | E

Northside | Morrison Hotel | Ormond Quay |·(353-1) 887-2420 |
www.morrisonhotel.ie

This "dramatic", two-story space with a striking staircase and "beautiful" minimalist design is in the fashionable Morrison Hotel on the banks of the Liffey; corporate types mainline Irish-International dishes, many with organic ingredients, or choose tastes from the tapas menu, and pick up pricey tabs in what, despite a renovation, is still one of the smartest dining rooms in the city.

Jacob's Ladder 🗷 🅼 *Irish/International*   22 | 20 | 22 | E

City Center | 4 Nassau St. | (353-1) 670-3865 | www.jacobsladder.ie

"A real winner" "bang in the center of town" is what supporters say about this chef-owned, bi-level Irish-International with "innovative", "enjoyable" cuisine and "solid service"; spectacular Georgian windows dominate the "pleasing" minimalist space and provide a "great view over Trinity College's playing fields."

Jaipur *Indian*   22 | 15 | 17 | M

City Center | 41 S. Great George's St. | (353-1) 677-0999 | www.jaipur.ie

It's "probably the best Indian in Dublin" declare devotees of this "authentic" Asian in a trendy part of the bustling City Center, where low-key decor – light wood, chrome and floor-to-ceiling windows – makes for a "nice environment"; prices are moderate to begin with, but there's a "great early-bird special" too, crow wallet-watchers.

🗷 L'Ecrivain 🗷 *Irish/French*   25 | 23 | 24 | VE

City Center | 109a Lower Baggot St. | (353-1) 661-1919 | www.lecrivain.com

This "high-end" Irish–New French remains one of the city's "top picks", largely for "loquacious" chef-owner Derry Clarke's "excellent, imaginative" fare; "staffers that make you feel like a guest in their home" preside over a quietly luxurious split-level setting that's "full of suits" during the week, while a pianist from Monday–Saturday attracts the "special-occasion" crowd.

	FOOD	DECOR	SERVICE	COST

Lobster Pot, The ⑤ *Seafood* — 22 | 17 | 21 | E

Ballsbridge | 9 Ballsbridge Terrace | (353-1) 668-0025 | www.thelobsterpot.ie
A local favorite is this long-standing, family-run, "old-school" sea-fooder (Mornay sauce, anyone?) with "frolicking fresh fish" in Ballsbridge, the embassy district, just south of the City Center; a "veteran staff" presides over a warm, "walking-back-into-a-time-machine" setting with an open fireplace, maritime memorabilia and a dessert cart.

Mermaid Café, The *French/American* — 21 | 18 | 22 | E

Temple Bar | 69-70 Dame St. | (353-1) 670-8236 | www.mermaid.ie
This "lively" stalwart, on the edge of Temple Bar, is still going strong with "exceptionally well-prepared" French-American fare served by a "professional staff"; the high-ceilinged, open-kitchen setting is simple, but that doesn't keep it from being "one of the city's best loved eateries"; N.B. the prix fixe lunch is one of Dublin's biggest bargains.

Mint Restaurant ⑤Ⓜ *French* — 24 | 20 | 21 | E

Ranelagh | 47 Ranelagh Village | (353-1) 497-8655 | www.mintrestaurant.ie
"Beautifully presented" and "inspired" New French cuisine makes for a "lovely dining experience" in Ranelagh; the small, stylish spot attracts tony types, who tout that it's in mint condition for prime people-watching, particularly at lunchtime; N.B. a post-Survey renovation may outdate the above Decor score.

O'Connells *Irish* — 23 | 19 | 19 | M

Ballsbridge | Bewley's Hotel | Merrion Rd. | (353-1) 647-3304 |
www.oconnellsballsbridge.com
This "excellent" traditional and modern Irish owned by foodie Tom O'Connell relies on organic "locally sourced ingredients"; some find the sprawling setting in Ballsbridge's Bewley's Hotel a bit like an "airport lounge", but a kitchen that's responsive to dietary needs (most menu items are gluten-free), reasonable prices, including an "incredible value early-bird", and an appealingly "quirky", affordable wine list win way more yeas than nays.

❷ One Pico ⑤ *French/Irish* — 25 | 23 | 23 | VE

City Center | 5-6 Molesworth Pl., Schoolhouse Ln. | (353-1) 676-0300 |
www.onepico.com
Set in an 18th-century coach house that's "tucked away" in a lane off St. Stephen's Green is chef-owner Eamonn O'Reilly's French-Irish "gem"; a "subtly elegant setting" is the backdrop for "wonderful", "top-quality" food, "very accommodating service" and "amazing wines"; of course, dining at "one of Dublin's better restaurants" comes at a price.

❷ Patrick Guilbaud ⑤Ⓜ *French* — 27 | 25 | 26 | VE

City Center | Merrion Hotel | 21 Upper Merrion St. | (353-1) 676-4192 |
www.restaurantpatrickguilbaud.ie
"Every city has its famous restaurant and this is Dublin's"; at Patrick Guilbaud's "excellent all-round" French in City Center, there's Guillaume Lebrun's "revelatory" cuisine, 500 "world-class wines", "outstanding service" and "amazing", "luxe surroundings" with 20th-century Irish art (and "it doesn't hurt that Bono may be at the

	FOOD	DECOR	SERVICE	COST

next table"); "if you really want to treat someone, this is the place", "so go on, blow the budget" – big, big, big time.

Peploe's *European/Irish*

| 20 | 20 | 18 | E |

St. Stephen's Green | 16 St. Stephen's Green | (353-1) 676-3144 | www.peploes.com

A "delightful addition to the Dublin dining scene", this "buzzing" wine bar features about 150 "fantastic selections" and a "good" though "not inspirational" European-Irish menu; its "perfect location" on the Green and chic "subterranean" space attract an "aspirational" clientele.

Poulot's 🗓 Ⓜ *French/Irish*

| 23 | 18 | 19 | E |

Donnybrook | Mulberry Garden | (353-1) 269-3300 | www.poulots.ie

On the site of the former Ernie's in Donnybrook is this French-Irish from chef-owner Jean-Michel Poulot, whose "delicious" cuisine relies on exceptional local produce, much of it organic, and is backed up by what some say is "the best wine list for value in Dublin"; the setting includes a bright modern interior decorated with contemporary paintings and an exterior with a "lovely" courtyard garden and fountain.

Roly's Bistro *Irish/French*

| 21 | 17 | 21 | E |

Ballsbridge | 7 Ballsbridge Terrace | (353-1) 668-2611 | www.rolysbistro.ie

"As reliable as old boots", this "boisterous" Irish-French "fixture" in Ballsbridge, near the sports stadium, is "bustling" with "lots of locals"; they come for "good plain food" like Dublin Bay prawns and a four-course lunch that's "one of the best values in town" (20 euros).

🄩 Seasons *Irish/European*

| 26 | 25 | 27 | VE |

Ballsbridge | Four Seasons Hotel | Simmonscourt Rd. | (353-1) 665-4000 | www.fourseasons.com/dublin

"Exactly what you'd expect from the Four Seasons" is what fans of this Irish-European in Ballsbridge say; "outstanding service", "excellent cuisine" and a "posh" setting with conservatory windows, a fireplace and an abundance of flowers add up to a "top-tier", "high-priced" experience; P.S. some swear the "Sunday brunch here is the best in the world."

🄩 Shanahan's on the Green *American/Steak*

| 25 | 24 | 26 | VE |

St. Stephen's Green | 119 St. Stephen's Green | (353-1) 407-0939 | www.shanahans.ie

"Great steaks, but gosh do you pay for them" at this opulent American chophouse "conveniently located" on St. Stephen's Green; "portions are mammoth" ("I hope they have a defibrillator on the premises"), and the glamorous Georgian setting is far from the typical "testosterone"-oriented atmosphere found in most meat meccas; throw in a seafood selection, an "amazing wine list", a celeb clientele and service that exudes "Irish charm" and no wonder it's "loved by the locals"; P.S. be sure to "check out JFK's rocker in the Oval Office bar."

🄩 Tea Room *Irish/International*

| 24 | 23 | 20 | E |

Temple Bar | The Clarence | 6-8 Wellington Quay | (353-1) 407-0813 | www.theclarence.ie

"A cathedral to fine food" in the "über-hip", U2-owned Clarence hotel is this "chic" and "spacious" Irish-International with a 20-ft. "soaring ceiling", "beautiful tall windows", "acres of blond wood" and "heavenly" cuisine; "it's perfect for romance, business" or "people-watching", so if you're big on "buzz" and "you're only in town for a short time", this is the place.

Z Thornton's Restaurant ⌧ Ⓜ *Irish/French* | 27 | 19 | 25 | VE |

St. Stephen's Green | Fitzwilliam Hotel | 128 St. Stephen's Green | (353-1) 478-7008 | www.thorntonsrestaurant.com

Voted No. 1 for Food in the city, chef Kevin Thornton's "highly personal and poetic" Irish-French cuisine, which relies on the "highest quality fresh local ingredients", is "unsurpassed" and served by a "perfect yet friendly" staff; sure, it's "very expensive", but most maintain it's a "great way to start or finish a trip to Dublin"; P.S. a major refurbishment may outdate the above Decor score and make some who found the Fitzwilliam Hotel setting "stark" change their minds.

Winding Stair *Irish* | 21 | 20 | 22 | M |

City Center | 40 Ormond Quay | (353-1) 872-7320 | www.winding-stair.com

New corporate owners have reopened this former City Center landmark that has a bookstore downstairs and an Irish cafe upstairs; the latter offers "reasonably priced", "good wholesome fresh" food made from "quality ingredients" (many of them organic) and an extensive wine list; the "bright, airy and open" setting is simple, but big windows provide "lovely" "views of the river Liffey."

Florence

TOP FOOD RANKING

	Restaurant	Cuisine
27	Enoteca Pinchiorri	Italian
	La Giostra	Tuscan
26	Alle Murate	Tuscan
	Fuor d'Acqua	Seafood
	Cibrèo	Italian
	Taverna del Bronzino	Italian
25	Omero	Tuscan
	Zibibbo	Italian/Mediterranean
	Villa San Michele	Italian
24	Cantinetta Antinori	Italian
	Sabatini	Tuscan
	Ora d'Aria	Tuscan/Mediterranean
	InCanto	Italian
	Il Latini	Tuscan
23	Olio & Convivium	Italian
	Buca Lapi	Tuscan
	Da Ruggero	Tuscan
22	Beccofino	Italian/Seafood
	Enoteca Pane E Vino	Tuscan
21	Cammillo Trattoria	Italian
20	Coco Lezzone	Tuscan
	Paoli	Italian
19	Dino	Tuscan

☑ Alle Murate Ⓜ *Tuscan* `26` `-` `24` `VE`

Duomo | 16R Via del Proconsolo | (39-55) 240-618 | www.artenotai.org
This "lovely, modern" Tuscan with an exceptional wine list is in a new Duomo locale, where a "friendly" staff oversees an "intimate" room with unearthed 14th-century frescoes; the "overall package puts them in a higher class", so expect to pay accordingly.

Beccofino Ⓢ *Italian/Seafood* `22` `20` `21` `E`

Santo Spirito | 1R Piazza Degli Scarlatti | (39-55) 290-076 |
www.beccofino.com
"Trendy", "tasty" Italian seafooder and "hot spot" in Santo Spirito that features a full "creative" menu with meat dishes as well as a wine bar with a "great selection" of vinos and lighter fare; the interior is "spare but chic", and there's also an appealing outdoor area overlooking the Arno.

Buca Lapi Ⓢ *Tuscan* `23` `19` `21` `E`

City Center | 1R Via del Trebbio | (39-55) 213-768 | www.bucalapi.com
At this "hospitable", "old" 1880 Tuscan in the basement of an 11th-century palazzo off tony Tornabuoni, the "famous *bistecca alla fiorentina* is the star" and the atmospheric setting with "postered walls still charms"; a few sniff it's "touristy" and say "unless you are a saber-toothed tiger the beef is too rare and big", but they're outvoted.

	FOOD	DECOR	SERVICE	COST

Cammillo Trattoria *Italian*
Oltrarno | 57R Borgo Sant Jacopo | (39-55) 212-427

| 21 | 17 | 19 | M |

This Italian "near the Ponte Vecchio" is noted for "excellently executed classic" meat and fish dishes and "efficient", old-world service; the rustic setting and moderate prices make it a "great family" place that's "always crowded"; N.B. closed Tuesday and Wednesday.

☑ Cantinetta Antinori ☒ *Italian*
Duomo | 3 Piazza Antinori | (39-55) 292-234 | www.antinori.it

| 24 | 23 | 23 | E |

"Owned by the famous wine family", this "wonderful" Italian in a Renaissance building in a "beautiful location" near the Piazza Duomo showcases 60 of their vintages (both by the bottle and the glass); "equally impressive" food is served by a "friendly" staff in a polished, wood-paneled setting filled with the fashionable who like to lunch here; N.B. closed Saturday and Sunday.

☑ Cibrèo ☒Ⓜ *Italian*
St. Ambrogio | 8R Via Andrea del Verrocchio | (39-55) 234-1100 | www.cibreo.com

| 26 | 21 | 23 | VE |

Chef-owner Fabio Picchi's "captivating" St. Ambrogio Italian is "one of the best in Florence" – the food is "original" (just note it's as likely to be "cock's combs and animal organs" as it is a signature ricotta, pesto and potato soufflé) and there's "no pasta" in sight; the tabs are high, but most maintain "even the memory feels satisfying"; N.B. on the same corner there is Picchi's less expensive Trattoria Cibrèo, which shares the same kitchen, as well as a cafe and the Teatro del Sale, with a buffet and entertainment.

Coco Lezzone ☒⊞ *Tuscan*
City Center | 26R Via del Parioncino | (39-55) 287-178

| 20 | 12 | 19 | M |

"Good solid cooking" ("you can make a meal of the *ribollita* that's always bubbling on the stove") and "reasonable prices" are an appealing combo at this "no-frills", family-run Tuscan housed in an antique Roman tower in the City Center; its "jammed communal tables" "can be fun if you don't mind sitting on top of a stranger"; N.B. note that where the wall paint changes color from yellow to white indicates the height the city's infamous flood rose to in 1966; N.B. closed Sundays and Tuesday evenings.

Da Ruggero *Tuscan*
Porta Romana | 89R Via Senese | (39-55) 220-542

| 23 | 16 | 18 | E |

At this rustic "little jewel" just outside Porta Romana, the chef-owner's "delicious", "well-prepared" Tuscan trattoria dishes lead loyalists to say "I dream of this place when I'm asleep in New York"; N.B. closed Tuesday and Wednesday.

Dino ☒ *Tuscan*
Santa Croce | 47R Via Ghibellina | (39-55) 241-452 | www.ristorantedino.it

| 19 | 15 | 17 | E |

"It's like being at grandma's all over again" at this "good", classic Tuscan with arches and wood-beamed ceilings housed in a 15th-century building near the Santa Croce church; surprisingly, for a small, family-run spot the wine list is sophisticated and international, but the smart thing is to stick to the luscious local reds.

	FOOD	DECOR	SERVICE	COST

Enoteca Pane E Vino 🕄 *Tuscan* 22 | 17 | 19 | E

Oltrarno | 3R Piazza di Cestello | (39-55) 247-6956 |
www.ristorantepaneevino.it

A "wonderful escape from the tourists" is this creative Tuscan in the Oltrarno district, which is known for its crafts people; an "amazing" 800-bottle wine list complements "excellent" cuisine, which is served in a minimal two-story setting.

☑ Enoteca Pinchiorri 🕄🅼 *Italian* 27 | 27 | 26 | VE

Santa Croce | 87 Via Ghibellina | (39-55) 242-757 |
www.enotecapinchiorri.com

"If there is a dining room in heaven, it's taking lessons" from this Santa Croce Italian, where Annie Féolde's "fantastic mix of flavors" and "masterful cuisine" is voted No. 1 for Food in Florence, partner Giorgio Pinchiorri's "incredible wine cellar" is praised as the "finest in Europe" and an "impeccable" staff presides over a "gorgeous", gardenlike setting with swagged drapes, massive flowers and the best crystal and china; while foes feel it's "more bloated than an old Englishman", most find the "incredible experience" is worth the "obscenely expensive" tab.

☑ Fuor d'Acqua 🕄 *Seafood* 26 | 19 | 21 | E

San Frediano | 37R Via Pisana | (39-55) 222-299

The darling of the fashion and entertainment set is this San Frediano seafooder where the "best fresh fish in town with a presentation to match" tempts the trendy; a vaulted-brick-ceiling setting with minimalist decor doesn't distract from "star- and people-watching."

☑ Il Latini 🅼 *Tuscan* 24 | 18 | 21 | M

City Center | 6R Via dei Palchetti | (39-55) 210-916 | www.illatini.com

"Be prepared to queue big-time" at this "eternally popular" "true Tuscan" in City Center where "hungry tourists" and locals are "packed in" at communal tables ("it's like eating with one giant Florentine family you never knew you had") to "revel in" gutsy food; "forget about the menu, let the waiter take care of you", then sit back and enjoy the "congenial" atmosphere and "inexpensive" prices.

InCanto *Italian* 24 | 22 | 22 | VE

Ponte Vecchio | Grand Hotel | 1 Piazza Ognissanti | (39-55) 271-61 |
www.starwoodhotels.com

"Grand views" of the Arno and the Ponte Vecchio can be had from this very "expensive" Italian "refuge" in the Grand Hotel; "fine food" and an "excellent wine list" are proferred in an intimate, "inviting" room with leather armchairs and an open kitchen.

☑ La Giostra 🌑 *Tuscan* 27 | 22 | 24 | E

Duomo | 12R Via Borgo Pinti | (39-55) 241-341 | www.ristorantelagiostra.com

"A wonderful restaurant with a chef who claims he's royalty" is what supporters say about this Tuscan near the Duomo where Prince Hapsburg Lorena and his "handsome" twin sons serve "delicious" food based on ancient recipes in a small, "romantic" setting where celebrity photos line the walls and "little white lights twinkle from the ceiling"; a few mutter it "oozes as much cheese as charm", but they're outvoted.

	FOOD	DECOR	SERVICE	COST

Olio & Convivium ☒ *Italian* — 23 | 21 | 23 | E

Oltrarno | 4 Via Santo Spirito | (39-55) 265-8198 |
www.conviviumfirenze.it

This classically decorated "tiny gem" with "inventive" Italian food in the Renaissance Palazzo Capponi is good for lunch if you're in the Oltrarno area; it's also a gourmet take-out shop where you can get picnic fixings, wines and a selection of about 40 olive oils.

Omero *Tuscan* — 25 | 21 | 22 | E

Arcetri | 11R Via Pian dei Giullari | (39-55) 220-053 |
www.ristoranteomero.it

"Take a taxi" and "go when it's light so you can enjoy" the "beautiful views of Florence" from the second dining room or terrace of this "unassuming", 106-year-old Tuscan trattoria in the cool hills of Arcetri, about five kilometers from the City Center; order the "best" fried chicken, rabbit and *bistecca alla fiorentina* and you'll join those who say: "eat here once and you'll want to return forever"; N.B. closed Tuesdays.

Ora d'Aria ☒ *Tuscan/Mediterranean* — 24 | 21 | 22 | E

Santa Croce | 3 CR Via Ghibellina | (39-55) 200-1699 |
www.oradariaristorante.com

"Wow" – "amazing food" (from "both their traditional and creative menus"), a "charming locale" in trendy Santa Croce, "elegant" modern decor with "ever-changing art on display" and "lovely service" make this Tuscan-Mediterranean "popular" with the "beautiful and stylish people", particularly after the theater; so "forget about the exchange rate" and focus on the "enchanting evening that awaits."

Paoli *Italian* — 20 | 21 | 21 | E

Duomo | 12R Via dei Tavolini | (39-55) 216-215

If it's ambiance you're after, you'll find it "sitting under tall, incredibly beautiful frescoed vaulted ceilings that make you feel like you're dining in pre-Renaissance times" at this Italian housed in a former church near the Duomo; there are no "fireworks from the kitchen", but the food is "reliable", the "service friendly" and the room "spectacular"; N.B. closed Tuesdays.

Sabatini Ⓜ *Tuscan* — 24 | 21 | 22 | VE

Duomo | 9A Via Panzani | (39-55) 282-802 |
www.ristorantesabatini.it

Since 1929 this "traditional", high-profile Tuscan with "excellent" but "expensive" food and "refined service" has been "one of the better Florentine restaurants", and it's conveniently located near the Duomo; fans of the surprisingly "spacious", "formal", wood-paneled room with paintings praise its lovely garden view, but others disdain the "dated setting."

Taverna del Bronzino ☒ *Italian* — 26 | 21 | 26 | E

Piazza Indipendenza | 25 Via delle Ruote | (39-55) 495-220

"No hype or hipness", just "wonderful food" is found at this Italian set in a 16th-century former artist's studio that's "a bit off the beaten path", near San Marco, where a "wonderful, attentive staff always tries to please the demanding international clientele that frequents" the place.

	FOOD	DECOR	SERVICE	COST

◪ Villa San Michele *Italian*

25 | 28 | 25 | VE

Fiesole | Hotel Villa San Michele | 4 Via Doccia | (39-55) 567-8200 | www.villasanmichele.com

"This is living" say sybarites about this Italian in Fiesole's Villa San Michele, a former 15th-century monastery with a facade attributed to Michelangelo; sure, the food is "very good", the "wine list outstanding", service "exceptional" and the dining areas "beautiful", but what surveyors "really remember is seeing night falling on Florence from a terrace table", "champagne glass in hand"; the less romantic also recall the "astronomical prices."

Zibibbo ◪ *Italian/Mediterranean*

25 | 20 | 25 | E

Careggi | 3R Via di Terzollina | (39-55) 433-383

Chef-owner Benedetta Vitali (ex co-founder Cibrèo) is a "magician" when it comes to cooking "great" Italian-Mediterranean cuisine at this "out-of-the-way temple of food" in the Careggi hills, about eight kilometers from the City Center; devotees declare it's "worth the trek" to dine on "outstanding" culinary combinations in her modern room with a skylight and Medici tower view.

Frankfurt

TOP FOOD RANKING

	Restaurant	Cuisine
25	Gargantua	French/Mediterranean
	Osteria Enoteca	Italian
24	Restaurant Français	French
23	Aubergine	German/Italian
	Sushimoto	Japanese
22	M Steakhouse	Steak
20	Medici	Mediterranean
	Erno's Bistro	French
	Edelweiss	Austrian
	Tiger	French/Mediterranean
19	Holbein's	German/International
	Charlot	Italian
	Signatures Veranda	German
	Rama V	Thai
18	Größenwahn	International/Italian
	Opéra	International
17	Die Leiter	International
16	Apfelwein Wagner	German
15	Garibaldi	Italian
14	Central Park Public Pantry	American/International

☑ Apfelwein Wagner ◑ *German* | 16 | 14 | 14 | M |

Sachsenhausen | Schweizer Str. 71 | (49-69) 612-565 |
www.apfelwein-wagner.com

For a taste of "typical Frankfurt", try this "typical apple-wine pub" in Sachsenhausen; the "down-to-earth" digs may be "bleak", the "simple" German fare "unexceptional" ("pork, pork and more pork") and the "rough", "gruff" staffers "uncouth", but "fast service", "moderate prices" and the city's "signature beverage" make it "popular among locals and tourists alike."

☑ Aubergine ☒ *German/Italian* | 23 | 22 | 23 | E |

City Center | Alte Gasse 14 | (49-69) 920-0780 | www.aubergine-frankfurt.de

A small red awning marks this "superb" City Center spot where one can expect "extravagant, freshly prepared" Italian-German fare as well as "attentive service" from a "nice, young, friendly" staff; owner and native Sardinian Paolo Vargiu's "incredible attention to detail" extends from the "excellent" wine list and "tasteful decor" "right down to the Versace plates" that grace the few tables.

Central Park Public Pantry ◑☒ *American/International* | 14 | 19 | 17 | M |

City Center | Kaiserhofstr. 12 | (49-69) 9139-6146 | www.central-park.com

The flagship of a family of five local venues, this "upscale" spot in City Center – "just off a wonderful street", the Goethestraße, and "near the Opera House" – exudes a "hip atmosphere", fueled in part by a "fun bar" where a "trendy" crowd congregates; its "eclectic" American-

FOOD DECOR SERVICE COST

International dishes make it "a place to escape the traditional meat-and-potatoes German" cuisine, and even those who find the casual fare merely "decent" declare "who cares about the food" when you can "look at the staff"?

Charlot *Italian*

19 | 17 | 17 | E

City Center | Opernplatz 10 | (49-69) 287-007
"A lot of thought goes into preparing" the "authentic Italian" fare at this "good, consistent" City Center establishment whose regulars report there's "no need to even look at a menu" – the "waiters are pros", so "just tell them what you like and they'll deliver something delicious"; the "small but attractive setting" is patronized "by smart people of all sorts", including a "celebrity crowd", making it "a good place to people-watch" too.

Die Leiter ⬧ *International*

17 | 12 | 12 | E

City Center | Kaiserhofstr. 11 | (49-69) 292-121 | www.dieleiter.de
When it opened nearly a quarter-century ago, this "super-centrally located" City Center spot quickly became a trendy destination, and it still attracts "the 'in' crowd" with an "extravagant" International menu of "appetizing" Italian- and Austrian-accented offerings; but foes fault "nothing-special" food, "excessive prices", "sober decor" and an "arrogant" staff that "seems burdened by having to wait on you."

⬧ Edelweiss *Austrian*

20 | 15 | 21 | M

Sachsenhausen | Schweizer Str. 96 | (49-69) 619-696 |
www.edelweiss-ffm.de
"Friendly service" from a "special" staff clad in lederhosen combined with a "relaxed atmosphere" lends a "holiday" feel to this "comfortable" Sachsenhausen pseudo-ski lodge where the "really good flavors" of "authentic Austrian food", including "wonderful dishes like Wiener schnitzel", are accompanied by a selection of "super brews to wash everything down"; N.B. don't miss the large heated terrace.

Erno's Bistro ⬧ *French*

20 | 15 | 21 | VE

Westend | Liebigstr. 15 | (49-69) 721-997 | www.ernosbistro.de
"Attentive" service from a "caring" staff overseen by longtime owner Eric Huber sets the tone at this "ultrareliable, top-flight French" in Westend, "a surprising oasis in a city full of heavy food", thanks to chef Valéry Mathis' "small but exquisite menu" of "excellent" fare; not only is it "a welcome break from German cuisine", but the "comfy atmosphere" of its "lively, friendly" digs makes it just the kind of place to which many "would go every day if they could."

⬧ Gargantua ⬧ *French/Mediterranean*

25 | 19 | 20 | VE

Westend | Liebigstr. 47 | (49-69) 720-718 | www.gargantua.de
It's the "creative, well-executed menu" of "incredible" New French-Mediterranean fare from chef-owner and cookbook author Klaus Trebes that makes this "exceptional small bistro" in Westend justifiably "famous", and earns it the ranking of No. 1 for Food in Frankfurt; "very good service", a winning wine list and shady terrace are other reasons it's "well worth" a visit; yes, it's quite expensive, but such an "excellent" experience offers "good value for the money."

	FOOD	DECOR	SERVICE	COST

Garibaldi ⌧ *Italian*
15 15 11 M

City Center | Kleine Hochstr. 4 | (49-69) 2199-7644

"Always crowded", this "hip spot" in City Center serves up "decent", "authentic Italian" fare "at a good price", but "you don't come here for the food" (or the "disappointing wine list") – rather, you come "to watch" the antics of the crowd and "listen to [the staff] sing 'Happy Birthday' several times an evening"; fun aside, though, some just "don't get what attracts people to" its "loud, smoke-filled" setting and "sometimes confused service."

Größenwahn *International/Italian*
18 13 15 M

Nordend | Lenaustr. 97 | (49-69) 599-356 | www.cafe-groessenwahn.de

For "more than 25 years", this "casual" Nordend "favorite" has been a "place for locals" to enjoy "a really nice evening" over a "varied", "creative" menu of Italian-International cuisine (including "fresh, delicious" vegetarian fare) that's "attractively" presented and "reasonably priced"; perhaps the decor is "nothing special" and the "service could be faster", but at least there's "always a smile on the faces" of the "friendly" staffers, ensuring that you "feel good" within the "warm", "cozy" setting.

🅉 Holbein's Ⓜ *German/International*
19 21 16 E

Sachsenhausen | Städel Kunstmuseum | Holbeinstr. 1 | (49-69) 6605-6666 | www.holbeins.de

"Beautiful, stylish decor" is the point at this "posh joint" that's "nicely located in the Städel museum" in Sachsenhausen, "a wonderful setting for a great meal" of "tasty" German-International fare made from "particularly fresh ingredients"; still, some complain of "long waits" and suggest that the generally "well-trained staff" is "not accommodating" when "stressed", "leaving the impression that guests have to be tolerated"; P.S. "in summer, sit on the terrace" overlooking the gardens.

Medici ⌧ *Mediterranean*
20 19 19 E

City Center | Weißadlergasse 2 | (49-69) 2199-0794 | www.restaurant-medici.de

Most maintain this centrally located City Center Mediterranean housed in an insurance company building is a "popular" and "secure bet for a business lunch or dinner"; for those who find the modern minimalist interior with its massive painting of bare-breasted females a "turnoff", there's alternate alfresco eating out on the terrace.

M Steakhouse ⌧ *Steak*
22 15 18 E

Westend | Feuerbachstr. 11A | (49-69) 7103-4050 | www.the-steakhouse.de

"A piece of America in Frankfurt", this Westend steakhouse packs in "lots of English-speaking customers" who come to sample its "delicious" fare – including "really tender" beef, "satisfying jumbo prawns" and "fantastic salads" – served by "good-humored" staffers in a "sparse" setting with "cowboy photos on the walls"; yes, it's "expensive", but most feel the "cost is appropriate given the quality" and "generous portions."

Opéra *International*
18 23 17 E

City Center | Alte Oper | Opernplatz 1 | (49-69) 134-0215 | www.opera-restauration.de

"Don't forget to look at the ceiling" while taking in the "spectacular old-world setting" of this "glamorous site" in a "stunning location"

FOOD DECOR SERVICE COST

"within the Opera House" in City Center, where a "polite", "professional" staff serves "well-presented" International fare and "expensive wines"; still, critics claim that the "erratic kitchen" produces "good but not great food" that should "be more ambitious to match" the "unbeatable ambiance."

🆉 Osteria Enoteca 🆉 Italian   25 | 18 | 23 | E

Rödelheim | Arnoldshainer Str. 2 | (49-69) 789-2216 | www.osteria-enoteca.de

Chef Carmelo Greco's "fresh", "delicious Italian food" (including "great antipasti") draws urbanites to this bi-level venue in the somewhat "remote suburb" of Rödelheim, where guests must ring a bell to gain access to the romantically lit, off-white dining room; add in a "good wine list" and an "accommodating, attentive" staff and you'll see why many lauders label it "a special-occasion place" that's "a bit out of the way but worth the trip."

Rama V ☾ Thai   19 | 15 | 15 | M

City Center | Vilbeler Str. 32 | (49-69) 2199-6488

"A must for Thai lovers", this City Center Siamese sports "an extensive menu" of "authentic" dishes that are "delicious and beautifully prepared"; the "stylish space, "tastefully decorated with art", is overseen by an "obliging staff" headed by "meticulous" owners whose "attention to detail is apparent in everything they serve", not to mention a "big golden Buddha" who "sits in the back watching you eat."

🆉 Restaurant Français 🆉 French   24 | 22 | 24 | VE

City Center | Steigenberger Frankfurter Hof | Am Kaiserplatz | (49-69) 215-118 | www.frankfurter-hof.steigenberger.de

Set "in Frankfurt's dowager hotel", City Center's Steigenberger Frankfurter Hof, this "formal special-occasion restaurant" has been "nicely upgraded" in recent years, and now attracts a "less-stuffy clientele" with its "gourmet New French selections", "excellent service" and "extremely civilized" decor with cream-colored walls and opulent oil paintings; "make sure you have plenty of room on your credit card", though, because "you may feel like royalty but you'll need access to the state treasury to settle the bill."

Signatures Veranda German   19 | 16 | 18 | E

City Center | InterContinental Frankfurt | Wilhelm-Leuschner-Str. 43 | (49-69) 2605-2452 | www.interconti.com

Serving from breakfast through dinner, this "very good" venue in the InterContinental Frankfurt in City Center features "delicious" German fare offered in "ample" à la carte portions or via "great buffets" that are "restocked like magic" by "competent and almost invisible" staffers; still, some surveyors damn with faint praise, purporting it "meets every expectation of a typical hotel restaurant."

🆉 Sushimoto 🅼 Japanese   23 | 16 | 18 | E

City Center | ArabellaSheraton Grand Hotel | Konrad Adenauer Str. 7 | (49-69) 298-1187 | www.arabellasheraton.com

Guests "wonder if you can eat so well in" Tokyo after a visit to this "unexpected" Japanese in City Center's ArabellaSheraton Grand; despite decor that "isn't world-shaking" and a staff that could use "a better knowledge of German" and English, it's "a must for fans" seeking "fan-

	FOOD	DECOR	SERVICE	COST

tastic and fresh meals" featuring "excellent sushi" and teppanyaki selections; P.S. those who find the tabs "too high" should check out the more "moderately priced set menu" at lunch.

Tiger 🅂🅼 *French/Mediterranean*　　　　20　19　18　E

City Center | Tigerpalast Varieté | Heiligkreuzgasse 16-20 |
(49-69) 920-02250 | www.tigerpalast.com

The "kitchen deserves high praise" at this "gourmet" French-Med venue in City Center's Tigerpalast Varieté theater, where the "extravagant", "delicious dishes and exclusive wines" come with "plenty of action" in the form of a "surprisingly" "smashing show" ("don't miss" it); additionally, the "cozy setup" is "nicely decorated" and the "obliging staffers" "know what they're doing", making for an "all-around aesthetic" experience that has even some with "tight wallets" conceding they "can't complain about the cost."

Geneva

TOP FOOD RANKING

Restaurant	Cuisine
29 Domaine de Châteauvieux	French
26 Auberge du Lion d'Or	French
25 Patara	Thai
24 La Vendée	French
Chez Jacky	French
Restaurant du Parc	French
La Favola	Italian
Miyako	Japanese
L'Auberge d'Hermance	French
Spice's	Asian Fusion
23 L'Entrecôte Couronnée	French
Vertig'O*	French/Mediterranean
Il Lago	Italian
Le Relais de l'Entrecôte	Steak
Le Chat-Botté	French
22 Roberto	Lombardian
21 L'Olivier de Provence	French
Le Buffet de la Gare	French/Mediterranean
20 Bistrot du Boeuf Rouge	Lyon
Thai Phuket*	Thai
La Perle du Lac	French

Z Auberge du Lion d'Or ⊠ *French*   26 | 24 | 25 | VE

Cologny | 5 Place Pierre Gautier | (41-22) 736-4432 | www.liondor.ch
"Worth" the trip "outside of town", this "excellent, old-school" inn in Cologny boasts a "contemporary" "gastronomic restaurant" and a "pretty", more casual bistro, "both of which serve fabulous French food"; the setting "overlooking the lake" is "magnificent" and the staff is "impeccable", ensuring "an experience that should not be missed."

Bistrot du Boeuf Rouge ⊠ *Lyon*   20 | 17 | 17 | M

Right Bank | 17 Rue Alfred-Vincent | (41-22) 732-7537 | www.boeufrouge.ch
A bastion of "Lyon in Geneva", this "reliable" Right Bank spot "is the place to go for" that French city's "excellent specialties" (like tripe), as well as some "local" favorites, all offered "at moderate prices"; the "small dining room" is sometimes "noisy", but its "original decor" featuring scads of quirky bric-a-brac and a collection of water carafes makes it "a fun place to eat."

Z Brasserie Lipp ◐ *French*   18 | 17 | 15 | E

Left Bank | 8 Rue de la Confédération | (41-22) 311-1011 |
www.brasserie-lipp.com
"Modeled on its Paris namesake", this "busy", "buzzy" Left Bank boîte is "everything you'd expect" in a "typical French brasserie" – "noisy" "art nouveau" digs "packed" with patrons at "too-small tables" enjoy-

---

* Indicates a tie with restaurant above

ing "consistently good" "traditional" fare ("shellfish is a specialty") "roughly served" by sometimes "rude" staffers; it also offers "salvation for those who don't eat on a strict Swiss timetable", as it's "seemingly always open"; P.S. you "must dine" on the "terrace overlooking the ramparts of the Old Town."

☑ Chez Jacky ☒ French   24 | 15 | 21 | E

Right Bank | 9-11 Rue Necker | (41-22) 732-8680 | www.chezjacky.ch

For a "distinguished dining experience", visit this "great little restaurant" whose "setting slightly off the beaten track" on the Right Bank "adds to its cachet as 'a find'"; eponymous "chef Gruber's truly imaginative" French food offers "value" (regulars recommend you "stick to the excellent, affordable set menu"), and a "friendly staff" further enhances the "pleasant" atmosphere; P.S. "dining on the patio is just wonderful."

☑ Domaine de Châteauvieux ☒Ⓜ French   29 | 25 | 27 | VE

Satigny | Domaine de Châteauvieux | Chemin de Châteauvieux 16, Peney-Dessus | (41-22) 753-1511 | www.chateauvieux.ch

"Wow!" is how fans sum up this "deluxe" venue in a "marvelous setting" overlooking the Rhône in Satigny that offers "the best table" around town, ranking No. 1 for Food in greater Geneva; "creative" chef "Philippe Chevrier's alchemy" produces "superb" New French fare, which is paired with a "fantastic wine list" and "impeccably served" by an "attentive, efficient" staff in "a lovely room" with "panoramic countryside views"; true, you'll need "a well-filled billfold", but everyone should experience such a "true gastronomic delight", "even if it's just once."

Il Lago Italian   23 | 26 | 23 | VE

Right Bank | Four Seasons Hôtel des Bergues | 33 Quai des Bergues | (41-22) 908-7110 | www.fourseasons.com/geneva

"If you like dining in hotels, this restaurant is as good as they come" say supporters of this Northern Italian in the Four Seasons Hôtel des Bergues on the Right Bank; "excellent" cuisine and a "great wine list" that includes bottles from France, Switzerland and The Boot are proffered in a "beautiful" "formal setting" with extravagant floral displays, paintings and Rhône views; of course, "prices that are off the charts" also make for an "elite" experience.

La Favola ☒ Italian   24 | 22 | 19 | E

Old Town | 15 Rue Jean Calvin | (41-22) 311-7437 | www.lafavola.com

It's no fairy tale: "a most memorable meal" can in fact be found at this "tiny gem", "a wonderful retreat" "in the heart of Old Town", where "fabulous Italian" "dishes and wines from Ticino" are served with "personalized attention" in a "cute" little "jewel-box" space; though both floors are "sweet", regulars recommend that "those who can navigate the tight staircase" should "make sure to get a table upstairs"; P.S. don't miss "the best tiramisu ever."

La Perle du Lac Ⓜ French   20 | 22 | 20 | VE

Right Bank | 128 Rue de Lausanne | (41-22) 909-1020 | www.laperledulac.ch

There's "fine New French" fare at this "divine" Right Bank venue, but it's the "magnificent view" (maybe the "most beautiful" in town) that keeps folks "coming back" to this "perfect location" in a "lovely lakeside setting" surrounded by "charming gardens"; it's "a must in

Geneva" for "all the tourists" for a "casual luncheon outdoors or formal dining indoors", "especially in spring and summer."

L'Auberge d'Hermance *French* | 24 | 23 | 24 | E |

Hermance | L'Auberge d'Hermance | 12 Rue du Midi | (41-22) 751-1368 | www.hotel-hermance.ch

Peripatetic patrons who are willing "to drive 15 minutes outside of the city" will be rewarded with an undeniably "great meal" at this "idyllic" French inn ensconced "in the medieval village" of Hermance, where a "friendly, professional" staff will seat you within the "intimate" "antique" dining room, in the "delightful" glass-walled winter garden or on the "beautiful terrace"; wherever you sit, though, expect "attractively presented dishes" from a "superb kitchen."

☑ La Vendée *French* | 24 | 17 | 20 | VE |

Petit-Lancy | Hostellerie de la Vendée | 28 Chemin de la Vendée | (41-22) 792-0411 | www.vendee.ch

"Inventive" French fare – including especially "well-prepared fresh-fish" dishes – served by a staff with "plenty of savoir faire" makes this "high-quality" destination in a Petit-Lancy hotel "worth the trip", despite its "steep" prices; some suggest the "rather somber" surroundings "don't suit the standing" of such an otherwise "first-class" venue, but all agree "the veranda is very nice."

Le Buffet de la Gare des Eaux-Vives ☑ *French/Mediterranean* | 21 | 15 | 17 | E |

Left Bank | 7 Avenue de la Gare des Eaux-Vives | (41-22) 840-4430 | www.lebuffetdelagare.ch

"Believe it or not", "haute cuisine" awaits at this "small place" in a "unique" "setting literally next to an old train station" on the Left Bank, where an "amazing selection" of "inventive", "refined" French-Med fare is "well served" along with "good wines"; perhaps the "modern decor" is "nothing special", but there's a "great terrace in summer", and though it's "not cheap", most insist it's "really worth it" – meaning "reservations are a must."

Le Chat-Botté *French* | 23 | 22 | 23 | VE |

Right Bank | Hôtel Beau-Rivage | 13 Quai du Mont-Blanc | (41-22) 716-6666 | www.beau-rivage.ch

"A favorite for many years", this "elegant" French venue in the Right Bank's Hôtel Beau-Rivage features "enchanting" cuisine and a "very nice wine list", all "effortlessly served" by an "impeccable" staff "in a refined setting" with decor resembling that of a "grand palace"; yes, "it will cost you", but most feel "the quality equals the price", though a few wonder "what's with the hype?", saying the fare would benefit from "a touch of originality."

L'Entrecôte Couronnée ☑ *French* | 23 | 18 | 19 | E |

Right Bank | 5 Rue du Pâquis | (41-22) 732-8445

Of course, this "lively" little French place on the popular Right Bank features an "excellent" namesake entrecôte with "endless frites", but other "quality" dishes (many based on local ingredients like fish fresh from the nearby lake) "will have you coming back for more"; wooden furnishings, mirrors and ceiling fans help produce an appealing archetypal bistro ambiance.

	FOOD	DECOR	SERVICE	COST

☑ Le Relais de l'Entrecôte ⑤ *Steak*   23 | 18 | 17 | M

Left Bank | 49 Rue du Rhône | (41-22) 310-6004

"Choice is not the strong" suit at this "single-dish" steakhouse "institution" on the Left Bank, but fans "know why they go" – for the "same quality" entrecôte "with a twist (an addictive sauce that's guaranteed to have you licking the plate)" and "classic frites" that are served at its Paris siblings; "the only disadvantage" is that it's "difficult to get a table" in the "noisy", "cramped" space, but most "don't mind standing in line" when "the meat is divine and the prices fair."

☑ Les Armures *French/Swiss*   19 | 19 | 17 | E

Old Town | Hôtel Les Armures | 1 Rue du Puits-Saint-Pierre | (41-22) 310-3442 | www.hotel-les-armures.ch

Just "steps from all the points of interest in Old Town", this "charming" "longtime favorite" "in the lovely" Hôtel Les Armures is "crowded" with "conventioneers and tourists" seeking "stereotypical" "Swiss-style" dining from a "traditional menu" with "wonderful specialties" such as "great fondue and raclette", along with classic French dishes; be warned, though, that the "overpowering smell" "of melted cheese" may stay with you "for a long" time.

L'Olivier de Provence ⑤ *French*   21 | 19 | 20 | E

Carouge | 13 Rue Jacques-Dalphin | (41-22) 342-0450 | www.olivierdeprovence.ch

This "treat" in an 18th-century building above the fountain on Place du Temple in Carouge welcomes guests with a "cozy" wood-beamed setting in which a "helpful" staff serves "good" classic French fare "with a Mediterranean touch", reminding some of "being in Provence."

Miyako ⑤ *Japanese*   24 | 18 | 22 | VE

Right Bank | 11 Rue de Chantepoulet | (41-22) 738-0120 | www.miyako.ch

"One of the best Japanese restaurants in Geneva", this Right Bank spot serves up "fresh", "delicious sushi and sashimi", plus "wonderful teppanyaki", to an "international and business clientele" amid "traditional" (some say "a bit stuffy") decor that makes "you think you're in" the East; though the "excellent" staffers are "all very willing to help" ensure that guests "enjoy a nice evening", some still wonder whether the experience "justifies the excessive prices."

☑ Patara *Thai*   25 | 19 | 19 | E

Right Bank | Hôtel Beau-Rivage | 13 Quai du Mont-Blanc | (41-22) 731-5566 | www.patara-geneve.com

"Part of a high-class chain" with branches in Singapore, Taipei and London, this "deluxe" Thai in a "great location" on the Right Bank offers "excellent" (albeit "high-priced") Siamese fare delivered by "attentive" staffers in a "pretty setting" with ceiling fans, wooden blinds and fresh flowers; still, some purists pout that the fare's "not authentic enough", while others opine that service suffers when it's "overcrowded."

Restaurant du Parc   24 | 25 | 20 | VE
des Eaux-Vives ⑤Ⓜ *French*

Left Bank | Hôtel du Parc des Eaux-Vives | 82 Quai Gustave-Ador | (41-22) 849-7575 | www.parcdeseauxvives.ch

"What a view!" exclaim enthusiasts of this "elegant" venue in the Left Bank's Hôtel du Parc des Eaux-Vives; a "wonderful menu" of "superb"

	FOOD	DECOR	SERVICE	COST

New French fare made from "quality ingredients" is presented in a "smart", "classical" interior with "the lake in the background"; true, "you pay for" the "enchanted setting", but the cost-conscious note that the downstairs "brasserie offers excellent food for decent prices"; P.S. "go when the roses are in bloom."

Roberto ⚅ *Lombardian*   22 | 18 | 21 | VE
Left Bank | 10 Rue Pierre-Fatio | (41-22) 311-8033

"Viva Roberto!" proclaim proponents of owner Mr. Carugati who have "nothing but positive things to say" about this "high-priced" eponymous "Italian institution in the center of Geneva's" Left Bank, where a "creative menu" of "delicious" Lombardian dishes is served by a "superb staff"; a "power-lunch" "favorite" of "the old-money" "business crowd", its "flashy red" room is "always busy" at midday, so regulars recommend you "go for dinner and relax."

Spice's ⚅ *Asian Fusion*   24 | 21 | 22 | VE
Right Bank | Hôtel Président Wilson | 47 Quai Wilson | (41-22) 906-6666 | www.hotelpwilson.com

"If you like great food but want something other than typical French cuisine", this "pleasant surprise" in the Right Bank's Hôtel Président Wilson "is for you"; its "creative", "excellent" Asian fusion cooking is served by an "impeccable" staff in a "hip", "modern" setting with "nice views"; no wonder most insist it's "worth" the "astronomical prices."

Thai Phuket *Thai*   20 | 18 | 17 | E
Right Bank | 33 Avenue de France | (41-22) 734-4100

"One of Geneva's best Thai addresses", this "solid" Right Bank spot features an "extensive menu" of "exotic" offerings served in a "modern", "no-fuss" space by a "welcoming staff"; some cynics say that the treats are "too tame", "tiny" and "expensive for what you get", but it's still "popular" "with the U.N. crowd" and "people from the other international organizations nearby" for a "business lunch", so midday "reservations are recommended."

Vertig'O ⚅ *French/Mediterranean*   23 | 22 | 24 | VE
Right Bank | Hôtel de la Paix | 11 Quai du Mont-Blanc | (41-22) 909-6066

Alright, you may well get vertigo from the "exorbitant" prices at this new French-Mediterranean that has replaced the former Café de la Paix in the venerable and recently renovated hotel of the same name; still, most maintain "very pleasing cuisine", "excellent service", "stunning" slate-blue and copper contemporary decor and a "beautiful location on the lake shore" make for a "winning" experience; N.B. closed Saturday and Sunday.

Hamburg

TOP FOOD RANKING

	Restaurant	Cuisine
25	Haerlin	French/Mediterranean
23	Jacobs	French/Mediterranean
	Landhaus Scherrer	German
	Le Canard Nouveau	Mediterranean/Turkish
	Doc Cheng's	Eurasian
	Fischereihafen	Seafood
	Saliba	Syrian
22	Stock's Fischrestaurant	German/Seafood
	Cox	French/Mediterranean
20	Tafelhaus	German/International
	Allegria	Austrian
19	Nil	German
18	Die Bank	French
	Windows	French/Mediterranean
17	Matsumi	Japanese
	Rive	Mediterranean/Seafood
16	Landhaus Flottbek	German/Mediterranean

Allegria 🅼 Austrian
20 | 17 | 22 | M

Eppendorf | Hudtwalcker Str. 13 | (49-40) 4607-2828 |
www.allegria-restaurant.de
"You'll be happy you went" to this "charming place" in Eppendorf, adjacent to the Winterhuder Komödie theater, as the staff is "attentive but not pushy" and will "answer all questions" about the "interesting" Med-influenced Austrian cuisine of "ingenious chef" Alexander Tschebull; the "modern" glass-and-steel setting is "chic [yet] cozy", and there's also delightful summer dining in the garden outside, with a good view of the river Alster.

🆉 Cox ◑ French/Mediterranean
22 | 15 | 18 | E

St. Georg | Lange Reihe 68 | (49-40) 249-422 |
www.restaurant-cox.de
Some "satisfied" surveyors are "surprised" by the "creativity" of the "excellent" New French–Med cuisine at this "place to meet people" in St. Georg, given its "restrained" decor, which elicits "contradictory opinions" – some term it "tasteful", while others call it "boring"; at least almost all agree that the "smooth-talking" staff offers "good advice" on what to order from the "innovative", if "short, menu."

Die Bank French
18 | 21 | 18 | E

Neustadt | Hohe Bleichen 17 | (49-40) 238-0030 |
www.diebank-brasserie.de
"This very hip-to-be-seen place" in Neustadt is in a "fantastic" and "beautiful" converted old bank with high ceilings, crystal chandeliers, a "big cool bar" and a "great terrace"; but since many maintain that the French food is "middle-of-the-road", "it's best to go for drinks and checking out the scene."

	FOOD	DECOR	SERVICE	COST

☑ Doc Cheng's ⑤ *Eurasian*   23 | 22 | 23 | E

Neustadt | Fairmont Hotel Vier Jahreszeiten | Neuer Jungfernstieg 9-14 |
(49-40) 349-4333 | www.hvj.de

An "all-round" winner, this "high-class establishment" in the Fairmont
Hotel Vier Jahreszeiten in Neustadt boasts "a nice team – both in" its
"show kitchen", where chefs who've "mastered the contrasting flavors"
of their "great Eurasian fusion fare" "prepare it in front of you", and on
the floor, where "accommodating and polite" staffers "make every effort" to ensure visitors "feel well cared for"; rounding out the "top-
notch dining" experience is the "posh, stylish Shanghai Express decor",
which also helps the "elevated prices" seem "quite appropriate."

Fischereihafen *Seafood*   23 | 14 | 19 | E

Altona | Große Elbstr. 143 | (49-40) 381-816 |
www.fischereihafenrestaurant.de

"Excellent quality and outstanding selection" are hallmarks of this "traditional" ("not trendy") fish house that "does honor to its name" with
"skillfully prepared", "classic seafood" that's "as fresh as it comes",
served by a "friendly and competent" staff that really "knows the menu";
some say its "dignified" decor is "a bit dowdy" and "could use an update", but all appreciate its "great" dockside location in Altona, complete
with a "wonderful view" – ask for a "table right next to the window."

☑ Haerlin ⑤Ⓜ *French/Mediterranean*   25 | 21 | 25 | VE

Neustadt | Fairmont Hotel Vier Jahreszeiten | Neuer Jungfernstieg 9-14 |
(49-40) 3494-3310 | www.hvj.de

Rated No. 1 for Food in Hamburg, this "top spot" in the Fairmont Hotel
Vier Jahreszeiten in Neustadt is "distinguished" by chef Christoph
Rüffer's "superb" French-Med cuisine, "gracious service" from staffers
who are "so attentive they know what you want before you do" and an
"excellent location" with "lovely views of the Alstersee through picture
windows"; in short, this "dream" of a place makes "you feel special",
even if you're not one of its "famous guests from radio, TV and politics."

☑ Jacobs *French/Mediterranean*   23 | 19 | 22 | VE

Nienstedten | Hotel Louis C. Jacob | Elbchaussee 401-403 |
(49-40) 8225-5405 | www.hotel-jacob.de

"Exquisite" French-Mediterranean fare, an "excellent wine list", a
"charming", "confident" staff and "classic decor" combine at this "elegant" establishment in Nienstedten's Hotel Louis C. Jacob; whether
you enjoy "top chef Thomas Martin's" "surprisingly" "imaginative
dishes" in an interior with a "wonderful collection of oil paintings" or
out on the "magnificent tree-shaded terrace overlooking the Elbe
river", the experience will "remain in your memory a very long time" –
but be sure to bring a "fat wallet."

Landhaus Flottbek ⑤⇨ *German/Mediterranean*   16 | 14 | 14 | E

Flottbek | Hotel Landhaus Flottbek | Baron-Voght-Str. 179 |
(49-40) 8227-4160 | www.landhaus-flottbek.de

"Lots of variety" on a menu of "good" German-Mediterranean dishes
means there's "something for everyone" at this "solid restaurant" in
the Hotel Landhaus Flottbek; the "rustic", "cottage-style decor"
makes for a "pleasant atmosphere", though some complain that "the
cost is quite high" for such a "simple" setting.

	FOOD	DECOR	SERVICE	COST

Z Landhaus Scherrer ⊠ *German* | 23 | 16 | 20 | VE |

Ottensen | Elbchaussee 130 | (49-40) 880-1325 | www.landhausscherrer.de
"Old-world charm, grace and quality abound" at this German in a former country house close to the river Elbe, where an "obliging" staff provides guests with "super recommendations from" the "creative menu's" "wide selection" of "first-class" modern dishes; some suggest its "decor could be better", but more insist that its "homelike atmosphere" makes it "ideal for a cozy get-together"; P.S. those who cry "oh, my poor wallet!" may find relief in its less-"expensive" bistro space.

Z Le Canard Nouveau Ⓜ *Mediterranean/Turkish* | 23 | 20 | 20 | VE |

Ottensen | Elbchaussee 139 | (49-40) 8812-9531 | www.lecanard-hamburg.de
"One of the best restaurants in town" also comes with perhaps "the most stunning view of the Elbe River" report respondents about this "excellent" Med with Turkish accents in Ottensen; it's "very expensive" but "always worth it", particularly if you get a seat on the terrace.

Matsumi ⊠ *Japanese* | 17 | 15 | 19 | E |

Neustadt | Colonnaden 96, 1st fl. | (49-40) 343-125 | www.matsumi.de
Expect "fast and friendly" service from the "attentive" staff at this "snug" spot in Neustadt, where "something different" from the usual comes in the form of "delicious" Japanese cuisine, including some of "the best sushi in the city" (if "the prices are high", "well, good fresh fish costs something"); still, critics "wouldn't give it high marks", claiming the "taste leaves something to be desired" and adding "there's nothing stunning" about the "standard" decor.

Nil ⊯ *German* | 19 | 16 | 13 | M |

St. Pauli | Neuer Pferdemarkt 5 | (49-40) 439-7823 | www.restaurant-nil.de
"All the beautiful people" still crowd this "relaxed yet classy" St. Pauli spot, "for years a trendsetter" with its "fresh", "delicious food" – lately "high-quality", "medium-priced" Med-influenced "new German cuisine"; insiders advise that you "enjoy the stylish", "colorful" gallery above and avoid "the poorly lit basement", while first-timers report that "folks have to be regulars to get a smile" from the merely "civil" staffers whose idea of service seems to be Nil; N.B. closed Tuesdays.

Z Rive ● *Mediterranean/Seafood* | 17 | 19 | 17 | E |

Altona | Van-der-Smissen-Str. 1 | (49-40) 380-5919 | www.rive.de
"For those romantic moments, a table by the window" or "on the wonderful, sunny [heated] terrace" of this "posh" Med seafooder in Altona "is a must" according to fans of its "fantastic location" and "exceptional view of the Elbe"; there's "something for everyone on its menu" of "fresh", "imaginative creations", though some are "disappointed" with the "simple", "nothing-special decor", "long waits", "ok service" and "high cost", declaring it "better for a light snack and drinks than an evening out."

Saliba *Syrian* | 23 | 20 | 19 | E |

Altona | Leverkusenstr. 54 | (49-40) 858-071 | www.saliba.de
"An adventure for the senses" awaits at this "wonderful" Altona venue, set in a former power station, that offers a break from the "monotonous" with its "delicious" Syrian fare (a "whole new taste experi-

ence"); neophytes needn't worry, as the "friendly, patient" staff "provides the necessary information" to those who "don't know" "this exceptional cuisine", and aesthetes add that its "imaginative, appealing decor" helps take you to "another world."

Stock's Fischrestaurant ⊠ *German/Seafood* | 22 | 15 | 21 | M |

Poppenbüttel | An Der Alsterschleife 3 | (49-40) 602-0043 | www.stocks.de
"Congratulations to Mr. Stock" say fans of this German seafooder set in a replica of a thatched, half-timbered 18th-century house "pleasantly located near Alstertal" Park in residential Poppenbüttel; "you get the feeling" that the "excellent local fish" "jumped directly out of the water onto your plate with a brief stopover in the frying pan", and you "can't complain" about the moderate cost, so it's no wonder most don't mind that the "simple decor" is a bit "meager."

Tafelhaus ●⊠ *German/International* | 20 | 22 | 18 | E |

Övelgönne | Neumühlen 17 | (49-40) 892-760 | www.tafelhaus-hamburg.de
This "wonderful place" blessed with "a great view of the harbor" in Övelgönne "exceeds expectations" with "sober but stylish decor" and "simply delicious" "German specialties" as well as some International dishes; still, surveyors are split over service, with some reporting "no complaints" about "caring" attendants who are "always at hand" and others offering "no special praise" for certain "slow" staffers.

Windows ⊠⊠ *French/Mediterranean* | 18 | 19 | 21 | E |

Pöseldorf | InterContinental Hamburg | Fontenay 10, 9th fl. | (49-40) 41420 | www.interconti.com
Set in a "beautiful location" – the penultimate floor of the InterContinental Hamburg hotel – this "expensive" fine-dining venue offers an equally "beautiful experience"; perhaps the "wonderful view over Lake Alster" and the city "tops" the "consistently good" French-Mediterranean cuisine, but most visitors nevertheless report being "thoroughly impressed with the restaurant."

Istanbul

TOP FOOD RANKING

	Restaurant	Cuisine
26	Borsa	Turkish
25	Körfez	Seafood/Turkish
	Develi	Turkish
	Seasons Restaurant	Mediterranean
	Tugra	Turkish/Ottoman
	Tike	Turkish
	Balikçi Sabahattin	Seafood
24	Lokanta	Turkish/Finnish
	Ulus 29	Turkish/International
	Laledan	Seafood
23	Feriye Lokantasi	Turkish/Ottoman
	Pandeli*	Turkish/Ottoman
	Del Mare	Seafood
	Kösebasi	Turkish/Mediterranean
	Sunset Grill & Bar	International
22	Paper Moon	Italian
	Mezzaluna	Italian
	Changa/Müzedechanga	Euro. Fusion/International
21	Asitane	Turkish
	Leb-i Derya	Turkish/Mediterranean
20	Yesil Ev	Turkish/International
	Vogue	International/Med.
19	360 Istanbul	Med./International

Asitane *Turkish*   21 | 16 | 19 | M

Edirnekapí | Kariye Hotel | Kariye Camii Sokak 18 | (90-212) 534-8414 |
www.kariyeotel.com

Dine like a sultan – as in Suleiman the Magnificent – for far less than the proverbial king's ransom at this "undiscovered gem" inside Edirnekapí's Kariye Hotel that features "authentic", "extensively researched" antique Turkish specialties from royal recipes dating back to 1539; while a few find the onetime Ottoman mansion "stuffy", dining in the "outdoor garden is lovely" and the live music on weekends is "interesting for tourists."

Balikçi Sabahattin/   25 | 17 | 20 | M
The Fisherman ❶ *Seafood*

Sultanahmet | Seyit Hasan Koyu Sokak 1 | (90-212) 458-1824 |
www.armadahotel.com.tr

"Wonderful", "authentic" and "freshly made mezes", "excellent fish and moderate prices" lure loyalists to this Sultanahmet seafooder in a restored mansion behind the Armada Hotel and "near the Blue Mosque"; menus are nonexistent – all meals are fixed-price and include drinks and dessert – so just "sit at an outside table", relax and enjoy the "classic Turkish experience."

---

* Indicates a tie with restaurant above

	FOOD	DECOR	SERVICE	COST

◪ Borsa ● Turkish — 26 | 16 | 25 | E

Harbiye | Istanbul Lütfi Kirdar Convention & Exhibition Ctr. |
(90-212) 232-4201 | www.borsarestaurants.com

Voted Istanbul's No. 1 for Food, this Harbiye institution is renowned for "excellent traditional" Turkish cuisine ("best doner kebab in town") ably presented by a courteous staff; the bonus of a "handy address" in the Lütfi Kirdar convention center ("five minutes from major hotels") draws a "businesslike" "older crowd" that also appreciates the "lovely" glassed-in terrace "overlooking the sea and the city."

Changa ◪ Euro. Fusion/International — 22 | 25 | 21 | E

Taksim | Siraselviler Caddesi 47 | (90-212) 249-1205

Müzedechanga ●Ⓜ Euro. Fusion/International

Emirgan | Sakip Sabanci Museum | Sakip Sabanci Cad. 22 |
(90-212) 323-0901
www.changa-istanbul.com

"The F word" – fusion – "still rules" at what some call "Istanbul's best" (and possibly only) multiculti eatery, where "good" International dishes are enhanced by local ingredients; located amid the sights and sounds of Taksim, the setting is equally eclectic, with a "historical" art nouveau exterior that belies its extremely stylish "modern" interior – small wonder it's popular with "the city's young movers and shakers"; N.B. the newer Müzedechanga offshoot is in the Sakip Sabanci Museum overlooking the Bosphorous.

Del Mare Seafood — 23 | 18 | 20 | E

Cengelköy | Kuleli Caddesi 53/4 | (90-216) 422-5762 | www.del-mare.com

The menu is extensive, the seafood is "delicious", the "service is kind" and the setting in a historic building is atmospheric at this Cengelköy spot; but it's "dining alfresco in the moonlight" on the expansive terrace with its "fantastic view of the Bosphorus" and bridge that's its "biggest asset" and what leaves most "breathless."

◪ Develi Turkish — 25 | 13 | 21 | M

Etiler | Tepecik Yolu 22 | (90-212) 263-2571
Kalamis | Kalamis Marina | Münir Nurettin Selçuk Caddesi |
(90-216) 418-9400
Samatya | Gümüsyüzük Sokak 7 | (90-212) 529-0833
www.develikebap.com

"Fun, frantic and fabulous", this trio of "outstanding kebab houses" specializing in spicy Southeastern Turkish–style fare is "where the locals go" to fill up for mere "pennies", but it's also "friendly to business travelers", who "can't go wrong" with any of the "multitude of meat selections" ("try the pistachio kebab"); ok, "the decor isn't great", but the Samatya original's "pleasant open-air rooftop" provides a panoramic "view of the harbor."

Feriye Lokantasi Turkish/Ottoman — 23 | 24 | 22 | E

Ortaköy | Çiragan Caddesi 124 | (90-212) 227-2216 | www.feriye.com

"Summer is the best time" to dine at this "beautiful" converted police station in Ortaköy because you'll want to sit on its "lovely terrace" to take in "one of Istanbul's most spectacular views" of the Bogazici Bridge ("unforgettable at sunset"); the location is so "breathtaking" it's "almost difficult to focus" on the "succulent" Turkish-Ottoman cuisine, comparatively extensive wine list and service that's "as good as it gets."

⊠ Körfez *Seafood/Turkish*

| 25 | 22 | 24 | VE |

Kanlica | Körfez Caddesi 78 | (90-216) 413-4314 | www.korfez.com
"Exquisite seafood" (e.g. "fantastic" salt-crusted sea bass) and "gorgeous" views of the Mehmet II Bridge and Rumeli Hisar make dinner at this pricey, nautical-themed Turkish "a great experience"; getting to the waterside villa can be half the "fun", since guests can choose to cross the Bosphorus on the restaurant's "private" ferry.

Kösebasi *Turkish/Mediterranean*

| 23 | 16 | 20 | M |

Beylikdüzü | Kaya Ramada Plaza Yani ES | (90-212) 886-6699
Fenerbahce | Fuatpasa Caddesi, Kurukahveciler Sokak | (90-216) 363-5856
Levent | Çamlik Sokak 153 | (90-212) 270-2433
Macka | Bronz Sokak 5 | (90-212) 230-3868
www.kosebasi.com.tr
"You can't miss" at this modern and "upscale" Turkish-Med chain, a "local favorite" with a "wide array" of "tantalizing", "sizzling" kebabs, "plentiful" meze and a large, affordable wine list; execs from the nearby business districts readily entertain foreign clients here, although a few folks fear the owners have now "opened too many branches" to sustain the high quality.

⊠ Laledan *Seafood*

| 24 | 27 | 26 | VE |

Besiktas | Çiragan Palace Kempinski | Çiragan Caddesi 32 | (90-212) 326-4646 | www.ciraganpalace.com
This "stunning" seafooder in the Çiragan Palace Kempinski has respondents rhapsodizing over its patio's "spectacular" Bosphorus views, gardens and elegant interiors ("like dining in a museum"); staffers deliver practically "perfect service" along with "world-class food and wine" to a well-heeled clientele, leaving a dazed few to sigh that with surroundings "so pretty" they "can't remember how the meal was."

Leb-i Derya *Turkish/Mediterranean*

| 21 | 22 | 19 | M |

Beyoglu | Richmond Hotel | Istiklal Caddesi 445 | (90-212) 243-4376
Tünel | Kumbaraci Yokusu 115/7 | (90-212) 243-9555
www.lebiderya.com
Capitalizing on the city's trend of opening chic eateries on rooftops, this Tünel Turkish-Mediterranean offers "stunning" historic and modern panoramas of "the Bosphorus, Golden Horn, Topkapi Palace and opposite Asian shore", both from its open outdoor terrace and glassed-in interior; the new branch atop the Richmond Hotel is built on the same concept – "amazing" views, "delicious", moderate priced fare and a "low-key but high-powered atmosphere"; P.S. at either one, "make a reservation for a table when the sun sets."

Lokanta ◗ *Turkish/Finnish*

| 24 | 18 | 19 | E |

Beyoglu | Mesrutiyet Caddesi 149/1 | (90-212) 245-6070 | www.lokantadaneve.com
What lures the thirtysomething crowds to this hip Beyoglu eatery is "talented" chef-owner Mehmet Gürs' "cool take" on Turkish treats, incorporating elements of Finnish cuisine; the modern interior is "under-

FOOD | DECOR | SERVICE | COST

stated", but for a truly "magical" experience, savor your fusion fare at a rooftop table overlooking the Golden Horn.

Mezzaluna ● *Italian*   22 | 15 | 18 | M

Nisantasi | Abdi Ipekçi Caddesi 38/1 | (90-212) 231-3142 | www.mezzaluna.com.tr

With a wood oven producing "wonderful pizzas" and an extensive menu full of "high-quality", affordable *cucina*, this big, colorful Italian mainstay in fashionable Nisantasi remains a "good choice" for an informal meal; the staff can be overwhelmed during the dinner rush, but overall this place is "always satisfactory" – which is why it's "always full."

Pandeli *Turkish/Ottoman*   23 | 20 | 20 | M

Eminönü | Misir Çarsisi 1 | (90-212) 522-5534

"Yes, it's a bit touristy" but this "bustling" "traditional" Turkish-Ottoman is nevertheless a "magical place" thanks to its "historic setting", a 17th-century edifice above the entrance to the Egyptian Spice Bazaar in Eminönü; colorfully tiled, domed rooms provide "Old Istanbul atmosphere" plus "excellent views" of the bustling market, and it's conveniently located for shoppers to stop in for a moderately priced midday meal (lunch only is served from noon–4 PM).

Paper Moon ● *Italian*   22 | 22 | 21 | VE

Etiler | Akmerkez Residence | Nispetiye Caddesi | (90-212) 282-1616

"Playboys, models" and other "beautiful" specimens populate the "scene" at this upscale Italian in Etiler's Akmerkez Residence hotel, so "go for the people-watching" but "stay for the food" too suggest surveyors; "good" pastas, risottos and wood-fired pizzas are served in the modern Milano-"chic" dining room or the garden, but because the experience can be "über-expensive", it's best for those "with expense accounts."

☑ Seasons Restaurant *Mediterranean*   25 | 26 | 27 | VE

Sultanahmet | Four Seasons Hotel | Tevkifhane Sokak 1 | (90-212) 638-8200 | www.fourseasons.com/istanbul

At the center of what was a "former prison" in Sultanahmet, this "intimate", "peaceful" glass-walled restaurant is now the place to "mingle with Istanbul's upper crust" over "marvelous" and costly Mediterranean meals ("order with abandon – it's all good") enhanced by "excellent Turkish wines"; best of all, report respondents, is the "extraordinary" service from an "attentive" and "friendly" staff, but then again all agree that's "typical Four Seasons quality."

Sunset Grill & Bar *International*   23 | 26 | 25 | VE

Ulus Park | Adnan Saygun Caddesi Yol Sokak 2 | (90-212) 287-0357 | www.sunsetgrillbar.com

"Out of the City Center" but nevertheless a "must-go", this Ulus Park destination with "terrace tables overlooking the whole city and the Bosphorus" is "one of Istanbul's best options for summer dining", plus the "magnificent" vistas are visible from the spare, open interior; "great" International eats (e.g. "unbeatable" but "expensive" sushi and steaks) come courtesy of a "wonderful" staff, so in all ways "it's worth the trip."

	FOOD	DECOR	SERVICE	COST

360 Istanbul ● *Mediterranean/International* — 19 | 24 | 20 | E

Beyoglu | Istiklal Caddesi 8/311, Misir Apt. 8th fl. | (90-212) 251-1042 |
www.360istanbul.com

The "food is delicious", but "the main draw is the unbelievable view
and the slick decor" declare "hip" habitués of this "trendy" Med-
International located on the eighth floor of a 19th-century building in
Beyoglu; true to its name, the 360-degree panorama from the glassed-in
interior and terrace provides "beautiful" vistas of Old Istanbul
and the Bosphorus.

Tike *Turkish* — 25 | 18 | 20 | E

Günesli | Koçman Caddesi Ziyal Plaza 38 | (90-212) 630-5930 ⊠
Kadiköy | Kazim Özalp Caddesi 58 | (90-216) 467-5914
Kemerburgaz | Göktürk Mahallesi Sadik Sok. 3A |
(90-212) 322-3255
Levent | Haci Adil Caddesi 4, Aralik 1 | (90-212) 281-8871
Nisantasi | Sair Nigar Sokak 4/A | (90-212) 233-3540
Sultanahmet | Senlikköy Mah Germeyan Sokak | (90-212) 574-0505
www.tike.com.tr

"Everyone knows" this burgeoning chain of "upscale kebab houses"
assert aficionados who say you've "got to love" its "delicious",
"perfectly seasoned" grilled meat skewers, "great vegetarian
dishes" and "tasty" meze and salads; all branches' "modern", "trendy"
settings and ample alfresco seating appeal to "crowds" of affluent
thirtysomethings, as do the indoor and outdoor bars featured at the
original Levent location.

Z Tugra *Turkish/Ottoman* — 25 | 28 | 27 | VE

Besiktas | Çiragan Palace Kempinski | Çiragan Caddesi 32 |
(90-212) 326-4646 | www.ciraganpalace.com

"Mind-blowingly beautiful, ornate and colorful", this "fabulous" jewel
box "overlooking the glittering Bosphorus" makes it clear you're "dining in the palace" of a sultan (now the Çiragan Palace Kempinski in
Besiktas); similarly exalted are the "wonderful", "perfectly" presented
Turkish and Ottoman specialties, a wine list that's among the city's
best, "excellent" live piano music performed nightly and tabs that may
necessitate dipping into the royal treasury.

Z Ulus 29 *Turkish/International* — 24 | 26 | 22 | VE

Ulus Park | Adnan Saygun Caddesi Yol Sokak 1 | (90-212) 358-2929 |
www.club29.com

Perched on a hilltop in residential Ulus, this "always 'in'" eatery offers "drop-dead" vistas – not only a "famous" panoramic Bosphorus
view of both bridges, but also glimpses of the "beautiful people"
who frequent this "elegant" mod-minimalist boîte to dine on "top-
level", premium-priced Turkish-International cuisine; after dinner the
young, fashionable crowd happily heads to the "fun" adjacent club for
late-night dancing.

Vogue ● *International/Mediterranean* — 20 | 25 | 21 | VE

Besiktas | BJK Plaza | Spor Caddesi 92, 13th fl. | (90-212) 227-4404 |
www.istanbuldoors.com

Still "in vogue" among "Turkish and foreign yuppies alike", this
10-year-old, minimalist International-Med with a sushi bar boasts
"the spectacular views one would expect" from its position "atop a

Besiktas Plaza office tower"; veterans advise "get one of the corner tables on the terrace" for a "romantic" (if pricey) "candlelit dinner."

Yesil Ev *Turkish/International* | 20 | 23 | 21 | M |

Sultanahmet | Yesil Ev Hotel | Kabasakal Caddesi 5 | (90-212) 517-6785 | www.istanbulyesilev.com

The name means "green house", which befits this "graceful" replica of an Ottoman mansion's emerald exterior and is also a pun on its "gorgeous", partially glassed-in "private garden", where four seasons of the year the hotel serves "fresh, well-prepared" Turkish-International fare around a cooling fountain; thanks to the "great" Sultanahmet location, plenty of tourists "come in for drinks" and "unbeatable", affordable meze "on a hot day."

Lisbon

TOP FOOD RANKING

	Restaurant	Cuisine
27	Varanda	French
	Ristorante Hotel Cipriani	Italian
	Sua Excelência	Portuguese
24	Gambrinus	International
	Casa da Comida	Portuguese
	Adega Tia Matilde	Portuguese
	O Mercado do Peixe	Seafood
	Olivier	Mediterranean
23	A Travessa	International
	Solar dos Presuntos	Portuguese
22	A Galeria Gemelli	Italian
	Solar dos Nunes	Portuguese
	Valle Flôr	French/Mediterranean
	Pap'Açorda	Portuguese
	A Casa do Bacalhau	Portuguese/Seafood
21	Ad Lib	French/Portuguese
	Conventual	Portuguese
	Tavares Rico	French/International
20	Alcântara Café	International
	BBC – Belém Bar Café*	French/Portuguese
	XL	Portuguese/International
19	Bica do Sapato	International/Japanese
17	Clara	Portuguese/International

A Casa do Bacalhau ⌷ *Portuguese/Seafood*   `22` `21` `17` `M`
Beato | Rua do Grilo 54 | (351-21) 862-0000 |
www.acasadobacalhau.restaunet.pt
You are at the 'House of the Codfish' at this Beato Portuguese specialist serving over 20 "good" versions of the revered local staple; prices are moderate, so if you're bananas for *bacalhau*, this is a good catch.

Adega Tia Matilde ◑ *Portuguese*   `24` `16` `21` `M`
Praça de Espanha | Rua da Beneficencia 77 | (351-21) 797-2172
Since 1937, locals have been flocking to this "delicious and authentic" Portuguese in Praça de Espanha for classic dishes; the spacious, tiled setting is traditionally decorated, and the price is right.

Ad Lib *French/Portuguese*   `21` `20` `21` `E`
Liberdade | Hotel Sofitel | Avenida da Liberdade 127 | (351-21) 322-8350 |
www.sofitel.com
Supporters spontaneously say this "good, innovative" French-Portuguese in the Hotel Sofitel "adds a bit of global chic to Avenida da Liberdade", the city's main thoroughfare, making it appropriate either for a business lunch or romantic dinner; it's a "beautiful find" in Downtown Lisbon, but "bring your wallet", as "it's expensive" by local "standards."

---

* Indicates a tie with restaurant above

	FOOD	DECOR	SERVICE	COST

A Galeria Gemelli ●⑤Ⓜ *Italian* 22 | 10 | 16 | E

Bairro das Mercês | Rua de São Bento 334 | (351-21) 395-2552 |
www.augustogemelli.com

Insiders insist "let owner Augusto Gemelli make the choice" as to
what you'll order at this Bairro Mercês "excellent Italian", where
many recipes rely on Portuguese products and there is always a
"nice surprise on the menu"; the bistro-style room is small but
"warm" and welcoming.

ⓩ Alcântara Café ● *International* 20 | 22 | 18 | E

Alcântara | Rua Maria Luísa Holstein 15 | (351-21) 363-7176 |
www.alcantaracafe.com

Even after 18 years it's "still one of the most beautiful rooms in Lisbon"
is what supporters say about this "stunning" Alcântara International
in "an old industrial setting" with steel beams, ornate mirrors, classic
statues, candlelight and a sexy bar; even though it's "more like a nightclub than a restaurant", the food is "surprisingly good", and the crowd
is a nice "mix of tourists and locals."

ⓩ A Travessa ●⑤ *International* 23 | 23 | 22 | E

Madragoa | Travessa do Convento das Bernardas 12 | (351-21) 390-2034 |
www.atravessa.com

This long-standing International in the 17th-century Convento das
Bernardas in Madragoa has "all the charm of a historic location";
a "nice" selection of "excellent Belgian dishes and local
Portuguese favorites" is served in an "inviting" setting by a "very
polite staff"; regulars recommend on a "warm night have dinner alfresco" on the terrace.

BBC - Belém Bar Café ●⑤Ⓜ *French/Portuguese* 20 | 23 | 20 | E

Belém | Avenida Brasília, Pavilhão Poente | (351-21) 362-4232 |
www.belembarcafe.com

In a "very beautiful location" in a "happening neighborhood" is this
well-frequented French-Portuguese restaurant/bar/club in Belém, a
"little far from the City Center" but in a popular redeveloped area with
a "good view" of the Tejo river and bridge; a "hip" crowd comes for a
"lively" time and an exceptionally "atmospheric" glassed-in setting.

ⓩ Bica do Sapato ⑤ *International/Japanese* 19 | 22 | 16 | E

Santa Apolónia | Avenida Infante D. Henrique, Armazém B, Cais da Pedra |
(351-21) 881-0320 | www.bicadosapato.com

"As cool as you can get in Lisbon" is this "trendy", "inventive"
Santa Apolónia International with a separate upstairs sushi bar in
a "huge waterfront warehouse" that's co-owned by actor John
Malkovich; "portions are small" ("the ideal quantity for models")
and service could be "friendlier and more attentive", but it's the
"grooviest" "place to see local celebs", and there are "beautiful views"
of the Tagus River too.

ⓩ Casa da Comida ⑤ *Portuguese* 24 | 23 | 22 | E

Jardim das Amoreiras | Travessa das Amoreiras 1 | (351-21) 388-5376 |
www.casadacomida.pt

Among the "tops in town" is this refined, "romantic" Portuguese in a
pretty, 18th-century townhouse in Jardim das Amoreiras; start by sipping a crisp white port while perusing the menu in the wood-paneled

lounge before moving into the "wonderful" interior garden room and enjoying an "excellent" meal served by a "cordial staff."

Clara ⊠ *Portuguese/International* | 17 | 20 | 21 | E |

Pena | Campo dos Mártires da Pátria 49 | (351-21) 885-3053 | www.lisboa-clara.pt

For over 30 years, this "pretty" Portuguese-International in Pena with "good food", an extensive wine list, "charming management" and a "comfortable setting" in an 18th-century mansion has been particularly popular for business lunches; in winter the fireplace is the focus, while in summer "exquisite garden" dining is the draw.

Conventual ⊠ *Portuguese* | 21 | 19 | 21 | E |

Bairro das Mercês | Praça das Flores 45 | (351-21) 390-9196

Many of long-standing chef-owner Dina Marques dishes are inspired by old recipes from Portuguese convents or monasteries, and the result is "deliciously flavored" "traditional" food; an "attentive" staff presides over the "sedate", white-walled space in the Bairro das Mercês that is, appropriately enough, decorated with "interesting religious art."

Ⓩ Gambrinus ❶ *International* | 24 | 20 | 24 | VE |

Baixa | Rua das Portas de Santo Antão 23-25 | (351-21) 342-1466

"Excellent seafood and game" are the focus at this International, "one of the oldest and most traditional restaurants" in the Baixa, where "waiters and customers seem to be longtime friends"; its decor – "dark-paneled rooms", stained glass and leather chairs – appeals to "mostly male" patrons, but everyone exclaims 'holy mackerel' when it comes to the "very expensive" prices.

Olivier ❶⊠ *Mediterranean* | 24 | 15 | 20 | E |

Bairro Alto | Rua do Teixeira 35 | (351-21) 343-1405 | www.restaurante-olivier.com

The menu at chef-owner Olivier da Costa's Bairro Alto dinner-only Mediterranean may be limited, but the cuisine is "unique", "sophisticated" and "delicious"; no wonder the charming, "tiny" wood-paneled room with paintings is always "full."

O Mercado do Peixe *Seafood* | 24 | 13 | 16 | E |

Monsanto | Estrada Pedro Teixeira, Vila Simão, Carmão da Ajuda | (351-21) 361-6070 | www.mercadodopeixe.web.pt

There's a "large diversity" of the "freshest" fish and shellfish on ice to choose from, and then you watch your selection being "grilled to perfection" in front of you at this favorite in Monsanto; aesthetes assert that the plain decor is not the lure, but even they insist the experience is "simple, direct and wonderful."

Pap'Açorda ⊠Ⓜ *Portuguese* | 22 | 17 | 19 | E |

Bairro Alto | Rua da Atalaia 57-59 | (351-21) 346-4811

Still "very popular" and "eternally trendy" "after more than 25 years" is this "Portuguese with a twist" up in the hopping Bairro Alto; dishes like the traditional namesake açorda (a bread stew cooked with shellfish, garlic and coriander) and an "excellent chocolate mousse" have their fans, but it's the "people-watching" that's the real order of the day.

	FOOD	DECOR	SERVICE	COST

☑ Ristorante Hotel Cipriani *Italian* | 27 | 25 | 27 | VE |

Lapa | Lapa Palace Hotel | Rua do Pau de Bandeira 4 | (351-21) 394-9494 | www.lapapalace.com

Set in the lush, "lovely" Lapa Palace Hotel in the "ritzy" embassy area is this "great" Italian with equally highly rated service; the softly lit room is patrician and pretty, plus in summer there's a "nice dining terrace overlooking a garden"; in sum, it's "very elegant" and "very expensive."

Solar dos Nunes ●Ⓩ *Portuguese* | 22 | 14 | 18 | M |

Alcântara | Rua dos Lusíadas 70 | (351-21) 364-7359 | www.solardosnunes.restaunet.pt

At this "Lisbon fixture" in the Alcântara, there's a "large choice" of "delightful" Alentejo specialties; a "friendly" staff, country casual decor and moderate prices add to its appeal.

Solar dos Presuntos ● *Portuguese* | 23 | 17 | 22 | M |

Baixa | Rua das Portas de Santo Antão | (351-21) 342-4253 | www.solardospresuntos.com

"Locals and tourists" hit this "very good" Restaurant Row pioneer in the Baixa for a plethora of "classic" and "simple" Portuguese staples ranging from meats to seafood dishes like "perfect paella", all complemented by a substantial wine cellar; "service is excellent", the decor is "traditional" and prices are "acceptable"; P.S. "try to get a table upstairs."

☑ Sua Excelência *Portuguese* | 27 | 16 | 22 | E |

Lapa | Rua do Conde 34 | (351-21) 390-3614 | www.suaexcelencia.co.nr

"Start with a chilled white port", sit back and let the "interesting" owner "recite the day's offerings" in several languages, including English if necessary, at this "excellent" Portuguese in the Lapa district; an "attentive and polite" staff presides over the small, unpretentious setting with white walls and wooden beams.

Tavares Rico Ⓩ *French/International* | 21 | 22 | 19 | E |

Chiado | Rua da Misericórdia 35-37 | (351-21) 342-1112 | www.tavaresrico.pt

"Still good after all these years" assert admirers of this 1784 Chiado French-International - maybe that's because its drop-dead opulent interior with gilt, mirrors and chandeliers was recently restored; the finest appointments - Vista Alegre china, Riedel crystal and Christofle silver - ensure this "institution" remains elegant.

Valle Flôr *French/Mediterranean* | 22 | 28 | 23 | VE |

Alcântara | Pestana Palace Hotel | Rua Jau 54 | (351-21) 361-5600 | www.pestana.com

"Probably the most beautiful and historic dining room in Lisbon" is this French-Mediterranean with frescoes, boiserie and garden views in the Pestana Palace Hotel, which is also a national monument; chef Aimé Barroyer does a "wonderful job modernizing classic dishes", and the result is an "expensive" but "great experience."

☑ Varanda *French* | 27 | 24 | 27 | VE |

São Sebastião da Pedreira | Four Seasons Hotel Ritz | Rua Rodrigo da Fonseca 88 | (351-21) 381-1400 | www.fourseasons.com/lisbon

Voted No. 1 for Food in the city is this "very expensive" French venue that "like most other Four Seasons' restaurants could easily stand on its own without the hotel"; an "impeccable" staff serves "exquisite" food in a luminous room with a view of Eduardo VII park; P.S. the "sumptuous and well-presented lunchtime buffet" is "where all of Lisbon meets."

XL ●☒ *Portuguese/International* | 20 | 18 | 20 | E |

Lapa | Calçada da Estrela 57-63 | (351-21) 395-6118
At this chef-owned Portuguese-International in the aristocratic Lapa district, "delicious steaks" and "good soufflés" are the stars; a "friendly, helpful" staff and "cool", "informal" vibe make it "a hit with a younger clientele."

London

TOP FOOD RANKING

	Restaurant	Cuisine
28	Chez Bruce	British
	Gordon Ramsay/68 Royal	French
	Hunan	Chinese
	Square, The	French
	Pétrus	French
	Pied à Terre	French
27	La Trompette	European/French
	Le Gavroche	French
	River Café	Italian
	Nobu London	Japanese/Peruvian
	Capital Restaurant	French
	Morgan M*	French
	Enoteca Turi	Italian
	Defune	Japanese
	Rasoi Vineet Bhatia*	Indian
26	L'Atelier Robuchon/La Cuisine	French
	Roussillon	French
	Zuma	Japanese
	Theo Randall	Italian

Capital Restaurant, The *French*   27 | 22 | 26 | VE

Knightsbridge | Capital Hotel | 22-24 Basil St., SW3 (Knightsbridge) | (44-20) 7591 1202 | www.capitalhotel.co.uk

"A piece of heaven in the middle of Knightsbridge" is how "discerning diners" view this "serene", "understated" hotel New French that "gives one the impression of eating in a rich relative's dining room"; provided by near-"perfect", "pukka service", chef Eric Chavot's cuisine is "a real treat" "not to be missed" – even if it does require "a second mortgage" on the *maison*; all told, a capital experience, if "not for the young and hip."

Z Chez Bruce *British*   28 | 21 | 25 | VE

Wandsworth | 2 Bellevue Rd., SW17 (Wandsworth Common B.R.) | (44-20) 8672 0114 | www.chezbruce.co.uk

"No restaurant can match the quality for the quid" of this "Wandsworth wonder", which has topped Gordon Ramsay at 68 Royal Hospital Rd. as London's No. 1 for Food with its "reliably fantastic", "flawlessly exe-cuted" Modern British cuisine; "everything [else] about it is class" too – the "knowledgeable" but "never intrusive" staff, "the extensive wine list and possibly the largest selection of cheese in town"; the "cozy" room can be "cramped", but really, "the only problem is getting a reservation."

Defune *Japanese*   27 | 16 | 20 | VE

Marylebone | 34 George St., W1 (Baker St./Bond St.) | (44-20) 7935 8311

There are those who "refuse to have sushi anywhere else" than this "serene", "friendly" Marylebone Japanese, maintaining its "marvel-

---

* Indicates a tie with restaurant above

				FOOD	DECOR	SERVICE	COST

lous, freshest" victuals are "perfect in size and consistency"; "you'll be shocked how much you're spending", especially since the "decor's nothing fancy", but "if you have an expense account, give it a try."

Enoteca Turi 🗷 *Italian* | 27 | 19 | 23 | E |

Putney | 28 Putney High St., SW15 (Putney Bridge) | (44-20) 8785 4449 | www.enotecaturi.com

"We have to keep reminding ourselves this is just across the Thames, not in the hills in Tuscany" say fans of this rustic ristorante that's "just about the best Italian in London" (and "the best in Putney by far"); the fare "never fails to impress" and there's "a phenomenal wine list too"; "tables are too close", but "personal attention from the owner and his wife ensures" a "pleasant evening."

Z **Gordon Ramsay at Claridge's** *European* | 25 | 24 | 24 | VE |

Mayfair | Claridge's Hotel | 45 Brook St., W1 (Bond St.) | (44-20) 7499 0099 | www.gordonramsay.com

"His kitchen might be hell, but the food is heavenly" at TV star/chef Gordon Ramsay's "art deco fantasy" ("red drapes, swirly light fixtures") in Claridge's, where the team led by exec toque Mark Sargeant is "inspired to deliver" "ever-so-imaginative" Modern European "refined classics" with "old-world charm"; sure, it's a "budget-buster" and, some believe, "a bit of a let-down lately", but most hail it as a "heady wonderland experience"; P.S. "lunch provides 80 percent of the experience at 20 percent of the cost."

Z **Gordon Ramsay at 68 Royal Hospital Rd.** 🗷 *French* | 28 | 24 | 28 | VE |

Chelsea | 68 Royal Hospital Rd., SW3 (Sloane Sq.) | (44-20) 7352 4441 | www.gordonramsay.com

"Dine at the altar of the master", Gordon Ramsay – a "superlative experience" for "serious foodies" in "crisp, chic" Chelsea quarters; the "rich and complex", "hellishly good" New French cuisine is ferried by a "suave staff" that delivers "royal treatment" that remains London's No. 1 for Service (manager Jean-Claude Breton "deserves to be as famous as Gordon"); it's "eye-wateringly expensive" – perhaps one reason it was edged out as No. 1 for Food this year – but all in all, Ramsay's "flagship is sailing high."

Z **Hunan** 🗷 *Chinese* | 28 | 14 | 22 | E |

Pimlico | 51 Pimlico Rd., SW1 (Sloane Sq.) | (44-20) 7730 5712 | www.hunanlondon.com

The trick is to let chef-owner Mr. Peng "know what you like and it will keep coming" at this "fine choice for the Chinese connoisseur" in Pimlico; admirers call it "incomparable" for its Hunanese dishes "dependant on the day's market" and delivered in "tasty little bites"; just be prepared to "ignore the cold surroundings" and "remember to say when you are full – otherwise they will keep feeding you!"

Z **J. Sheekey** ◗ *Seafood* | 25 | 21 | 23 | VE |

Covent Garden | 28-32 St. Martin's Ct., WC2 (Leicester Sq.) | (44-20) 7240 2565 | www.j-sheekey.co.uk

The "peerless seafood has barely stopped breathing" at this "discreet" Theatreland "bastion" where "the warmly lit, woody interior complements the conviviality"; throw in "unerring service" and a "chance to celeb-spot" among all "the thespians after a show", and this "slick outfit" "is "rightly revered", "like her sister, The Ivy."

L'Atelier de Joël Robuchon ◗ *French*   26 | 24 | 24 | VE

Covent Garden | 13-15 West St., WC2 (Leicester Sq.)

La Cuisine *French*

Covent Garden | L'Atelier de Joël Robuchon | 13-15 West St., WC2 (Leicester Sq.)

(44-20) 7010 8600 | www.joel-robuchon.com

Super-chef Joël Robuchon has "hit town with his fantastic creativity" at this "thrilling" Theatreland yearling; there's a "chic" red/black eatery with a "wall of green plants" and counter seating, and up above, a "black and white kitchen"-themed restaurant, La Cuisine, both offering different iterations of "divine *nouvelle cuisine française*"; given the "minuscule mains", it's all too "pricey" and "pretentious", pessimists protest, but "if you really want to impress, this is where to come"; P.S. there's also a "boudoirlike bar" on the top floor.

La Trompette *European/French*   27 | 21 | 25 | VE

Chiswick | 5-7 Devonshire Rd., W4 (Turnham Green) | (44-20) 8747 1836 | www.latrompette.co.uk

Surveyors "sound the trumpets" for this "hidden" "blessing for Chiswick locals" (sister of Chez Bruce), an "elegant" venue with "expertly prepared" Modern European–New French cooking, a "wine list to dive into" and "attentive, but not cloying service"; while the "fixed-price menus make for excellent cost control", it's "great to impress for business or that second date (may be a bit flashy for a first)."

☑ Le Gavroche ⊠ *French*   27 | 24 | 26 | VE

Mayfair | 43 Upper Brook St., W1 (Marble Arch) | (44-20) 7408 0881 | www.le-gavroche.co.uk

"As expensive as it gets, but as fabulous as it can be" sums up Michel Roux Jr.'s "magnificent" Mayfair "bastion" of haute cuisine in a "sumptuous" "snug basement setting with a real sense of exclusivity"; the "*superbe*" kitchen doesn't "miss a beat", and "every detail is attended to" by an "exemplary" staff; modernists may mutter "this 1950s rendition of fancy French" "needs updating", but the overwhelming opinion is "the old style still works."

Morgan M ⊠ *French*   27 | 17 | 22 | VE

Islington | 489 Liverpool Rd., N7 (Highbury & Islington) | (44-20) 7609 3560 | www.morganm.com

"A real mecca for food lovers", "dedicated chef"-owner Morgan Meunier's "hidden gem" offers Islingtonians "the rare pleasure of an eponymous restaurant with the namesake firmly in control"; the experience involves "delectable" New French fare (including an "outstanding vegetarian" tasting menu), "quirky amuse-bouches and entremets", plus a "staff that's trained to please"; P.S. the "refurbishment provides a better", more formal setting.

☑ Nobu London *Japanese/Peruvian*   27 | 20 | 21 | VE

Mayfair | Metropolitan Hotel | 19 Old Park Ln., W1 (Hyde Park Corner) | (44-20) 7447 4747 | www.noburestaurants.com

Even after 10 years, Nobu Matsuhisa's "sizzling" Old Park Lane "flagship is firing on all cylinders", with an "exotically marvelous"

Japanese-Peruvian menu ("sushi-lovers' heaven") that "exceeds expectations"; ok, the "stark" decor "could do with a splash of paint", the "efficient service sometimes looks harassed" and "booking a table takes creativity"; but few deny this "celestial" spot – rammed with "A- through C-list celebs" – is "definitely a treat, especially if someone else drops the credit card."

☑ Pétrus ⑤ French
28 | 25 | 26 | VE

Belgravia | Berkeley Hotel | Wilton Pl., SW1 (Hyde Park Corner) | (44-20) 7235 1200 | www.gordonramsay.com

"Luxuriate in Marcus Wareing's sublime creations" – the epitome of New French "cooking at its most cutting edge", backed by "wines that live up to the name" – at this "beautiful" Belgravia venue where an "utterly professional" staff "provides tip-top service"; perhaps it's *un peu* "pretentious", with "eye-popping prices", but it's also "everything a modern fine-dining institution should be" – "so pick a special occasion, forget the cost and book it."

Pied à Terre ⑤ French
28 | 22 | 25 | VE

Fitzrovia | 34 Charlotte St., W1 (Goodge St.) | (44-20) 7636 1178 | www.pied-a-terre.co.uk

"Hats off to chef Shane Osborne for the culinary masterpieces" he creates at this "small" but "stunning" New French in Fitzrovia; from the "star wine list" to the "extremely knowledgeable servers", it has "everything you could possibly want in a restaurant" (except perhaps the decor – "chic, but nothing eye-grabbing"), and so it's "worth the prices" – "you'll pay for the *pied,* but you'll leave *la terre* for *le ciel!*"

Rasoi Vineet Bhatia ⑤ Indian
27 | 19 | 23 | VE

Chelsea | 10 Lincoln St., SW3 (Sloane Sq.) | (44-20) 7225 1881 | www.vineetbhatia.com

With an "exquisite Indian" menu of "dishes that tempt and surprise", chef-owner Vineet Bhatia's "charming" Chelsea townhouse (recently given a light refurb) is "always a pleasure", smoothed along by "superb service"; if a few flinch at the "high-end prices", even they are "entertained" by this "epicurean delight."

River Café Italian
27 | 22 | 24 | VE

Hammersmith | Thames Wharf | Rainville Rd., W6 (Hammersmith) | (44-20) 7386 4200 | www.rivercafe.co.uk

Boasting "joyful" "unfussy dishes that showcase exquisite ingredients to beautiful effect", this Italian "evergreen" "never fails to delight", even after 20-plus years; "decor and ambiance display a similar lack of pretension, and the informally clad staff clearly enjoys working here"; yes, the Hammersmith "location is a problem", but it's "so worth the trip" – especially if you "sit on the terrace (the view's as good as the food)."

Roussillon ⑤ French
26 | 23 | 25 | VE

Pimlico | 16 St. Barnabas St., SW1 (Sloane Sq./Victoria) | (44-20) 7730 5550 | www.roussillon.co.uk

"Deserves to be better known than it is" say fans of this "quiet" Pimlico place with a pleasantly "informal" feel ("like walking into someone's lounge"), though there's nothing casual about chef/co-owner Alexis Gauthier's "high-end, creative" New French cooking that "emphasizes vegetables"; with perks like "pampering" service and a "fabulous wine list with one of the smartest sommeliers", it's "worth going on a special occasion – or just to treat yourself."

NEW Skylon *European*

-	-	-	E

South Bank | Royal Festival Hall | Belvedere Rd., SE1 (Waterloo) | (44-20) 7654 7800 | www.skylonrestaurant.co.uk

Named after an iconic attraction from the 1951 Festival of Britain, this confident newcomer in the newly revamped Royal Festival Hall offers a dramatic panoramic view across the Thames; a casual, hardwood-floored grill and smarter, retro-looking restaurant – both serving different incarnations of a Modern European menu from chef Helena Puolakka (ex Fifth Floor) – act as stylish bookends to an airy cocktail bar in the center of the cavernous space.

☑ Square, The *French*

28	24	26	VE

Mayfair | 6-10 Bruton St., W1 (Bond St./Green Park) | (44-20) 7495 7100 | www.squarerestaurant.com

"Fantastic food", "faultless service", "my favorite" fawn fans of this "grown-up", "elegant eatery off Bond Street" that maintains its edge with an "inventive take on Classic French" food, a "gigantic wine list" and "understated" decor that has gotten "warmer after a makeover"; "though the set lunch is reasonable, it's very expensive for dinner" – better "bring your Black Amex" – but that doesn't stop it from being "simply the best all-rounder in London."

Theo Randall at The InterContinental *Italian*

26	21	24	VE

Mayfair | InterContinental Park Ln. | 1 Hamilton Pl., W1 (Hyde Park Corner) | (44-20) 7318 8747 | www.theorandall.com

Although it's still "unknown to many", this newly renovated hotel restaurant is "a change for the positive at Hyde Park Corner"; the "wonderful", "innovative Italian food" is "in the tradition of the River Café" (the ex-home of the eponymous chef) and is served by a "genial" staff; only the room – "slick" but "somewhat sterile" – sets some back.

NEW Wild Honey *British*

-	-	-	E

Mayfair | 12 St. George St., W1 (Oxford Circus) | (44-20) 7758 9160 | www.wildhoneyrestaurant.co.uk

After the success of Soho yearling Arbutus, owners Anthony Demetre and Will Smith have opened this offshoot in clublike, wood-paneled Mayfair premises that used to house the Drones Club; it serves a similar formula of innovative Modern British cooking at commendable prices for the quality and neighborhood, and also offers the same clever oenological policy of making the 80-strong wine list available in mini-carafe size (about two large glasses) to encourage experimentation.

Zuma *Japanese*

26	24	21	VE

Knightsbridge | 5 Raphael St., SW7 (Knightsbridge) | (44-20) 7584 1010 | www.zumarestaurant.com

If you can breach the "obnoxious reservation system", you too can join the "ultrathin women, middle-aged bankers" and "expense-account types" at this "buzzy to the extreme" Knightsbridge "nouveau Japanese"; ranging from rave-worthy robata to "superb" sushi, the "food's mind-blowing" – and "it's easy to blow a fortune" on it as well; but despite that, and a "staff that's not quite up to" handling the "hot, heaving" scene, this hipster still seems "sensational."

Madrid

TOP FOOD RANKING

	Restaurant	Cuisine
28	Santceloni	Mediterranean
27	Zalacaín	International
	Goizeko Kabi/Wellington	Basque
26	Príncipe de Viana	Basque/Navarraise
	Combarro	Galician/Seafood
	Viridiana	International
	La Terraza del Casino	Spanish
	El Chaflán	Mediterranean
25	Horcher	International
	Jockey	International
	El Amparo	Basque
	Goya	International/Spanish
	Kabuki	Japanese/Mediterranean
24	Asia Gallery	Chinese
	Arce	Basque
	El Pescador	Seafood
	La Broche	Mediterranean
	La Trainera	Seafood
23	El Bodegón	Basque
	El Olivo	Mediterranean
	Shiratori	Japanese

Arce ◐⊠ Basque
24 | 16 | 21 | E

Centro | Augusto Figueroa 32 | (34-91) 522-0440 |
www.restaurantearce.com
Admirers advise on planning for an interactive evening at this
"fine" modern Basque in El Centro, where "attentive" chef-owner
Iñaki Camba may "come out of the kitchen and help you design
your meal", which can be complemented with wine from an impressive 900-bottle list; the cozy, "comfortable" setting reminds some of
"eating at home."

Asia Gallery ◐ Chinese
24 | 24 | 24 | E

Centro | Hotel Westin Palace | Plaza las Cortes 7 | (34-91) 360-0049 |
www.palacemadrid.com
"It's hard to find Asian food this good in Spain" say supporters of this
Chinese in the Hotel Westin Palace; an "amazing", "luxurious" setting
with silks and antiques and "great service" add to the experience,
making it "ideal for a romantic evening."

⊠ Balzac ◐⊠ Mediterranean
22 | 19 | 21 | E

Retiro | Moreto 7 | (34-91) 420-0177
"An epicurean delight" is how devotees like to describe the cuisine
at this "inventive" and "modern" Mediterranean in the Retiro, near
the Prado Museum; "pleasing" service and a series of softly lit,
minimally decorated rooms with modern art help to provide
the "enjoyable atmosphere."

⊠ Botín Restaurante ● *Castilian*   22 | 22 | 21 | E

Centro | Cuchilleros 17 | (34-91) 366-4217 | www.casabotin.com
"Although touristy, it's no trap" assert admirers of this 1725 Castilian "institution" and former Hemingway haunt off Plaza Mayor that bills itself as "the oldest restaurant in the world"; the food is "great" ("particularly roast suckling pig, baby lamb" and "mouthwatering Iberian ham"), the "warren of rickety rooms" is "atmospheric" and service is "gracious", making it "a must-see" and "must-do" in Madrid.

⊠ Combarro ● *Galician/Seafood*   26 | 18 | 21 | E

Tetuán | Reina Mercedes 12 | (34-91) 554-7784 | www.combarro.com
Many surveyors say this Tetuán establishment is the "best place in town" for simply prepared seafood with a Galician accent; it imports its fin fare from its own fish farm in that region, along with local wines like the crisp Albariños; the "bill can add up", but "you'll leave satisfied."

El Amparo ⊠ *Basque*   25 | 22 | 22 | VE

Salamanca | Calle Puigcerdá 8 | (34-91) 431-6456 |
www.arturocantoblanco.com
"It really doesn't get much better than this" "outstanding" Basque in the "ritzy" Salamanca district, where "perfectly prepared" modern cuisine and an "excellent wine list" are proffered by a solidly rated staff in a "relaxing", "romantic" triplex setting.

El Bodegón ⊠ *Basque*   23 | 21 | 21 | E

Salamanca | Pinar 15 | (34-91) 562-8844 | www.grupovips.com
Housed in a stone cottage in Salamanca is this Basque bastion serving "quality" "classic" cooking; "top-notch service" and a comfortable and "tasteful dining room" with wood beams and "beautiful art" make it "excellent for entertaining clients."

El Chaflán *Mediterranean*   26 | 22 | 24 | VE

Chamartín | Hotel Aristos | Avenida de Pío XII 34 | (34-91) 350-6193 |
www.elchaflan.com
One of the most talked about restaurants in town is cutting-edge chef Juan Pablo Felipe's "inventive" modern Mediterranean, which makes the most of white Alba truffles in autumn; housed in the Hotel Aristos, the "minimalist" pale-green-and-white space is enlivened by a sky-light and gleaming open kitchen.

El Olivo ●⊠ *Mediterranean*   23 | 18 | 22 | E

Chamartín | General Gallegos 1 | (34-91) 359-1535 |
www.elolivorestaurante.es
As its name implies, this "first-class" Mediterranean in Chamartín is devoted to olives as well as their oils (there's a trolley of them for sampling and for sale), and the ingredient turns up in "subtle and delicate" dishes, even including a signature ice cream; a "kind" staff, "comfortable" setting and swell selection of 120 sherries are added attractions.

El Pescador ●⊠ *Seafood*   24 | 15 | 20 | E

Salamanca | José Ortega y Gasset 75 | (34-91) 402-1290
"Fabulous fresh seafood" like "big-as-a-whale sole" is the lure at this long-standing "no-attitude" spot in Salamanca; the "casual nautical decor" could use "refurbishing", but that doesn't keep the likes of the Royal Family from frequenting the place.

	FOOD	DECOR	SERVICE	COST

Z Goizeko Kabi ●🅵 *Basque*   27 | 19 | 20 | VE
Tetuán | Comandante Zorita 37 | (34-91) 533-0214
Z Goizeko Wellington ●🅵 *Basque*
Salamanca | Wellington Hotel | Villanueva 34 | (34-91) 577-0138
www.goizekogaztelupe.com

"A bastion of the fur-wearing Tetuán ladies and their banking husbands" is this very expensive Basque that boosters boast is "one of the best choices in town", with "fine food" and a "great wine list"; P.S. those who find the ambiance here "stuffy" prefer the newer, more modern and relaxed branch in the Wellington Hotel.

Goya *International/Spanish*   25 | 26 | 26 | VE
Retiro | Hotel Ritz | Plaza de la Lealtad 5 | (34-91) 701-6767 |
www.ritzmadrid.com

This "grand" Spanish-International on the ground floor of the Ritz comes with "pampering" service that's a "tribute to the art of fine dining"; the interior, with its chandeliers and palms, evokes "old-world elegance to the nth degree", and in summer, eating in the "garden is magical"; like one of its namesake's paintings, its cost is "excessive", but the "well-heeled" clientele doesn't dwell on such mundane matters.

Horcher 🅵 *International*   25 | 24 | 26 | VE
Retiro | Alfonso XII 6 | (34-91) 522-0731 | www.restaurantehorcher.com
Family-owned International dowager with a German accent near Retiro Park that's been turning out "classic" cuisine like stroganoff and game dishes since 1943; an "excellent" solicitous staff ("in his heyday Franco would not have been treated better") works an "old-world" room with floral fabrics and porcelain figurines; of course, you pay for a "formal evening out" like this "big time"; N.B. jacket and tie required.

Jockey ●🅵 *International*   25 | 23 | 25 | VE
Chamberí | Amador de los Ríos 6 | (34-91) 319-2435 |
www.restaurantejockey.net

This "old-school", über-expensive International in Chamberí has been putting itself through its paces since 1945 and still draws a formally dressed crowd of the "who's who of the Madrid business and aristocratic worlds"; they come for "classic" cuisine, a "great wine list", "attentive service" and a "clubby" setting with paintings and prints; N.B. jacket and tie required.

Kabuki ●🅵 *Japanese/Mediterranean*   25 | 16 | 19 | E
Chamartín | Presidente Carmona 2 | (34-91) 417-6415
For the "best toro in town" and other "top-quality sushi", loyalists head to this chef-owned Japanese-Mediterranean in Chamartín, where a "charming" and "friendly" staff presides over a small, minimalist black-and-yellow setting that spills over onto an appealing terrace in summer.

La Broche 🅵 *Mediterranean*   24 | 24 | 23 | VE
Chamberí | Miguel Ángel Hotel | Miguel Ángel 29-31 | (34-91) 399-3437 |
www.labroche.com

Top toque and Ferran Adrià disciple Sergi Arola's modern Med in the Miguel Ángel Hotel is "controversial": aficionados admire his "unbelievable imagination" and "exquisite and daring" deconstructed dishes, while detractors declare them "weird" and the puzzled plead "who wants to eat rooster combs?"; note that the "stark white setting" "couldn't be more minimalist", and the tab is about the "price of a Picasso"; N.B. closed Saturday and Sunday.

La Terraza del Casino 🗷 Spanish
26 | 24 | 25 | VE

Puerta del Sol | Casino de Madrid | Alcalá 15 | (34-91) 532-1275 | www.casinodemadrid.es

"You'll feel like a king" (or at least "Cary Grant") dining in a "breath-taking" rooftop room in one of the city's oldest "exclusive" clubs just off the Puerta del Sol; El Bulli's touted Ferran Adrià is the consulting chef, and his "high-quality", "high-tech" deconstructed Spanish dishes with foams are complemented by "great wines" and served by an "incredibly attentive" staff in a see-and-be-seen-in space; it's "quite expensive", but the experience is "incomparable."

🗷 La Trainera 🗷 Seafood
24 | 15 | 19 | E

Salamanca | Lagasca 60 | (34-91) 576-0575 | www.latrainera.es
For "simple, satisfying and consistently excellent" "classical" dishes like clams and the signature turbot, fanatics flock to this sprawling seafooder in Salamanca; just be warned that its "unassuming" decor – "wood paneling" and a "nautical theme" with ships' lanterns and wheels – "belies how expensive it is."

🗷 Príncipe de Viana ●🗷 Basque/Navarraise
26 | 18 | 25 | VE

Chamartín | Manuel de Falla 5 | (34-91) 457-1549
"They don't take risks" at this "classic" Basque-Navarraise in Chamartín, but "top ingredients" and "extremely fresh, tasty and delicate food" make it "one of Madrid's perennial greats"; an older crowd appreciates the comfortable split-level space and serious service and can cope with the "pricey" tabs.

🗷 Santceloni 🗷 Mediterranean
28 | 25 | 28 | VE

Chamberí | Hotel Hesperia | Paseo de la Castellana 57 | (34-91) 210-8840 | www.restaurantesantceloni.com

Voted No. 1 for Food in Madrid is star chef Santi Santamaría's (of the acclaimed Can Fabes outside Barcelona) "fantastic", "cutting-edge" Med that's "never over the top", set in the Hotel Hesperia; the staff is the "best", plus there's a "great wine list, good sommelier advice" and a "chic" white skylit setting that provides well-spaced tables and "lots of privacy"; not surprisingly, such an "extraordinary experience" is "very, very expensive."

Shiratori 🗷 Japanese
23 | 21 | 23 | E

Salamanca | Avenida de la Castellana 36-38 | (34-91) 577-3733
After the long-standing Suntory shuttered its doors in 2004, its former manager and chef upgraded its interior and opened this "centrally located" renamed Japanese in Salamanca; for "those who cannot do without sushi in Spain", or without sashimi or teppanyaki for that matter, it's an "upscale", "well-managed" option.

🗷 Viridiana ●🗷 International
26 | 18 | 21 | VE

Retiro | Juan de Mena 14 | (34-91) 523-4478 | www.restauranteviridiana.com
Fans of chef-owner Abraham García and his "innovative-in-all-senses" International near Retiro Park say he's been doing "superb" "fusion cuisine in his own inimitable style for nigh on 20 years", making it al-

most "impossible not to be surprised here"; an "attentive professional" staff presides over a black-and-white setting dominated by
stills from the Buñuel film for which it is named; considered "one of
Madrid's best", it's "worth taking out a mortgage for."

Z Zalacaín ⊠ *International* | 27 | 24 | 27 | VE |

Salamanca | Álvarez de Baena 4 | (34-91) 561-4840 |
www.restaurantezalacain.com

"It's seldom that a restaurant can keep its standards up for more than
30 years", but this "winner" in Salamanca has done it; "innovative"
International cuisine using the best seasonal ingredients is served by
an "excellent professional" staff in a "handsome" setting with salmon-
colored walls and dark wood; you'll need "mucho dollars, but you'll see
it as a good investment", as it's a gastronomic landmark that "lives up to
its large reputation"; P.S. "jackets and ties are mandatory for gents."

Milan

TOP FOOD RANKING

	Restaurant	Cuisine
29	Il Luogo di Aimo e Nadia	Italian
28	Sadler	Italian
27	Ristorante Cracco	Italian
25	Da Giacomo	Seafood/Tuscan
	Boeucc	International/Italian
	Il Teatro	Italian/Mediterranean
24	Joia	Vegetarian
	Armani/Nobu	Japanese/Peruvian
	Bebel's	Italian/Mediterranean
23	Giannino	Italian
	La Veranda	International/Italian
	Park, The	Italian/Mediterranean
	Dal Bolognese	Emilian
22	Innocenti Evasioni	Italian
	Trussardi alla Scala	International/Italian
	Don Lisander	Lombardian/Milanese
	Trattoria Bagutta	Lombardian/Tuscan
	Bice	Tuscan
	Al Giararrosto	Tuscan
21	Shambala	Thai/Vietnamese
	Alla Cucina delle Langhe	Piedmontese
20	Gold	Mediterranean/Tuscan
	La Briciola	Milanese

Al Girarrosto *Tuscan* | 22 | 17 | 22 | E |

San Babila | Corso Venezia 31 | (39-02) 7600-0481

This "always reliable" Tuscan trattoria with "an efficient" and "knowledgeable staff" is near Milan's commercial center, Piazza San Babila, and is particularly popular for business lunches; the warm interior with watercolors hasn't changed since the Michi family opened the restaurant in 1943, and their four daughters intend to keep it that way; P.S. closed Saturdays, "but it's one of the few good restaurants here open for Sunday dinner."

Alla Cucina delle Langhe 🗷 *Piedmontese* | 21 | 15 | 19 | E |

Garibaldi | Corso Como 6 | (39-02) 655-4279

A "very fashionable" crowd frequents this sprawling stalwart on trendy Corso Como, where "excellent", "honest" food from the Langhe district in the Piedmont is complemented by a "good selection" of the area's red wines and a "warm welcome" from the owners.

🗷 Armani/Nobu *Japanese/Peruvian* | 24 | 22 | 21 | VE |

Montenapoleone | Via Pisoni 1 | (39-02) 6231-2645 | www.armaninobu.it

"What could possibly be more chic" than this "internationally acclaimed" Japanese-Peruvian housed in a stylish Armani shop in the heart of the fashion district in Montenapoleone?; "excellent", "inventive" and "artistic" cuisine, "hip" Eastern decor with screens and natural wood and a "stylish crowd" lead customers to conclude "beautiful food, people and ambiance", but "terrible prices."

Bebel's *Italian/Mediterranean*   24 | 19 | 20 | E

Brera | Via San Marco 38 | (39-02) 657-1658

This long-standing, popular Italian-Med on the edge of the Brera district serves "fantastic authentic" grilled meat, fish and pizzas to locals like Miuccia Prada; the long, narrow room has art nouveau accents and stained-glass windows, plus there are "wonderful market displays" of the day's "fresh vegetables, seafood and cheeses."

☒ Bice ☒ *Tuscan*   22 | 19 | 21 | VE

Montenapoleone | Via Borgospesso 12 | (39-02) 7600-2572 | www.bicemilano.it

"Good things never change" at this 1926 Montenapoleone Tuscan, the original "flagship" of a third-generation, family-run franchise; "loyal patrons" like its "reliable", "classic" cuisine and "chic" clientele and setting, but cynics shrug at the "rich, tourist-trap" prices and conclude "better for ogling – I kept tripping over all the tall models' feet – than eating."

☒ Boeucc *International/Italian*   25 | 22 | 24 | VE

Duomo | Piazza Belgioioso 2 | (39-02) 7602-0224 | www.boeucc.com

This "distinguished" 1696 Italian-International, near the Duomo, with "312 years of experience" excels with "excellent" "classic" dishes, a "wine list that's a bible of Italian vintages", "impeccable service" and an "exquisite setting" with antique columns and vaulted ceilings; a few sniff it's "stuffy", but "power brokers and beautiful people" pronounce it "the only choice for business dinners and special occasions"; N.B. closed Saturdays.

☒ Da Giacomo *Seafood/Tuscan*   25 | 20 | 23 | E

Porta Vittoria | Via Pasquale Sotto Corno 6 | (39-02) 7602-3313 | www.dagiacomoristorante.it

The "seafood-laced spaghetti is a triumph" at this long-standing Tuscan fish house near Porta Vittoria, but you can also order *bistecca alla fiorentina* complemented by a "serious" wine list that's strong on that region's reds; an "in" crowd of fashionistas and arty types frequents the gracious space with arches and mosaic-tiled floors.

Dal Bolognese ☒ *Emilian*   23 | 19 | 20 | E

Repubblica | Piazza della Repubblica 13 | (39-02) 6269-4843

This hot Emilian next door to the stylish Hotel Principe di Savoia is a "posh" "place to see and be seen", just like its legendary flagship in Rome; foodies may fume about "unexciting" cuisine, but that doesn't stop fashionistas from praising the "delightful" dishes, then hitting its smoky bar, surveying the scene and declaring it a "must when in Milan."

Don Lisander ☒ *Lombardian/Milanese*   22 | 18 | 20 | E

Piazza della Scala | Via Alessandro Manzoni 12A | (39-02) 7602-0130 | www.ristorantedonlisander.it

Near the newly restored Teatro alla Scala Opera House is this "historical" Lombardian with "good, reliable" "classic" Milanese dishes; whether eating in the "cozy interior in winter", the former chapel of an aristocratic family, or in the "marvelous garden in summer", it's "delightful."

	FOOD	DECOR	SERVICE	COST

Giannino ● *Italian*　　　　23　20　21　E

Repubblica | Via Vittor Pisani 6 | (39-02) 6698-6998 | www.giannino.it
A Milan landmark since 1899, this Italian has changed hands (and even addresses), but its new Repubblica incarnation that opened last year is still offering "excellent" traditional fare and "first-class service"; its "cool New York–style interior" and expansive terrace are also a "hangout" for "beautiful women and soccer players."

Gold *Mediterranean/Tuscan*　　　20　25　21　VE

Porta Venezia | Via Carlo Poerio 2/A | (39-02) 757-7771 | www.dolcegabbanagold.it
If you're going for the Gold, you'll need to "bring plenty of it to pay for your meal" at this "trendy" new Porta Venezia Tuscan-Med with a first-floor restaurant, ground-floor bistro and small food shop; owned by fashion darlings Dolce & Gabbana, it emphasizes glitz not gourmet food, so look for "stylish-till-it-hurts" sparkling yellow accents "everywhere – on the walls, toilets, tables" and even in some of the dishes.

ⓩ Il Luogo di Aimo e Nadia ☒ *Italian*　29　20　28　VE

Bande Nere | Via Montecuccoli 6 | (39-02) 416-886 | www.aimoenadia.com
Voted No. 1 for Food in Milan is Aimo and Nadia Moroni's "superb from start to finish" "innovative" and expensive Italian with top-notch ingredients, "sparkling, fresh" flavors, the "best wine list" and "incredible service"; it's a "bit out of the way" in Bande Nere and some don't care for "the room decorated with modern art", but proponents proclaim don't let that keep you from "one of the most rewarding eating experiences of your life."

ⓩ Il Teatro ☒ *Italian/Mediterranean*　25　26　26　VE

Montenapoleone | Four Seasons Hotel | Via Gesù 8 | (39-02) 7708-1435 | www.fourseasons.com/milan
"Everything is exceptional" at this Italian-Med in the Four Seasons Hotel – from chef Sergio Mei's "superb creative cuisine" and "excellent wines" to the "reliably efficient" service and "warm, comfortable" and "serene setting"; of course, it's so "blindingly expensive", "it will cost you your shirt", but you're in Milan, so "just visit Zegna for another."

Innocenti Evasioni ☒ *Italian*　　22　20　20　E

Certosa | Via Privata della Bindellina | (39-02) 3300-1882 | www.innocentievasioni.com
At this intimate Italian in Certosa there's "excellent", "innovative cuisine", an "extensive wine list" and "friendly but discreet service"; the "warm and welcoming", rustically "romantic" room with well-spaced tables overlooks "a wonderful garden" with Asian accents and adds to the opinion that dining here is "a treat for all the senses."

Joia ☒ *Vegetarian*　　　　24　18　24　VE

Porta Venezia | Via Panfilo Castaldi 18 | (39-02) 2952-2124 | www.joia.it
Wags wager the "best place to go with a model on a diet" is probably chef-owner Pietro Leemann's "very pricey" vegetarian in Porta Venezia, where "beautifully presented" "creative" cuisine "with a lively twist" is served in a wood-and-stone setting that reflects his attraction to an Asian aesthetic.

FOOD | DECOR | SERVICE | COST

La Briciola ☒ *Milanese*

20 | 18 | 18 | E

Brera | Via Solferino 25 | (39-02) 655-1012 | www.labriciola.com
Owner Gianni Valveri knows everyone in town, so even after 30 years his spacious Milanese "favorite" in Brera is still "trendy" and "full of beautiful young Italians"; it's "good for carpaccio and beef and the women at the next table."

La Veranda ◐ *International/Italian*

23 | 26 | 25 | VE

Montenapoleone | Four Seasons Hotel | Via Gesù 8 | (39-02) 7708-1478 |
www.fourseasons.com/milan
The less-formal sister of the Four Seasons' Il Teatro is this Italian-International in Montenapoleone, the center of Milan's fashion scene; "good across-the-board" is the verdict on "excellent food" (with light choices for the style-conscious clientele), a "gracious" staff and an "airy setting" with frescoes and a "great view" of a cloistered courtyard.

Park, The ☒ *Italian/Mediterranean*

23 | 25 | 23 | VE

Duomo | Park Hyatt Milan | Via Tommaso Grossi 1 | (39-02) 8821-1234 |
www.milan.park.hyatt.com
On the ground floor of the luxurious Park Hyatt Milan, this Italian-Mediterranean makes a strong "modern" design statement with expanses of cool, cream travertine marble and black leather banquettes; "creative and delicious" dishes and "the nicest staff in town" add up to a "high-end" and "enjoyable" experience.

☒ Ristorante Cracco ☒ *Italian*

27 | 22 | 24 | VE

(fka Cracco-Peck)

Duomo | Via Victor Hugo 4 | (39-02) 876-774
Chef Carlo Cracco is no longer affiliated with the nearby prestigious gourmet shop Peck, but his experimental recipes and innovative techniques continue to make this "top-class" Italian a "temple of modern cuisine"; a "wonderful wine list" and "amazingly knowledgeable staff" are added pluses, and if a few fault the cellar setting, most maintain the elevated eating experience offsets it and the "expensive" prices.

☒ Sadler ☒ *Italian*

28 | - | 24 | VE

Navigli | Via Ascanio Sforza 77 | (39-02) 5810-4451 | www.sadler.it
"One of the best restaurants in town" is what supporters say about this "wonderful" Italian "institution" that after 21 years in a tiny Navigli space has moved to new digs in that same neighborhood; celebrity chef-owner Claudio Sadler's "excellent", "creative" cuisine with "well-balanced flavors" is complemented by an extensive wine list and a "friendly and efficient staff."

Shambala ◐ *Thai/Vietnamese*

21 | 26 | 19 | E

Ripamonti | Via Ripamonti 337 | (39-02) 552-0194 |
www.shambalamilano.it
It's decidedly out of the way in Ripamonti, about a 15-minute cab ride from the City Center, but if for some reason you must have Thai-Vietnamese instead of Milanese, this "excellent" fusion venue features dishes like *branzino* cooked in banana leaves; the interior is "impressive", with "lots of candles and cushions of every color", but "the garden is the best place you can go on a hot summer night."

	FOOD	DECOR	SERVICE	COST

☑ Trattoria Bagutta ☒ *Lombardian/Tuscan*   22 | 19 | 19 | E

San Babila | Via Bagutta 14 | (39-02) 7600-2767 | www.bagutta.it
Since 1924, this big, "vibrant" San Babila trattoria has been feeding cultural icons and business leaders from a Lombardian-Tuscan menu that has been "consistently good over the years", particularly the "wonderful pastas and antipasti"; the setting is "charming", with wood-beamed ceilings and walls lined with frescoes and photos, but the alfresco-oriented advise "sit in the garden if the weather permits."

Trussardi alla Scala ☒ *International/Italian*   22 | 23 | 21 | E

Piazza della Scala | Piazza della Scala 5 | (39-02) 8068-8201 |
www.trussardiallascala.com
Set in Piazza della Scala and with a great view of its legendary and now restored opera house is this Italian-International in the Trussadi building, which is owned by the fashion family; patrons are "singing the praises" of chef Andrea Berton's "terrific" cuisine, which is served in a "spectacular" contemporary red-and-white setting with columns and leather seating.

Moscow

TOP FOOD RANKING

	Restaurant	Cuisine
25	Mario	Italian
24	Palazzo Ducale	Italian
23	Café Pushkin	French/Russian
	Cantinetta Antinori	Tuscan
22	Vogue Café	International
21	Bistrot	Italian
	Cheese	Italian
	Uzbekistan	Uzbeki/Chinese
20	Galereya	International
	Shinok	Ukrainian
	Vanil	French/Japanese
19	White Sun of the Desert	Uzbeki/Chinese
	Scandinavia	Scandinavian
18	Café des Artistes	European/Med.
	CDL	Russian/Italian
	Maharaja	Indian

Bistrot ◐ *Italian* | 21 | 21 | 17 | VE |

Savvinskaya naberezhnaya | Bolshoi Savvinskiy pereulok 12/2 | (7-495) 248-4045 | www.restsindikat.com
The setting and menu of the award-winning Bistrot in Italy's Forte dei Marmi inspired this new collaboration in the up-and-coming neighborhood of Savvinskaya naberezhnaya between the owner of the aforementioned Tuscan and some Russian restaurateurs; the result is a "great looking" re-created two-storied villa with a courtyard and fountain, serene white-and-cream decor, working fireplaces and candlelight that's a backdrop for "very good food" from The Boot; but wallet-watchers note "as always, Moscow restaurants are overpriced."

Café des Artistes ◐ *European/Mediterranean* | 18 | 19 | 18 | E |

Tverskaya | Kamergersky pereulok 5/6 | (7-495) 692-4042 | www.artistico.ru
Its "great location" close to Tverskaya ulitsa and opposite the Moscow Art Theater makes this European-Med ideal for a pre- or post-play dinner; the "food is good not great", but it's a "reliable" place with a romantic, candlelit art nouveau setting displaying the works of local artists, and in summer its "relaxing" sidewalk cafe on a pedestrian-only street is a prime perch for "people-watching" and "taking in the local scene."

ⓩ Café Pushkin ◐ *French/Russian* | 23 | 27 | 23 | E |

Tverskaya | Tverskoy bulvar 26a | (7-495) 629-5590
This "delicious", "classic" Russian-French "must" is set in a "richly decorated mansion" in Tverskaya that's overseen by an "attentive", graceful staff that's been trained by a ballet-master; the "magical" multilevel space consists of a first floor decorated like a "beautiful" 19th-century chemist's shop that's open 24/7 so "you can indulge in

caviar and champagne at 6 AM", and a "more expensive" and formal "upstairs Imperial library" where jackets are required; either way, it's "high-priced and touristy", but most say don't miss the chance to hang with an "illustrious" clientele of "movers, shakers and mafia."

☑ Cantinetta Antinori ❶ *Tuscan*

| 23 | 23 | 20 | VE |

Arbat | Denezhny pereulok 20 | (7-495) 241-3771 | www.antinori.it

"The latest hangout for oligarchs" is this "fashionable" Tuscan in the Arbat, an affiliate of the Florence-based namesake original; Antinori family wines (100 by the bottle and 30 by the glass) are complemented by "superb" "authentic" cuisine and a rustically chic setting with a fireplace; for some "it's hard to justify the price", but sybarites simply cite the "buzz" and say "when you're sick of sour cream and borscht, this is the place."

CDL ❶ *Russian/Italian*

| 18 | 24 | 20 | VE |

Sadovoe Ring | Povarskaya ulitsa 50 | (7-495) 291-1515 | www.cdlrestaurant.ru

Set in an 1899 Sadovoe Ring building that formerly housed the Soviet Writers' Union, this Russian-Italian exudes "tremendous history", "lots of cachet" and "impressive decor" – richly burnished interiors with oak paneling, tapestries and chandeliers; "traditional food" and "exquisite service" make for an "impressive", very expensive "taste and feel of old Moscow" and "for a super evening if you have the time."

Cheese ❶ *Italian*

| 21 | 20 | 17 | VE |

Tsvetnoy Boulevard | Sadovaya-Samotechnaya ulitsa 16/2 | (7-495) 650-7770 | www.cheese-restaurant.ru

So you've always wanted to know what it's like to sit inside a huge, hollow chunk of cheese? well, here's your chance, because that's what the first-floor decor of this Italian near Tsvetnoy Boulevard looks like; an open kitchen turns out expensive, "high-quality" dishes like octopus carpaccio and "great pasta"; for a less-cheesy experience, head for the more conventionally decorated burgundy-colored dining room upstairs.

☑ Galereya ❶ *International*

| 20 | 21 | 18 | E |

Boulevard Ring | Petrovka ulitsa 27 | (7-495) 937-4544 | www.novikovgroup.ru

"If you like beautiful women who are taller than you are" and "would give Claudia and Giselle inferiority complexes", then head to the Boulevard Ring and one of the "trendiest" spots in town, owned by Russian restaurant czar Arkady Novikov; the "beautifully presented" International food is "fine" and the gallerylike space with changing artwork is dramatic, but the "crowd is better", and it's open 24/7; "it costs an arm and a leg", but scenesters sniff "who cares?"

Maharaja *Indian*

| 18 | 10 | 18 | M |

Kitai Gorod | Starosadsky pereulok 2/1 | (7-495) 621-9844 | www.maharaja.ru

Proponents pronounce this basement-level stalwart in the Kitai Gorod area, the old center of the city, the "best Indian in Moscow" for "authentic" and "tasty" cooking; the decor is nonexistent, but that doesn't stop the crowds – "mostly expats" and their families – from coming back for moderately priced meals.

	FOOD	DECOR	SERVICE	COST

Z **Mario** ● *Italian* | 25 | 15 | 19 | VE |

Presnya | Klimashkina ulitsa 17 | (7-495) 253-6505

Voted No. 1 for Food in the city and judged by many to be the "best Italian" in town, this split-level spot in Presnya offers "excellent" pasta and fish dishes; outside there's an expansive summer garden and Ferraris and Lamborghinis in the parking lot, inside there's glam owner Tatiana Kurbatskaya and a clubby, salon vibe that attracts rich young Russians who all seem to know each other; "prices are outrageous" and the "service is like the weather, but the kitchen is Gibraltar."

Z **Palazzo Ducale** ● *Italian* | 24 | 22 | 21 | VE |

Tverskaya | Tverskoy bulvar 3/1 | (7-495) 789-6404

"Great pasta for the price of caviar" can be had at this über-expensive, "authentic" Italian in Tverskaya run by the owner of Mario; while a few fume about it being a "poseur paradise", most maintain a "wine list strong on Tuscan reds", "top-notch service" and "rich decor" evocative of a Venetian palace with paintings, mirrors, chandeliers and a gilded, gondola-shaped bar make it "a good place for romantic dinners."

Z **Scandinavia** *Scandinavian* | 19 | 16 | 18 | E |

Tverskaya | Malye Palashevsky pereulok 7 | (7-495) 937-5630 | www.scandinavia.ru

A "popular expat place" in Tverskaya that's "consistently good" is this Scandinavian with a "varied menu" that ranges from herring to halibut; a "friendly" staff presides over a "sleek, chic" but cozy Swedish country house setting, and in summer its "famous garden" with a less-expensive menu is "one of the best outdoor hangouts in Moscow."

Z **Shinok** ● *Ukrainian* | 20 | 23 | 18 | E |

Presnya | 1905 Goda ulitsa 2 | (7-495) 255-0888 | www.shinok.ru

To say this 24-hour Ukrainian in Presnya has the most "unique decor of any restaurant in the world" may be an understatement, since it consists of a glassed-in "faux farmhouse in the center" filled with "live domestic animals" like cows, hens and horses tended to by a lady who sits and knits when not otherwise occupied with her charges; the rustic food is "filling" and "satisfying", but clearly it plays second fiddle to the setting.

Uzbekistan ● *Uzbeki/Chinese* | 21 | 25 | 20 | E |

Tsvetnoy Boulevard | Neglinnaya ulitsa 29/14 | (7-495) 623-0585 | www.uzbek-rest.ru

This Uzbeki-Chinese near Tsvetnoy Boulevard shares space and the same menu with sister restaurant The White Sun of the Desert; a "cavernous" palatial space filled with sofas, pillows and carpets makes guests "feel like a sultan" and encourages lingering over "tasty" dishes; a summer garden and belly dancing add to the indolent atmosphere.

Vanil *French/Japanese* | 20 | 19 | 18 | VE |

Kropotkinskaya | Ostozhenka ulitsa 1/9 | (7-495) 202-3341 | www.novikovgroup.ru

Admirers enamored of this "trendy" French-Japanese fusion in posh Kropotkinskaya assert "if you bring your better half here for a date, all your sins will be forgiven", thanks to pricey but "very good" food and a comfortable, candlelit modern setting with brick walls, banquettes and views of the reconstructed 19th-century Christ the Savior Cathedral.

	FOOD	DECOR	SERVICE	COST

☑ Vogue Café ● *International* — 22 | 19 | 19 | E

Bolshoy Theatre | Kuznetsky most ulitsa 7/9 | (7-495) 623-1701 | www.novikovgroup.ru

Not surprisingly, given its moniker and affiliation with the Russian magazine of the same name, the "fashionable" flock to this "trendy" International, another venue from Moscow restaurant magnate Arkady Novikov, located near the Bolshoi Theatre; a few sniff it's more for "meeting than eating", but proponents praise "very good food" that's fairly priced for "such quality" and the "stylish" setting.

White Sun of the Desert, The ● *Uzbeki/Chinese* 19 | 23 | 18 | E

Tsvetnoy Boulevard | Neglinnaya ulitsa 29/14 | (7-495) 209-6015 | www.bsp-rest.ru

Named after and inspired by a cult Soviet film, this Uzbeki-Chinese theme restaurant near Tsvetnoy Boulevard shares space and the same menu with its sibling, Uzbekistan; a kitschy setting – a tree trunk, life-size papier-mâché soldiers and wizened hookah smokers – is the bizarre backdrop for "fresh and authentic" dishes that feature some "startling options", like an "entire roast lamb on a spit" that you can pre-order.

Munich

TOP FOOD RANKING

	Restaurant	Cuisine
27	Tantris	International
25	Vue Maximilian	Bavarian/International
	Schuhbeck's	Bavarian
	Boettner's	International
24	Königshof	French/International
	Mark's	Med./International
	Dallmayr	Mediterranean/Seafood
23	Sushibar	Japanese
	Retter's	German
	Acquarello	Italian
22	Fleming's Koscher	Kosher
	Paulaner am Nockherberg	German
	Käfer-Schänke	Italian/International
	Hippocampus	Italian
	Austernkeller	French/Seafood
21	Mangostin Asia	Pan-Asian
20	Brenner	Mediterranean
	Garden*	Mediterranean
19	Weichandhof	Bavarian/International
	Geisel's Vinothek	Italian/Mediterranean
18	Lenbach	International
	Terrine	French

Acquarello *Italian*   23 | 15 | 21 | VE
Bogenhausen | Mühlbaurstr. 36 | (49-89) 470-4848 |
www.acquarello.com
Touted by some as "the best Italian in town", this small spot in residential Bogenhausen draws diners with "excellent" fare that "reflects
the creativity of the chef", served by "friendly" staffers who are
"knowledgeable" about the expansive wine list; despite its "good reputation", though, detractors cite "too-expensive" eats and "dismal decor" bordering on "kitsch" as evidence that it may be "overhyped";
P.S. the special menus available on Truffle Evenings during the fall are
especially "worth" sampling.

Austernkeller *French/Seafood*   22 | 19 | 21 | E
Innenstadt | Stollbergstr. 11 | (49-89) 298-787 |
www.austernkeller.de
This "favorite" in the Altstadt section of Innenstadt has been serving
up "quality" French cuisine for more than 25 years; the "romantic" interior manages to be a bit "opulent", despite its "cellar" setting, and
the service is reliably "friendly", but the "highlight" that keeps regulars
returning is the "fantastic seafood", such as "excellent lobster
Thermidor" and (as the name indicates) some of "the best" oysters in
town – including a platter of 24 featuring four varieties in season.

---

* Indicates a tie with restaurant above

	FOOD	DECOR	SERVICE	COST

☒ Boettner's ⊠ *International* — 25 | 22 | 26 | VE

Innenstadt | Pfisterstr. 9 | (49-89) 221-210

For a "terrific slice of old Munich", locals head to this elegant Innenstadt International (in a "great location" in the historic Altstadt section) that's been run by the same family for more than a century; its "innovative chef brings the world to" German palates with his "grand selection of specialties", and the "attentive, competent" staff also helps ensure that its "beautiful" interior is the "perfect place for a really good meal."

Brenner ● *Mediterranean* — 20 | 23 | 20 | E

Innenstadt | Maximilianstr. 15 | (49-89) 452-2880 | www.brennergrill.de

Set behind the opera house, in the Altstadt section of Innenstadt, this former royal stable has been restored and modernized, creating a bright, expansive space with "big" pillars and vaulted ceilings; the "unparalleled" interior is divided into "various dining areas", with chefs at a "large open grill" cooking up up Med specialties for a chic clientele that "enjoys" the "satisfying" fare.

☒ Chinesischen Turm Restaurant & Biergarten *German/International* — 15 | 16 | 12 | M

Schwabing | Englischer Garten 3 | (49-89) 3838-730 | www.chinaturm.de

"A trip to Munich would not be complete without an afternoon spent" in the "beautiful", "truly Bavarian" beer garden of this landmark in Schwabing, whose "special" "Chinese Tower" serves as the backdrop for what most maintain is only "standard", "self-serve" German fare; the restaurant's interior offers an International menu that's generally considered "much better" foodwise, but then you miss out on the "festive" "Oktoberfest experience."

☒ Dallmayr *Mediterranean/Seafood* — 24 | 20 | 21 | E

Innenstadt | Dienerstr. 14-15 | (49-89) 213-50 | www.dallmayr.de

An Innenstadt "institution", this "upmarket" venue in the Altstadt section features a "gourmet emporium" "downstairs" that's "akin to a food museum" thanks to a "tremendous selection of delicacies", some of "the finest coffee" in town and a champagne-and-oyster bar for "hedonists" seeking "paradise"; "upstairs", there's a "top-notch restaurant" serving "delicious" Mediterranean and seafood dishes, which are complemented by a "posh" setting and "smart" service – but "don't expect to get a table without a reservation, even for lunch."

Fleming's Koscher Restaurant *Kosher* — 22 | 19 | 22 | E

Innenstadt | St.-Jakobs-Platz 18 | (49-89) 202-400-333 | www.flemings-hotels.de

"The chopped liver can actually compete with your own *bubbe*'s" boast boosters of this new spot in Innenstadt that claims to be the only glatt kosher restaurant in Bavaria; Israeli and Eastern European specialties are also served "by a knowledgeable staff" in an expansive "modern" setting located within the Jewish community center.

Garden *Mediterranean* — 20 | 19 | 19 | E

Innenstadt | Bayerischer Hof | Promenadeplatz 2-6 | (49-89) 212-0993 | www.bayerischerhof.de

Both the "beautiful" terrace and the menu at this Innenstadt spot sport "Mediterranean flair" in the midst of "oh-so-traditionally German" surroundings; while some surveyors are split on the service ("expert" vs. "unfriendly") and find the "modest" interior "dowdy", the majority maintains the overall experience "leaves a lasting impression."

Geisel's Vinothek *Italian/Mediterranean*

19	21	19	E

Innenstadt | Hotel Excelsior | Schützenstr. 11 | (49-89) 5513-7140 | www.geisel-hotels.de

"Nice for oenophiles", this "lovely hotel restaurant" in Innenstadt is all about vintages, and "friendly, service-oriented" staffers are "dedicated" to providing "good recommendations" about the "excellent list's" "extraordinary variety" of labels (more than 400) from all over the world; a "nice", "down-to-earth" Italian-Med menu and "cozy", "country" dining room with vaulted, frescoed ceilings add to the "outstanding" ambiance.

Hippocampus *Italian*

22	21	21	E

Bogenhausen | Mühlbauerstr. 5 | (49-89) 475-855 | www.hippocampus-restaurant.de

"Anyone with a hippocampus" will remember that it's expensive joke jesters about this Italian in Bogenhausen, but "always fresh" and "absolutely delicious" cuisine keeps the crowds returning and the place "quite popular"; the "exquisite" setting consists of dark-walnut paneling, marble floors and bronze art nouveau lamps, as well as a torch-lit terrace in summer.

☑ Käfer-Schänke ⓩ *Italian/International*

22	20	19	E

Bogenhausen | Prinzregentenstr. 73 | (49-89) 416-8247 | www.feinkost-kaefer.de

"Excellent Italian food" and "out-of-the-ordinary" International dishes are served in an "old-world", country house–style dining area or in one of 12 "beautiful" private rooms at this "classic" in suburban Bogenhausen; the service is generally "friendly", even if it "sometimes takes too long" when things get "hectic", but "great people-watching" helps pass the time; P.S. "don't miss their gourmet store downstairs", "the ultimate German delicatessen."

☑ Königshof *French/International*

24	21	24	E

Innenstadt | Hotel Königshof | Karlsplatz 25 | (49-89) 551-360 | www.geisel-hotels.de

With "superior" New French–International creations courtesy of chef Martin Fauster and "accommodating" service from a "discreet" staff, this "fine-dining" venue in the Hotel Königshof offers an "elegant experience" befitting a "king's court"; the "exclusive ambiance" is enhanced by "plush" design details, a dramatic view of Innenstadt's Karlsplatz and live piano music on Friday and Saturday evenings; P.S. the prix fixe "gourmet dinner, including wines with each course, is spectacular."

Lenbach ⓩ *International*

18	20	18	E

Innenstadt | Ottostr. 6 | (49-89) 549-1300 | www.lenbach.de

"Hip comes to Munich" in the form of this 19th-century Innenstadt palace-turned-"modern" urban ode to the Seven Deadly Sins, thanks to the "über-trendy" design of Sir Terence Conran; a "fast", "friendly", "pretty" staff serves International dishes (including "great sushi") that are "varied" and "fanciful" – though some quip "you may need to view them with a magnifying glass"; the "catwalk atmosphere" and late-night hours also help keep it "in vogue."

	FOOD	DECOR	SERVICE	COST

Mangostin Asia *Pan-Asian*

| 21 | 19 | 16 | E |

Thalkirchen | Maria-Einsiedel-Str. 2 | (49-89) 723-2031 | www.mangostin.de

"Unusual atmosphere and unusually delicious" Pan-Asian fare make it "easy to think you're in a different country" at this Thalkirchen "jewel" near the zoo, where "authentic", "attractive" dishes are delivered within a trio of Japanese-, Thai- and Colonial-style dining rooms (or outside in the beer garden); some cynics say "it's past its prime" and find the service "lacking", but most maintain it's "a real joy", especially for its "great" dinner and Sunday brunch buffets.

Mark's *Mediterranean/International*

| 24 | 21 | 24 | VE |

Innenstadt | Mandarin Oriental | Neuturmstr. 1 | (49-89) 2909-8862 | www.mandarinoriental.com

Chef Mario Corti's "inspired" Med-International cuisine is "perfectly executed and flawlessly" delivered by a "well-trained, friendly" staff at this "awesome place" in the Mandarin Oriental hotel, in the Altstadt section of Innenstadt; a few find the "quiet, elegant" dining room a "little boring" and say the "surreal prices" make for "excessive" tabs, but the monthly changing, six-course menu (including wine) and the special late-night, three-course dinner offered during the Opera Festival in summer are especially "worth a try."

Paulaner am Nockherberg *German*

| 22 | 20 | 18 | M |

Giesing | Hochstr. 77 | (49-89) 459-9130 | www.nockherberg.com

The Paulaner brewery folks are behind the "authentic Bavarian feel" of this "typical beer garden" in Giesing, and they continue to have one of the largest Oktoberfest tents each year (it's "enormous", as are all those "liter brews everyone's drinking"); suds aside, though, the moderately priced, "good German" fare – such as "well-made" and well-priced Weißwurst and roast pork – is itself "worth stopping" for.

Retter's 🗺Ⓜ *German*

| 23 | 18 | 22 | E |

Innenstadt | Frauenstr. 8 | (49-89) 2323-7923 | www.retters.de

Oenophile Nicole Retter has opened this new German restaurant/wineshop in Innenstadt, and while the cuisine is "creative" and "inspired" (often by the ingredients in the adjacent Viktualienmarkt or food market), it's the potential "great pairings" with any of 250 "excellent" selections by the bottle and 25 by the glass that's generating the buzz; the setting is a handsome, wood-paneled townhouse with ample garden seating in summer.

🄩 Schuhbeck's Restaurant in den Südtiroler Stuben 🗺 *Bavarian*

| 25 | 20 | 25 | VE |

Innenstadt | Platzl 6 + 8 | (49-89) 216-9900 | www.schuhbeck.de

"Traditional Bavarian cuisine" is given a "contemporary cutting-edge" (read: "not so heavy") slant at this gourmet spot, owned by "famous" TV-chef Alfons Schuhbeck, just next door to the Hofbräuhaus in the Altstadt section of Innenstadt; "clever" food combinations, "exceedingly attentive" service and a "superb" wine selection may come at a price that's even "beyond expense-account" status, but it adds up to one of "the best restaurants in Munich" for a truly "adult dining" experience.

	FOOD	DECOR	SERVICE	COST

Sushibar *Japanese*   23 | 19 | 21 | E

Innenstadt | Maximilianstr. 34 | (49-89) 2554-0645 🗲🖻
Schwabing | Marschallstr. 2 | (49-89) 3889-9606
www.sushibar-muc.de

Like the name says, sushi is showcased here at this small specialist that some say serves the "freshest raw fish in town", including sashimi; the setting is light, modern and urbane, and the location is in one of the quieter quarters of tourist hot spot Schwabing; N.B. the new Maximilian Strasse offshoot opened post-Survey.

🗲 Tantris 🖻🅼 *International*   27 | 23 | 26 | VE

Schwabing | Johann-Fichte-Str. 7 | (49-89) 361-9590 | www.tantris.de
Austrian chef Hans Haas incorporates regional influences and culinary trends at his "outstanding" International out in Schwabing, earning it the ranking of No. 1 for Food in Munich; his "superb" daily changing prix fixe menus are paired with sommelier Paula Bosch's "inspired wines" and complemented by "remarkable service" ("you'll feel like a king!"), so though a few fault the "truly weird" "over-the-top" decor and "outrageous" prices, most insist "you get what you pay for" at this "classic."

Terrine 🖻🅼 *French*   18 | 15 | 24 | E

Maxvorstadt | Amalienpassage | Amalienstr. 89 | (49-89) 281-780 | www.terrine.de
"Attentive" service creates a "warm atmosphere" at this "little" stalwart near the university in Maxvorstadt, making it "great" for a relaxing evening of "excellent wine" and "tasty" French dishes, served either in the "unobtrusive" bistro interior or out on the terrace; though it shares the same ownership with the highly rated and more expensive Tantris, its "fairly priced" prix fixe menus offer real "value", leaving some amazed that you can "get something so good for so little"; a post-Survey chef and decor change may outdate the above scores.

🗲 Vue Maximilian *Bavarian/International*   25 | 23 | 25 | VE

Innenstadt | Hotel Vier Jahreszeiten Kempinski | Maximilianstr. 17 | (49-89) 2125-2125 | www.vue-maximilian.de
This venue in the historic Hotel Vier Jahreszeiten Kempinski takes its name from the wonderful view of Maximilian Strasse, the city's most beautiful and exclusive boulevard; the redone interior, a lighter, less "stuffy" room than what went before, is a "lovely" but "very expensive" backdrop for "top-notch" Bavarian-International cuisine, which relies on local and seasonal ingredients.

Weichandhof *Bavarian/International*   19 | 17 | 21 | M

Obermenzing | Betzenweg 81 | (49-89) 891-1600 | www.weichandhof.de
"Everyone should visit" this "good place to dine" along the river Würm in rural Obermenzing, where the "attentive" staff "never stops being friendly" and the "fine" Bavarian-International fare includes "good wild game dishes"; perhaps the "cozy", "rustic" refurbished farmhouse setting with a beer garden is "slightly outmoded" by city standards, but most feel that's more than compensated for by modest prices.

Paris

TOP FOOD RANKING

	Restaurant	Cuisine
28	Taillevent	Haute Cuisine
	Le Cinq	Haute Cuisine
	Guy Savoy	Haute Cuisine
	L'Astrance	New French
	Pierre Gagnaire	Haute Cuisine
	L'Ambroisie	Haute Cuisine
	Alain Ducasse	Haute Cuisine
	L'Atelier de Joël Robuchon	Haute Cuisine
	Le Grand Véfour	Haute Cuisine
	Les Ambassadeurs	Haute Cuisine/New French
27	Lasserre	Haute Cuisine
	Michel Rostang	Classic French
	La Braisière	Gascony
	Le Bristol	Haute Cuisine
	Dominique Bouchet	Haute Cuisine
	Le Meurice*	Haute Cuisine
	Le Pré Catelan	Haute Cuisine
	Relais d'Auteuil	Haute Cuisine
26	Apicius	Haute Cuisine
	Au Trou Gascon	Southwest
	Hiramatsu	Haute Cuisine
	Carré des Feuillants	Haute Cuisine

☑ Alain Ducasse
au Plaza Athénée ⌧ *Haute Cuisine*

28 | 27 | 27 | VE

8ᵉ | Plaza-Athénée | 25, av Montaigne (Alma Marceau/Franklin D. Roosevelt) | (33-1) 53 67 65 00 | www.alain-ducasse.com

The legendary Alain Ducasse serves up "a meal of a lifetime" at his Paris flagship, an "*ancien régime* meets high-tech" setting in the Plaza-Athénée; "from the *amuse-bouches* to the delightful candy cart" and tea made from "live herbs snipped by white-gloved waiters", the Haute Cuisine is "probably similar to what the angels are eating", while "exceptional" service "without the starch" makes each diner feel like "the most important client in the world"; it's all "divine", but if the bill seems "hellish", consider it "tuition toward the art of eating."

Apicius ⌧ *Haute Cuisine*

26 | 26 | 26 | VE

8ᵉ | 20, rue d'Artois (George V/St-Philippe-du-Roule) | (33-1) 43 80 19 66 | www.restaurant-apicius.com

It's easy to "fall in love" with "movie-star handsome" chef-owner Jean-Pierre Vigato and his Haute Cuisine establishment, a "stunning" mansion in the centrally located 8th with "spectacular decor" and a "hidden garden", plus "welcoming service" that's "close to perfection"; "but the food trumps all", "combining the very best of the French classics with creative modern influences"; in short, supporters swear this place "outshines" the rest, though "alas, it's impossible to get a reservation."

---

* Indicates a tie with restaurant above

Au Trou Gascon ☒ *Southwest*

26	19	24	E

12ᵉ | 40, rue Taine (Daumesnil) | (33-1) 43 44 34 26 | www.autrougascon.fr

"Let's hear it for the Southwest!" shout supporters of Alain Dutournier's original "off-the-beaten track" eatery in the 12th that's "worth every travel minute"; "a mixture of classics and innovations", its Gasçon cuisine includes "the best confit de canard ever had", "transcendent cassoulet" and other "superb heart-attack food" served in "spare but elegant surroundings"; though the wine list's "a little short" on by-the-glass offerings, that's "made up for by a huge selection of armagnacs", so for most "the real trick is to get up from the table after a meal" here.

Carré des Feuillants ☒ *Haute Cuisine*

26	23	25	VE

1ᵉʳ | 14, rue de Castiglione (Concorde/Tuileries) | (33-1) 42 86 82 82 | www.carredesfeuillants.fr

"One of the great ones", this Haute Cuisine table "adjacent to the Place Vendôme "deserves more recognition" than it gets, since "inventive veteran" Alain Dutournier prepares "divine", "classical" food with Southwestern flavors, plus, in autumn, "possibly the best game menu in Paris", accompanied by a "wine list that's tops" and service that's almost "at the level of the food"; while "elegant", "the decor reminds one of the Ice Queen's palace", but overall, the experience is still "memorable", so "order with abandon if your wallet can afford it."

Dominique Bouchet ☒ *Haute Cuisine*

27	21	24	VE

8ᵉ | 11, rue Treilhard (Miromesnil) | (33-1) 45 61 09 46 | www.dominique-bouchet.com

Although it's "hidden" in the upper 8th, those who find this Haute Cuisine haven declare it "delivers 100% on the promise of greatness reflected in Bouchet's résumé", which includes Les Ambassadeurs; a "joy of a man", the chef-owner makes "creative preparations" of French classics while steering clear of trendy "foams and froths", and converts also compliment the "modern but warm interior" and "polite, attentive service from English-speaking waiters"; so, travelers, take note: "this is the food you went to Paris for."

☒ Guy Savoy, Restaurant ☒Ⓜ *Haute Cuisine*

28	25	27	VE

17ᵉ | 18, rue Troyon (Etoile) | (33-1) 43 80 40 61 | www.guysavoy.com

Clearly, his "ventures in Las Vegas haven't distracted" chef-owner Guy Savoy – his "modern", "elegantly understated" Rue Troyon flagship remains "consistently superior in every way"; the "innovative" cooking "brings Haute Cuisine as close to art as it can come", the "formal but friendly" service hits a "high watermark" ("the staff all but spoon-fed us"), "and – unusual for a big-name chef – M. Savoy often is actually at the restaurant"; yes, they charge "ridiculous prices", but since "you can't take it with you, leave some of it here."

Hiramatsu ☒ *Haute Cuisine*

26	25	26	VE

16ᵉ | 52, rue de Longchamp (Boissière/Trocadéro) | (33-1) 56 81 08 80 | www.hiramatsu.co.jp

The "meticulous attention to detail, immaculate presentation and delicate sauces and flavors" offer a "spectacular experience" at this Haute Cuisine destination owned by chef Hiroyuki Hirmatsu in the

FOOD DECOR SERVICE COST

16th; though some feel it's "becoming more Frenchified", the fare still offers "an uncanny union of Gallic complexity and Japanese elegance", while waiters who are "responsive, helpful and elegant without being stuffy" warm the slightly "cold", if "refined", dining room; most are "just waiting to go back", even though it's "sooo expensive."

La Braisière ⊠ *Gascony*   27 | 19 | 23 | E

17ᵉ | 54, rue Cardinet (Malesherbes) | (33-1) 47 63 40 37
The "quiet contented murmurings" attest to the "masterful" cuisine found in this "hidden gem" for "imaginative" Gasçon gastronomy in the 17th, with connoisseurs claiming it offers "more value for the money than the better-knowns"; the "neutral" decor was recently redone, but the ambiance is still "cozy" and "down-to-earth", while the "relaxed service encourages you to linger over your meal and savor every bite."

L'Ambroisie ⊠ Ⓜ *Haute Cuisine*   28 | 27 | 26 | VE

4ᵉ | 9, pl des Vosges (Bastille/St-Paul) | (33-1) 42 78 51 45
It's like "dining in a nobleman's home" at this "smoothly run", "aptly named" Haute Cuisine haven "serving food of the gods" along with a "top flight wine list" that helps to "rationalize" the "damage the bill inflicts"; "the most intimate of Paris' grand restaurants" (only 40 seats), it's also possibly the "toughest table in town" – and beware of "being exiled to the back room" – but "who wouldn't want to be king of the Place des Vosges, even just for a few hours?"

Lasserre ⊠ *Haute Cuisine*   27 | 28 | 28 | VE

8ᵉ | 17, av Franklin D. Roosevelt (Franklin D. Roosevelt) | (33-1) 43 59 02 13 | www.restaurant-lasserre.com
Experience "elegance personified" at this "old-world" "orchid-filled" establishment in an 8th-arrondissement mansion; combining "great classics with innovations", chef Jean-Louis Nomicos' "brilliant" Haute Cuisine bags bushels of compliments, as does the "flawless" staff, but the real raves are for the "fabulously '60s" technical touches, "from the James Bond entrance by the mini-lift" to the "unique open roof" (it's the "best topless place in town!"); "it all adds up to one magical evening for which you'll pay – but without the sense of being robbed."

🔟 L'Astrance ⊠ Ⓜ *New French*   28 | 22 | 27 | VE

16ᵉ | 4, rue Beethoven (Passy) | (33-1) 40 50 84 40
"Young, passionate" chef/co-owner Pascal Barbot "manages to wow the most blasé palates" with "inventive" New French cuisine that's "otherworldly", "intellectual" and always "surprising" (especially at dinner, where the "no-choice" tasting menu is the only option) at this "hard-to-get-into" table in the 16th; a near-"flawless" staff with a "personal touch" services the small, "sophisticated" room; aesthetes argue "they could rethink the decor, but with bookings two months in advance, why – and when?"

🔟 L'Atelier de Joël Robuchon ● *Haute Cuisine*   28 | 24 | 24 | VE

7ᵉ | Hôtel Pont Royal | 5, rue de Montalembert (Rue du Bac) | (33-1) 42 22 56 56 | www.joel-robuchon.com
In the tony 7th, the idolized chef's "Asian-sleek" "canteen for the rich" has them queuing at the door, then sitting "on a stool at a counter" ("singles welcomed") and watching the kitchen turn out "sublime", "cutting-edge" Haute Cuisine; tapas-size portions offer "a great way

to sample the offerings" from the Robuchon repertoire, though the "hearty of appetite" must be "prepared to pay a fortune"; the "attentive" service displays "typical French insouciance", but the only really "irksome" item is the no-reservations policy (except for very early and very late).

⚡ La Tour d'Argent Ⓜ *Haute Cuisine* | 25 | 28 | 26 | VE |

5ᵉ | 15-17, quai de la Tournelle (Cardinal Lemoine/Pont-Marie) | (33-1) 43 54 23 31 | www.latourdargent.com

Defiant (and dominant) devotees "don't care if it's considered uncool" – this Haute Cuisine table "is still one of the most magical of Parisian places", with its "spectacular views of Notre Dame"; "make sure you ask for a window table when you book, and for heaven's sake order the pressed duck" "with its numbered certificate" – though new chef Stéphane Haissant has "finally updated" the menu with some "excellent" options, served by an initially "haughty", but truly "outstanding staff"; so let the grouches grimace she's "a grande dame in decline" – this tower remains "a reason to sell off your worldly goods for one meal here before you die."

Le Bristol *Haute Cuisine* | 27 | 28 | 27 | VE |

8ᵉ | Hôtel Le Bristol | 112, rue du Faubourg St-Honoré (Miromesnil) | (33-1) 53 43 43 40 | www.lebristolparis.com

When an "extravagant experience" is in order, this "special-night-out kind of place" in the 8th is "close to perfect", with "two separate dining rooms, depending upon the season": an oak-paneled, "sumptuous circular room" in winter and an "exquisite" garden in summertime; chef Eric Frechon's "phenomenal", "cutting-edge" Haute Cuisine is worth the "oooh-la-la" prices, "particularly for those who like strong tastes in original combinations", while the "exceptional" service extends to "a silver tray of cleaning items" in case a customer should splash gravy on his recommended jacket.

⚡ Le Cinq *Haute Cuisine* | 28 | 29 | 28 | VE |

8ᵉ | Four Seasons George V | 31, av George V (Alma Marceau/George V) | (33-1) 49 52 71 54 | www.fourseasons.com/paris

"Come here for the meal of your life" swoon sated surveyors who promise this Haute Cuisine table in the George V, voted Tops in Decor and Service, is "perfect in every way", from the "delectable", oft-"adventurous" menu to the "exquisite" classic decor with "vases of flowers everywhere" to the "surprisingly friendly service", "as personal as it is professional" (even offering "a box of reading glasses" to farsighted diners); yes, this "splendid splurge" "will just about rob you of every last euro", but "the experience is so wonderful, somehow one doesn't mind."

⚡ Le Grand Véfour Ⓩ *Haute Cuisine* | 28 | 29 | 28 | VE |

1ᵉʳ | Palais Royal | 17, rue de Beaujolais (Palais Royal-Musée du Louvre) | (33-1) 42 96 56 27 | www.grand-vefour.com

Chef Guy Martin's "exquisite" Haute Cuisine offers "a glorious feast for the senses in the midst of old-world luxury" at this "mythic address" in the Palais-Royal; "dripping with atmosphere", the "exceptional setting", a gilded box of a room with a painted ceiling and brass plaques engraved with the names of its celebrated clientele (Colette,

Maria Callas), is animated by a staff that's "professional, courteous and welcoming"; true, this "royal treatment needs a royal treasury" when the bill comes – but "it meets each and every expectation."

Le Meurice 🅢 *Haute Cuisine* — 27 | 28 | 27 | VE

1ᵉʳ | Hôtel Meurice | 228, rue de Rivoli (Concorde/Tuileries) | (33-1) 44 58 10 55 | www.meuricehotel.com

"One of the great French chefs in one of Paris' prettiest dining rooms" sums up "the Haute Cuisine experience" at the Hôtel Meurice; loaded with luxe items like truffles and caviar, "culinary wizard" Yannick Alléno's "food is just exquisite", and "the cuisine's matched" by the "ballet-like service" "gliding" within the "grand, gorgeous" and "gilded" space recently redone with Philippe Starck's silver chairs and abstract glass sculpture; "yes, it's expensive" – but "the experience is magnificent."

Le Pré Catelan 🅢 🅜 *Haute Cuisine* — 27 | 28 | 26 | VE

16ᵉ | Bois de Boulogne, Route de Suresnes (Pont-de-Neuilly/Porte Maillot) | (33-1) 44 14 41 14 | www.precatelanparis.com

"Haute Cuisine of the highest order", "impeccable service" and of course that "beautiful location" in the Bois de Boulogne – small wonder that a "phenomenal dining experience" awaits at this "elegant, enduring" classic; though recently redone in contemporary tones of beige, bronze and gray, the decor retains its "magical" imperial aura; even advocates allow the "prices are budget-busting", but "cost be damned" – "lunch in the garden on a summer afternoon is pure bliss."

Les Ambassadeurs 🅜 *Haute Cuisine/New French* — 28 | 29 | 28 | VE

8ᵉ | Hôtel de Crillon | 10, pl de la Concorde (Concorde) | (33-1) 44 71 16 16 | www.crillon.com

The "sumptuous" "gold and marble" surroundings of the Crillon hotel are like eating "inside a jewel box", a "perfect showplace" for the "incredibly inventive" New French Haute Cuisine of chef Jean-François Piège (who has "enchanted" "serious foodies" ever since he was at Alain Ducasse); the 1,100-label wine list is *"extraordinaire"*, the service is "choreographed to perfection" while remaining "refreshingly friendly", and though the experience may "relieve you of many euros", "you get a lot for the price"; N.B. "the lunch menu at 75€ is a delight" – and a relative deal.

Michel Rostang 🅢 *Classic French* — 27 | 24 | 27 | VE

17ᵉ | 20, rue Rennequin (Péreire/Ternes) | (33-1) 47 63 40 77 | www.michelrostang.com

"Where charm and sophistication intersect", you find chef-owner Michel Rostang's "chic" table in the 17th, whose "every detail is perfect", from the "superb" cuisine ("rich, rich", "but delicious none the same") to the "charming maitre d'" and "flawless staff" to the "wood-paneled beauty" of the decor; yes, it's "a bit too pricey" – but after 30 years, this is "still among the best of the Classic French" establishments; P.S. "in season, ask to be truffled for the entire meal."

🅩 Pierre Gagnaire 🅢 *Haute Cuisine* — 28 | 25 | 27 | VE

8ᵉ | Hôtel Balzac | 6, rue Balzac (Charles de Gaulle-Etoile/George V) | (33-1) 58 36 12 50 | www.pierre-gagnaire.com

"Let your senses explore uncharted territory" during a "breathtaking meal" at this "brilliant", completely "unforgettable" Haute Cuisine haven in the 8th, serving what many describe as "the most innovative food" in Paris ("Pierre Gagnaire is to gastronomy what Picasso was to contemporary art"); yes, the master's "science experiment"–like creations, while "out of this world", are "too out there" for some; but the "exceptional service" in the discreet dove-gray and blonde wood dining room makes you "feel like royalty", and to the vast majority, it's "worth every euro (damn dollar)."

Relais d'Auteuil "Patrick Pignol" 🛇Ⓜ *Haute Cuisine*

27 | 20 | 26 | VE

16ᵉ | 31, bd Murat (Michel-Ange-Molitor/Porte d'Auteuil) | (33-1) 46 51 09 54

"If you're adventuresome", join the "well-to-do neighborhood clientele" that congregates at this Haute Cuisine table out toward the Porte d'Auteuil; while "outrageously expensive", it's "one of the best in Paris" for the eponymous chef-owner's traditional French food and "outstanding wine", plus the "warm welcome of Madame Pignol", within the wood-paneled, slightly "dim" setting; a "really lovely" experience, all round.

🆉 Taillevent 🛇 *Haute Cuisine*

28 | 28 | 28 | VE

8ᵉ | 15, rue Lamennais (Charles de Gaulle-Etoile/George V) | (33-1) 44 95 15 01 | www.taillevent.com

"You're at home the minute you enter" this "elegant", "spectacular modern art"-adorned townhouse in the 8th, which – though mourning the loss of legendary owner Jean-Claude Vrinat – shines on as Paris' No. 1 for Food and Popularity; guests would "gladly borrow from the kids' college fund" to sample "service that's not just an art form, but a religion" as it delivers chef Alain Solivérès' "classic", sometimes "inventive", but always "decadent and luscious" Haute Cuisine, backed by "a prodigious wine list"; in short, "why wait for heaven, when you can go to Taillevent?"

Prague

TOP FOOD RANKING

	Restaurant	Cuisine
26	Allegro	Italian/Mediterranean
25	Aquarius	Czech/Mediterranean
	David	Czech/International
	V Zátiší	Czech/International
	Essensia	Asian/International
24	Flambée	French/International
	U Zlaté Hrušky	Czech/International
	Rybí trh	International/Seafood
	U Modré Ruze	Czech/International
23	U Modré Kachnicky	Czech
	Kampa Park	International/Seafood
	Mlýnec	International
	Oliva	Mediterranean
	Coda	Mediterranean
	La Perle de Prague*	French
	Bellevue	Czech/International
22	Hergetova Cihelna	Czech/International
	Pravda	International
	Pálffy Palác	International
21	C'est La Vie	International/Seafood
	Square*	Italian/Spanish
	Alcron, The	Seafood
	U Vladare	Czech/International
	Barock	Asian/Mediterranean

Alcron, The ⑤ *Seafood* — 21 | 19 | 22 | E

New Town | Radisson SAS Alcron Hotel | Stĕpánská 40 | (420) 222-820-000 | www.radissonsas.com

A "private" refuge for well-heeled travelers, businessmen and in-the-know locals, this "wonderful little seafood restaurant" in New Town's Radisson SAS Alcron Hotel is home to chef Jirí Stift, who fans feel is "great with fish", as evidenced by dishes like sea bass roasted in salt crust; his creations are served in an "art deco setting" sporting a "lovely" curved mural, but those who are "a bit jaded" judge the atmosphere "not very warm."

Ⓩ Allegro *Italian/Mediterranean* — 26 | 24 | 27 | VE

Old Town | Four Seasons Hotel | Veleslavínova 2A | (420) 221-426-880 | www.fourseasons.com/prague

"Not your typical hotel dining" room, this "truly first-rate" Old Town venue "wows" with an "ultimate experience" that's just as "wonderful" "as you'd expect" from the Four Seasons; indeed, it's ranked No. 1 for Food in Prague for "fantastic" Italian-Med cuisine, "beautifully presented" in "a lavish environment" by "charming" staffers who treat guests "as visiting royalty"; P.S. "come early to get a window seat" for

---

* Indicates a tie with restaurant above

subscribe to ZAGAT.com

a "particularly" "spectacular view" of "the Vltava River's Charles Bridge" and the "fairy-tale" castle; N.B. a recent chef change may outdate the above Food score.

☒ Aquarius *Czech/Mediterranean* | 25 | 23 | 19 | E |

Little Quarter | Alchymist Grand Hotel & Spa | Tržiště 19 | (420) 257-286-019 | www.alchymisthotel.com

This Czech-Med is located in the Little Quarter's Alchymist Grand Hotel & Spa, four richly and romantically refurbished 16th-century buildings; "great" cuisine and a "fantastic" setting – a vaulted, mirrored space that opens to a courtyard on one side – make for "an enchanting experience", plus the practial pronounce "the price is a very good value"; N.B. there's live jazz on Saturdays.

Barock *Asian/Mediterranean* | 21 | 23 | 21 | E |

Old Town | Parízská 24 | (420) 222-329-221 | www.barockrestaurant.cz

"Still hip" and "happening", this "trendy little" Old Town "hangout" in a "great location near the luxury shopping in the Jewish Quarter" is known for "nice eye candy" thanks to its posse of "lively young" patrons and photos of "supermodels" adorning the walls of its "stylish" interior; service is "friendly", and the "flavorful options" on its "well-executed" Asian-accented Mediterranean menu (including an extensive sushi selection) offer a "terrific break from the routine."

☒ Bellevue *Czech/International* | 23 | 23 | 24 | VE |

Old Town | Smetanovo nábrezí 18 | (420) 222-221-443 | www.zatisigroup.cz

"An incredible dining experience" is in store for guests of this "grand" Old Town venue who enjoy a "magnificent view of the river, Charles Bridge and Prague Castle" as "impeccable" staffers deliver "delicious", "up-to-date" Czech-International cuisine; some suggest the same can't be said about the somewhat "faded" decor, but more maintain the "elegant setting" is "stylish and romantic", saying they'd "happily return again and again."

C'est La Vie *International/Seafood* | 21 | 19 | 21 | E |

Little Quarter | Rícní 1 | (420) 721-158-403 | www.cestlavie.cz

"A favorite for locals and tourists alike", this International-seafooder in the historic Little Quarter has a cozy, atmospheric interior with nooks and crannies, but it's the "beautiful" riverside terrace setting with its view of the Charles Bridge and boats that leaves lifers proclaiming "we'll be back."

Coda *Mediterranean* | 23 | 23 | 23 | E |

Little Quarter | Hotel Aria | Tržiště 9 | (420) 225-334-761 | www.aria.cz

The "beautiful Hotel Aria" "comes through" with this Mediterranean "hot spot" on its premises that offers "exceptional food" and "exceedingly friendly service"; the rich red dining room is "sexy", but the "great view" from the "gorgeous" terrace includes St. Nicholas Church, Prague Castle and a medley of romantic terra-cotta rooftops.

☒ David *Czech/International* | 25 | 22 | 24 | E |

Little Quarter | Tržiště 21 | (420) 257-533-109 | www.restaurant-david.cz

For "a fantastic trip to another era", step inside the "country-style dining rooms" of "this relaxing haven" "tucked into a hillside" "in a quiet corner" of the Little Quarter, where "carefully prepared", "delicious"

	FOOD	DECOR	SERVICE	COST

Czech-International cuisine (including "hearty, traditional game dishes") is "augmented by an excellent wine list"; fans also "can't say enough good things about" the "gracious" service and "charming", "tiny space", insisting you're guaranteed a "most memorable" meal.

☑ Essensia *Asian/International* | 25 | 25 | 25 | VE |

Little Quarter | Mandarin Oriental Hotel | Nebovidská 459/1 | (420) 233-088-888 | www.mandarinoriental.com

"A cut above the competition" and "one of the best" "places to take business clients" is this new Asian-International in the Mandarin Oriental Hotel, which is housed in a converted 14th-century monastery and courtyard; the "brilliant" cuisine is served in a series of five "beautiful", softly lit vaulted rooms by an "attentive staff", and if it's pricey, pragmatists point out "expensive eating in Prague would be considered cheap in London or Paris."

Flambée ● *French/International* | 24 | 25 | 26 | E |

Old Town | Husova 5 | (420) 224-248-512 | www.flambee.cz

"Truly a treasure", this "gem" of a French-International in Old Town is manned by a "hospitable", "attentive staff" that "puts you at ease" the moment you descend to its "distinctive Gothic cellar", which "dates back to the 11th century" but has been updated with modern accents including "red-velvet seating"; "great chef" Dušan Jakubec's "culinary art reaches the highest standards", and when coupled with the "impeccable service" and "striking" setting justifies the "astronomical" prices.

Hergetova Cihelna *Czech/International* | 22 | 25 | 21 | E |

Little Quarter | Cihelná 2b | (420) 296-826-103 | www.kampagroup.com

The "fantastic view of the Charles Bridge" from its "window seats and terrace" "is alone worth the visit" to this "special treat" "with an amazing location" "in an old brick factory" "on the riverbank" in the Little Quarter; within the "*très chic*" atmosphere of its "dramatic yet romantic setting", a "modern" menu of "excellent" International offerings "as well as regional Czech dishes" is served by a "very good" staff, making it "a must-stop when in town."

☑ Kampa Park *International/Seafood* | 23 | 24 | 22 | E |

Little Quarter | Na Kampe 8B | (420) 296-826-102 | www.kampagroup.com

Perennially "popular", this "renowned" "favorite" "beautifully located" on the Little Quarter's "historic Kampa Island" (right "under the famous Charles Bridge") offers two terraces for "contemporary fine dining at the water's edge"; loyalists also laud the "lovely" interior and "inventive", "top-quality" International menu focusing on "properly cooked fish entrees", but surveyors are split on the "efficient" staffers, with some swearing they "couldn't be more friendly" and others opining that they "need an attitude adjustment."

La Perle de Prague ☒ *French* | 23 | 25 | 22 | VE |

New Town | Tancící Dum | Rašínovo nábrezí 80 | (420) 221-984-160 | www.laperle.cz

"Both the beautiful views and good cocktails will make you giddy" at this "fantastic location atop" 'The Dancing House', architect Frank "Gehry's whimsical" creation in New Town; some say the "surroundings are far better than" the "overpriced" fare, but more insist the "excellent" New French cuisine – offered in a "funky", "contemporary" interior with "pampering service" – "matches the splendor of" the "amazing" vistas of the winding river, Old Town and Prague Castle on the horizon.

Mlýnec *International*

23 | 21 | 21 | E

Old Town | Novotného Lávka 9 | (420) 221-082-208 | www.zatisigroup.cz

With its "great location" on a pier "at the foot of the Charles Bridge" in Old Town, this "superb" spot offers "very nice views" to accompany its "wonderful food" and "top-flight service"; the "interesting" International "menu challenges the traditional Prague palate", since there's "nothing local" on it, but the "good-quality wine list" does feature some Moravian selections.

Oliva ⊠ *Mediterranean*

23 | 21 | 22 | M

New Town | 4 Plavecká | (420) 222-520-288 | www.olivarestaurant.cz

In-the-know locals have taken to this "stylish" Mediterranean newcomer in New Town that, like the name says, pays homage to the olive and its oil in some of its "delicious" dishes and also in the pale-green color on its walls; "fresh food", "friendly owners" and fair prices make many say they "wish this favorite were in their neighborhood."

Pálffy Palác *International*

22 | 24 | 19 | E

Little Quarter | Valdštejnská 14 | (420) 257-530-522 | www.palffy.cz

"Difficult to find but worth the effort", this delightful" "favorite" features a "romantic", "candlelit" setting "in an old nobleman's palace close to the castle" in the Little Quarter, where "excellent" International food is served along with "good local wines" by an "able" staff; P.S. the "ancient building" also houses a "music conservatory", so sometimes "you dine to the sounds" of its students.

☑ Pravda *International*

22 | 23 | 22 | E

Old Town | Parízská 17 | (420) 222-326-203 | www.pravdarestaurant.cz

Set "on smart" "Parízská Street, next to the Old-New Synagogue" "in the Jewish Quarter" of Old Town, this "classy" International "celebrates tastes from all over the world"; the "simple", "modern, open space offers views of the bustling" thoroughfare ("during the summer months the outdoor tables" provide particularly "great people-watching"), and "excellent cocktails" add to the "lively", "trendy" vibe.

Rybí trh *International/Seafood*

24 | 19 | 23 | E

Old Town | Týnský Dvur 5 | (420) 224-895-447 | www.rybitrh.cz

You might not expect "simply divine" "seafood in a land-locked country", but you'll find it at this Old Town "fish market/restaurant" set "on the charming Týnský Dvur courtyard"; its "excellent" International menu offers a "great choice" of "creatively prepared" fin fare, the savvy staff has a knack for "fulfilling unspoken wishes" and the "understated" interior is appropriately decorated with "nice aquariums"; as for the cost, surveyors wax philosophical, saying "what can you do? – quality is expensive."

☑ U Modré Kachnicky *Czech*

23 | 23 | 21 | E

Little Quarter | Nebovidská 6 | (420) 257-320-308

☑ U Modré Kachnicky II *Czech*

Old Town | Michalská 16 | (420) 224-213-418
www.umodrekachnicky.cz

"Those wanting to taste the true local flavor" of Prague "must stop" for a "cultural experience" 'At the Blue Duckling' (the English translation of this "quaint" and "cozy" Little Quarter "stalwart's" name); like "someone's grandmother's house", its "rustic" rooms are "quirky" but "comfortable", providing a "charming" setting in which to "relish" "exceedingly well-done" "homestyle Czech cooking" with "an emphasis on game" and "regional specialties", proffered by a "warm, gracious" staff; N.B. there's a newer offshoot in the Old Town.

U Modré Ruze *Czech/International*   24 | 21 | 22 | E
Old Town | Rytírská 16 | (420) 224-225-873 | www.umodreruze.cz
"Step down into" the "lovely subterranean setting" of this "first-class establishment" (whose name means 'At The Blue Rose') "located in a 15th-century cellar" in Old Town, where "authentic Czech cuisine" and some International offerings are backed up by a "small but reliable wine list" with "good [domestic] selections" at "moderate prices"; the "charming" barrel-vaulted stone walls lend "a medieval feel" to the setting, which is made all the more "romantic" by "a great piano player."

U Vladare ● *Czech/International*   21 | 18 | 19 | M
Little Quarter | Maltézské námestí 10 | (420) 257-534-121 | www.uvladare.cz
"Near the Charles Bridge" in the Little Quarter, this "charming" venue offering "excellent" Czech-International cuisine occupies "one of the oldest restaurant spaces in Prague", having been home to various eating establishments since 1776; perhaps the "service is not the best", but at least the staff is "friendly" and you can choose between three settings – the cozy antiques-filled dining room, the low-ceilinged wine cellar or the earthy club area.

U Zlaté Hrušky *Czech/International*   24 | 23 | 21 | M
Castle Quarter | Nový svet 3 | (420) 220-514-778 | www.uzlatehrusky.cz
"A golden find", this "cozy, quaint" "sleeper a little off the beaten track" in the Castle Quarter, "on a beautifully picturesque and quiet cobbled street", boasts a "menu offering traditional Czech food" (including "wonderful game and fish") as well as some International fare; the "pleasantly furnished, comfortable" interior "immediately transports one to another century" and is peopled by "lots of locals", all enjoying the "authentic" cuisine and "gracious service."

Z V Zátiší *Czech/International*   25 | 20 | 23 | E
Old Town | Liliová 1 | (420) 222-221-155 | www.zatisigroup.cz
Think all Czech "cuisine is heavy"? – you'll "think again" after sampling the "excellent local specialties" "exquisitely cooked" with an International, "modern take" at this "lovely restaurant" "just off Betlemska Square" in the Old Town; its "feasts are fit for bohemian royalty", thanks to "creative" cuisine, "first-rate wines", "impeccable service" and an "intimate" setting; a few feel "there are equally good places" charging "much less money", but most insist it's "a truly wonderful dining experience" worthy of "a prompt return visit."

Rome

TOP FOOD RANKING

	Restaurant	Cuisine
26	Vivendo	Italian
	La Pergola	Italian/Mediterranean
	Alberto Ciarla	Seafood
	La Rosetta*	Seafood
	Agata e Romeo	Roman
	Mirabelle	Italian
	Sora Lella*	Roman
25	Al Vero Girarrosto	Tuscan
	Quinzi e Gabrieli	Seafood
	Antico Arco	Italian
	L'Altro Mastai*	Mediterranean
	Baby	Neapolitan/Med.
24	Il San Lorenzo	Neapolitan/Seafood
	Il Convivio Troiani	Italian
	Piperno	Roman/Jewish
	Da Tullio	Tuscan
	I Sofa' di Via Giulia	Italian/Mediterranean
	Antica Pesa	Roman
	Camponeschi	Italian

Z Agata e Romeo ⊠ *Roman*   26 | 22 | 24 | VE

Esquilino | Via Carlo Alberto 45 | (39-06) 446-6115 | www.agataeromeo.it
"Superior ingredients" help make for "brilliant" "creative" interpretations of Roman cuisine at this tiny, "family-run delight" where wife Agata Parisella is the chef, husband Romeo Caraccio is the host-sommelier and daughter Mariantonietta delivers the delicious goods; "a perfect meal" is complemented by an "outstanding wine list" and a "chic but cozy setting"; besides the expensive tabs, the only downside is the near-the-train-station location in Esquilino; N.B. closed Saturday and Sunday.

Z Alberto Ciarla ●⊠ *Seafood*   26 | 20 | 24 | VE

Trastevere | Piazza San Cosimato 40 | (39-06) 581-8668 | www.albertociarla.com
The "food practically flops off your plate and into your mouth it's so fresh" at this "great", old famous seafooder that specializes in raw fish (*crudo*) in Trastevere; some find the decor – black walls, sofas and mirrors – "tacky", but proponents point out the space has been updated and insist "if you get the right spot it can be romantic", or head for the outdoor area.

Al Vero Girarrosto Toscano ● *Tuscan*   25 | 20 | 23 | E

Via Veneto | Via Campania 29 | (39-06) 482-1899 | www.alverogirarrostotoscano.com
This "wonderful" Tuscan right behind the Via Veneto and only steps from Villa Borghese is "a true classic" that's been serving "abundant

---

* Indicates a tie with restaurant above

antipasti" and "the best steak Florentine" since 1969; "gracious service" and a "warm" and "cozy" basement setting combine to make customers feel "at home the minute they walk in."

Antica Pesa ● *Roman*

24	20	20	E

Trastevere | Via Garibaldi 18 | (39-06) 580-9236 | www.anticapesa.it

"Be sure to bring an empty stomach" to this "terrific" Roman "taste treat" in Trastevere; though it dates back to 1922, its menu focuses on "excellent" modern interpretations of traditional ingredients like lamb, and the "wonderfully romantic" setting – contemporary frescoes on the walls, a fireplace, enchanting garden and exceptional wine cellar – has become a celebrity hang since its recent association with Robert De Niro's Tribeca Film Festival and the new Rome Film Fest.

Antico Arco ●⊠ *Italian*

25	20	23	E

Gianicolo | Piazzale Aurelio 7 | (39-06) 581-5274 | www.anticoarco.it

It's "off the beaten path", up in the Janiculum Hill near the American Academy, but the "young and the beautiful are all here" at this popular, "innovative" Italian with "decently priced" "divine food", "exceptional wines" and "gracious service"; it's "minimalist in a NYC Village kind of way", there's a "hip vibe" and the experience is "special from entrance to exit."

Baby Ⓜ *Neapolitan/Mediterranean*

25	24	25	E

Parioli | Aldrovandi Palace Hotel | Via Ulisse Aldrovandi 15 | (39-06) 321-6126 | www.aldrovandi.com

This "great" Neapolitan-Med in the Aldrovandi Palace Hotel in Parioli is the baby of star chef Alfonso Iaccarino, whose celebrated flagship restaurant, Don Alfonso 1890, is near the Amalfi Coast; "excellent", "creative" cuisine is "enriched by the finest ingredients" and served by a "great staff" in a "fantastic setting", whose "crisp white decor" and "view of a swimming pool" "make it feel like the Caribbean" and a "great date place."

Camponeschi ●⊠ *Italian*

24	23	23	VE

Piazza Farnese | Piazza Farnese 50 | (39-06) 687-4927 | www.ristorantecamponeschi.it

"*Bella Italia* at its very best" is found at this "top-class", "they-do-everything-well", expensive Italian facing Michelangelo's Palazzo Farnese; there's "excellent food" and "superb service", and the "elegant setting", with hand-painted boiserie, is one of the most "romantic" rooms in Rome, but sitting outside looking at the exquisite square is also appealing; N.B. their wine bar next door serves the family's own wines along with about 500 others.

Ⓩ Dal Bolognese Ⓜ *Emilian*

23	19	20	E

Piazza del Popolo | Piazza del Popolo 1 | (39-06) 361-1426

"All of Rome passes through" this 65-year-old Emilian "classic" and its alfresco patio "perfectly positioned" on the Piazza del Popolo; "great" traditional food like *tagliatelle al ragu* and the trolley of boiled meats merit almost as much attention as the "wonderful people-watching", so if a few snipe that "service can be snippy", for most it's a "must."

	FOOD	DECOR	SERVICE	COST

Da Tullio ⊠ *Tuscan* — 24 | 18 | 23 | E

Piazza Barberini | Via San Nicola da Tolentino 26 | (39-06) 474-5560 | www.tullioristorante.it

This "simple" Tuscan near Piazza Barberini has "been in business forever, and for good reason" – "well-prepared" "authentic" dishes like *ribollita* and *bistecca alla fiorentina,* which are complemented by a "great" regional wine list.

⊠ Harry's Bar ● ⊠ *International/Mediterranean* — 18 | 21 | 20 | VE

Via Veneto | Via Veneto 150 | (39-06) 484-643 | www.harrysbar.it

"Bellini, panini and people-watching on the Via Veneto" are the point at this "clubby", 1958 International-Med "watering hole" "where you can feel the history"; it's "overpriced", "there are loads of Yanks" and some say "it's lost some of its charm", but most maintain "everyone has to go here at least once just to say they've been."

Il Convivio Troiani ⊠ *Italian* — 24 | 22 | 23 | VE

Piazza Navona | Vicolo dei Soldati 31 | (39-06) 686-9432 | www.ilconviviotroiani.com

The brothers Troiani "have consistently had one of Rome's best restaurants" is what surveyors say about this Italian near Piazza Navona; "outstanding" traditional and creative dishes, "attentive service" and a "classy", "soigné setting" – three rooms with frescoes or paintings – add up to a "pleasurable" evening; of course, the bill also adds up to "very expensive."

Il San Lorenzo ● *Neapolitan/Seafood* — 24 | 20 | 21 | E

Campo dei Fiore | Via dei Chiavari 4/5 | (39-06) 686-5097

This new Neapolitan seafood specialist "conveniently located" near Campo dei Fiore "wins a lot of points" – there's "excellent food", "respectful service" and "very pretty" multilevel dining rooms dotted with modern art, as well as an oyster-shell-studded bar where you can sip a glass of champers with your crustaceans; no wonder most maintain "it's a must when you are in Rome."

⊠ Imàgo *International/Italian* — 24 | – | 25 | VE
(fka Hassler Rooftop)

Trinitá dei Monti | Hotel Hassler | Trinità dei Monti 6 | (39-06) 699-34726 | www.hotelhasslerroma.com

"A must for everyone who can afford it" declare devotees of the Hotel Hassler's International-Italian with "a commanding rooftop view of the Eternal City" from its "perch atop the Spanish steps"; "delicious" "creative food, an impressive wine list" and "wonderful service" also add to the "romantic", "rarefied experience"; it's a "super-swank" hang for "the glitterati", so be prepared for "over-the-top prices for an over-the-top" evening; N.B. a post-Survey redo and name change make for a more modern and luminous setting, but the rest remains the same.

NEW I Sofa' di
Via Giulia ● *Italian/Mediterranean* — 24 | 22 | 22 | E

Piazza Farnese | St. George Hotel | Via Giulia 62 | (39-06) 686-611 | www.stgeorgehotel.it

"Great food" is found at this Italian-Mediterranean in the new luxury St. George Hotel, "excellently located" on central Rome's loveliest

| | FOOD | DECOR | SERVICE | COST |

street, Via Giulia; a "wonderful staff" presides over an elegant setting that mixes minimalist modern decor with classic touches in travertine, plus there's a tranquil courtyard garden for warm-weather dining.

L'Altro Mastai ⊠Ⓜ *Mediterranean*   25 | 24 | 24 | E

Piazza Navona | Via Giraud 53 | (39-06) 6830-1296 | www.laltromastai.it
Supporters of rising star chef Fabio Baldassarre, a former protégé of La Pergola's acclaimed Heinz Beck, say his four-year-old Mediterranean near Piazza Navona is among "the best in Rome today"; a "formal" setting with modern art, marble and mosaics is the backdrop for his brand of innovative fine dining; N.B. a move to a new location at Via delle Terme di Traiano, 4a, in the Colosseum area, is scheduled for spring 2008.

❏ La Pergola ⊠Ⓜ *Italian/Mediterranean*   26 | 26 | 26 | VE

Monte Mario | Cavalieri Hilton | Via Alberto Cadlolo 101 | (39-06) 3509-2152 | www.cavalieri-hilton.it
"A German chef in an American hotel serving Italian-Med food results in one of the finest dining experiences imaginable" assert admirers of Heinz Beck and his "exceptional cuisine" at the Cavalieri Hilton; there's also an "impressive wine list", "outstanding staff" and "beautiful" rooftop room, which provides "an amazing view of Rome"; a few mutter about its "out-of-the-way" Monte Mario locale and "tad-over-the-top" ways – there's gold cutlery and a "mineral water menu with 40 choices" – but they're outvoted.

❏ La Rosetta ⊠ *Seafood*   26 | 20 | 23 | VE

Pantheon | Via della Rosetta 8 | (39-06) 686-1002 | www.larosetta.com
For "mind-blowing" fish with a Sicilian accent, finatics urge you to try this family-owned stalwart with a "wonderful location near the Pantheon", where a "solicitous staff" presides over a "cozy, convivial" setting with frescoes; "prices are insane", but that doesn't prevent a jet-set crowd from streaming through the door.

❏ La Terrazza *Italian/Mediterranean*   23 | 26 | 24 | VE

Trinitá dei Monti | Hotel Eden | Via Ludovisi 49 | (39-06) 4781-2752
There's a "romantic" and "unbelievable" "knockout view of Rome" from this Italian-Mediterranean on the Hotel Eden's rooftop; also on offer are "wonderful food, wine and service" as well as a "lovely piano bar with great cocktails", so "although prices are as lofty" as the vista, most maintain "it's worth the splurge."

Mirabelle *Italian*   26 | 24 | 24 | VE

Via Veneto | Hotel Splendide Royal | Via di Porta Pinciana 14 | (39-06) 4216-8838 | www.mirabelle.it
An "absolutely spectacular" "view over Rome" and the Villa Medici gardens "caps what is an excellent evening" sigh sybarites about this Italian atop the Hotel Splendide Royal; chef Giuseppe Sestito's "superb" cuisine, "first-class service" and a "beautiful" room make for a "perfect" and "extremely expensive" "marriage."

Piperno Ⓜ *Roman/Jewish*   24 | 18 | 21 | E

The Ghetto | Monte de' Cenci 9 | (39-06) 6880-6629 | www.ristorantepiperno.it
"For the best fried artichokes and stuffed zucchini blossoms", "forget your cholesterol problems" and head for this 1860 Roman-Jewish

"must" that's a "bit hard to find" in front of historic Palazzo Cenci in the Ghetto; the rooms are looking a "bit worn", but dining out on the small outdoor space on the piazza is pleasing.

Quinzi e Gabrieli ⊠ *Seafood*

| 25 | 18 | 19 | VE |

Pantheon | Via delle Coppelle 5/6 | (39-06) 687-9389 | www.quinziegabrieli.it
"The freshest seafood money can buy in Rome" is found at this "fashionable" fish house, near the Pantheon, where "exquisite", "unbelievably expensive" dishes are served raw or lightly cooked at the table; a "serene" room is decorated with murals of three seaport cities, and there's also appealing outdoor eating for the alfresco-oriented.

Sora Lella ⊠ *Roman*

| 26 | 20 | 21 | E |

Isola Tiberina | Via di Ponte Quattro Capi 16 | (39-06) 686-1601 | www.soralella.com
This long-standing, "family-run" Roman is set on Isola Tiberina, an island on the Tiber River, and features traditional dishes such as *rigatoni all'amatriciana* as well as more creative ones like leg of lamb with artichokes and pecorino cheese – all backed up by an extensive wine list.

⊠ Vivendo ⊠ *Italian*

| 26 | 27 | 25 | VE |

Piazza della Repubblica | St. Regis Grand Hotel |
Via Vittorio Emanuele Orlando 3 | (39-06) 4709-2736
Voted No. 1 for Food in Rome is this Italian in the "magnificent" St. Regis Grand Hotel, where "exceptional" "creative" cuisine is served by a "flawless staff" in a "lovely", quietly "lavish" room with satin fabrics and contemporary paintings; it all adds up to an experience that's quite expensive and "exquisite in every way."

TOP FOOD RANKING

	Restaurant	Cuisine
28	Paul & Norbert	French/Swedish
	Wedholms Fisk	Swedish/Seafood
27	F12	International
26	Lux Stockholm	International/Swedish
	Ulriksdals Wärdshus	Swedish/International
	Vassa Eggen	International
25	Eriks Bakficka	International/Swedish
24	Operakällaren	French/International
	Pontus!	Seafood/Swedish
	Leijontornet	Scandinavian
	Edsbacka Krog	Swedish/French
23	Prinsen	Swedish/French
22	Kungsholmen	International
	Den Gyldene Freden	Swedish
	Eriks Gondolen	French/Swedish
	Restaurangen™	Swedish/International
21	Clas på Hörnet	French/Swedish
	Grands Veranda	International/Swedish
20	Sturehof	Swedish/Seafood
19	Pontus by the Sea	French/Swedish
	KB	Swedish
	Rolfs Kök	Swedish/Mediterranean
	Berns Asian	Asian

ⓩ Berns Asian *Asian*   19 | 24 | 18 | E

Norrmalm | Berns Hotel | Berzelii Park | (46-8) 5663-2222 | www.berns.se
"You have to love" the "fabulously over-the-top" interior of "this massive place" in Norrmalm; its "trendy, aristocratic" crowd ensures there's always "excitement in the air", but even they admit you "go for the drinks" and "scene", as service is only "adequate" and the "competent" kitchen's Asian fare can sometimes be "an afterthought."

Clas på Hörnet ⓩ *French/Swedish*   21 | 20 | 20 | E

Södermalm | Hotel Clas på Hörnet | Surbrunnsgatan 20 | (46-8) 165-136 | www.claspahornet.se
This "charming" French-Swedish in a "quaint" 1731 Södermalm inn serves "tasty" traditional fare, with an emphasis on fish; a "lovely" candlelit Gustavian-style setting overlooking a garden and "stellar service" lead loyalists to say "this is the place to go for an adult evening."

Den Gyldene Freden ⓩ *Swedish*   22 | 24 | 23 | E

Gamla Stan | Österlånggatan 51 | (46-8) 249-760 | www.gyldenefreden.se
"Beautiful old-world surroundings" dating from the 18th century define this "charming, historic" Gamla Stan "favorite" "in a cellar in the Old Town"; almost "everyone loves this place" for its combination of "cozy" ambiance, traditional local dishes (plus some International of-

ferings) and "efficient service", even if some say it's "too bad" it's "getting a little staid" and "somewhat touristy" of late; P.S. "the Swedish Academy dines there on Thursdays."

Edsbacka Krog ✉ *Swedish/French*   24 20 22 VE

Sollentuna | Sollentunavägen 220 | (46-8) 963-300 | www.edsbackakrog.se
"A tribute to the art of food", this "exquisite" restaurant in a 17th-century building "is surely worth the journey" to Sollentuna, "on the outskirts of town", as its "top" staff "delivers a symphony of exceedingly well-balanced" dishes from an "excellent" Swedish-French menu; a stellar wine cellar and an idyllic setting further enhance the "extraordinary experience."

Eriks Bakficka *International/Swedish*   25 17 24 E

Östermalm | Fredrikshovsgatan 4 | (46-8) 660-1599 | www.eriks.se
"Owned by one of Sweden's best chefs", Erik Lallerstedt, "this charming bistro" is "a favorite haunt of locals" in the "expensive residential quarter" of Östermalm – indeed, the "well-heeled" guests seem to "all know each other" as they gather within its "more formal dining room" or "cozier bar section" to enjoy "fine" Swedish-International cuisine; true, it's "a little pricey", but insiders insist it offers "excellent value."

Eriks Gondolen ●☻✉ *French/Swedish*   22 26 22 VE

Södermalm | Stadsgården 6 | (46-8) 641-7090 | www.eriks.se
Though it's the "fantastic atmosphere" and "breathtaking view of Stockholm" (including "spectacular" vistas of "the harbor" and "Old Town") that "really make it stand out", advocates avow you'll also "enjoy a fine meal" of "wonderful" Swedish-French cuisine and "excellent service" at this "great place to watch the sunset" suspended high above Södermalm; even those who feel the "very expensive" fare is "not outstanding" and "only secondary" to the venue's visual delights declare do "come for a drink" and "mingle at the nice bar."

Ƶ F12 ✉ *International*   27 22 24 VE

Norrmalm | Fredsgatan 12 | (46-8) 248-052 | www.f12.se
A "favorite" for many, this "consistently excellent and stylishly" "mod locale" in Norrmalm is run by "people who care about food" – namely "talented" chef-owners Melker Andersson (a "god in Stockholm") and Danyel Couet, whose "flavorful" International fare is served by an "incredibly friendly and helpful staff" in a "first-rate setting"; still, some who resent "very expensive", "tiny portions" warn that "you may not like" their "innovative approach", which allows guests "to assemble their meal from a number of small dishes."

Grands Veranda *International/Swedish*   21 23 22 E

Norrmalm | Grand Hôtel | Södra Blasieholmshamnen 8 | (46-8) 679-3586 | www.grandhotel.se
"For a true Grand Hôtel experience", supporters suggest you "snag a table with" a "to-die-for view" of "the Royal Palace, the parliament building "and the harbor" at this Swedish-International in Norrmalm; "the service is excellent", and "they always have" a "wonderful smörgåsbord" "filled with" so many "tempting foods" that "it's easy to fill *yourself* to bursting" – though those with less voracious appetites aver there's "nothing wrong with their à la carte menu" of "delicious, high-quality food", either.

	FOOD	DECOR	SERVICE	COST

KB *Swedish* | 19 | 21 | 21 | E

Norrmalm | Smålandsgatan 7 | (46-8) 679-6032 | www.konstnarsbaren.se
"When visiting Stockholm", locals say, stop at this "cozy" "artists' hangout" in an "excellent" Norrmalm location that's "still lots of fun" after more than 70 years; regulars "enjoy the art in the dining room" even more than the "great traditional *husmanskost*" (down-home Swedish fare), which "perhaps could be more inspired"; it "gets a little hectic and noisy late" in the evening, but it's "perfect as a business lunch place."

NEW Kungsholmen *International* | 22 | 22 | 20 | E

Kungsholmen | Norr Mälarstrand | (46-8) 5052-4450 |
www.kungsholmen.com
Swedish restaurant guru Melker Andersson of the highly rated F12 "has done it again" with this "trendy" International in Kungsholmen, right on the waterfront, where patrons mix and match their meal from a variety of seven "upmarket" "gourmet food courts" serving everything from sushi to soups and salads; throw in a "delightful setting" that includes a terrace where you can have "drinks by the sea where the sun never sets" and no wonder a "hip crowd congregates" here.

Leijontornet ⊠ *Scandinavian* | 24 | 27 | 23 | VE

Gamla Stan | Victory Hotel | Lilla Nygatan 5 | (46-8) 5064-0080 |
www.leijontornet.se
An "authentic medieval room" in an "Old Town cellar" is the "wonderful setting" of this "great place to eat" in Gamla Stan's "small, high-class" Victory Hotel ("don't just eat at the restaurant – stay at the hotel too"); as if the "fabulous" environment weren't enough, you can also expect "splendid art from the kitchen" in the form of "superb" Scandinavian cuisine, served by a "staff that tries hard to please"; no wonder most predict you'll "enjoy the experience."

Z Lux Stockholm ⊠ⓂⒸ *International/Swedish* | 26 | 19 | 22 | E

Kungsholmen | Primusgatan 116 | (46-8) 619-0190 | www.luxstockholm.com
Set "in a tastefully redone" "old Electrolux building" (hence the name) on Lilla Essingen island near Kungsholmen, "just outside central Stockholm", this "amazing" venue peopled by a "hip, beautiful staff and clientele" is "so trendy it hurts", but even the "cool atmosphere" "can't match the fabulous", "first-class modern Swedish"-International fare or "warm", "attentive service"; its "spacious dining room" is "beautifully minimalist" to some, "a bit too austere" for others, but all adore the "gorgeous view."

Z Operakällaren ⊠Ⓜ *French/International* | 24 | 27 | 23 | VE

Norrmalm | The Royal Opera House | Karl XII:s Torg | (46-8) 676-5801 |
www.operakallaren.se
"One can only say bravo!" about this "magnificent" "landmark" in the "lovely" Royal Opera House in Norrmalm that's "so popular it's almost a cliché now" thanks to the hordes of "hip see-and-be-seen" people who "go for the scene" and to "check out the latest fashions"; most report the "grand" "opulent" interior, "delicious" French-International fare and "classic", "formal" service are also "superb", and "worth every penny" of the "astronomical price" here ("no, you can't sing for your supper").

	FOOD	DECOR	SERVICE	COST

ⓩ Paul & Norbert ⌧ *French/Swedish* — 28 | 23 | 25 | VE

Östermalm | Strandvägen 9 | (46-8) 663-8183 | www.paulochnorbert.se
"Truly" a "favorite", this "dining delight" in Östermalm is rated No. 1 for
Food in Stockholm on the strength of its "superb" French-Swedish cuisine created by "excellent chef" Norbert Lang; you'll also "enjoy wonderful service" from an "exceptional" staff, a "nice atmosphere" and a "great
wine selection", making it "satisfying" for a "private, romantic" "meal of
a lifetime" that will "never be forgotten" – "but bring a lot of krona because you'll need them"; N.B. if you'd like an interactive evening, you can
be a cook for the night and prepare your own meal alongside Lang.

Pontus! ⌧ *Seafood/Swedish* — 24 | – | 23 | VE
(fka Pontus in the Green House)

Norrmalm | Brunnsgatan 1 | (46-8) 5452-7300 | www.pontusfrithiof.com
"Relax and enjoy" a "fantastic" experience at this Swedish seafooder,
a bastion of "great dining" whose habitués "humbly bow to chef"
Pontus Frithiof and his "artful kitchen" for delivering "delicious"
dishes; other pluses are some "reasonably priced gems on the wine
list" and a "friendly staff", so admirers advise "if you have the money
to spare", "don't miss it"; N.B. post-Survey, the restaurant moved from
Gamla Stan to this new location in Norrmalm.

Pontus by the Sea *French/Swedish* — 19 | 21 | 21 | E

Gamla Stan | Skeppsbrokajen, Tullhus 2 | (46-8) 202-095 |
www.pontusfrithiof.com
Once just a "wonderful summer restaurant", Pontus Frithiof's "expensive" Gamla Stan spot "in the heart of the Old Town" now offers its
"friendly service" year-round and, as befits its setting "by the sea",
continues to be known for a "solid" French-Swedish menu starring
"colorful plates" of "perfectly cooked fish" dressed with "delicate
sauces"; for many, though, "it's all about" the "excellent view", as
there's "something amazing about dining next to the water."

Prinsen *Swedish/French* — 23 | 22 | 23 | E

Norrmalm | Mäster Samuelsgatan 4 | (46-8) 611-1331 |
www.restaurangprinsen.se
"The food is excellent and the service is accommodating" at this
Norrmalm "classic that never disappoints" with its "innovative"
Swedish-French fare, whether enjoyed "at one of the outside tables"
or within the "impressive interior" of its "more formal" "wood-paneled
dining room"; it's a "power-lunch" favorite for "the cognoscenti of the
financial industry" as well as a "terrific evening" haunt of "tourists",
and though it's "a bit on the expensive side", most insist it "always
gives you value for your money."

Restaurangen™ ⌧ *Swedish/International* — 22 | 21 | 18 | E

Norrmalm | Oxtorgsgatan 14 | (46-8) 220-952 | www.restaurangentm.com
Supporters of "sampling" swear by the "Scandinavian-tapas concept" of
this Norrmalm Swedish-International (from the "same owner as F12")
"where you order by numbers" – choosing three, five or seven "tasty,
small" "courses, each" "well-paired" with a "different wine" "that complements its flavor"; it "is a fun way to try a variety" of "great food" that's
"not the usual fare", and the "noisy room" packed with "pretty people"
adds to the experience ("if only I could eat like this every night").

	FOOD	DECOR	SERVICE	COST

Rolfs Kök ● *Swedish/Mediterranean* — 19 | 19 | 20 | E

Norrmalm | Tegnérgatan 41 | (46-8) 101-696 | www.rolfskok.se
This casual "old favorite" Swedish-Med in Norrmalm is "still going strong" say some who cite fare that is "fresh and beguiling", an "excellent" staff and a modern, open-kitchen setting that caused a buzz when it was built in the late '80s; the less-enthused lament food that is "not always exciting", a once-bold minimalist design that is now only "alright" and downright "cramped" quarters.

☒ Sturehof ● *Swedish/Seafood* — 20 | 18 | 18 | E

Stureplan | Sturegallerian 42 | Stureplan 2 | (46-8) 440-5730 | www.sturehof.com
A "smart", "stylish crowd" of locals and "hip tourists" hails this "huge, fun place" "conveniently located" "in the hub of Stockholm's cool Stureplan district" for its "high-quality" "traditional Swedish" menu with a "seafood specialty" and "friendly, professional" staff (including "sommeliers knowledgeable" about the "nice wine list"); three "lively" bars and a generally "buzzing atmosphere" mean it's "too bustling" "for those who like quiet dining", but "lively" sorts love the "great people-watching" – especially from the "wonderful terrace in summertime."

☒ Ulriksdals Wärdshus *Swedish/International* — 26 | 23 | 26 | VE

Solna | Ulriksdals Slottspark | (46-8) 850-815 | www.ulriksdalswardshus.se
"Well worth every minute of travel" to its "out-of-the-way" but "choice location" – "in the country by a bay" within the "peaceful and relaxing" park of Ulriksdals Castle in Solna – this "gem" is "a rite of passage" "when visiting Stockholm" thanks to "excellent" Swedish-International cuisine (including a "fine smörgåsbord" served weekends and holidays); throw in a "superb wine cellar" and "formal" service from a "thoughtful and courteous staff" and it's no wonder fans insist this "favorite" is "perfect for festive occasions."

Vassa Eggen ☒ *International* — 26 | 17 | 23 | VE

Stureplan | Elite Hotel Stockholm Plaza | Birger Jarlsgatan 29 | (46-8) 216-169 | www.vassaeggen.com
Named after W. Somerset Maugham's novel *The Razor's Edge,* this "eggstravagant" venue in the Elite Hotel Stockholm Plaza in Stureplan showcases "stunning" International cuisine (gourmets "strongly recommend the six-course dinner with corresponding wines - a rare experience"); still, some find the food "overly fancy", even "a little pretentious", and the service somewhat "impersonal", while others opine that the "sterile" setting is "not very attractive"; N.B. a recent major renovation may outdate the above Decor score.

☒ Wedholms Fisk ☒ *Swedish/Seafood* — 28 | 21 | 26 | VE

Norrmalm | Nybrokajen 17 | (46-8) 611-7874 | www.wedholmsfisk.se
"Do not leave Stockholm before" visiting this "old-school" Swedish seafooder on Norrmalm's Nybrokajen wharf, where the "first-rate" "chef rightly trusts his ingredients" (namely, "fresh", "fantastic fish"), which results in "superb, simply prepared" "traditional dishes" that are "not too elaborate" but truly "exceptional"; perhaps "the decor is rather plain" and the "atmosphere quiet" (like a "hospital waiting room" some quip), but the "efficient" staff provides "excellent service" – yet another reason to "book in advance."

Venice

TOP FOOD RANKING

	Restaurant	Cuisine
27	Vini da Gigio	Venetian
26	Da Ivo	Tuscan/Venetian
	Osteria Da Fiore	Italian/Seafood
	Corte Sconta	Venetian/Seafood
25	Fortuny	Italian
	Club del Doge	Venetian/Mediterranean
	De Pisis*	Italian
	Osteria alle Testiere*	Italian/Seafood
	Al Covo	Seafood
24	Do Leoni	Italian/Seafood
	Fiaschetteria Toscana	Venetian
	La Cusina	Venetian/International
	Cip's Club	Venetian
	Hostaria da Franz	Venetian
	Ai Gondolieri	Venetian
	Antico Pignolo	Venetian/Seafood
23	La Terrazza	Italian/International
	Vecio Fritolin	Venetian/Seafood
	L'Osteria di Santa Marina	Venetian
	Il Ridotto	Italian/Seafood
	Antico Martini	Venetian
22	Do Forni	Venetian

Ai Gondolieri *Venetian*   24 | 19 | 23 | E

Dorsoduro | Fondamenta de l'Ospedaleto 366 | (39-041) 528-6396 |
www.aigondolieri.com

Carnivores adrift in this seafood-loving city head to this Venetian in residential Dorsoduro, near the Guggenheim foundation, where "only land
creatures are served", like the signature calf's liver, plus pork, lamb and
"wonderful risottos"; an "impeccable yet warm and friendly" staff presides over a "low-key, comfortable" rustic setting; N.B. closed Tuesdays.

Z Al Covo *Seafood*   25 | 20 | 23 | E

Castello | Campiello della Pescaria 3968 | (39-041) 522-3812

"Amazingly fresh", "superb" Adriatic seafood is the focus at this "warm,
welcoming" stalwart in Castello, run by a "great" Italo-American couple
with "high standards", chef Cesare Benelli and his wife, hostess/pastry
chef, "delightful Diane"; the room is small but flower-filled, and the terrace has a sweet view of the square; N.B. closed Wednesday–Thursday.

Antico Martini ◑ *Venetian*   23 | 22 | 22 | VE

San Marco | Campo San Fantin 1983 | (39-041) 522-4121 |
www.anticomartini.com

It's "ideal for dinner after the fat lady has sung at the Fenice Opera
house next door" is what un-PC admirers assert about this "wonder-

---

* Indicates a tie with restaurant above

fully located" "landmark" Venetian with "outrageously expensive" but "memorable" meals; a "refined crowd" fills a "lovely", rosy room with Persian carpets and paintings, plus there's a "romantic terrace" and a late-night piano bar; N.B. closed Tuesdays.

Antico Pignolo *Venetian/Seafood* | 24 | 22 | 25 | E |

San Marco | Calle dei Specchieri 451 | (39-041) 522-8123

"Convenient to St. Mark's Square" is this "good, dependable" Venetian seafooder with a "fantastic wine list", "outstanding service" and a big, beautiful garden for "delightful" outdoor dining; while wallet-watchers warn "bring buckets of euros", the philosophical simply shrug "but that's Venice."

Cip's Club *Venetian* | 24 | 25 | 26 | VE |

Isola della Guidecca | Hotel Cipriani | Isola della Giudecca 10 | (39-041) 520-7744 | www.hotelcipriani.com

Everyone wants to join this "wonderful", dinner-only club in the Cipriani with its "great view of St. Mark's Square" and the lagoon; "go only when the weather is good", "take the hotel's private power boat over" to the Isola della Giudecca, "sit outside on the terrace" and order something from the "tasty" Venetian menu along with "a glass of champagne"; of course, you'll "need a big bank roll", but for most it's a "must."

Club del Doge *Venetian/Mediterranean* | 25 | 26 | 26 | VE |

San Marco | Hotel Gritti Palace | Campo Santa Maria del Giglio 2467 | (39-041) 794-611 | www.starwoodhotels.com

"Why die when you can go to heaven here?" at this "stunning and elegant" Venetian-Med in the "grand" Hotel Gritti Palace that's "beautifully situated on the Grand Canal"; the "glorious view" from the veranda, "great food" and the "best service" add up to an extremely "expensive" but "transporting experience."

☑ Corte Sconta ⑤Ⓜ *Venetian/Seafood* | 26 | 17 | 20 | E |

Castello | Calle del Pestrin 3886 | (39-041) 522-7024 | www.ristorantibuonaaccoglienzavenezia.it

"Unfussy" but "exceptional seafood" from "passionate owners" is the lure at this "off-the-beaten-path" Venetian near the Arsenale, the city's historic shipyard; the round of briny appetizers is legendary and the *moeche* (soft-shell crab) "sublime", leading surveyors to say a "first-rate meal" makes for a "memorable" and expensive evening.

☑ Da Ivo ⑤ *Tuscan/Venetian* | 26 | 21 | 23 | VE |

San Marco | Ramo dei Fuseri 1809 | (39-041) 528-5004

It's "cool to arrive by gondola", but this "top" Tuscan-Venetian is also just a five-minute walk from St. Mark's Square; "gracious" chef-owner Ivo Natali prepares "wonderful" dishes like "huge, excellent *bistecca alla fiorentina*" or fresh Adriatic seafood, "pops out of the kitchen to ensure your pleasure" and presides over a "tiny, atmospheric, low-lit" "romantic" room that leads devotees to decree "just leave me here forever."

De Pisis *Italian* | 25 | 24 | 25 | VE |

San Marco | Il Palazzo at the Hotel Bauer | San Marco 1459 | (39-041) 520-7022 | www.bauervenezia.com

"The view, the food, the romance" and "the gracious service" leave sybarites sighing over this über-"expensive" Italian in the "grand"

18th-century Il Palazzo at the Hotel Bauer; the interior is opulent, and the "breathtaking terrace" vista of the Grand Canal and St. Mark's basin is better than namesake Italian artist De Pisis might have ever imagined.

Do Forni ❶ Venetian

| 22 | 19 | 19 | E |

San Marco | Calle dei Specchieri 457 | (39-041) 523-0663 | www.doforni.it

Surveyors are split on this big, pricey, "always-packed" Venetian classic "conveniently located" "just off Piazza San Marco"; loyalists like its huge menu with lots of "good, hearty" meat and seafood dishes and the dining rooms with burnished-wood-and-brass "Orient Express decor", but detractors declare the experience "crowded, loud" and "touristy."

Do Leoni Italian/Seafood

| 24 | 23 | 23 | E |

Schiavoni | Hotel Londra Palace | Riva degli Schiavoni 4171 | (39-041) 520-0533 | www.hotelondra.it

"Excellent cuisine and high-quality service" are the hallmarks of this Italian seafooder in the Hotel Londra Palace; the "beautiful" contemporary interior is stylish but soothing, and in warm weather the terrace is great for "people-watching" and a panoramic view that goes from the Grand Canal to the Lido.

Fiaschetteria Toscana Venetian

| 24 | 17 | 21 | E |

Cannaregio | San Giovanni Grisostomo 5719 | (39-041) 528-5281 | www.fiaschetteriatoscana.it

Name to the contrary (it was once an outlet for Tuscan wines), this is a true, family-run Venetian in Cannaregio, and one of the tops in the city, serving "divine dishes" like tagliolini with lobster, risottos and other "fantastic" fish-oriented appetizers and entrees; "the decor is better downstairs, but the staff is charming no matter where you sit" in the "warm", "winning" place; N.B. closed Tuesdays.

ⓩ Fortuny Italian
(fka Cipriani)

| 25 | 26 | 25 | VE |

Isola della Guidecca | Hotel Cipriani | Isola della Giudecca 10 | (39-041) 520-7744 | www.hotelcipriani.com

This "fabulous, famous" and "formal" Italian in the Hotel Cipriani recently changed its name, but still "has everything that makes Venice memorable – the view, the water, the romance"; the "impressive" experience starts with the "short private shuttle-boat ride from St. Mark's Square" and goes on to an "excellent staff" serving "exquisite" Italian cuisine in a "beautiful" room with mirrors or out on a "magical" terrace; even those who complain about "outrageous prices" urge "eat here once before you die just to say you did."

ⓩ Harry's Bar International/Venetian

| 19 | 19 | 18 | VE |

San Marco | Calle Vallaresso 1323 | (39-041) 528-5777 | www.cipriani.com

It's Cipriani's "original" 1931 "mythic bar", the birthplace of the Bellini and former Hemingway hang in San Marco, and it's still packing "tourists" in, however controversially: the mellow cite the International-Venetian's "history and scene" and shrug just stick to the signature cocktail, but the many who are no longer wild about Harry hiss "what a disappointment – we came in search of the legendary, found the ordinary and paid stratospherically."

	FOOD	DECOR	SERVICE	COST

Hostaria da Franz *Venetian*
24 | 18 | 25 | E

Castello | Fondamenta San Giuseppe 754 | (39-041) 522-0861 |
www.hostariadafranz.com

"They serve wonderful food and treat you like long-lost rich relatives"
at this father-and-son-run Venetian "gem" in Castello, near the
Biennale Gardens; "fresh, delicious" dishes, "superb service" and a
"great" summertime setting with outdoor tables along a tiny canal
make it a big "pleaser"; N.B. closed mid-November to mid-February.

Il Ridotto *Italian/Seafood*
23 | 20 | 21 | E

Castello | Camp San Filippo e Giacomo 4609 | (39-041) 520-8280

In a city "where a good meal can be difficult to find", this Italian seafood newcomer in Castello is a "gem" say those who cite "outstanding
tastes" and a "mind-blowing wine list"; the contemporary space is a
bit "cramped", but still the experience is "truly exceptional."

La Cusina *Venetian/International*
24 | 24 | 23 | VE

San Marco | The Westin Europa & Regina | Larga XXII Marzo 2159 |
(39-041) 240-0001 | www.westin.com/europaregina

This "very good" Venetian-International in The Westin Europa &
Regina boasts a "beautiful" backdrop – a "grand view of the Grand
Canal" – from its terrace and an interior that's a series of elegant, inti-
mate rooms filled with marble and Murano glass.

Z La Terrazza *Italian/International*
23 | 26 | 24 | VE

San Marco | Hotel Danieli | Riva degli Schiavoni 4196 | (39-041) 522-6480 |
www.starwoodhotels.com

Romantics say "request a window table" or eat outside on the terrace at
this "absolutely stunning" Italian-International with "spectacular views"
of the Grand Canal, the lagoon and the Island of San Giorgio from the
rooftop of the "opulent Hotel Danieli"; opinions on the food ("wonderful" vs. "average") and service ("terrific" vs. "stuffy") vary, but there's
consensus that the astronomical tab would be "VE even for Bill Gates."

L'Osteria di Santa Marina ⊠Ⓜ *Venetian*
23 | 20 | 20 | M

Castello | Campo Santa Marina 5911 | (39-041) 528-5239 |
www.osteriadisantamarina.it

At this chef-owned Venetian in Castello, there are "fairly priced", "delicious" traditional dishes as well as "beautifully presented imaginative combinations" with an emphasis on "exceptional seafood", all
backed up by an "extensive wine list"; the wooden interior is "charming", and there's a terrace for candlelit dining.

Osteria alle Testiere ⊠Ⓜ *Italian/Seafood*
25 | 18 | 24 | E

Castello | Calle del Mondo Novo 5801 | (39-041) 522-7220 |
www.osterialletestiere.it

An "outstanding" "place for lovers of good fish" is this popular, "minuscule" Italian off Campo Santa Maria Formosa; "wonderfully prepared", "intriguingly flavored" dishes are served by a "top-notch" staff
in a casual setting, making enthusiasts exclaim it's "not to be missed."

Z Osteria Da Fiore ⊠Ⓜ *Italian/Seafood*
26 | 22 | 24 | VE

San Polo | Calle del Scaleter 2202A | (39-041) 721-308 | www.dafiore.net

Among the very "best in Venice" is the Martini family's "innovative"
Italian piscine palace in San Polo that some wish could be the "location

of their last meal on earth"; "wonderful" cuisine that's "all about the ingredients", "gracious service" and a "comfortable yet elegant setting" add up to a feeling of "pure joy" for most; N.B. not to be confused with the similarly named Trattoria da Fiore near San Marco or Ristorante Osteria da Fiore in Santa Croce.

Vecio Fritolin Ⓜ *Venetian/Seafood*   23 | 22 | 23 | E

Rialto | Calle della Regina 2262 | (39-041) 522-2881 | www.veciofritolin.it

They are famous for their *fritolini* (little deep-fried fish) at this "top-notch", "classic" Venetian seafooder near the Rialto bridge, but there are also "delicious pastas", homemade breads and desserts, all served by a "helpful staff"; a "great" Northern Italian wine list and warm, wood-lined 16th-century interior add to the "always-a-pleasure" experience.

Ⓩ Vini da Gigio Ⓜ *Venetian*   27 | 19 | 25 | E

Cannaregio | Fondamenta San Felice 3628A | (39-041) 528-5140 | www.vinidagigio.com

A "little difficult to find" but "oh what a find" is this family-run Venetian in Cannaregio that's Voted No. 1 for Food in the city; "terrific" "simply and honestly prepared" meat and fish dishes and an "out-of-this-world wine list" are proferred in a "down-to-earth" setting by a "friendly" staff; it's "not the fanciest or most expensive" spot, but it is a "wonderful experience"; N.B. closed Monday and Tuesday.

Vienna

TOP FOOD RANKING

	Restaurant	Cuisine
28	Steirereck	Austrian/International
26	Imperial	Austrian/International
25	Coburg	Austrian/International
24	Demel	Austrian/International
	Walter Bauer	Austrian/International
	Mraz & Sohn	Austrian/International
	Korso bei der Oper	Austrian/French
	Kim Kocht	Asian/International
	Drei Husaren	Austrian/International
23	Julius Meinl am Graben	French/International
	Zum weiß. Rauchfangkehrer	Austrian
22	Österreicher im MAK	Viennese
	DO & CO	Austrian/International
	Plachutta	Austrian
	Goldene Zeiten	Chinese
21	Fabios	Italian/Mediterranean
	Indochine 21*	French/Vietnamese
	Mörwald im Ambassador	International
	Ella's	Greek
	Vestibül	Austrian/International
	Wrenkh*	Vegetarian
	Weinkellerei Artner	Austrian

Z Coburg 🗚Ⓜ *Austrian/International* | 25 | 22 | 23 | VE |

Innere Stadt | Palais Coburg | Coburgbastei 4 | (43-1) 5181-8800 |
www.palaiscoburg.at

"Expensive, but justifiably" so, this Austrian-International housed
in Innere Stadt's "breathtaking" Palais Coburg hotel showcases
chef Christian Petz's "excellent" cuisine, which is expertly paired
with "outstanding" selections from an "incredible wine cellar"; a
"young but well-trained" staff provides "courteous" service amid
the "elegant" surroundings, and for many satisfied diners, eating
out on the "beautiful" terrace that overlooks the Stadtpark is
an "unparalleled" experience.

Z Demel *Austrian/International* | 24 | 22 | 18 | E |

Innere Stadt | Kohlmarkt 14 | (43-1) 5351-7170 | www.demel.at

"Expand your waistline and thin out your wallet" at this "posh"
"pastry nirvana" on the Innere Stadt's tony Kohlmarkt, where a
"fantastic array" of "beautifully decorated" cakes (some 50 varieties) and other desserts are showcased in "world-famous window
displays"; the Austrian-International menu, by contrast, is "unim-
pressive", and service can be "iffy", so many prefer to just sit back
with some "fabulous" *"kaffee und kuchen"* and "watch master
bakers at work."

---

* Indicates a tie with restaurant above

	FOOD	DECOR	SERVICE	COST

DO & CO Albertina ◑ *Austrian/International* | 22 | 21 | 20 | E |

Innere Stadt | The Albertina | Albertinaplatz 1 | (43-1) 532-9669

DO & CO Stephansplatz ◑ *Austrian/International*

Innere Stadt | Stephansplatz 12 | (43-1) 535-3969
www.doco.com

A "reliable mix of Austrian and International cuisine" (including "superb Japanese" dishes) "prepared in front of you" along with "stunning views of St. Stephan's Cathedral" and the beautiful Stephansplatz attract a "well-dressed crowd" to this "see-and-be-seen" spot atop the Haas Haus in Innere Stadt; the "modern, urban" interior has a "NY feel", and the service is "competent" and "friendly"; N.B. it has a younger sibling in the Albertina museum.

☑ Drei Husaren *Austrian/International* | 24 | 23 | 23 | VE |

Innere Stadt | Weihburggasse 4 | (43-1) 5121-0920 |
www.drei-husaren.at

"Everything is top-drawer" at "Vienna's most famous" venue (circa 1933) in Innere Stadt near Stephansplatz, where you "feel like a Kaiser" (but you also better "have his bank account") thanks to "terrific" Austrian-International cuisine, including an "incredible hors d'oeuvre cart", "polite", "efficient" service and a "refined", "old-fashioned" setting with live music; while some find it "stuffy" and "not what it once was", for others it's still a "real experience."

Ella's *Greek* | 21 | 21 | 19 | M |

Innere Stadt | Judenplatz 9 | (43-1) 535-1577 | www.ellas.at
Owner Eleftherios Dermitzakis' new modern Hellenic in Innere Stadt has surveyors salivating over its "exceptional fare" (including "eyebrow-raising food combinations" such as foie gras with Granny Smith sorbet) and moderate prices; the "modern, minimalist" space features white tablecloths and black banquettes set against deep-red and orange walls, but in the summer "make a reservation for outside" on the "beautiful" terrace on Judenplatz.

Fabios ◑▣ *Italian/Mediterranean* | 21 | 21 | 20 | VE |

Innere Stadt | Tuchlauben 6 | (43-1) 532-2222 | www.fabios.at
"You can always meet the people who count" at this "hot spot" in Innere Stadt, just a short walk from Graben, where "authentic" Italian-Med cuisine is served by a "friendly" staff in a "trendy, modern" space with "large tinted windows", lots of "dark wood" and leather, and a "simple but elegant" lounge; still, some find the "masculine" setting "oppressive" and the service "overbearing", while wallet-watchers warn you're "paying for the atmosphere" and "good location."

Goldene Zeiten ◑ *Chinese* | 22 | 21 | 20 | E |

Innere Stadt | Dr. Karl Lueger-Platz 5 | (43-1) 513-4747 |
www.goldenezeiten.at
This Chinese may be the "best there is in Vienna" say supporters who praise the chef-owner, who peppers his "authentic" menu with elaborate Shanghainese and Sichuan dishes, which are complemented by an extensive wine list that sparkles with some rare Austrian vintages; recently relocated from the suburbs to Innere Stadt, the bright new modern digs feature butter-yellow walls and soaring ceilings that are punctuated by enormous red lamps.

	FOOD	DECOR	SERVICE	COST

Ⓩ Imperial *Austrian/International* ⟮ 26 | 26 | 27 | VE ⟯

Innere Stadt | Hotel Imperial | Kärntner Ring 16 | (43-1) 5011-0356 |
www.starwoodhotels.com

"You're treated like an emperor" at this "superlative" Austrian-
International housed in Innere Stadt's "grand" Hotel Imperial that provides "friendly", "flawless" service and "outstanding" cuisine in a
"plush", wood-paneled Victorian room with Hapsburg portraits; a "marvelous pianist adds to the mood" of "old-world elegance and charm",
making it a "slice of heaven on earth" for many – albeit at "hellish prices."

Indochine 21 ● *French/Vietnamese* ⟮ 21 | 19 | 19 | E ⟯

Innere Stadt | Stubenring 18 | (43-1) 513-7660 | www.indochine.at
Across the street from the Museum für Angewandte Kunst (MAK) in
Innere Stadt, this French-Vietnamese is a "nice change of pace" "from
Viennese and Italian cooking", offering "delectable" dishes with "unusual taste combinations" and "competent" service in a "trendy" yet
"comfortable" "cafelike" room with bamboo accents and Buddhist
icons; the only complaint is that it's "overpriced."

Julius Meinl am Graben Ⓩ *French/International* ⟮ 23 | 17 | 21 | E ⟯

Innere Stadt | Graben 19 | (43-1) 532-3334-6000 | www.meinlamgraben.at
For a "culinary adventure", a "cosmopolitan clientele" gravitates to
Graben and this "upmarket" French-International on the second
floor of "Vienna's leading gourmet store", which carries nearly
"everything the heart desires"; a "courteous staff" serves chef
Joachim Gradwohl's "innovative" fare in a "lovely" room with "stunning views" of the street, though some find it hard to "escape the fact
that it is a supermarket."

Kim Kocht ●Ⓩ Ⓜ *Asian/International* ⟮ 24 | 18 | 20 | E ⟯

Alsergrund | Lustkandlgasse 6 | (43-1) 319-0242 | www.kimkocht.at
A "gourmet experience" awaits at this boîte in Alsergrund near the
Volksoper, where chef-owner Sohyi Kim's "inventive" Asian-
International cuisine emphasizing organic ingredients is "unbelievably
tasty and healthy" and "needs are fulfilled immediately" by a "courteous" staff; "even first-time visitors feel at home" here – those who can
get into the "mini" (24-seat) space, that is, which leads some to gripe
that it's "impossible to get a table unless you know her well."

Ⓩ Korso bei der Oper *Austrian/French* ⟮ 24 | 25 | 25 | VE ⟯

Innere Stadt | Hotel Bristol | Mahlerstr. 5 | (43-1) 5151-6546 |
www.luxurycollection.com
The "best bet after the opera" is this "classic, opulent" nearby venue
in Innere Stadt's Hotel Bristol, where celeb chef "Reinhard Gerer has
reinvented Viennese cuisine" via his "superb" Austrian-French creations; service is "polished and professional", the wine list "excellent"
and the "beautifully appointed" room evokes "old Vienna" in all its
"elegance" – so "don't look at the prices and enjoy a special evening."

Mörwald im Ambassador *International* ⟮ 21 | 17 | 21 | E ⟯

Innere Stadt | Ambassador | Neuer Markt 5/Kärnter Str. 22 |
(43-1) 9616-1161 | www.moerwald.at
Freunden give a "big thank you" to the chef of this "wonderful" International that also offers a "first-class choice" of wines at "reasonable

prices" in the Ambassador hotel in Innere Stadt; moreover, the staff is "not intrusive" yet "always there" in the "upscale" space that's at once "modern" and "cozy"; P.S. "don't miss" the winter garden.

Mraz & Sohn ⊠ *Austrian/International*

24	21	19	E

Brigittenau | Wallensteinstr. 59 | (43-1) 330-4594 | www.mraz-sohn.at
This "excellent, high-quality" Austrian-International may be located in the downscale neighborhood of Brigittenau, but foodies flock to the 45-seater to sample the creations of chef Markus Mraz, a molecular gastronomy pioneer in Vienna; the "casual" setting belies such sophisticated touches as a legendary wine list and choice selection of cheeses.

Österreicher im MAK ❷ *Viennese*

22	23	21	E

Innere Stadt | Museum für Angewandte Kunst | Stubenring 5 | (43-1) 714-0121 | www.oesterreicherimmak.at
"One of the best chefs in Austria", Helmut Österreicher (ex the highly rated Steirereck), brings *his* culinary art to The MAK (Museum for Applied Arts) at this expansive venue, and the result is "well-done" "traditional and slightly modernized" Viennese food; the "wonderful location" is only exceeded by the "even greater interior design", which includes soaring ceilings and a chandelier made from 200 wine bottles.

Plachutta *Austrian*

22	14	19	E

Döbling | Heiligenstädterstr. 179 | (43-1) 370-4125
Hietzing | Auhofstr. 1 | (43-1) 8777-0870
Innere Stadt | Wollzeile 38 | (43-1) 512-1577
www.plachutta.at
"If you like *tafelspitz*, you can't go wrong" at this "dependable", "authentic" trio of Austrians where that signature Viennese dish and other "varieties of traditional boiled beef" are "unbeatable" if a bit "expensive"; you feel "like you're in good hands" with a "charming", "helpful" staff that presides over "simple", "bourgeois" digs that are "comfortable" even when they get "noisy and crowded."

☑ Steirereck ⊠ *Austrian/International*

28	25	26	VE

Landstrasse | Im Stadtpark | Am Heumarkt 2A | (43-1) 713-3168 | www.steirereck.at
"By far the best" restaurant in the city and voted No. 1 for Food here, this Landstrasse landmark is a "fairy-tale" experience, featuring chef Heinz Reitbauer's "exquisite" Austrian-International cuisine, "cheese and bread carts that put others to shame", an "excellent" wine cellar and "first-class" service; the move in 2005 to its current Stadtpark address "has been a fantastic success", thanks to the "exquisite" renovation of a century-old pavilion into a "knockout" location with "no shortage of space."

Vestibül ⊠ *Austrian/International*

21	24	20	E

Innere Stadt | Dr. Karl Lueger Ring 2 | (43-1) 532-4999 | www.vestibuel.at
Blessed with a "perfect location" in the Burgtheater (in what was formerly the emperor's secret entrance), this Innere Stadt Austrian-International (a sibling of Hansen) is "ideal for business meetings and impressing foreigners" thanks to its "sensational" "marble ballroom" interior and "quiet, classy" ambiance; still, surveyors are split over the cuisine – while some feel it "doesn't justify the prices", to others it's a "pleasant surprise."

	FOOD	DECOR	SERVICE	COST

☑ **Walter Bauer** ⓢ *Austrian/International* — 24 | 18 | 26 | E

Innere Stadt | Sonnenfelsgasse 17 | (43-1) 512-9871
Regulars have "never been disappointed" by this "hidden gem" in
a small medieval house (circa 1505) "on a quiet street" near
Stephansplatz in one of the oldest parts of Innere Stadt; a "wide-
ranging" Austrian-International menu is complemented by a "superb
wine list", an "attentive staff" and an "intimate" setting.

Weinkellerei Artner *Austrian* — 21 | 20 | 18 | E

Wieden | Floragasse 6 | (43-1) 503-5033 | www.artner.co.at
The Artner family makes up for an "unglamorous" Wieden location
with a "creative" regional menu that's a "welcome relief from typical
Austrian cuisine", as well as "great goat cheese" and wines from their
farm and winery in Höflein; the "brightly furnished", "modern" room is
an "attractive place to eat and watch folks" in a "relaxing" atmosphere, although sometimes service is "not very attentive."

Wrenkh ⓢ *Vegetarian* — 21 | 14 | 19 | M

Innere Stadt | Bauernmarkt 10 | (43-1) 533-1526 | www.wrenkh.at
Chef-owner Christian Wrenkh's meatless cuisine is "as good as vegetarian can be" swear fans of this Innere Stadt spot near Stephansplatz,
which offers a "wide selection" of flesh-free fare, including "salad
dressings that are poetry" to the palate, as well as a "small but good
wine list"; the '90s decor is "nothing out of the ordinary", but the
"friendly" staff is "witty" and "patient."

Zum weißen Rauchfangkehrer ⓢ Ⓜ *Austrian* — 23 | 20 | 23 | E

Innere Stadt | Weihburggasse 4 | (43-1) 512-3471 |
www.weisser-rauchfangkehrer.at
For a "taste of Vienna", fans tout this "lovely old place" (circa 1844)
near Stephansplatz in Innere Stadt offering "outstanding" organic
"takes on traditional Viennese fare"; it's a bit "pricey", but "high-
quality" *essen,* "personable, professional service" and a "classic setting" with lots of "country-style" "charm" make it "worth a return visit"
for many; N.B. live piano music daily.

Warsaw

TOP FOOD RANKING

	Restaurant	Cuisine
25	Rest. Polska Tradycja	Polish
	Dom Polski	Polish
23	U Kucharzy	Polish
	Parmizzano's	Italian
22	Malinowa	Polish
	Michel Moran Bistro/Paris	French
	Belvedere	International/Polish
21	Qchnia Artystyczna	International
	Boathouse	Italian/Mediterranean
	Oriental, The	Asian/Sushi
19	Chianti	Italian
	La Bohème	International
18	Santorini	Greek
	Dom Rest. Gessler	Polish
17	U Fukiera	Polish
16	Blue Cactus	Southwestern/Tex-Mex

Ƶ Belvedere *International/Polish*　　22 | 26 | 23 | E

Srodmiescie | ul. Agrykola 1 | (48-22) 841-2250 | www.belvedere.com.pl
After "a welcome revamp" of its "stupendous location" – a "grand", "glass-facaded" 19th-century "orangery in Lazienki Park" with an "adjacent open-air terrace" overlooking "lush grounds" – this "classic" "fine-dining" venue in Srodmiescie is now not only "posh but trendy", attracting those who "enjoy people-watching" while "indulging" in "well-executed" Polish-International fare; it's an "excellent" place "for that special dinner", as long as "you have money to throw around."

Ƶ Blue Cactus *Southwestern/Tex-Mex*　　16 | 15 | 14 | M

Mokotów | ul. Zajaczkowska 11 | (48-22) 851-2323 | www.bluecactus.pl
Amigos assess this "usually crowded" Southwestern spot in Mokotów as "a fun place to get a bite to eat and have some drinks with friends" thanks to the "Latin flair" of its "good Tex-Mex" eats and its "lively" atmosphere; enemigos, though, judge it "a bore", blaming "food that's mediocre at best", "loud decor" and a staff that makes "you feel not wanted."

Boathouse *Italian/Mediterranean*　　21 | 17 | 17 | E

Saska Kepa | Wal Miedzeszynski 389a | (48-22) 616-3223 | www.boathouse.pl
"Ideal for groups" and families, this spacious "haven" "right on the river" in Saska Kepa is "a lovely place to dine" on "excellent" Italian-Med fare; it's especially "noteworthy" "in the summer" for the "charming outdoor seating" "with its pretty garden views" – just "beware the mosquitoes!"

Chianti *Italian*　　19 | 19 | 20 | M

Srodmiescie | ul. Foksal 17 | (48-22) 828-0222 | www.kregliccy.pl
"Run by well-known restaurateurs" Agnieszka Kreglicka and Marcin Kreglicki, this "reliable", "simple trattoria" "conveniently located" in

	FOOD	DECOR	SERVICE	COST

Srodmiescie, in the hip bar district next to Nowy Ýöwiat, is "still providing quality Italian fare" such as "good homemade pastas" and "one of the best tiramisus in town"; still, a few sigh that it "has run out of steam", saying there are now "better" venues in Warsaw for food from The Boot.

⛷ Dom Polski *Polish*   25 | 21 | 21 | E

Saska Kepa | ul. Francuska 11 | (48-22) 616-2488 | www.restauracjadompolski.pl

"If you want to taste real", "traditional Polish" fare, "look no further" than this "fabulous restaurant" in Saska Kepa, a beautiful residential area on the Vistula River's right bank; it's "still one of the best" of its kind, and a "great place to get to know" the cuisine thanks to a kitchen that "excels at old", "tried-and-true recipes" ("particularly" the "excellent desserts") – just "be hungry when you come, as the portions are big"; N.B. a recent expansion and the addition of a winter garden may outdate the above Decor score.

Dom Restauracyjny Gessler *Polish*   18 | 24 | 20 | E

Stare Miasto | Rynek Starego Miasta 21/21a | (48-22) 887-0344 | www.gessler.pl

Its "excellent location" in Stare Miasto, "at the very center" of the Old Town, and a "unique setting" of "low-beamed rooms" in a 16th-century house is what "pulls in" the crowds of "mostly wealthy" travelers at this "obviously touristy" spot; but since its "hearty Polish" fare is only "alright", foodies feel "let down by the quality."

La Bohème ● *International*   19 | 22 | 19 | E

Srodmiescie | Plac Teatralny 1 | (48-22) 692-0681 | www.laboheme.com.pl

Blessed with a "spectacular location", a stone's throw from the National Theatre, a "sophisticated" setting and "nice terrace", this Srodmiescie "oasis" "crowded with businessmen, politicians" and artists offers "satisfying" International fare and an "extensive wine list"; supporters say it's "simply one of the finest overall dining experiences" around, but cynics snipe it's "too expensive for the quality of the food."

⛷ Malinowa *Polish*   22 | 21 | 27 | VE

Srodmiescie | Le Royal Méridien Bristol | ul. Krakowskie Przedmiescie 42/44 | (48-22) 551-1000 | www.starwoodhotels.com

An "intelligent staff" oversees this "very expensive", "elegant restaurant in the famous" Le Royal Méridien Bristol hotel in Srodmiescie, where the mostly "traditional" Polish menu features "some modern variations"; a few find it "a bit unexciting", saying "Warsaw has developed more interesting [venues] in recent years", but a majority reports an experience "worth repeating"; P.S. "Sunday brunch is fabulous."

Michel Moran Bistro de Paris ⊠ *French*   22 | 16 | 19 | E

Srodmiescie | pl. Pilsudskiego 9 | (48-22) 826-0107 | www.restaurantbistrodeparis.com

Amis assert *"mercis beaucoup"* are due to this Srodmiescie French in the rear of the National Theatre, where "talented" chef Michel Moran prepares "very good" cuisine that emphasizes seafood and relies on "excellent ingredients"; the "elegant" wood-paneled setting provides a view of Norman Foster's Metropolitan building, and in season the impressive, columned terrace makes for a prestigious perch that comes with a "charming summer menu."

Oriental, The *Asian/Sushi*

21 | 19 | 22 | E

Srodmiescie | Sheraton Warsaw Hotel | ul. Prusa 2 | (48-22) 450-6705 | www.sheraton.pl

The "most-attentive service" from a "staff that couldn't be more helpful" "makes meals exceptional" at this "good bet" situated in Srodmiescie's Sheraton Hotel; folks who "walk in to see what smells so delicious" usually "stay" for the "authentic", "quality" Asian fare (as well as sushi) served in a "pleasant", "atmospheric" space.

⧣ Parmizzano's *Italian*

23 | 18 | 21 | E

Srodmiescie | The Marriott Warsaw | al. Jerozolimskie 65/79 | (48-22) 630-5096 | www.marriott.com/wawpl

"Forget the usual hotel-type places" – this Srodmiescie spot "is a true gem of an Italian restaurant", "in spite of being located" on the second floor of The Marriott Warsaw, thanks to a staff providing "great service", a "chef who's really passionate" about turning out "heavenly" dishes and a setting that reminds some of "a nice, quiet place in Sicily"; P.S. business sorts also say "it's a safe choice" for an "excellent light lunch."

Qchnia Artystyczna *International*

21 | 21 | 17 | E

Srodmiescie | al. Ujazdowskie 6 | (48-22) 625-7627 | www.qchnia.pl

Supporters of this "stylish" Srodmiescie venue "set in Ujazdowskie Castle" (home to the Center for Contemporary Art) say it possesses an "artistic" kitchen that produces "imaginative" International dishes within a "vibrant" space with "a great view of the park"; it's "popular with the hip and wealthy" for a "lovely lunch" or "a romantic dinner", even though some say "the service should be more professional and less arty."

⧣ Restauracja Polska Tradycja *Polish*

25 | 25 | 25 | E

Mokotów | ul. Belwederska 18a | (48-22) 840-0901 | www.restauracjatradycja.pl

"Outstanding in every way", "this fabulous find on a quiet little street" in Mokotów, "an elegant residential area", is rated No. 1 for Food in Warsaw on the strength of its "authentic and oh-so-good" "traditional Polish cuisine", which is complemented by a "great wine list" and "first-class" staff; its "magical setting", "a beautiful old" renovated "villa close to Lazienki Park", is always "bustling with people enjoying themselves", making it "a wonderful place for a romantic dinner, business" gathering or any "special-occasion" "celebration."

Santorini *Greek*

18 | 18 | 19 | M

Saska Kepa | ul. Egipska 7 | (48-22) 672-0525 | www.kregliccy.pl

"If you've a hankering for" Hellenic fare, "check out this" "charming", "established" spot in Saska Kepa that offers "a real taste of Greece" that includes a "good choice of meze"; visually, its "first impression is not good", but insiders say look past the facade of its "ugly communist-style building", as "inside" awaits a "nice" blue-and-white taverna that brings "a touch of the Mediterranean to Eastern Europe."

	FOOD	DECOR	SERVICE	COST

U Fukiera *Polish*   17 | 23 | 18 | E

Stare Miasto | Rynek Starego Miasta 27 | (48-22) 831-1013 | www.ufukiera.pl

Given its "beautiful" "central" setting in Stare Miasto, it comes as no surprise this "upscale", "atmospheric place" "has become a touristy" "favorite" of "rich" travelers, who tout its "attentive service" and Polish menu featuring "a fabulous selection of game"; still, foes who "expected more" assert it's "too expensive" and "banks on location" too heavily.

Z U Kucharzy ☉ *Polish*   23 | 20 | 21 | E

Srodmiescie | Hotel Europejski | ul. Ossolinskich 7 | (48-22) 826-7936 | www.gessler.pl

At this new Polish venue set in the vast kitchen of the Hotel Europejski, which is currently closed for renovation, the chefs not only prepare "delicious" meals out in the open (using organic ingredients from the restaurant's own farm), they serve them in a series of white-tiled rooms as well; but surveyors are split on whether they find the overall experience here "unique" or "uneven."

Zurich

TOP FOOD RANKING

	Restaurant	Cuisine
27	Petermann's Kunststuben	French
26	Rest. Français/Le Pavillon	French/Mediterranean
	Lindenhofkeller	Swiss/International
24	Ginger	Japanese
	Casa Aurelio	Spanish
	Ristorante Orsini	Italian
23	Casa Ferlin	Italian
	Sala of Tokyo*	Japanese
	Asian Place	Asian
	Sein	International
	Accademia	Italian
	Emilio*	Spanish
	Il Giglio	Italian
22	Widder	International
	Rive Gauche	Mediterranean
	Zentraleck	International
	Ristorante Bindella	Italian
	Blu	Mediterranean/Italian
	Haus Hiltl	Vegetarian/Indian
	Veltliner Keller	Swiss/French
	Kronenhalle	Swiss/French
21	Sonnenberg	Swiss

Accademia Ⓢ Italian

23 | 18 | 23 | VE

Kreis 4 | Rotwandstr. 62 | (41-44) 241-4202

"One of Zurich's stalwarts", this "classic Italian" in Kreis 4 features "superb food" (including "extremely good pastas") made from "fresh ingredients" and offered amid "authentic decor"; expect "excellent service as well", even if a few feel "the formal staff" is "a little stuffy" and perhaps "slightly supercilious if you don't arrive dressed in an Armani suit"; just be warned that the "exceptional food comes at an exceptional price" – leading the cost conscious to exclaim "ouch!"

Asian Place ⓈAsian

23 | 17 | 20 | E

Glattbrugg | Renaissance Zurich Hotel | Talackerstr. 1 | (41-44) 874-5721 | www.asianplace.ch

The descriptive "name says it all" about this "delightful surprise" located "in the Renaissance Zurich Hotel, near the airport" in Glattbrugg, that makes "you feel as if you were in Asia" with its "wide selection" of "exciting", "exotic dishes" "from Japan, China and Thailand", all of which are "graciously served" by a "friendly and efficient" staff; some consider the prices "inflated", but others say they're "justified by the quality of the food", not to mention the "tranquil" location.

---

* Indicates a tie with restaurant above

	FOOD	DECOR	SERVICE	COST

Blu *Mediterranean/Italian*

22 | 23 | 16 | E

Kreis 2 | Seestr. 457 | (41-44) 488-6565

With its "beautiful setting" and "modern but charming" decor featuring multi-"meter-high windows", this Kreis 2 spot boasts "wonderful views of Lake Zurich", not to mention a "lovely" menu of Med-Italian specialties; still, critics among its "trendy crowd" contend that the "young, overtaxed" staff "does its best, but service is not really at the level it should be for the cost."

☑ Brasserie Lipp *French*

18 | 17 | 16 | E

Kreis 1 | Uraniastr. 9 | (41-43) 888-6666 | www.brasserie-lipp.ch

Like its famed Parisian namesake, this "must-see" spot in Kreis 1 is "a true French brasserie" in every respect – from its "authentic" decor, "suitable furnishings" and "high noise level" to its "nostalgic bar", "big wine list" and "dependable" (if "expected") menu sporting "specialties from *plateau de fruits de mer* to Alsatian choucroute"; most find it "enjoyable", even if the fact that it's "always crowded" means you may "have to wait and wait."

☑ Casa Aurelio ☒ *Spanish*

24 | 17 | 18 | E

Kreis 5 | Langstr. 209 | (41-44) 272-7744 | www.casaaurelio.ch

"There's always something special about eating at" this "Spanish place in Zurich's" Kreis 5, which is perennially "popular" with an interesting mix of locals and celebrities for its "substantial portions" of "outstanding food" and "nice wine list" offered by an "obliging staff"; some say the environment is "somewhat noisy" and "slightly worn-out", but then sometimes "patrons are the best decor."

Casa Ferlin ☒ *Italian*

23 | 16 | 21 | E

Kreis 6 | Stampfenbachstr. 38 | (41-44) 362-3509 | www.casaferlin.ch

"It's been around a long time, but it holds up well" is the consensus on this family-owned Italian in Kreis 6, where "large portions" of "excellent traditional dishes", particularly "fresh pasta" like "the best homemade ravioli", are served by an "attentive" staff; some find the decor "dark and dated", but devotees declare "that's just part of the charm."

Emilio *Spanish*

23 | 9 | 18 | E

Kreis 4 | Zweierstr. 9 | (41-44) 241-8321 | www.restaurant-emilio.ch

A genuine "Spanish feel" pervades this Kreis 4 spot that "always delivers the same good quality" with its authentic fare, including "paella that can't be beat" and some of "the best chicken in the world" (which "is worth the nearly obscene price"); still, the "sometimes not-so-attentive service" "could be better" – and as for the "rather poor" decor, "well . . ."

☑ Ginger ☒ *Japanese*

24 | 18 | 19 | VE

Kreis 8 | Seefeldstr. 62 | (41-44) 422-9509 | www.shinsen.ch

Some of the "very best and freshest sushi in town" can be found at this "small", "cool" Japanese venue in Kreis 8, where "creative" chefs fashion "great" "authentic" fare; sit at the H-shaped bar and choose from the fin fare that "revolves before you" on a carousel or is "obligingly served" to you in one of the few booths; remember, though, that it all comes "at a premium price", and those "little plates add up quickly."

	FOOD	DECOR	SERVICE	COST

Haus Hiltl *Vegetarian/Indian* | 22 | 12 | 16 | M

Kreis 1 | Sihlstr. 28 | (41-44) 227-7000 | www.hiltl.ch

"Europe's first vegetarian restaurant", this "definite don't-miss" "institution" with an Indian accent in Kreis 1 "opened its doors in 1898" and has since been serving a "marvelous selection" of "healthy" dishes that "make eating without meat a pleasure"; the "approachable staffers" help novices navigate the "reasonably priced" International menu, even though they're "often stressed" by the "hectic", crowded setting; N.B. a recent renovation may outdate the above Decor score.

Il Giglio 🄵 *Italian* | 23 | 16 | 19 | E

Kreis 4 | Weberstr. 14 | (41-44) 242-8597 | www.ilgiglio.ch

Locals "love this small, intimate [Southern] Italian place" in Kreis 4 for its "nice, clean" dishes, many of which are accented with tomatoes imported from Calabria; the decor may be "nothing special", but the "pleasant" staff always provides "polite service"; P.S. look for "excellent wines of the month at moderate prices."

🄵 Kronenhalle *Swiss/French* | 22 | 24 | 22 | VE

Kreis 1 | Rämistr. 4 | (41-44) 262-9900 | www.kronenhalle.com

"The owner's splendid collection" of art treasures including "original works by Picasso, Chagall and Matisse" "makes for a wonderful atmosphere" at this "pricey" "perennial favorite" in Kreis 1, but there are "masterpieces on the plate", as well, in the form of "fabulous traditional Swiss-French fare" "elegantly served" by an "expert" staff; P.S. to watch "celebrities fight for tables", "get a seat on the main floor."

🄵 Lindenhofkeller 🄵 *Swiss/International* | 26 | 20 | 24 | E

Kreis 1 | Pfalzgasse 4 | (41-44) 211-7071 | www.lindenhofkeller.ch

"Outstanding meals" await at this "upmarket" venue in Kreis 1, where the "very good wine list" has "depth and breadth" and the "excellent" menu "changes with the seasons", but always features "imaginative nouvelle Swiss"-International fare that's "more sophisticated than the typical" indigenous cuisine; additionally, the "pleasant, competent" staff is "amenable to customers' wishes", leading some who love "to linger" within the "cozy, comfortable" interior or in the "beautiful garden" to quip "when can I move in?"

🄵 Petermann's Kunststuben 🄵🄼 *French* | 27 | 24 | 26 | VE

Küsnacht | Seestr. 160 | (41-44) 910-0715 | www.kunststuben.com

"Absolutely one of the finest restaurants in Switzerland", this "splendid" French "classic" is "first rate in every way" and ranks No. 1 for Food in Zurich; "outstanding cook Horst Petermann" maintains the "highest standards", producing "unbelievably good culinary" creations that are "almost too beautiful to eat", while "his wife, Iris, a wonderful hostess", presides over the "special" staff and "intimate setting"; all told, it's "an unforgettable dining experience" that's "worth the short trip to Küsnacht" – just be warned that "the bill will also be unforgettable."

🄵 Restaurant Français/ Le Pavillon *French/Mediterranean* | 26 | 23 | 26 | VE

Kreis 1 | Baur au Lac | Talstr. 1 | (41-44) 220-5020 | www.bauraulac.ch

"Top-class all the way", these "exceptional" Kreis 1 spaces, "in one of Europe's classiest hotels", are facets of a single "Zurich institution", offering "outstanding meals" of "grand" fare, along with an "excellent wine selection"; from October to April, an "extremely attentive staff" presides over the "relaxing, elegant" main dining room and its French cuisine, then from April to October guests order from the Med menu "in the heavenly pavilion" with "a view of the garden and canal"; yes, it's very "expensive", but "you get what you pay for and then some."

Ristorante Bindella *Italian*   22 | 17 | 21 | E

Kreis 1 | In Gassen 6 | (41-44) 221-2546 | www.bindella.ch
"Centrally located" in Kreis 1, this "very nice" venue "is convenient after shopping", "popular with the business crowd" and "always a good place for friends or couples" thanks to a "frequently changing menu" of "delicious" Northern Italian fare that's prepared "with Swiss attention to detail"; an "extensive wine list", "friendly" staff and "smart" surroundings boasting "subdued lighting" add to the experience.

Ristorante Orsini *Italian*   24 | 19 | 25 | VE

Kreis 1 | Hotel Savoy Baur en Ville Paradeplatz | Am Münsterhof 25 | (41-44) 215-2727 | www.savoy-baurenville.ch
"Superb service" from an "attentive" "old-school" staff "satisfies" visitors to this "reliable" "businessman-and-banker hangout" in Kreis 1's Savoy Baur en Ville hotel, while "cuisine purists" praise the kitchen for its "no-nonsense" Italian fare, calling it nothing short of "splendid"; factor in the "excellent selections" on its "good wine list" and the "bright, classic decor" of its "formal" dining room and you'll see why patrons predict "you will not be disappointed."

Rive Gauche ⊠ *Mediterranean*   22 | 22 | 22 | VE

Kreis 1 | Baur au Lac | Talstr. 1 | (41-44) 220-5020 | www.agauche.ch
As "the informal restaurant for the very formal Baur au Lac hotel", this Mediterranean draws a mix of local professionals, affluent guests and celebrities to its "central location" in Kreis 1; with its "classic" clubby decor and an "excellent" selection of "inventive cuisine" that emphasizes light seasonal dishes and is "served with Swiss efficiency and grace", no wonder that for many it's a "favorite place to dine in Zurich."

Sala of Tokyo ⊠Ⓜ *Japanese*   23 | 15 | 19 | VE

Kreis 5 | Limmatstr. 29 | (41-44) 271-5290 | www.sala-of-tokyo.ch
"Quality and presentation" "make lunch or dinner always a great experience" at this "traditional" spot in Kreis 5; of course there's "excellent sushi", but the "varied" menu also features "all the Japanese specialties (such as shabu-shabu, sukiyaki, robatayaki, tempura)"; many consider the decor "nice", but even those who see it as merely "ok" concede it "could be worse" – and the "ever-so-charming presence of [chef/co-owner] Sala" Ruch-Fukuoka adds to the ambiance.

Sein ●⊠ *International*   23 | 20 | 21 | E

Kreis 1 | Schützengasse 5 | (41-44) 221-1065
"Innovative" International fare, "luxurious" tapas at the bar and "real Swiss service" cater to dueling crowds at this Kreis 1 restaurant/bar: "suits and ties" at lunch vs. hip types at night; a "bold, beautiful and bright" vibe permeates this vibrant mirrored red space, luring in all who just want to be "Sein."

	FOOD	DECOR	SERVICE	COST

Sonnenberg *Swiss*

| 21 | 22 | 21 | VE |

Kreis 7 | Hitzigweg 15 | (41-44) 266-9797 | www.sonnenberg-zh.ch
A "favorite", this "winner" "on a hillside overlooking the city and lake" in Kreis 7 scores on all counts – from its "majestic views" (especially "magnificent" "at sunset") and "star chef Jacky Donatz's" "excellent" cuisine ("a testimony to Swiss perfectionism") to the "obliging service"; P.S. "the place belongs to FIFA", the Fédération Internationale de Football Association, so "you may see Europe's soccer heroes" at the next table.

Veltliner Keller 🗷 *Swiss/French*

| 22 | 23 | 23 | E |

Kreis 1 | Schlüsselgasse 8 | (41-44) 225-4040 | www.veltlinerkeller.ch
"Everything is just right" at this "charming" Kreis 1 venue "in a medieval townhouse" "near St. Peter's church in Old Town": the "classy ambiance" of its dark-wood setting replete with "beautiful carvings" is matched by the "formal but warm service" from its "professional" staff, and the "delicious, if heavy", "traditional Swiss-French food" (including "good regional selections") "wins you over with its simple style", leading acolytes to assert that "the price is irrelevant."

🗷 Widder *International*

| 22 | 23 | 23 | VE |

Kreis 1 | Widder Hotel | Rennweg 7 | (41-44) 224-2526 | www.widderhotel.ch
A "classy" hotel composed of a series of historic Kreis 1 townhouses that "blend modern and old superbly" provides the "lovely setting" for this "upmarket" "fine-dining" venue; its "true professionals" "take pride in what they do, and it shows" in the "discreet service" and "great menu" of "excellent" International dishes they provide; with such "all-around quality", it's no wonder the place is "popular" – and a visit to the Widder "Bar afterward", with its live piano music and "phenomenal jazz" concerts twice a year, is "the cherry on the cake."

Zentraleck 🗷 *International*

| 22 | 20 | 21 | E |

Kreis 3 | Zentralstr. 161 | (41-44) 461-0800 | www.zentraleck.ch
The young chef/co-owner of this small Kreis 3 International concocts "creative" dishes that are matched with "excellent wines" and served by a "flawless" staff in a simple, "cozy" setting of polished wood set against a sea of white; in sum, most proponents pronounce it a "Swiss delight!"

UNITED STATES
RESTAURANT
DIRECTORY

Atlanta

TOP FOOD RANKING

	Restaurant	Cuisine
29	Bacchanalia	American
28	Quinones Room	American
	Rathbun's	American
	Ritz/Buckhead Din. Rm.	French/Mediterranean
27	Aria	American
	Bone's	Steak
	Tamarind Seed	Thai
	Park 75	American
	di Paolo	Italian
26	Floataway Cafe	French/Italian
	MF Sushibar	Japanese
	McKendrick's Steak	Steak
	Taka	Japanese
	Nan Thai	Thai
	Chops/Lobster Bar	Seafood/Steak
	JOËL	French
	La Grotta	Italian
	Madras Saravana	Indian/Vegetarian
	New York Prime	Steak
	Restaurant Eugene	American
	Sotto Sotto	Italian

Z Aria ⑤ *American*   27 | 25 | 25 | E

Buckhead | 490 E. Paces Ferry Rd. NE (Maple Dr.) | 404-233-7673 |
www.aria-atl.com

"Gerry Klaskala continues to be at the top of his game" at this
Buckhead "beauty" where he creates "amazing" New American
cuisine "with a soul", while pastry chef Kathryn King's desserts are
some of the "best in town"; the "gorgeous" space (which includes
a "cozy" patio) has recently been renovated, and though the scene
can get "way too loud" at times, "superb" service makes "you feel
like a million bucks"; it's "expensive" too, but "you get what
you pay for."

Z Bacchanalia ⑤ *American*   29 | 25 | 28 | VE

Westside | Westside Mktpl. | 1198 Howell Mill Rd. (bet. 14th St. &
Huff Rd.) | 404-365-0410 | www.starprovisions.com

"Any conversation about Atlanta's best" must include this "seamless" Westside New American – voted both the city's Most Popular
and No. 1 for Food – with a "big-time wow factor" that "could make
a rainy Tuesday seem like a special occasion"; "husband-and-wife
team" Anne Quatrano and Clifford Harrison's "focused" cuisine
virtually guarantees "gastronomic ecstasy" that's considered a
"bargain despite the price", and though the "refined" warehouse
space has a "laid-back" atmosphere, the "sublime" service
("choreographed like a ballet") provides further evidence of its
"top-tier status."

	FOOD	DECOR	SERVICE	COST

☒ Bone's Restaurant *Steak*   27 | 22 | 26 | E

Buckhead | 3130 Piedmont Rd. (Peachtree Rd.) | 404-237-2663 |
www.bonesrestaurant.com

"Impeccable" right "down to the bone", this "carnivore central" in
Buckhead delivers a "wow experience" "time and again" with "classic"
steaks "Fred Flintstone would die for", "generous sides", "big, cold
drinks" and a "phone book" of a wine list; "polished" servers and "fabulous bartenders" "take excellent care" of the crowd of "serious
business-lunchers", "power players" and others in a "plush red", "old-
world" setting that's "drenched in testosterone" as well as "tremendous history and personality"; this "local legend lives on."

☒ Chops/Lobster Bar *Seafood/Steak*   26 | 24 | 24 | E

Buckhead | Buckhead Plaza | 70 W. Paces Ferry Rd. (Peachtree Rd.) |
404-262-2675 | www.buckheadrestaurants.com

A "bit of heaven on earth" for "carnivores and their fish-loving brethren",
this "consistently spectacular" Buckhead Life production offers "exemplary" steaks and "unbeatable seafood", paired with a "phenomenal
wine list", and "pampering" service that "makes you feel like royalty";
there's a "good bar scene" peopled by the "'in' crowd" in the "elegant",
"man's man" chophouse upstairs, while the "dungeon of deliciousness"
downstairs boasts an "awesome" "Grand Central Station"–inspired look.

di Paolo Ⓜ *Italian*   27 | 21 | 25 | M

Alpharetta | Rivermont Sq. | 8560 Holcomb Bridge Rd. (Nesbit Ferry Rd.) |
770-587-1051 | www.dipaolorestaurant.com

The "magnificent obsession" of a "loyal army of regulars", Atlanta's
No. 1 Italian is "worth the drive to the end of the earth" (i.e. Alpharetta)
for "superb" Northern Italian creations from an open kitchen that'll
"knock your socks off" and "impeccable" service; there's a "surprise
with every detail" in the "relaxing" dining room, and though the "old
strip-mall location doesn't do it justice", for many it's the "perfect
choice for any occasion"; N.B. a post-Survey redo of the interior is not
reflected in the above Decor score.

Floataway Cafe Ⓢ Ⓜ *French/Italian*   26 | 22 | 24 | E

Emory | Floataway Bldg. | 1123 Zonolite Rd. NE (bet. Briarcliff &
Johnson Rds.) | 404-892-1414 | www.starprovisions.com

Intowners "never tire of" this "foodies' delight", the "more informal"
dinner-only sibling of Bacchanalia and Quinones that wins props for
"deceptively simple" and "stunning" French-Italian cuisine emphasizing "local organic produce", an "eclectic" wine list and "gracious" service; nestled in an "oasis of artists' studios" amid an "industrial
wasteland" near Emory, the "sleek" space with "ethereal curtains" cultivates an "energetic" vibe – if they could "just get rid of the noise", it
"would be the perfect place."

🆕 French American Brasserie Ⓢ *American/French*   - | - | - | M
(aka F.A.B.)

Downtown | Southern Company | 30 Ivan Allen Jr. Blvd. (W. Peachtree St.) |
404-266-1440 | www.fabatlanta.com

Fans of the late Brasserie Le Coze take note: chef Kaighn Raymond has
returned from NYC (where he trained with Le Bernardin's Eric Ripert)

to take the kitchen reins at this Downtown restaurant offering an expanded menu of New American and French brasserie fare; cheery tiles, lampposts and columns were resurrected from the original venue, and the expansive multilevel art nouveau space also includes street level and rooftop outdoor dining.

JOËL ☒ *French* | 26 | 26 | 24 | E |

Buckhead | The Forum | 3290 Northside Pkwy. NW (W. Paces Ferry Rd.) | 404-233-3500 | www.joelrestaurant.com

Joël Antunes is a "true artist" creating "brilliant" French cuisine in the "lavishly appointed kitchen" of his Buckhead establishment; the food is paired with a "formidable" wine list and service that strikes a few as "snooty" but nevertheless "superb", which may explain why most keep this "standout" "high on their list for special occasions"; still, "perfection" may not be "for the faint of pocketbook"; P.S. an August 2007 redo has transformed the "stunning" interior into an intimate dining room with fewer than 50 seats.

La Grotta ☒ *Italian* | 26 | 22 | 25 | E |

Buckhead | 2637 Peachtree Rd. NE (bet. Lindbergh Dr. & Wesley Rd.) | 404-231-1368

La Grotta Ravinia ☒ *Italian*

Dunwoody | Crowne Plaza Ravinia Hotel | 4355 Ashford Dunwoody Rd. (Hammond Dr.) | 770-395-9925
www.lagrottaatlanta.com

"La Grade A" is what aficionados call this "anniversary-worthy" duo where "fabulous" Northern Italian cuisine that "never disappoints" and "exemplary" service from a "professional" staff represent "fine dining at its very best"; an "older, affluent crowd" is unfazed by the Buckhead original's "strange basement location", enjoying a "sense of calm" and "great acoustics" during dinner, while the Dunwoody offshoot (which also serves lunch) provides an "elegant", "plush" setting overlooking a garden and waterfalls.

Madras Saravana Bhavan *Indian/Vegetarian* | 26 | 10 | 14 | I |
(nka Saravana Bhavan)

Decatur | North Dekalb Sq. | 2179 Lawrenceville Hwy. (N. Druid Hills Rd.) | 404-636-4400 | www.saravanabhavan.com

Faithful fans wish they had "more arms than Vishnu to shovel in all the wonderful delights" at Atlanta's No. 1 Indian, this "superb vegetarian" in Decatur offering "incredible", "extremely spicy" fare at "affordable prices"; service can be a "crapshoot" and the decor resembles something like "tiki hut meets" the subcontinent, but aficionados just "close their eyes" and "wallow in the smells and tastes" that "take you to India for the price of three coffees from Starbucks."

McKendrick's Steak House *Steak* | 26 | 21 | 25 | E |

Dunwoody | Park Place Shopping Ctr. | 4505 Ashford Dunwoody Rd. NE (bet. Hammond Dr. & Perimeter Ctr.) | 770-512-8888 | www.mckendricks.com

This "high-end" "power" spot in Dunwoody "competes with the best of Buckhead" via "fabulous" steaks that are "worth the cholesterol", "huge", "tasty sides", an "impressive wine list" and "wonderful" "old-fashioned" service that "makes you feel special"; the atmosphere is "vibrant" (and a "little noisy") in "quintessential" steakhouse surroundings of "dark oak" and "white tablecloths" – just be sure to "bring lots of money" because "everything's à la carte."

MF Sushibar *Japanese*

| 26 | 23 | 21 | M |

Midtown | 265 Ponce de Leon Ave. (Penn Ave.) | 404-815-8844 | www.mfsushibar.com

At this Midtown Japanese serving the "best sushi in town", "lovingly prepared" offerings of "amazingly fresh" fish are "literally art" and the "fresh wasabi" is "not to be missed"; located in a "wonderfully renovated section" of Ponce, the "modern" space attracts crowds of "hip", "eye-appealing" types (the "cool factor is high"), so "make reservations" and be prepared to "pay extra" or "forget about eating here."

Nan Thai Fine Dining *Thai*

| 26 | 27 | 24 | E |

Midtown | 1350 Spring St. NW (16th St. NW) | 404-870-9933 | www.nanfinedining.com

Voted Atlanta's No. 1 for Decor, this "smoothly sexy" "high-end" Midtown Thai (and Tamarind sibling) is "like a trip to Bangkok without the airfare" thanks to a "dazzlingly dramatic" Johnson Studio–designed space that "gushes Asian sophistication and charm" ("even the restroom is gorgeous"); the cuisine is "art on your plate" that's delivered with "impeccable" grace by a "gorgeous" staff, making it "an experience you don't want to miss" and the "best place" to "impress your friends, clients or in-laws."

New York Prime *Steak*

| 26 | 22 | 24 | E |

Buckhead | Monarch Tower | 3424 Peachtree Rd. NE (Lenox Rd.) | 404-846-0644 | www.newyorkprime.com

"Oh yeah, baby" crow carnivores who "rejoice" over this "prime" Buckhead chain link that's "rising in the ranks" with "perfect" steaks that "melt in your mouth", side dishes "to die for" and a "phenomenal" wine list; the "special occasion"- and "expense account"-worthy experience is set in a "masculine" space where there's a staff of "real pros" with "attention to detail" and "a happening happy hour" ("better not mind cigar smoke").

Park 75 *American*

| 27 | 25 | 28 | E |

Midtown | Four Seasons Atlanta | 75 14th St. (bet. Peachtree & W. Peachtree Sts.) | 404-253-3840 | www.fourseasons.com

The "elegant" Four Seasons "lives up to its image" with this "flawless" New American showcasing the "extraordinary flavors" of chef Robert Gerstenecker's "sublime" cuisine, including a "beyond-belief brunch"; the service is "off the charts", mapping "power meals" for "neighborhood lawyers, bankers, headhunters" and other "who's who" guests who gather for "white-tablecloth dining" in the "handsomely appointed" room; P.S. the "divine" chef's table in the kitchen is a "fantastic experience."

☑ Quinones Room at Bacchanalia 🗷Ⓜ *American*

| 28 | 27 | 28 | VE |

Westside | Courtyard of Bacchanalia | 1198 Howell Mill Rd. (bet. 14th St. & Huff Rd.) | 404-365-0410 | www.starprovisions.com

Bacchanalia may have "one-upped" itself with this "truly remarkable" New American prix fixe–only "experience" in the same Westside complex, where "every bite" offers an "unforgettably superb taste" and "fantastic wine pairings" "won't disappoint"; "impeccable", "synchronized" service and a "gorgeous", "intimate" room with "wonderful linens" add to the "$$$'s no object special-occasion" experience that's "worth every penny" according to fans, who feel it should be on everyone's "once-before-I-die list."

☑ Rathbun's ☒ American   28 | 25 | 25 | E

Inman Park | Stove Works | 112 Krog St. NE (bet. Edgewood Ave. & Irwin St.) | 404-524-8280 | www.rathbunsrestaurant.com

"The raves are true" about this "trendy but not pretentious" New American in a "refurbished industrial area" of Inman Park: it "leaves the hip pretenders in the dust" thanks to Kevin Rathbun's "spectacular", "visually appealing" "creations" that offer "something for everyone" and "every budget", topped off with "small and perfect" desserts; daily "hand-scrawled" menus and "homey" "greetings from the man himself" are part of the "charming" service, and the "beautiful" "rehabbed stove plant" resonates with a "lively" vibe (but "bad acoustics") that "makes life seem glam and fun."

Restaurant Eugene American   26 | 25 | 24 | E

South Buckhead | The Aramore | 2277 Peachtree Rd. NE (Peachtree Memorial Dr.) | 404-355-0321 | www.restauranteugene.com

"Tradition and innovation pat each other on the back" in the kitchen of this "first-class" New American in South Buckhead, where the "husband-and-wife duo has got it going on" with a "constantly changing menu" of "fresh", Southern-accented fare emphasizing "local" ingredients and an "impressive boutique wine list"; "impeccable" service "makes everyone feel special and welcome" in the "beautiful" "quiet" room, and satisfied surveyors go so far as to say it's "a pleasure to pay the bill."

☑ Ritz-Carlton Buckhead   28 | 27 | 28 | VE
Dining Room ☒Ⓜ French/Mediterranean

Buckhead | Ritz-Carlton Buckhead | 3434 Peachtree Rd. NE (Lenox Rd.) | 404-237-2700 | www.ritzcarlton.com

Near "perfect from beginning to end", this "elegant", upscale "grande dame" in Buckhead was voted Atlanta's No. 1 for Service thanks to a "kind" and "impeccable" staff that "makes all diners feel special", a "knowledgeable" sommelier who is "helpful" with her "wine novella" and "the best maitre d' in town"; chef Arnaud Berthelier's New French–Med cuisine "holds a universe of remarkable flavors" that are "simply unforgettable", and the green damask setting with "cozy" booths is another "treat for the senses" that "makes you feel like a Rockefeller"; N.B. jackets required.

Sotto Sotto Italian   26 | 19 | 21 | M

Inman Park | 313 N. Highland Ave. NE (Elizabeth St.) | 404-523-6678 | www.sottosottorestaurant.com

"Riccardo Ullio continues to set the bar" high for "elegant" Northern Italian cuisine with "dazzling performances in the kitchen" of his "super trattoria" that's the "highlight of Inman Park", where "heavenly" dishes are paired with a "well-chosen" wine list and the signature chocolate soup dessert is "divine"; the "courteous" service "seduces with small touches", "acoustical ceiling tiles" have "improved the din" in the "cozy" space and a "nifty little" patio offers a respite for "claustrophobes."

Taka ☒ *Japanese* | 26 | 14 | 21 | M |

Buckhead | 375 Pharr Rd. NE (Grandview Ave.) | 404-869-2802
"Insiders" are tickled by the "hilarious" e-mails they receive from chef Taka Moriuchi, an "absolute delight" who turns out "artistic" sushi and "sashimi that will make your head swim" at his Buckhead Japanese; even the "waiters are a joy" and "good about making recommendations" in the "small" venue that's "never crowded"; boosters say it's one of the "best in town – without the attitude."

Tamarind Seed Thai Bistro ● *Thai* | 27 | - | 23 | M |

Midtown | Colony Sq. | 1197 W. Peachtree St. NE (14th St.) | 404-873-4888 | www.tamarindseed.com
"As genuine as the best in Bangkok", this "off-the-charts" Midtown Thai (and elder sibling of Nan) serves "perfect", "beautifully presented" cuisine that's "worth every penny", and an "impeccable staff" delivers "tip-top" service that "leaves an impression"; though it's moved to a new location down the street post-Survey, odds are you'll still "see famous golfers", as "it's a favorite of Masters champions."

Trois *French* | - | - | - | E |

Midtown | 1180 Peachtree St. NE (14th St.) | 404-815-3337 | www.trois3.com
This polished Midtown offering from the Concentrics group (ONE. midtown kitchen, TAP) swings into full Gallic gear with white-clad servers delivering superstar chef Jeremy Lieb's New French cuisine; in keeping with the name, sweeping staircases link three floors: a top-story event space, a mid-tier dining room with artwork suspended from poles and a street-level bar with aluminum flooring that's pierced to let light stream into the room.

Baltimore

TOP FOOD RANKING

	Restaurant	Cuisine
28	Sushi Sono	Japanese
27	Charleston	American
	Samos	Greek
	Peter's Inn	American
	Prime Rib	Steak
	Tersiguel's	French
	Mari Luna	Mexican
26	Chameleon Cafe	American
	Trattoria Alberto	Italian
	Aldo's	Italian
	Helmand	Afghan
	Linwoods	American
	Roy's	Hawaiian
	Black Olive	Greek/Seafood
25	Milton Inn	American/Continental
	Boccaccio	Italian
	Oregon Grille	Seafood/Steak
	Ambassador Dining	Indian
	Pierpoint	American
	Edo Sushi	Japanese

Aldo's *Italian*　　　　　　　　　26 | 25 | 25 | E

Little Italy | 306 S. High St. (Fawn St.) | 410-727-0700 | www.aldositaly.com
"Decadent" Southern Italian "indulgences" from woodworker-"turned-chef" and owner Aldo Vitale are "just part of the experience" at this Little Italy "special-occasion" destination that will make you "feel like a king", given "attentive" service and an "elegant" setting that's "like being in someone's exquisitely decorated home" with "lots of little rooms" and a colonnaded atrium; still, some nitpickers note "you pay for the tux-and-luxe formula."

Ambassador Dining Room *Indian*　　　25 | 26 | 24 | M

Homewood | Ambassador Apts. | 3811 Canterbury Rd. (bet. 39th St. & University Pkwy.) | 410-366-1484 | www.ambassadordiningroom.com
In a "dark", "hushed" apartment house dining room that will "transport you to colonial India", patrons savor the "gourmet twists on traditional" dishes that make this the "best Indian in Baltimore"; its Homewood location is "hard to find", but once you do, "sit on the [enclosed] patio" – it's especially "romantic" "in winter with the fireplace roaring" – or in the "lush" garden "overlooking the fountain."

Black Olive, The *Greek/Seafood*　　　26 | 20 | 22 | E

Fells Point | 814 S. Bond St. (Shakespeare St.) | 410-276-7141 | www.theblackolive.com
"Nicely renovated" twin Fells Point townhouses are the setting for this "cozy" Greek seafooder that has "a winning formula": a "market-style" icebox allows diners to "select their own fish", which is "filleted table-

side", then "grilled to perfection" using "simple preparations" and mostly organic ingredients; of course, this "platonic ideal of a taverna" totals up to a "tsunami of a bill", though most find it "worth the splurge."

Boccaccio *Italian* | 25 | 21 | 23 | E |

Little Italy | 925 Eastern Ave. (bet. Exeter & High Sts.) | 410-234-1322 | www.boccaccio-restaurant.com

Catch this "solid performer" on "a good night" and the "flavorful" Northern Italian cuisine "will be the best you ever had", as will the "professional" service; with "tables far apart", it lends itself to "romance or closing the big deal", so while the unimpressed gripe about "mega bills", the majority agrees it's "a cut above the other Little Italy restaurants" and "worth it."

Chameleon Cafe 🖼️Ⓜ️ *American* | 26 | 18 | 24 | M |

Northeast Baltimore | 4341 Harford Rd. (bet. Montebello Terr. & Overland Ave.) | 410-254-2376 | www.thechameleoncafe.com

Husband-and-wife-team Jeffrey Smith and Brenda Wolf Smith's "dedication shines through" at this Northeast Baltimore "foodie's find" featuring "innovative, artistic, delicious" French-inflected New American entrees; while the "small" setting strikes some as "too casual for the menu", an open kitchen and "adept" servers "with a lot of heart" make you feel like you're "eating in the owners' home"; N.B. sidewalk seating adds appeal.

🅩 Charleston 🖼️ *American* | 27 | 26 | 27 | VE |

Harbor East | 1000 Lancaster St. (S. Exeter St.) | 410-332-7373 | www.charlestonrestaurant.com

"One of Baltimore's best" is "even better" thanks to a "strikingly elegant" makeover and a relatively new set-price format that lets diners "try more" of chef/co-owner Cindy Wolf's "cutting-edge", "Southern-style" New American small plates offered in three-, five- and six-course "create-your-own tasting menus"; though a few are perturbed about the now-"tiny portions", the "celestial" tabs at this Harbor East experience are justified by the "exceptional service" and an "exquisite wine list" from co-owner Tony Foreman.

🅩 Clyde's *American* | 18 | 21 | 19 | M |

Columbia | 10221 Wincopin Circle (Little Patuxent Pkwy.) | 410-730-2829 | www.clydes.com

While this "original" American "dining saloon" has "created a vast legion of copycats", it remains a "staple" that's "always good, year after year" (it's the Most Popular restaurant in the Baltimore Survey); with "fresh" oysters, "delicious" crab cakes, "the best" burgers and other "bar food, par excellence" served in a "brash" setting amid "nostalgic decor", it's "reliably good"; P.S. the two newest branches – a "gorgeous" Victorian "sight to see" at Gallery Place and a tavern complex in Broadlands, VA – are "great for just hanging out."

Edo Sushi *Japanese* | 25 | 17 | 23 | M |

Inner Harbor | Harborplace Pratt Street Pavilion | 201 E. Pratt St. (South St.) | 410-843-9804
Timonium | Padonia Village Shopping Ctr. | 53 E. Padonia Rd. (York Rd.) | 410-667-9200

(continued)

(continued)

Edo Mae Sushi *Japanese*

Owings Mills | Boulevard Corporate Ctr. | 10995 Owings Mills Blvd.
(bet. I-795 & Reisterstown Rd.) | 410-356-6818
www.edosushimd.com

"Watch chefs" create "beautiful sushi" and sashimi at these Japanese where the "innovative" specials are made from "fish that tastes like it just jumped out of the sea"; "attentive servers", a no-corkage BYO policy at most locations and a drum you "bang for good luck" help overcome the "strip-mall atmosphere"; N.B. Harborplace opened post-Survey.

Helmand *Afghan* 26 | 20 | 23 | M

Mt. Vernon | 806 N. Charles St. (bet. Madison & Read Sts.) | 410-752-0311 | www.helmand.com

At this Mt. Vernon "institution", "your taste buds will dance" to the "delicious diplomacy" of "complex, eye-opening" Afghan dishes that "go far, far beyond the kebab" "without being offputting" (don't miss the "bliss-on-a-plate pumpkin appetizer"); "vegetarians and meat eaters alike" "may fall in love with" its "exotic character" and "reasonable prices", and if "seating can be crowded", most feel "the food is worth the coziness."

Linwoods *American* 26 | 25 | 25 | E

Owings Mills | 25 Crossroads Dr. (bet. McDonogh & Reisterstown Rds.) | 410-356-3030 | www.linwoods.com

After nearly 20 years, surveyors can still "count on" this "upscale" Owings Mills "gold standard" "blessed with many" "consistently delicious" "spins on New American fare"; "owner Linwood Dame knows his business well", and his "clubby" restaurant "is all class" "without pretense", with an open kitchen and "professional service" to boot; some note, however, that a meal here can "put a dent in your wallet."

Mari Luna Mexican Grill Ⓜ *Mexican* 27 | 13 | 20 | I

Pikesville | 102 Reisterstown Rd. (Seven Mile Ln.) | 410-486-9910 | www.mariluna.com

"Set in a converted Carvel store", this Pikesville "gem" "may not have a ton of curb appeal", but it does have "divine", "authentic" "Mexican (not Tex-Mex)" fare; locals say it's "easy to get hooked on" this "friendly, family-owned" "find" that's both "small" and "popular as all get-out", so expect to "fight for a table"; P.S. BYO makes it even more of a "value."

Ⓩ McCormick & Schmick's *Seafood* 21 | 20 | 20 | E

Inner Harbor | Pier 5 Hotel | 711 Eastern Ave. (S. President St.) | 410-234-1300 | www.mccormickandschmicks.com

The "daily fresh catch can't be beat" say habitués hooked on this "clubby" chain where the "plethora of choices" "cooked as simply or as complicated as one would like" and "knowledgeable servers" make it "safe for a biz lunch" or "excellent for a family celebration"; though the "disappointed" call the "overpriced" "fish factory" fare a "let-down", barflies insist the "great" happy-hour specials deliver "real value."

Milton Inn *American/Continental* 25 | 26 | 24 | E

Sparks | 14833 York Rd. (3 mi. north of Shawan Rd.) | 410-771-4366 | www.miltoninn.com

For that "romantic celebration", gas up "your Range Rover" and "take your gold card" to this "charming" 1740 Sparks inn, a "cozy" "place to be pampered" with "gracious, attentive service" and Traditional American–Continental cuisine; it's "like dining at your millionaire uncle's", with "fireplaces in winter and a garden in summer", but a few find it "a little stuffy" and quite "pricey", so "definitely try the $36 chef's tasting menu."

Oregon Grille *Seafood/Steak*

25 | 25 | 24 | E

Hunt Valley | 1201 Shawan Rd. (Beaver Dam Rd.) | 410-771-0505 | www.theoregongrille.com

Be sure to "hold on to your wallet" at this Hunt Valley "place for special occasions", but "if you have the bucks, they have the steaks": "excellent" dry-aged cuts as well as serious seafood; some surveyors find it "stuffy" – "what do you expect in horse country?" – but most admit the service is "top-notch" and the atmosphere is "stunning" (they now have a spacious patio too); still, casual customers wish they'd "get rid of" the "archaic" jacket-required evening dress code.

☑ Peter's Inn ⑤Ⓜ *American*

27 | 15 | 20 | M

Fells Point | 504 S. Ann St. (Eastern Ave.) | 410-675-7313 | www.petersinn.com

"Defining Baltimore quirkiness" with its "strange collision" of "leather-clad biker" and "gourmet", this "teeny-tiny" Fells Point "hangout" may "look like a dive", but it's "as culinary as places twice as fancy and four times as dull", with a "limited" but "surprisingly ambitious" New American menu that "rotates weekly"; "get there early" since "it can get crowded" and "noisy", though regulars reveal "it's much more pleasant" "now that it's nonsmoking."

Pierpoint Ⓜ *American*

25 | 16 | 22 | E

Fells Point | 1822 Aliceanna St. (bet. Ann & Wolfe Sts.) | 410-675-2080 | www.pierpointrestaurant.com

Fells Point fine-dining pioneer "Nancy Longo knows how to cook", turning out an "adventurous" menu of Maryland-inspired New American cuisine (try the "must-get smoked crab cake") that now includes half-plates; still, some say it "needs to be updated" – "please redo the interior!"; N.B. it also serves a Sunday brunch.

☑ Prime Rib ❶ *Steak*

27 | 24 | 26 | E

Downtown North | 1101 N. Calvert St. (Chase St.) | 410-539-1804 | www.theprimerib.com

"Classy, swanky and all dressed up", this black-lacquered "old-fashioned supper club" in Baltimore's Downtown North is the quintessential spot to celebrate anniversaries or the "close of a big deal" over "massive cuts of buttery, beefy, masculine prime rib", the "most succulent" crab and "perfect" martinis brought to table by "impeccable" tuxedoed waiters.

Roy's *Hawaiian*

26 | 24 | 24 | E

Harbor East | 720B Aliceanna St. (President St.) | 410-659-0099 | www.roysrestaurant.com

"If you can't get to Hawaii, then at least your taste buds can" at this Harbor East link in Roy Yamaguchi's chain, appreciated for its "artful", "assertively flavored" fusion fare featuring "funky twists" on "super-fresh seafood"; it "breaks the mold", from "polished" service and an "exciting ambiance" to a "splash of Baltimore" "attitude", making some "wish they were open for lunch" too; P.S. order the "gooey" chocolate soufflé "as soon as you sit down."

	FOOD	DECOR	SERVICE	COST

☑ Ruth's Chris Steak House *Steak* | 24 | 21 | 23 | E |

Inner Harbor | 600 Water St. (bet. Gay St. & Market Pl.) | 410-783-0033
Inner Harbor | Pier 5 Hotel | 711 Eastern Ave. (S. President St.) |
410-230-0033
Pikesville | 1777 Reisterstown Rd. (Hooks Ln.) | 410-837-0033
www.ruthschris.com

"Everything's big" at these "high-end" beef houses – the steaks "sizzling in butter, the sides, the drinks, the bill!" – but "so what?" since you'll "check your diet at the door and rip into" a slab that "melts in your mouth", with a "great bottle of wine"; the "well-timed" service also "pampers" and the dark-wood digs are just right for business, but some insist these choices are "not as good" as the city's other chophouses.

☑ Samos ☒⇌ *Greek* | 27 | 12 | 20 | I |

Greektown | 600 S. Oldham St. (Fleet St.) | 410-675-5292 |
www.samosrestaurant.com

Meet the "Greektown family you never knew you had": chef-owner Nick Georgalas, "there every day" with "capable son Michael at his side", along with "hometown waitresses" who "call you 'hon' and mean it" as they bring around "huge portions" of "divinely zesty" "delights"; it's "no-frills" and "doesn't take reservations", but diners have determined it's "far and away" "Baltimore's top Greek", with a "BYO that makes it easy on the wallet" too; N.B. cash only.

☑ Sushi Sono ☒ *Japanese* | 28 | 19 | 24 | M |

Columbia | 10215 Wincopin Circle (Little Patuxent Pkwy.) | 410-997-6131 |
www.sushisonomd.com

"Lovely views" "overlooking serene Lake Kittamaqundi" "add to the Zen ambiance" at "Columbia's pristine Japanese haven", rated No. 1 for Food in the Baltimore Survey; "unmatched sushi and sashimi" and a "mouth-watering" "selection of specialty rolls" are "served with grace and charm" by a "kimono-clad" staff that has "a way of making you feel welcome"; "it's like being in another world" (especially after a few cups of sake), but be advised that it can be "quite pricey" and "packed."

Tersiguel's *French* | 27 | 23 | 26 | E |

Ellicott City | 8293 Main St. (Old Columbia Pike) | 410-465-4004 |
www.tersiguels.com

"Allow chef/co-owner Michel Tersiguel to take you on a tour" of "fine French country cuisine" at this "first-rate", family-run Gallic "in the heart of Ellicott City"; it "has a following" for its "rich", "fabulous food" (they even "grow their own vegetables"), and the "extensive wine" list and "wonderful service" help to ensure it's "perfect for a special occasion"; a "whopping bill" doesn't deter fans who note they've "paid three times as much for offerings that don't compare."

Trattoria Alberto ☒ *Italian* | 26 | 17 | 24 | E |

Glen Burnie | 1660 Crain Hwy. S. (bet. Hospital Dr. & Rte. 100 overpass) |
410-761-0922 | www.trattoriaalberto.com

Way out "in the 'burbs" near Glen Burnie is this "upscale" Northern Italian serving "exceptional" cuisine that's all the more "amazing" when you consider "the strip center it's in"; "from food to service, it's so old-world", but some note that specials can induce "sticker shock" and ask "for these prices, couldn't they hire a decorator?"

Boston

TOP FOOD RANKING

	Restaurant	Cuisine
28	L'Espalier	French
	Oishii	Japanese
	Clio/Uni	French
27	No. 9 Park	French/Italian
	Aujourd'hui	French
	Lumière	French
	La Campania	Italian
	Blue Ginger	Asian Fusion
	Saporito's	Italian
	Oleana	Mediterranean
	Mistral	French/Mediterranean
	Coriander Bistro	French
	Zabaglione*	Italian
	Sweet Basil	Italian
	Craigie St. Bistrot	French
	Helmand	Afghan
26	Hamersley's Bistro	French
	Il Capriccio	Italian
	Sage	American/Italian
	Meritage	American
	Marco Cucina	Italian
	Salts	American/French

Z Aujourd'hui *French*   27 | 27 | 28 | VE

Back Bay | Four Seasons Hotel | 200 Boylston St. (bet. Arlington & Charles Sts.) | 617-351-2037 | www.fourseasons.com

All of "life should be lived" as it is at the Four Seasons' "lavish" yet "serene" dining "retreat" overlooking the Common in the Back Bay: surrounded by "smooth-as-silk" staffers – again voted No. 1 for Service in Boston – who appear "devoted to your table" throughout an "exquisite" New French "experience" that's "worth the extra credit cards"; factor in a "fabulous Sunday brunch", and you'll be chiming in when the Francophiles chant *"Oui, oui, j'adore Aujourd'hui!"*

Z Blue Ginger *Asian Fusion*   27 | 22 | 25 | E

Wellesley | 583 Washington St. (Church St.) | 781-283-5790 | www.ming.com

Celebrity chef Ming Tsai all but "defined East-meets-West" cuisine, and his Asian fusion "classic" – still "the shining star" of "swanky Wellesley" – "continues to wow" with its "fantabulous" "explosion of flavors"; indeed, the "luxuriousness" of the food leaves some "surprised" by the comparatively "sparse" surroundings and service that, though "unfailingly" "well-versed", isn't always "warm" – but "Master" "Sigh" compensates ("when present") by giving "personal attention" to "each dish" and "every table", justifying the "exorbitant prices."

---

* Indicates a tie with restaurant above

	FOOD	DECOR	SERVICE	COST

☑ Clio/Uni *French* | 28 | 25 | 26 | VE

Back Bay | Eliot Hotel | 370A Commonwealth Ave. (Mass. Ave.) |
617-536-7200 | www.cliorestaurant.com

Whether or not it "holds the local record for the highest price per calorie served", this seriously "swanky" New French "supernova" in the Back Bay's Eliot Hotel "transports" "serious gourmets" who taste "brilliance" "beyond belief" in "every morsel" of chef Ken Oringer's "arresting", "complex" and "dramatic" presentations; even the miffed minority to whom the "extremely professional" staffers' "show of knowledge" comes across as a little bit "condescending" admits that Uni, the "incredible" sashimi bar right next door, reestablishes "cozy" "intimacy."

Coriander Bistro ⊠Ⓜ *French* | 27 | 22 | 26 | E

Sharon | 5 Post Office Sq. (bet. Billings & S. Main Sts.) | 781-784-5450 |
www.corianderbistro.com

As "reasons to leave the city" go, this Sharon bistro is "difficult to top": a chef who "loves doing what he does best" and his "affable" wife know how to deliver "fantastic" "gourmet" French goods "artfully", using ingredients from "the farm down the street"; abetted by a "solicitous staff", they "make recommendations" from a wine list of "carefully chosen treasures", "adding a homey touch" to a "simple" space that's as "welcoming" as it is "welcome."

Craigie Street Bistrot Ⓜ *French* | 27 | 19 | 25 | E

Harvard Square | 5 Craigie Circle (bet. Brattle St. & Concord Ave.) |
Cambridge | 617-497-5511 | www.craigiestreetbistrot.com

In this "wee, cozy" "basement from heaven" (transported to Harvard Square), "daring" "gourmets" "stop all conversation" except "oohs and aahs" as chef-owner Tony Maws makes their culinary "dreams come true" via "constantly new", "unfailingly memorable" French "challenges" that incorporate "whatever's freshest that day", while "smart", "sincere" servers offer "terrific" tips on "phenomenal" wines; if a few "meat-and-potato" types, "claustrophobes" and thwarted walk-ins feel "alienated", most swear its "stars are aligned"; P.S. the twice-weekly Chef's Whim prix fixe "blows away" "thrifty adventurers."

☑ Hamersley's Bistro *French* | 26 | 23 | 25 | E

South End | 553 Tremont St. (Clarendon St.) | 617-423-2700 |
www.hamersleysbistro.com

The South End's "pacesetter" for 20 years and counting, "master chef" Gordon Hamersley still runs the kitchen of his "handsome", "sunny-yellow" country French bistro, and "it shows on the plate": though "uncontrived", the cooking "pops" with "complex flavors" (the famed chicken has "changed lives"); his "dedicated long-time staff" continues to serve with "silver-spoon" "verve", so it's no wonder upstarts who opine it "needs a shot of 'now'" are drowned out by worshipers who pray it never "succumbs to trendiness."

Helman *Afghan* | 27 | 23 | 20 | M

East Cambridge | 143 First St. (Bent St.) | Cambridge | 617-492-4646 |
www.helmandrestaurantcambridge.com

"In the desert" of East Cambridge, an exquisite "oasis" filled with "beautiful blues and maizes" and an "aroma they could charge for" awaits; as it is, you get "exceptional value" from the "distinctive", "hearty" and "intriguingly spiced" assortment of Afghani specialties that "never change, but neither do their quality", from "smashing" baby pumpkin to "savory" lamb to "piping-hot flatbread" that warms your cockles – even when servers as "distant" as Kabul don't.

Il Capriccio ⌷ *Italian*   26 | 21 | 24 | E

Waltham | 888 Main St. (Prospect St.) | 781-894-2234

"Leave the kids at home" for "an evening to remember" at this "dark, private" Waltham "hideaway" where "rich" yet "crystal-pure" *piatti* complement a "world-class wine list" that has remained "devout in its homage to all things Italian" "for some 26 years"; while the "very seriousness" of the culinary endeavor leaves a few fun-lovers chirping "lighten up!", most just wish they "could afford to eat here more" often.

La Campania ⌷Ⅿ *Italian*   27 | 25 | 25 | E

Waltham | 504 Main St. (bet. Cross & Heard Sts.) | 781-894-4280 | www.lacampania.com

"Are we in Waltham" or a "rustic" "village" "inn"? wonder suburban Italophiles "swept away" by this "small" "blessing" with an "artist" for a chef and "a wine god" for a manager (oenophiles dream of running "loose in his cellar"); while some small spenders balk at the "steep" bill, sensualists say it's so "sublime from start to finish", they'll just have to "get over" it.

⊠ Legal Sea Foods *Seafood*   22 | 18 | 20 | M

Back Bay | Copley Pl. | 100 Huntington Ave. (bet. Dartmouth & Exeter Sts.) | 617-266-7775

Back Bay | Prudential Ctr. | 800 Boylston St. (Ring Rd.) | 617-266-6800

Park Square | 26 Park Plaza (Columbus Ave.) | 617-426-4444 ●

Waterfront | Long Wharf | 255 State St. (Atlantic Ave.) | 617-227-3115

Harvard Square | 20 University Rd. (Eliot St.) | Cambridge | 617-491-9400

Kendall Square | 5 Cambridge Ctr. (bet. Ames & Main Sts.) | Cambridge | 617-864-3400

Chestnut Hill | Chestnut Hill Shopping Ctr. | 43 Boylston St. (Hammond Pond Pkwy.) | 617-277-7300

Braintree | South Shore Plaza | 250 Granite St. (I-95, exit 6) | 781-356-3070

Peabody | Northshore Mall | 210 Andover St./Rte. 114 (Rte. 128) | 978-532-4500

Framingham | 50-60 Worcester Rd./Rte. 9 (Ring Rd.) | 508-766-0600
www.legalseafoods.com

"Come one, come all" to the "Ellis Island of fish", the "Oktoberfest of lobster", the "seafood-starved tourist" "zoo": "after all these years and all that expansion", Boston's Most Popular "institution" still draws the "teeming hordes" by providing more "impeccable consistency" "than any chain has a right to", all while getting the balance between culinary "simplicity" and "innovation" "down to a science" and honing its formula for "cheerful" decor and service; in short, it may be a "cliché", but it's a largely "beloved" one.

⊠ L'Espalier *French*   28 | 28 | 28 | VE

Back Bay | 30 Gloucester St. (bet. Commonwealth Ave. & Newbury St.) | 617-262-3023 | www.lespalier.com

The city's "best all-around dining experience" is how many view this "luxe-to-the-max" gourmet "adventure", rated No. 1 in Boston for both Food and Decor: in an "opulent" Back Bay brownstone you'll "wish you could live in", chef-owner Frank McClelland "takes you beyond the stretch of your imagination" with *"fantastique"* prix fixe menus that incorporate "impeccable" New England ingredients into "transcendent" New French meals overseen by "beyond impeccable" servers who "think about everything for you"; of course it's all "staggeringly" "cost-prohibitive" – "but what price culinary genius, yes?"

Lumière *French*

27 | 22 | 25 | E

Newton | 1293 Washington St. (Waltham St.) | 617-244-9199 | www.lumiererestaurant.com

A "surefire" *"bon soir"* awaits both "special-occasion" observers and "lucky" regulars at this "splendid" West Newton bistro, whose "clean and cool", "quiet and refined" design sets the tone for the "precision" kitchen's New French output, "cleverly" "streamlined" to "let the ingredients show through" – and "really classy service" "has it right" too; N.B. sticklers for "'oomph' for the price" might try the "superb" "weekday prix fixe."

Marco Cucina Romana ☒ *Italian*

26 | 21 | 23 | E

North End | 253 Hanover St., 2nd fl. (bet. Cross & Parmenter Sts.) | 617-742-1276 | www.marcoboston.com

Within a "rustic" "brick-walled" roost "above the hubbub of Hanover Street", Pigalle's Marc Orfaly has "hidden" a *"fantastico"* trattoria that "walks the line between traditional and modern flavors" with "lively" antipasti, "delicious pastas" and "reasonably priced wines"; if "elbow room" is scarce and the "courteous" servers can be occasionally "slow", so much the better for feeling "as close to Italy as you can get."

Meritage ☒ *American*

26 | 26 | 26 | E

Waterfront | Boston Harbor Hotel | 70 Rowes Wharf (Atlantic Ave.) | 617-439-3995 | www.meritagetherestaurant.com

Gourmet "synergy" suffuses "exceptional chef" Daniel Bruce's Waterfront monument to pairing, where guests essentially "make their own tasting menus" from an "opulent, indulgent" array of seasonal New American dishes, available in small or large sizes and coordinated with the "enormous wine list" – though "distinguished" servers can "provide direction" too; of course, "those little plates add up to big $$$", but "no one whines" – perhaps because the "dynamite" harbor view takes their breath away.

Mistral *French/Mediterranean*

27 | 26 | 25 | E

South End | 223 Columbus Ave. (bet. Berkeley & Clarendon Sts.) | 617-867-9300 | www.mistralbistro.com

Still "the Rolls-Royce" of restaurants in the South End, Jamie Mammano's French-Mediterranean "stronghold" "has it all": "out-of-this-world" "indulgences" paired with a "wide spectrum" of wines presented by a veritable "battalion" of "polished" floor staffers in a "regal", "high-ceilinged" space; granted, given the "buzz" the bar crowd of "young power brokers" and "models" generates, the "noise level" can rise to "absurd" heights – just like the "eye-popping" checks.

☒ No. 9 Park ☒ *French/Italian*

27 | 24 | 26 | VE

Beacon Hill | 9 Park St. (bet. Beacon & Tremont Sts.) | 617-742-9991 | www.no9park.com

"You have arrived" when you enter Barbara Lynch's "suave" "flagship" on Beacon Hill – and you'll "stay for the duration" as "superior mixologists", a "wonderful sommelier" and "passionate" "waiters who speak like chefs" administer an "extraordinary" "crossover French-Italian" meal you're actually "excited to eat", coming from a kitchen that's "on a different level altogether"; so while the usual holdouts harrumph over "minuscule portions" that leave them "hungry but appreciably poorer", the "'in' crowd" insists this fledgling "legend" is "worth your arm and leg."

⚡ Oishii Ⓜ *Japanese*   28 | 14 | 21 | E

Chestnut Hill | 612 Hammond St. (Boylston St.) | 617-277-7888
Sudbury | Mill Vill. | 365 Boston Post Rd./Rte. 20 (Concord Rd.) | 978-440-8300

⚡ Oishii Boston ●Ⓜ *Japanese*

South End | 1166 Washington St. (E. Berkeley St.) | 617-482-8868 | www.oishiiboston.com

The Chestnut Hill senior's "smaller than a Tokyo karaoke bar", the Sudbury junior's a "neighborhood joint" and the "ultracontemporary" South End freshman defines "chichi" – but all three serve as "shrines to the art of sushi" and "what it's supposed to taste like"; you may "panic at the cost" (not to mention the "hour-plus waits"), but once you've had one "mm-worthy" bite of some "dreamy" "departure" from the "spicy tuna" norm, you'll be "ready to spend exorbitant" sums on "the omakase – a guaranteed thrill ride."

Oleana *Mediterranean*   27 | 22 | 23 | E

Inman Square | 134 Hampshire St. (bet. Elm & Norfolk Sts.) | Cambridge | 617-661-0505 | www.oleanarestaurant.com

Inman Square's intelligentsia consider it "an unbelievable privilege" to "educate their taste buds" at this "remarkable" Arabic-Mediterranean "destination": "each bite" of chef-owner Ana Sortun's "refreshingly" "gutsy" and "complex" creations shows she "knows her spices", and her "well-versed" "staff can describe every ingredient" (if in an occasionally "condescending" manner); quick studies have also learned to "sharpen their elbows" when seated at the "closely placed tables" – or arrive early for places on the "magical" patio.

Sage *American/Italian*   26 | - | 22 | E

South End | 1395 Washington St. (bet. Pelham & Union Park Sts.) | 617-248-8814 | www.sageboston.com

Eat "art" at Anthony Susi's "serious" Italian–New American "standout" where the seasonal menu is "short" but "refined", "thoughtful" and "spot-on", from "unsurpassed gnocchi" to "melt-in-your-mouth meats" – and do it all in newfound comfort: after over a decade, the North End "hallway" has moved to more spacious South End digs, with more seating and a full bar to round out the "well-selected" wine list.

Salts ⅀Ⓜ *American/French*   26 | 22 | 26 | E

Central Square | 798 Main St. (bet. Cherry & Windsor Sts.) | Cambridge | 617-876-8444 | www.saltsrestaurant.com

Balance is this "quiet" "little" Central Square destination's "brilliant" gift; its "manicured yet homey" dining room sets the tone for French-New American cuisine that's simultaneously "earthy" and "ethereal", "approachable" and "elegant" – just as the "class acts" who serve it, led by "earnest" owners, embody both "amiability" and "total professionalism"; P.S. if your heart's set on the signature duck for two, "order it in advance" – sometimes "they run out."

	FOOD	DECOR	SERVICE	COST

Saporito's Ⓜ *Italian*   27 | 20 | 24 | E

Hull | 11 Rockland Circle (George Washington Blvd.) | 781-925-3023 | www.saporitoscafe.com

A "summer cottage" to the diplomatic, a "beach shack" to the blunt, Hull's "gold standard" for Northern Italian cuisine is a "little treasure" by most accounts, including those of urbanites who "schlep" southward to be "accommodated" by "stellar" servers bearing "frequently changing" creations; indeed, even the downsides – "uncomfortable" "wooden booths" and "NYC prices" – are upsides, insofar as they "turn off" "the tourists, who leave it alone."

Sweet Basil Ⓜ🍴 *Italian*   27 | 11 | 20 | M

Needham | 942 Great Plain Ave. (Highland Ave.) | 781-444-9600

Long generating "conspiratorial excitement" among BYO-toting Needhamites with the "garlicky" "intensity" of its "abundant" "bellywarmers", this Italian "walk-in closet" has finally upped the ante with a recent size-doubling expansion (which may outdate the Decor score); provided the "adorable" chef-owner and his much-"appreciated" staff "continue their legacy" of "down-to-earth" "personality and flavor" at "prices that allow frequent visits", the new "place to breathe" should be "sweet indeed."

Zabaglione *Italian*   27 | 18 | 24 | E

Ipswich | 10 Central St. (Market St.) | 978-356-5466

Zabaglione Cafe *Italian*

Ipswich | 1 Market St. (Central St.) | 978-356-6484

"It's hard to choose just one entree" at this "intimate" Ipswich "secret", whose "out-of-this-world" Italian creations – abounding in "clever", "artfully showcased" ingredients – are supplemented by "evening specials" "brought out to view" by a "staff that dotes on you"; but whatever you select will be "worth every penny" (just "don't pass up dessert" or "you will regret it"); P.S. the "cute cafe" "right down the street" keeps things "informal" and more "affordable."

Chicago

TOP FOOD RANKING

	Restaurant	Cuisine
29	Carlos'	French
28	Les Nomades	French
	Tru	French
	Alinea	American
	Tallgrass	French
	Arun's	Thai
27	Topolobampo	Mexican
	Charlie Trotter's	American
	Everest	French
	Vie	American
	Spring	American/Seafood
	Barrington Country Bistro	French
	Oceanique	French/Seafood
	Blackbird	American
26	Courtright's	American
	Frontera Grill	Mexican
	Spiaggia	Italian
	Mirai Sushi	Japanese

☑ Alinea ☒ American `28` `27` `28` `VE`

Lincoln Park | 1723 N. Halsted St. (bet. North Ave. & Willow St.) | 312-867-0110 | www.alinearestaurant.com

Astronomic scores support the "sheer genius" of chef-owner Grant Achatz and the "astonishing flavors" of his "fabulous" "experimental" New American cuisine at this Lincoln Park "thrill ride" that "engages all your senses" and "expands your concept of fine dining"; the space is "understated and serene", the nearly 700-bottle wine list is "superb" and the "polished service" (ranked No. 1 in Chicago) is near "perfect"; be prepared, though, as this "surreal" "journey" will be "looong" and "ungodly expensive"; N.B. open Wednesday–Sunday for dinner only.

Arun's ☒ Thai `28` `24` `26` `VE`

Northwest Side | 4156 N. Kedzie Ave. (bet. Irving Park Rd. & Montrose Ave.) | 773-539-1909 | www.arunsthai.com

Arun Sampanthavivat's "inventive", "customized" 12-course tasting-only menu of "transcendental" Thai is tantamount to "edible art", "served with care and courtesy" in a "elegant gallery" setting with a "great wine cellar"; sure, it's "in an industrial/residential neighborhood" on the Northwest Side, but it's "as good as the best in Thailand" and "a whole lot easier to get to", even if it "can seem wildly expensive" – in other words, "make sure this is on your 'things to do before I die' list."

Barrington Country Bistro ☒ French `27` `21` `24` `E`

Barrington | Foundry Shopping Ctr. | 700 W. Northwest Hwy. (Hart Rd.) | 847-842-1300 | www.barringtoncountrybistro.com

Toques off to the "top-quality traditional bistro fare" at this "hidden gem" situated in an "inauspicious" Northwest Suburban mall; it's a "continual favorite" for its "pleasant country-French setting" (including comfortable outdoor seating), "excellent service" and the presence of a particularly "gracious owner"; P.S. "lunch is a special treat."

Blackbird ⓈⒶ *American* | 27 | 20 | 23 | E |

West Loop | 619 W. Randolph St. (bet. Desplaines & Jefferson Sts.) | 312-715-0708 | www.blackbirdrestaurant.com

Make sure this "fabulously polished" West Loop "classic" is on your list for "pure tastes in a pure space", featuring "local, organic and unique ingredients" in "exquisite" New American cuisine that "makes you proud to be from Chicago"; the setting may be "stark" ("the whole white-on-white thing"), the "tables cramped" and the "din" "astonishing", but there's "plenty of eye candy", plus "consummately professional" service and "one of the highest-quality wine selections in the city, at all price ranges"; N.B. the Food rating may not reflect the addition of Mike Sheerin (ex NYC's WD-50) as chef de cuisine, taking over the kitchen reins from owner Paul Kahan.

Ⓩ Carlos' *French* | 29 | 25 | 28 | VE |

Highland Park | 429 Temple Ave. (Waukegan Ave.) | 847-432-0770 | www.carlos-restaurant.com

A "memorable evening" awaits visitors to this 26-year-old North Shore "treasure", a "fine-dining" "temple on Temple Avenue" that's ranked No. 1 for Food among Chicagoland restaurants on the strength of its "superb", "very creative" New French fare, which is accompanied by a "fantastic wine list" and served by a "staff that knows when to be friendly and when to be reserved"; the feel is "formal yet extremely comfortable, with cozy booths and soft lighting", making it a "great celebration place" – "if you can afford it"; N.B. jackets required.

Ⓩ Charlie Trotter's ⓈⒶ *American* | 27 | 25 | 27 | VE |

Lincoln Park | 816 W. Armitage Ave. (Halsted St.) | 773-248-6228 | www.charlietrotters.com

"A religious experience" "worth a mortgage payment" awaits at this Lincoln Parker, the "epitome of [New] American gastronomy" and Chicagoland's Most Popular restaurant, where customers are "dazzled" by "brilliant" chef Charlie Trotter's daily changing menu (with "fantastic pairings" from an "exceptional wine cellar") and "cosseted" by a "masterfully courteous and knowledgeable" staff; a few find the "formal" feel "churchlike" and the whole experience a bit "precious", but most maintain it's "absolutely sublime", especially if you "get a reservation at the kitchen table"; N.B. jackets required, and be aware that it's only open on some Mondays.

Courtright's Ⓜ *American* | 26 | 25 | 26 | E |

Willow Springs | 8989 S. Archer Ave. (Willow Springs Rd.) | 708-839-8000 | www.courtrights.com

Excursionists to the Southwest Surburbs eagerly enthuse about this "excellent out-of-the-way" "destination restaurant" where "marvelous", "creative seasonal" New American "meals are carefully planned, expertly prepared and exquisitely presented" in a "classic atmosphere" with "beautiful gardens" ("grazing deer appear magically as if on cue outside the [nearly] floor-to-ceiling windows"); P.S. "the wine alone is worth the trip."

	FOOD	DECOR	SERVICE	COST

DeLaCosta *Nuevo Latino* — | - | - | - | E

River North | 465 E. Illinois St. (bet. Lake Shore Dr. & McClurg Ct.) | 312-464-1700 | www.delacostachicago.com
Chef Douglas Rodriguez (of Miami's OLA empire) makes his Midwestern debut with this River North supper club serving pricey Nuevo Latino cuisine paired with six styles of sangria and sexy 'pop-tails' (cocktail popsicles); the 12,000-sq.-ft. setting includes multiple high-style environments, including a ceviche bar, a private wine room and a 'solarium' overlooking Ogden Slip.

Everest 🅂🅼 *French* — | 27 | 26 | 27 | VE

Loop | One Financial Pl. | 440 S. LaSalle St., 40th fl. (Congress Pkwy.) | 312-663-8920 | www.everestrestaurant.com
Financiers feel an affinity for this "romantic", "formal" "expense-account haven", "still at its peak" thanks to Jean Joho's "delectable" New French–Alsatian cuisine, an "exemplary wine list", "totally professional service" and "a breathtaking view" from "the top of the [Loop] Financial District"; a recent face-lift may appease fans who felt that the "nouveau riche" decor was "stuck in the '80s", though it may do little for those more concerned that the "attitude" "is loftier than the location."

Z Frontera Grill 🅂🅼 *Mexican* — | 26 | 21 | 22 | M

River North | 445 N. Clark St. (bet. Hubbard & Illinois Sts.) | 312-661-1434 | www.fronterakitchens.com
"Top-of-the-line Mexican [food] with a focus on fresh ingredients" comes courtesy of "culinary hero Rick Bayless" at this River North "treasure" with a "national reputation"; "bold, bright" and "somewhat raucous", it's "less expensive and more casual" than its "refined big brother", Topolobampo, with the same "superb wine selections" and "great margarita-tequila menu", but some say "service can be spotty when it's busy – which is always."

Z Les Nomades 🅂🅼 *French* — | 28 | 26 | 28 | VE

Streeterville | 222 E. Ontario St. (bet. Fairbanks Ct. & St. Clair St.) | 312-649-9010 | www.lesnomades.net
This "refined" former private club in Streeterville "still satisfies" thanks to chef Chris Nugent, who uses "generous quantities of luxury ingredients" in his "excellent" New French cuisine, which is backed by a "fine" wine list and "superb service"; the "formal" (some say "stuffy") setting has an "understated", "hushed" tone that befits "a romantic rendezvous" or "an important business dinner" for a "cut-above" clientele that can afford "top-of-the-line prices."

Mirai Sushi 🅂 *Japanese* — | 26 | 20 | 20 | E

Wicker Park | 2020 W. Division St. (Damen Ave.) | 773-862-8500
"In the face of a Chicago sushi explosion", this "hip" Wicker Park Japanese "remains the best" per raters who prefer its "pricey" but "pristine fish" – the "unusual" "maki don't disappoint, but the quality of the straight-up sashimi sets this place apart" – or "put themselves in the chef's hands for a sublime omakase dinner"; add the "divine sake" (over 30 varieties) and the "scene", especially "upstairs", where it's "definitely darker and more swank", and it's no surprise satisfied surveyors make this their "go-to" for raw fin fare.

☑ Morton's, The Steakhouse *Steak*

26 | 21 | 24 | E

Loop | 65 E. Wacker Pl. (bet. Michigan & Wabash Aves.) | 312-201-0410
Gold Coast | Newberry Plaza | 1050 N. State St. (Maple St.) | 312-266-4820
Rosemont | 9525 W. Bryn Mawr Ave. (River Rd.) | 847-678-5155
Northbrook | 699 Skokie Blvd. (Dundee Rd.) | 847-205-5111
Schaumburg | 1470 McConnor Pkwy. (Meacham Rd.) | 847-413-8771
Westchester | 1 Westbrook Corporate Ctr. (22nd St.) | 708-562-7000
www.mortons.com

"Still the standard" for "scrumptious slabs of the best [prime] beef known to man", this "granddaddy" (tops among Chicago steakhouses) is a "candy store for carnivores" complete with the "show-and-tell" presentation cart, "huge sides" and "soufflés meant to be shared", a "great wine list" and a "professional staff"; decor at various locations may stray from the "quintessential", "manly" Gold Coast "mother ship", and some raters reckon it's "resting on its laurels", but a well-fed majority insists this "class act" is "worth" its "break-the-bank prices."

Oceanique ☒ *French/Seafood*

27 | 21 | 24 | E

Evanston | 505 Main St. (bet. Chicago & Hinman Aves.) | 847-864-3435 | www.oceanique.com

"Unpretentious" "fine dining" is the house special at this North Suburban New French "treasure" where chef-owner Mark Grosz creates "a flawless assortment of beautifully prepared dishes" featuring the "best seafood in the Chicago area", plus "plenty of alternate choices for meat people"; expect an "excellent wine list" and "well-educated staff" in a "pleasant" setting where you can "enjoy the food and your companions without dressing to the nines" (though luxe-lovers would "upgrade" the atmosphere); P.S. try "the $39 three-course dinner Monday–Friday."

Osteria di Tramonto *Italian*

- | - | - | M

Wheeling | Westin Chicago North Shore | 601 N. Milwaukee Ave. (N. Wolf Rd.) | 847-777-6570 | www.cenitare.com

Rick Tramonto (ex Tru) cooks up classic and contemporary multiregional Italian cuisine in Wheeling's new Westin Chicago North Shore hotel; the seasonal menu is at once rustic and modern, a philosophy that's carried through in the decor with its exposed brick, 10,000-bottle glass wine wall and an open kitchen with dining counter; N.B. breakfast includes goodies from partner Gale Gand's on-site coffee bar.

NEW Sepia *American*

- | - | - | M

Market District | 123 N. Jefferson St. (bet. Randolph & Washington Sts.) | 312-441-1920 | www.sepiachicago.com

At this sophisticated Market District newcomer, toque Kendal Duque's impressive string of celeb-chef mentors (Julian Serrano, Alice Waters, etc.) comes through in his seasonal, simply presented New American cuisine (with a wine list to match); set in a remodeled printing house, it blends modern and vintage elements, including extravagant light fixtures, an 800-bottle floor-to-ceiling wine wall and – in a nod to the name – a late-19th-century antique camera.

Spiaggia *Italian*

26 | 27 | 25 | VE

Gold Coast | One Magnificent Mile Bldg. | 980 N. Michigan Ave., 2nd fl. (Oak St.) | 312-280-2750 | www.spiaggiarestaurant.com

Expect a "peak dining experience" at this "honed-to-perfection", "luxury" Gold Coaster boasting a "sumptuous" setting with "spectacular views" of the Michigans (both Lake and Avenue), chef Tony Mantuano's "sublime", "incomparable Italian" cuisine, an "excellent", "extensive wine list" and "superlative service"; most maintain it's "one of the few places where the high price tag is worth it", though a segment of surveyors submits that the staff's "snooty" and the "small portions" are "overpriced" (served only in the cafe, "lunch is a lot less expensive"); N.B. jackets required, jeans not allowed.

Spring Ⓜ American/Seafood | 27 | 25 | 25 | E |

Wicker Park | 2039 W. North Ave. (Damen Ave.) | 773-395-7100 | www.springrestaurant.net

Shawn McClain's "incredible creations" of "perfectly prepared" New American seafood "with a slight Asian slant" inspire acolytes to ask "is it impolite to lick the plate?" at this "hip" Wicker Park place that's "as fresh and exciting as the season it's named after"; the "quietly elegant setting" "in a converted bathhouse" is "beautiful and peaceful", the service is "polished but not overwhelming" and there's an "outstanding wine list", all of which adds up to "a wonderful experience" – so if you don't have a "special occasion, just come up with one."

Ⓩ Tallgrass Ⓜ French | 28 | 24 | 25 | VE |

Lockport | 1006 S. State St. (10th St.) | 815-838-5566 | www.tallgrassrestaurant.com

"Spectacular", "innovative" New French fare and a "deep wine list" (600 labels strong) fuel this "venerable" "foodie's paradise" "in the middle of nowhere" – aka historic Southwest Suburban Lockport – that's "well worth the drive from anywhere"; gourmets gush they "would go broke if they [lived] nearby", returning for chef-partner Robert Burcenski's "fine haute cuisine" with "wonderful presentation" in a "very private", "romantic" space; N.B. jackets are suggested.

Topolobampo Ⓢ Ⓜ Mexican | 27 | 23 | 25 | E |

River North | 445 N. Clark St. (bet. Hubbard & Illinois Sts.) | 312-661-1434 | www.rickbayless.com

"This is what the food in heaven must taste like" posit praisers of this "pinnacle" of Mexican "alta cucina" in River North, where "every bite" of "creative genius" Rick Bayless' cuisine is "utterly swoon-worthy", the tequila list is "to die for" and the "passionate staff" "pampers" patrons; most feel it's "more elegant than its attached sister restaurant, Frontera Grill", with fare that "really is better", even if a handful of heretics wonder "is it worth the price difference?"; P.S. "book well ahead", as getting "weekend reservations can take forever."

Ⓩ Tru Ⓢ French | 28 | 27 | 28 | VE |

Streeterville | 676 N. St. Clair St. (bet. Erie & Huron Sts.) | 312-202-0001 | www.trurestaurant.com

"Art and food meet and really, really like each other" at this jackets-required Streeterville "temple of excess" that "amazes" with "progressive, daring" New French plates plus sommelier Scott Tyree's "divinely inspired" 1,400-bottle wine selection, all borne by a virtually "flawless" staff within a "stark, simple" setting sporting an "original Andy Warhol" and "a lovely little tuffet for Madame's handbag"; "sticker shock" aside, it's a "magical experience" that "will become a lasting memory"; N.B. the Food score was tallied when founding chefs Rick Tramonto and Gale Gand were still at the helm.

Vie ⓩ *American*

| 27 | 23 | 23 | E |

Western Springs | 4471 Lawn Ave. (Burlington Ave.) | 708-246-2082 | www.vierestaurant.com

"Wow"-ed West Suburbanites feel "lucky to have" this New American in the "quaint", "sleepy" town of Western Springs, where chef-owner "Paul Virant brings many of his Blackbird sensibilities" to his "haute" "seasonal" "dishes with excellent flavor combinations", paired with a "very interesting wine list"; just "steps from the train station", it's even "worth the reverse commute for adventurous Chicagoans", though some call the "modern, minimalist" decor "cold" and others purport it would be "perfect" "if the service could catch up with the brilliance of the food."

ⓩ Wildfire *Steak*

| 23 | 21 | 21 | M |

River North | 159 W. Erie St. (bet. LaSalle Blvd. & Wells St.) | 312-787-9000
Lincolnshire | 235 Parkway Dr. (Milwaukee Ave.) | 847-279-7900
Glenview | 1300 Patriot Blvd. (Lake Ave.) | 847-657-6363
Schaumburg | 1250 E. Higgins Rd. (National Pkwy.) | 847-995-0100
Oak Brook | Oakbrook Center Mall | 232 Oakbrook Ctr. (Rte. 83) | 630-586-9000
www.wildfirerestaurant.com

Spreading like their namesake, this "insanely popular" passel of Traditional American steakhouses from the "Lettuce Entertain You group" keeps carnivores "coming back" with "hearty Midwest-sized portions" from a "crowd-pleasing menu" of "awesome wood-fired" fare ("juicy" steaks and chops), "delicious chopped salad" and "great martini flights" in a "classy", "clubby" "'40s-style" setting; salivating surveyors swear it's "worth the wait" ("even with reservations"), but wet blankets rank these "noisy" "madhouses" "really rather ordinary, just on a grand scale."

Dallas/Ft. Worth

TOP FOOD RANKING

Restaurant	Cuisine
28 French Room	American/French
Tei Tei Robata	Japanese
Local	American
Teppo Yakitori	Japanese
Abacus	Eclectic
27 York Street	American
Saint-Emilion	French
Yutaka Sushi	Japanese
Bonnell's	Southwestern
Lanny's Alta Cocina	Eclectic/Mexican
Aurora	American
Bijoux	French
Stephan Pyles	Southwestern
Del Frisco's	Steak
Mercury Grill	American
Amici	Italian
Nana*	American
Lola	American
Pappas Bros.	Steak
62 Main	American
26 Mercury Chop	Steak
Lonesome Dove	Southwestern

Abacus 🅩 Ⓢ *Eclectic*   28 26 27 VE

Knox-Henderson | 4511 McKinney Ave. (Armstrong Ave.) | Dallas | 214-559-3111 | www.abacus-restaurant.com

"Hands down one of the best restaurants in town" recommend regulars of this "inventive" Knox-Henderson Eclectic (ranked our Survey's Most Popular in Dallas) helmed by Kent Rathbun, whose "truly memorable" "California, French and Asian" style dishes – including those signature lobster shooters, which "deserve all the hype" that they get – "never fail to delight or impress"; a "meticulous" service staff attends to the "noisy", "trendy, neo-industrial" dining room, where the only downside seems to be that eating here is so "expensive", you may "need to bring along an abacus to total the bill."

Amici Ⓢ Ⓜ *Italian*   27 17 24 E

Carrollton | 1022 S. Broadway Rd. (Belt Line Rd.) | 972-245-3191 | www.amicisignature.com

A "delightful find" rave fans of this Carrollton "hideaway" overseen by a "charming chef-owner" who sends out "first-class" French-inflected Italian cuisine, including "excellent game specials"; the digs are "dark" and modern, and because it's BYO, prices are a relative "bargain."

---

* Indicates a tie with restaurant above

Aurora 🅾 *American* | 27 | 24 | 27 | VE |

Oak Lawn | 4216 Oak Lawn Ave. (Wycliff Ave.) | Dallas | 214-528-9400 | www.auroradallas.com

Don't hesitate to "max out your credit cards" at this "over-the-top" Oak Lawn New American that "stands out among the many temples of haute cuisine" thanks to "master" chef Avner Samuel, who serves up "beautifully presented" plates matched with wine from an "outstanding" 500-label list; bejeweled and designer-draped cognoscenti fill the art-deco inspired space and coo over its "luxury, sophistication and polish", though some find the "strip center" drive-up an incongruous welcome.

Bijoux 🅾🅼 *French* | 27 | 25 | 25 | VE |

West Lovers Lane | 5450 W. Lovers Ln. (bet. Inwood Rd. & Preston Park Dr.) | Dallas | 214-350-6100 | www.bijouxrestaurant.com

Expect "impeccable everything" at Scott Gottlich's "consistently superb" West Lovers Lane "star that has not lost its luster", luring foodies and "special occasion" celebrators with "ultra-refined" French food and "fabulous, attentive service"; "tables are spaced nicely" in the artful, "sedate" space, so your conversation is your own, just know that prix fixe menus (which can pair with "affordable wines") are the only option.

Bonnell's 🅾🅼 *Southwestern* | 27 | 23 | 26 | E |

Southwest | 4259 Bryant Irvin Rd. (Southwest Blvd.) | Ft. Worth | 817-738-5489 | www.bonnellstexas.com

"A safari of fine foods" is rounded up by "wonderfully inventive" chef Jon Bonnell who is "true to Texas cuisine" at this moderately priced Southwestern "favorite" where "innovative" wild game preparations wow "adventurous" and timid types alike; "don't be fooled by the outside appearance" "next to the freeway" on the Southwest side of town, as "inside is cozier", trimmed in stylish "cowboy and Western motifs" and serviced by "top-quality" staff.

🆉 Del Frisco's Double Eagle Steak House *Steak* | 27 | 24 | 25 | VE |

North Dallas | 5251 Spring Valley Rd. (Dallas N. Tollway) | Dallas | 972-490-9000

Downtown Ft. Worth | 812 Main St. (8th St.) | Ft. Worth | 817-877-3999 www.delfriscos.com

Born in Dallas, this "high-end" franchise attracts a "see-and-be-seen" crowd with its "Texas-size" steaks and sides backed up by a "fantastic wine list"; sure, it's "way expensive", but in return you get sleek settings, "flawless service" from "attractive" staffers and "no chain feeling."

🆉 French Room 🅾🅼 *American/French* | 28 | 29 | 29 | VE |

Downtown Dallas | Hotel Adolphus | 1321 Commerce St. (Field St.) | Dallas | 214-742-8200 | www.hoteladolphus.com

"Smitten" surveyors find an "off-the-charts experience" at this Downtown "icon", voted No. 1 for Food, Decor and Service in Dallas/Ft. Worth, where "stupendous" French-New American cuisine is served with "unparalleled attention to detail" inside the "opulent" crystal-chandeliered and marble-columned dining room of the Hotel Adolphus; sure, it's "expensive", but "close to perfect" for a "good old-fashioned splurge" – especially if you opt for the tasting menu with "excellent" wine pairings.

	FOOD	DECOR	SERVICE	COST

Lanny's Alta
Cocina Mexicana ⑤Ⓜ *Eclectic/Mexican*   27 | 25 | 26 | E

Cultural District | 3405 W. Seventh St. (Boland St.) | Ft. Worth |
817-850-9996 | www.lannyskitchen.com

"Simply awesome" declare those dazzled by chef Lanny Lancarte's
"haute" Eclectic-Mexican eatery in Ft. Worth's Cultural District offering "clever takes" on South-of-the-border classics (like elk mole and
pomegranate margaritas) plus "inventive" international dishes all
served by a "friendly and efficient" staff; yes, it's "expensive", but an
"inviting" atmosphere with a "beautiful patio" make it all "worth it."

ⓩ Local ⑤Ⓜ *American*   28 | 24 | 25 | E

Deep Ellum | 2936 Elm St. (1 block west of Hall St.) | Dallas | 214-752-7500 |
www.localdallas.com

A "hidden gem" in Deep Ellum, chef Tracy Miller's "funky and modern"
venue set in the historic Boyd Hotel charms connoisseurs with "great
wines" and a "zingy, fresh-flavored" New American menu that utilizes
"local, seasonal ingredients", which make it "one of the few places in
Dallas where it's possible to eat both healthy and well"; solid service
is a plus, though some demur on tabs they call "pretty pricy" for the
area; N.B. there is private parking adjacent to the restaurant.

Lola ⑤Ⓜ *American*   27 | 23 | 25 | VE

Uptown | 2917 Fairmount St. (Cedar Springs Rd.) | Dallas | 214-855-0700 |
www.lola4dinner.com

"Romantics" adore this "quaint old house" Uptown where "outstanding" New American cuisine is presented in "exquisite" prix fixe menus
and matched with wines from an "incredible", "reasonably priced" list;
add in high-level service, and it's the "perfect spot for a special
evening"; P.S. the separate chef's tasting room with a 10-course menu
is "one of the city's great fine-dining experiences."

Lonesome Dove
Western Bistro ⑤Ⓜ *Southwestern*   26 | 23 | 23 | E

Stockyards | 2406 N. Main St. (24th St.) | Ft. Worth | 817-740-8810 |
www.lonesomedovebistro.com

Chef-owner Tim Love's "haute cowboy cuisine" earns legions of fans at
this fine-dining "treasure" in Ft. Worth's Stockyards that "hits the mark"
with "huge portions" of "impressive", "experimental" Southwestern
specialties like braised wild boar ribs and buffalo ribeye; given the "sophisticated" saloon setting and staff who lays on the "Texas charm",
it's "a must" for visitors, especially those on "expense account."

Mercury Chophouse *Steak*   26 | 23 | 23 | E
(fka Fort Worth Chophouse)

Sundance Square | 301 Main St. (2nd St.) | Ft. Worth | 817-336-4129 |
www.mcrowd.com

There's "never a bad meal" at this "solid" Downtown steakhouse in
Sundance Square (recently taken over by the M Crowd restaurant
group) that's an "excellent place for a business lunch" and "one of the
best in Ft. Worth for conversation"; the "great" fare features a "perfect
fillet", and the "intimate" room is both "comfortable and luxurious",
with "big velvety drapes" and "club chairs" to bring you "back in time
to the '40s."

Mercury Grill *American*

27 | 23 | 24 | E

Preston Forest | Preston Forest Vill. | 11909 Preston Rd. (Forest Ln.) | Dallas | 972-960-7774 | www.mcrowd.com

"Talented" chef Chris Ward "gets it right" at this "fashionable" Preston Forest "place to be seen" with his "sublime" New American menu from which loyalists recite their litany of "favorites" ("heavenly mushroom risotto", braised short ribs); despite the fact that it's "tucked into a strip center", this is "one happening spot", with a staff so personable "we wished our waiter could have joined us for the meal" – just "watch out for the tab."; N.B. there's an expanded lounge and rooms for private groups.

☑ Mi Cocina *Tex-Mex*

21 | 19 | 20 | I

Lake Highlands | 7201 Skillman St. (Kingsley Rd.) | Dallas | 214-503-6426

Park Cities | Highland Park Vill. | 77 Highland Park Vill. (bet. Mockingbird Ln. & Preston Rd.) | Dallas | 214-521-6426

Preston Forest | Preston Forest Vill. | 11661 Preston Rd. (Forest Ln.) | Dallas | 214-265-7704

West Village | West Vill. | 3699 McKinney Ave. (Lemmon Ave.) | Dallas | 469-533-5663

Sundance Square | Sundance Sq. | 509 Main St. (bet. 4th & 5th Sts.) | Ft. Worth | 817-877-3600

Southlake | Southlake Town Sq. | 1276 S. Main St. (Carroll Ave.) | 817-410-6426

www.mcrowd.com

Admirers assert this "upscale" chain with locations in Highland Park, North Dallas and all the nearby suburbs is the "standard setter" for Tex-Mex cuisine, with "light", "fresh-tasting" "contemporary" fare and "killer 'ritas" attracting a "noisy" crowd of "pretty folk" and their offspring; "modern" atmosphere (no "south-of-the-border clichés" here) plus "solid value", even considering the "expensive drinks", means you can "go to any of them and leave satisfied."

Nana *American*

27 | 27 | 27 | VE

Market Center | Hilton Anatole Hotel | 2201 Stemmons Frwy. (Market Center Blvd.) | Dallas | 214-761-7470 | www.nanarestaurant.com

It's tough to compete with "absolutely stunning" "panoramic" views of Downtown Dallas, yet chef Anthony Bombaci captivates diners with equally "amazing" New American dishes prepared in "imaginative" ways (think ahi tuna tartare with wasabi ice cream) at this elegant aerie atop the Hilton Anatole Hotel in Market Center; prices are "expensive", but the "superb" staff "executes at a high level", making it a top ticket for "special occasions."

Pappas Bros. Steakhouse ☒ *Steak*

27 | 24 | 25 | E

Love Field | 10477 Lombardy Ln. (Northwest Hwy.) | Dallas | 214-366-2000 | www.pappasbros.com

"The Pappas family does it right" at this "standout" meatery in Dallas, which keeps "packing them in" to its "sumptuous" quarters for a "phenomenal" combo of "awesome" beef, "killer wines" and "outstanding service" that's "worth every dollar" of the "very high" price tag; its "warm" atmosphere is "great for business dinners or a night out with the guys", so expect a strong showing of "men in suits."

Saint-Emilion ⊠ Ⓜ *French* | 27 | 24 | 27 | E |

Cultural District | 3617 W. Seventh St. (Montgomery St.) | Ft. Worth | 817-737-2781

A "country French delight" in Ft. Worth's Cultural District, this "small jewel" warmed by brick walls and a wood-beamed ceiling is "perfect for dates" and "special occasions", presenting "amazing" "daily black-board specials" matched by a "fabulous" wine list and "hospitality on the same delicious level as the food"; fans say the prix fixe option offers a real "value in fine dining" and, as tables are limited, recommend making "reservations on peak nights."

62 Main Restaurant ⊠ Ⓜ *American* | 27 | 23 | 26 | E |

Colleyville | 62 Main St. (bet. Hwy. 26 & Main St.) | 817-605-0858 | www.62mainrestaurant.com

It's "big-city dining in the 'burbs" proclaim chain-weary fans who flock to chef-owner David McMillan's "upscale" New American spot that serves "inventive" "masterpieces" with "sauces and flavors that are right on"; "tucked away" on the second floor of the Village at Colleyville development, the rustic room has a Napa feel, enhanced by "friendly" service and costs that are "a bit pricey, but an overall fair value", causing most to concur that it's "worth the drive."

Z Stephan Pyles ⊠ *Southwestern* | 27 | 28 | 26 | E |

Arts District | 1807 Ross Ave. (St. Paul St.) | Dallas | 214-580-7000 | www.stephanpyles.com

"Father of Southwestern cuisine" Stephan Pyles "has his groove back" say fans of this "elegant but relaxed" Dallas Arts District "hot spot" where he reprises some of his "classic" menu items while also branching out into newer territory", mixing ingredients "you never expect to mesh"; though some say it can get "way too noisy", most concur that the "great lighting and architecture" create a package "beyond phenomenal", "classy down to the waiter's attire" – making it "worth every cent and more."

Z Tei Tei Robata Bar Ⓜ *Japanese* | 28 | 23 | 23 | E |

Knox-Henderson | 2906 N. Henderson Ave. (Willis Ave.) | Dallas | 214-828-2400 | www.teiteirobata.com

"Some of the best sushi in Dallas" shout aficionados at this "noisy" Knox-Henderson Japanese (and sib of Teppo) catering to a "hip" crowd with "fantastic", "fresh fish" and a "wonderful" selection of grilled dishes served by a "warm" staff; it's "often very crowded", but fans find it's "worth the wait" and the somewhat "pricey" tabs.

Z Teppo Yakitori & Sushi Bar Ⓜ *Japanese* | 28 | 22 | 25 | E |

Greenville Avenue | 2014 Greenville Ave. (Prospect Ave.) | Dallas | 214-826-8989 | www.teppo.com

It's "like a top yakitori restaurant in Tokyo" rave devotees of this "real-deal" Japanese, a Greenville Avenue sibling of Tei-Tei Robata, that dishes out "killer sushi" and "great grilled" meats by chefs who clearly show "care in the preparation" of "fresh, fresh, fresh" food; adding to the "wonderful experience", its minimally decorated space (with semi-private tatami rooms for parties) feels "swanky yet comfortable", prices are "reasonable" and the staff is "welcoming" – just "be prepared for a long wait."

FOOD DECOR SERVICE COST

York Street 🅂 🅼 *American* | 27 | 20 | 26 | E |

Lakewood | 6047 Lewis St. (Skillman St.) | Dallas | 214-826-0968 |
www.yorkstreetdallas.com

Chef-owner Sharon Hage's "artistry" makes for "world-class", "beautifully conceived and executed" New American dishes incorporating
"locally fresh" ingredients at this "teeny-tiny", hard-to-find "old
house" on the outskirts of Lakewood; while some find the space
"sparse" and "cramped", most agree the servers are "wonderful"
(even if they sometimes "concentrate on regulars"), and the food offers "substantial rewards" at "fair prices" for those willing to "reserve
well in advance."

Yutaka Sushi & Bistro *Japanese* | 27 | 19 | 22 | E |

Uptown | 2633 McKinney Ave. (Routh St.) | Dallas | 214-969-5533 |
www.yutakasushibistro.com

"Locals" lament "the secret is out" at this Uptown Japanese that's
"packed" with fin-addicts feasting on "outstanding sushi" and "phenomenal grilled dishes" all best appreciated via an "omakase meal"
that's "to die for"; the space is "small", but "down-to-earth prices" and
a "friendly" staff compensate for occasional "waits."

Denver Area & Mountain Resorts

TOP FOOD RANKING

	Restaurant	Cuisine
28	Mizuna	American
	Frasca	Italian
	Fruition	American
	Sushi Den	Japanese
27	Sushi Sasa	Japanese
	Six89 Kitchen/Wine	American
	Matsuhisa	Japanese
	Keystone Ranch	American
	Del Frisco's	Steak
	Kevin Taylor	French
	Splendido/Chateau	American
26	Sweet Basil	American
	Piñons	American
	Flagstaff House	American
	Luca d'Italia	Italian
	rioja	Mediterranean
	La Tour	French
	Barolo Grill	Italian
	Z Cuisine Bistrot	French
	Juniper	American
	Montagna	American
25	John's	American
	Potager	American

Z Barolo Grill Ⓩ Ⓜ *Italian*　　　26 | 23 | 25 | E

Cherry Creek | 3030 E. Sixth Ave. (bet. Milwaukee & St. Paul Sts.) | Denver | 303-393-1040 | www.barologrilldenver.com

"You'd have to travel to Tuscany to find better fare" than at this "elegant" Cherry Creek "favorite" where "beautiful people" sit by the "romantic fireplace" and savor "heavenly" Northern Italian cuisine that's "a study in flavor", especially when paired with selections from the "amazing wine list"; in fact, the staff itself "visits Italy every year", resulting in service that surveyors describe as "somewhat pretentious" but "knowledgeable and eager to help."

Del Frisco's　　　27 | 24 | 26 | E
Double Eagle Steak House *Steak*

Greenwood Village | Denver Tech Ctr. | 8100 E. Orchard Rd. (I-25, Ext. 198) | 303-796-0100 | www.delfriscos.com

This "clubby" Greenwood Village "cow palace" corrals all types – from "power brokers" and "local sports celebrities" to "high rollers and those looking to hit on them" – for "consistently excellent" steaks "prepared to perfection" plus "huge sides" and an "extensive wine list" that "reads like *War and Peace*"; "exceptional service" and a "separate cigar lounge" also add appeal, but be prepared – you'll need "some large bills" to pay the tab at this "carnivore's delight."

Flagstaff House *American*

26 | 27 | 27 | VE

Boulder | 1138 Flagstaff Rd. (on Flagstaff Mtn.) | 303-442-4640 |
www.flagstaffhouse.com

"Make the drive up" Flagstaff Mountain to this "treasure in the sky"
where "resplendent views" "overlooking Boulder and beyond" ("so
beautiful at sunset!") are just the beginning: chef Mark Monette's
"simply superb" New American cuisine, an "amazing wine list with incredible sommeliers to match" and "impeccable" service "timed to the
second" also add to the "absolutely first-class" package; it's "not for
the weak of wallet", but you should "go at least once in a lifetime."

☑ Frasca Food and Wine ⑤ *Italian*

28 | 24 | 27 | E

Boulder | 1738 Pearl St. (18th St.) | 303-442-6966 |
www.frascafoodandwine.com

"Words cannot adequately express how divine" Colorado's Most
Popular restaurant really is, so you'll just have to "call two months
ahead and pray" that you get a reservation at this "beacon in Boulder",
where chef Lachlan Mackinnon-Patterson and master sommelier
Bobby Stuckey (both French Laundry alums) "specialize in the food
and wine of [Italy's] Friuli region; it's also No. 1 for Service, courtesy
of a "friendly, knowledgeable staff" that helps make this "truly world-
class experience" "deserving of all the hype."

☑ NEW Fruition Ⓜ *American*

28 | 21 | 26 | E

Country Club | 1313 E. Sixth Ave. (bet. Lafayette & Marion Sts.) |
Denver | 303-831-1992 | www.fruitionrestaurant.com

"Absolutely incredible" "plates that look like a Cézanne still life" are
the hallmark of this "top-tier destination" situated between Capitol
Hill and Country Club that has come to "fruition indeed", courtesy of
"talented" chef/co-owner Alex Seidel, who "goes above and beyond"
with his "fantastic", "expertly crafted" New American cuisine; "deft
and friendly service" adds to the "sterling experience", which means
"the only chink in the armor" is the "cozy" but "very tiny space."

John's ☒ Ⓜ *American*

25 | 19 | 24 | E

Boulder | 2328 Pearl St. (bet. 23rd & 24th Sts.) | 303-444-5232 |
www.johnsrestaurantboulder.com

"It's like visiting the home of a wealthy friend" announce acolytes of
this "hidden gem" offering "creative", "wonderful" New American cuisine plus a "well-chosen wine list" in a "nicely renovated old house" in
Boulder; the "delightful dining experience" is "perfect for any occasion" thanks to "attentive" service and the type of "peaceful setting"
that's "quiet" enough for a "pleasant conversation with friends."

Juniper *American*

26 | 20 | 22 | E

Edwards | 97 Main St. (Hwy. 6) | 970-926-7001 |
www.juniperrestaurant.com

"A charming surprise" situated a few miles from Vail in "unassuming"
Edwards, this New American "gem" is "well worth the drive" for "excellent" "seasonal" cuisine served by an "enthusiastic" staff, plus its
"happening local scene" and "sublime" deck with tables "overlooking
the Eagle River"; nevertheless, a few fret about "cramped quarters"
and a "snooty attitude", recommending patrons "sit at the bar for op-
timal location and attention."

Kevin Taylor 🗷 French

| 27 | 25 | 26 | VE |

Downtown Denver | Hotel Teatro | 1106 14th St. (Arapahoe St.) | Denver | 303-820-2600 | www.ktrg.net

Step into "a magical world where all your desires come true" at this "benchmark of excellence" in the Downtown theater district offering "exquisite" New French cuisine from "accomplished" and "uncompromising" chef-owner Kevin Taylor; situated in a "classic white-tablecloth" setting in the Hotel Teatro, it's an "elegant" (if "pricey") experience that's elevated by a "superior wine list" and "attentive but unobtrusive service."

Keystone Ranch 🗷 American

| 27 | 27 | 26 | VE |

Keystone | Keystone Ranch Golf Course | 1437 Summit County Rd. 150 (Rd. D) | 970-496-4386 | www.keystone.snow.com

"As good as it gets", this "rustic" "reminder of a time gone by" is No. 1 for Decor in Colorado, offering "consistently wonderful" regional New American cuisine and "superb service" amid the "spectacular" ambiance of an "elegant" "turn-of-the-century" Keystone ranch house; such a "memorable" evening could only end with dessert in a "cozy" sitting room "complete with roaring fire and overstuffed leather sofas"; in short, it may be "costly, but who cares?"

La Tour French

| 26 | 20 | 24 | E |

Vail | 122 E. Meadow Dr. (I-70) | 970-476-4403 | www.latour-vail.com

Have your "French food and wine fantasy fulfilled" at this "hidden" "must-do in the Vail Valley", where chef/co-owner Paul Ferzacca offers "heaven on a plate" in the form of "creative", contemporary Gallic cuisine ("the Dover sole is truly inspired"); it's all served by a "friendly", "attentive staff that knows the menu" and can suggest the "perfect wine pairing", helping to make this both a "place to impress a date" and "a tough ticket in-season."

Luca d'Italia 🗷🅼 Italian

| 26 | 19 | 26 | E |

Capitol Hill | 711 Grant St. (bet. 7th & 8th Aves.) | Denver | 303-832-6600 | www.lucadenver.com

Overseen by chef-owner Frank Bonanno ("the mind behind Mizuna"), this "splendid Italian noshery" on Capitol Hill is "a truly superior experience" offering "interesting culinary combinations" full of "unexpectedly wonderful flavors" plus homemade "pastas from the heavens"; although a few frown upon the "simple", "sterile" surroundings, they're outvoted by those who appreciate the "excellent tasting menu", "knowledgeable staff" and "great people-watching."

Matsuhisa Japanese

| 27 | 23 | 24 | VE |

Aspen | 303 E. Main St. (Monarch St.) | 970-544-6628 | www.matsuhisaaspen.com

"A mile-high Nobu" that "lives up to its reputation", this Aspen eatery from the eponymous restaurateur is a "fabulous" "treat" delivering "jaw-dropping Japanese fusion" fare and "amazingly fresh" sushi; the "food outshines everything else", but the basement-level dining room has a "hip vibe" and the upstairs lounge is also a "happening" place to sip "chilled sake served in bamboo carafes"; still, "astronomical prices" have some insisting "it's not the lack of oxygen in the air that leaves you breathless – it's the bill."

	FOOD	DECOR	SERVICE	COST

Ⓩ Mizuna 🅢Ⓜ *American* — 28 | 23 | 27 | E

Capitol Hill | 225 E. Seventh Ave. (bet. Grant & Sherman Sts.) | Denver | 303-832-4778 | www.mizunadenver.com

Rated No. 1 for Food in Colorado, this "consistently excellent" Capitol Hill "favorite" "still leads the pack" when it comes to "culinary genius" Frank Bonanno's "undeniably brilliant" New American menu (including "to-die-for lobster mac 'n' cheese"); it has "all the components of a wonderful evening" – a "well-rounded wine list", "impeccable service" and an "intimate, romantic" ambiance – so although prices are steep, it's "worth every penny" in order to "sweep a first date or long-time girlfriend off her feet."

Montagna *American* — 26 | 26 | 25 | VE

Aspen | The Little Nell Hotel | 675 E. Durant Ave. (Spring St.) | 970-920-6330 | www.thelittlenell.com

"Nestled in The Little Nell Hotel" in Aspen, this "place to see and be seen" draws a "fabulous crowd" with its "equally fabulous food": chef Ryan Hardy's "sophisticated menu" of "inventive, well-executed" New American cuisine is coupled with an "opulent", "encyclopedic wine list" overseen by "maestro Richard Betts"; "unsurpassed service" adds to a "beautiful experience" that's costly and to some "a bit stuffy" but for most is "just magnificent" – "what more could you want?"

Piñons *American* — 26 | 24 | 26 | VE

Aspen | 105 S. Mill St. (E. Main St.) | 970-920-2021 | www.pinons.net

Still "an outstanding dining experience" "after all these years", this "timeless" Aspen "favorite" draws "locals and VIPs" (hence there's "excellent people-watching") with its "superb" "Rocky Mountain haute cuisine", including meats that "practically 'moo' from your plate"; but whether you relax in the "elegant" interior or "outside on a perfect summer evening", be sure to take note of the "great mountain views" and take advantage of the "bargain", "early prix fixe dinner."

Potager 🅢Ⓜ *American* — 25 | 21 | 23 | E

Capitol Hill | 1109 Ogden St. (bet. 11th & 12th Aves.) | Denver | 303-832-5788

"A seasoned toque in every sense", chef/co-owner Teri Rippeto is "truly dedicated" to using "seasonal, locally raised and mostly organic" ingredients at her "lovely" Capitol Hill New American, a "unique experience" with "something for everyone" on a menu that's "ever-changing" yet "never bends to hip food trends"; "a boutique wine list just adds to the culinary magic", as does an "attentive but not obtrusive" staff and an "intimate backyard garden"; P.S. get here "early, since they don't take reservations."

Ⓩ rioja *Mediterranean* — 26 | 23 | 23 | E

Larimer Square | 1431 Larimer St. (bet. 14th & 15th Sts.) | Denver | 303-820-2282 | www.riojadenver.com

Chef/co-owner Jennifer Jasinski "is nothing short of amazing", and her "cosmopolitan" restaurant in "hip Larimer Square" rewards its "loyal following" with "mouthwatering" Med cuisine that "makes use of seasonal and local ingredients" and is paired with "some fine Spanish wines"; a "knowledgeable" staff that "goes above and beyond" adds to the "inviting" and "always energetic" (if occasionally "noisy.") ambiance; P.S. try to "get a seat at the chef's counter."

Six89 Kitchen/Wine Bar Ⓜ American

27 | 22 | 25 | E

Carbondale | 689 Main St. (7th St.) | 970-963-6890 | www.six89.com

"Skip the scene in Aspen" and take a "trip down-valley" to this "swank" "favorite" that's "worth the drive" to Carbondale for "unusual", "truly creative" New American cuisine from chef-owner Mark Fischer, a proprietor who "knows no wrong"; the "food and wine combinations" are "coveted by locals", who also appreciate the "exceptional staff" and a "fantastic atmosphere" that includes a welcoming patio and a dining room "where you can carry on a conversation."

Splendido at the Chateau American

27 | 27 | 26 | VE

Beaver Creek | Beaver Creek Resort | 17 Chateau Ln. (Scott Hill Rd.) | 970-845-8808 | www.splendidobeavercreek.com

"An outstanding experience" "from start to finish", this New American in the Beaver Creek Resort offers a "splendid blending of food, service and atmosphere": chef David Walford "runs a first-class kitchen" that turns out "imaginative" preparations of local game, while a "fantastic" staff treats guests "like royalty" as they dine in the "beautiful", "elegant room" or sip cocktails in the "delightful piano bar"; yes, it's "expensive", but it's "worth the cost" "for a special occasion."

Ⓩ Sushi Den Japanese

28 | 23 | 21 | E

South Denver | 1487 S. Pearl St. (E. Florida Ave.) | Denver | 303-777-0826 | www.sushiden.net

For "absolutely flawless" "fish so fresh you can't believe you're eating it in Colorado", set sail for this South Denver Japanese where "shockingly" "inspired sushi" and "unique rolls" are served in a "stylish" space that gets "crowded" with "local stars, sports celebrities" and other "beautiful people"; there are often "outrageous waits" and servers can be "a bit snooty", but most agree it's "worth the suffering" to experience "the magic unfold"; P.S. "they don't take reservations."

Ⓩ Sushi Sasa Japanese

27 | 22 | 23 | E

Highlands | 2401 15th St. (Platte St.) | Denver | 303-433-7272 | www.sushisasadenver.com

At this "upscale" Japanese in the "increasingly popular Highlands neighborhood", chef-owner Wayne Conwell "is a magician" who will "tantalize your taste buds" with his "delicious seafood dishes" and "brilliantly crafted", "impeccably fresh sushi"; a "simple", "modern space" with "white everything" serves as a counterpoint to the "dynamic" cuisine, while a "friendly" staff adds to the "pleasant experience."

Ⓩ Sweet Basil American

26 | 23 | 24 | E

Vail | 193 E. Gore Creek Dr. (Bridge St.) | 970-476-0125 | www.sweetbasil-vail.com

"Still as sweet as ever", this "high-altitude gem" is "the gold standard of the Vail Valley" courtesy of "cutting-edge", "practically flawless" New American cuisine from chef Paul Anders plus a "killer wine list" and an "engaging staff"; a "glitzy crowd" gathers here "after a hard day playing in the powder", so although the "delightful setting" was "just refurbished and enlarged", it remains "tough to score a reservation"; P.S. "ask for a creekside window table."

Z Cuisine Bistrot & Parisian Bar ⓈⓂ *French* | 26 | 20 | 22 | M |

Highlands | 2239 W. 30th Ave. (Wyandot St.) | Denver | 303-477-1111 | www.zcuisineonline.com

Be "transported to Paris" "without the jet lag" at this "labor of love" located "off the beaten path" in Highlands, where "talented" chef/co-owner Patrick DuPays pleases patrons with a "terrific" blackboard menu of "truly incredible, authentic bistro" classics that "pair perfectly with the lovely wine list"; the "intimate", "postage stamp–sized" space is being expanded, which is certain to appease frustrated Francophiles who say "the no-reservations policy is a crock of cassoulet"; N.B. closed Sunday–Tuesday.

Honolulu

TOP FOOD RANKING

	Restaurant	Cuisine
28	Alan Wong's	Hawaii Reg.
27	La Mer	French
26	Hoku's	Pacific Rim
	Roy's	Hawaiian
	Chef Mavro	French/Hawaii Reg.
	Roy's Ko Olina	Hawaiian
	Orchids	American
	3660 on the Rise	Pacific Rim
	Hy's Steak House	Steak
25	Ruth's Chris	Steak
	Michel's	French
24	Sansei	Japanese
	Mekong	Thai
	Pineapple Room	Hawaii Reg.
	Hiroshi Eurasian	Eurasian
	Bali by the Sea	Pacific Rim
23	Side Street Inn	Hawaii Reg.
	Indigo	Asian Fusion
	Olive Tree Café	Greek
	Nick's Fishmarket	Seafood

Z Alan Wong's *Hawaii Reg.* `28` `20` `26` `E`

Ala Moana | McCully Ct. | 1857 S. King St., 3rd fl. (bet. Hauoli & Pumehana Sts.) | 808-949-2526 | www.alanwongs.com

Ranked Most Popular and No. 1 for Food in Honolulu, this restaurant "away from the tourist fray" in Ala Moana "never ceases to amaze" fans of notable chef Alan Wong's "creative brilliance"; with Hawaii Regional dishes like the "heavenly ginger-crusted onaga", "amazing" tasting menus and "stealthlike", "unobtrusive service", it's "Pacific meets perfection", despite its "nondescript" second-floor space and "limited street parking"; P.S. be sure to make reservations "well in advance."

Bali by the Sea ☒ *Pacific Rim* `24` `26` `24` `E`

Waikiki | Hilton Hawaiian Village | 2005 Kalia Rd. (Ala Moana Blvd.) | 808-941-2254 | www.hiltonhawaiianvillage.com

"Expertly prepared seafood" that's "so fresh" "you swear it was just caught" and an "arty" chocolate replica of Diamond Head (it "smokes" via dry ice) delight diners at this Pacific Rim spot that's "really by the sea" in an "idyllic" location in the Hilton Hawaiian Village; you may have to book a few days in advance for the most "dramatic views", but with such a "warm, welcoming" atmosphere, you'll "dream about coming back."

NEW Cassis by Chef Mavro *French* `-` `-` `-` `E`

Downtown | 66 Queen St. (Nimitz Hwy.) | 808-545-8100 | www.cassishonolulu.com

Top chef George Mavrothalassitis (of the highly regarded Chef Mavro in Ala Moana) draws on his Provençal heritage at this trendy Downtown addition where an attractive staff serves up island-inflected French bistro fare – think grilled ahi niçoise – and a hip wine bar offers daily flights; the cavernous former Palomino space retains a slightly institutional feel despite an extensive renovation, so aesthetes are advised to grab a window seat to take in the Honolulu Harbor views; N.B. it gets packed at lunch.

Z Chef Mavro M *French/Hawaii Reg.*

26 | 23 | 26 | VE

Ala Moana | 1969 S. King St. (McCully St.) | 808-944-4714 | www.chefmavro.com

"From the moment you enter until the end of your meal", dining here is an "experience for all the senses" say fans of the "inspired" New French–meets–Hawaii Regional cuisine of chef George Mavrothalassitis, who "often greets guests himself"; service is very "knowledgeable", the "wine pairings are outstanding" and the interior is "beautiful", so even if its Ala Moana location "leaves a bit to be desired" and "portions are tiny", most take one bite of the "homemade malasadas" dessert and declare it "fabulomavrous!"

Z Duke's Canoe Club *Seafood*

17 | 22 | 17 | M

Waikiki | Outrigger Waikiki on the Beach | 2335 Kalakaua Ave. (bet. Dukes Ln. & Kaiulani Ave.) | 808-922-2268 | www.dukeswaikiki.com

"Wild, wacky" and "tons of fun", this "always packed", open-air, oceanfront seafooder in the Outrigger Waikiki on the Beach is a "tourist mecca" with a "great" breakfast buffet, "classic mahi sandwiches", "kitschy Hawaiian cocktails" and a "famous hula pie", all delivered with "a smile"; there's lots of "memorabilia" honoring the "great surfing legend" Duke Kahanamoku, and when the "hotties" show up for live music after sunset, it becomes "*the* happening place."

Hiroshi Eurasian Tapas *Eurasian*

24 | 20 | 23 | E

Restaurant Row | 500 Ala Moana Blvd. (South St.) | 808-533-4476 | www.dkrestaurants.com

The small-plates concept makes its way to Hawaii in the form of this "innovative" Restaurant Row Eurasian where the "classic techniques" of chef Hiroshi Fukui are coupled with the talents of master sommelier Chuck Furuya, who offers "interesting wine flights"; "every plate is a piece of art" (though it's too bad the same can't be said of the "drab" decor), and the staff serves it amiably, but hungry wallet-watchers warn that all those "too tiny" tapas add up to one big bill.

Z Hoku's *Pacific Rim*

26 | 26 | 26 | E

Kahala | Kahala Hotel & Resort | 5000 Kahala Ave. (Kealaolu Ave.) | 808-739-8780 | www.kahalaresort.com

For "sublime dining" with a "beautiful view of the ocean", this Kahala Hotel & Resort restaurant is a "stunning" choice; feast on a recently revamped menu of "creative", "phenomenal" Pacific Rim fare among the "movers and shakers", revel in the "gracious" service and soak up the "romantic" ambiance "at sunset" with the one you love; sure, it might just "break the bank", but the experience leaves you "happy to pay"; N.B. no casual attire is permitted in the evenings.

Hy's Steak House *Steak*

26 | 23 | 25 | E

Waikiki | Waikiki Park Heights Hotel | 2440 Kuhio Ave. (Uluniu Ave.) | 808-922-5555 | www.hyshawaii.com

"Excellent" slabs of beef grilled "exactly how you ordered" right "before your eyes" on a kiawe-wood fire make this "wonderful anachronism" in the Waikiki Park Heights Hotel a "superb" steakhouse "throwback to the '60s or '70s"; a dimly lit, "old-world" setting complete with "curved booths for cuddling" and "impeccable" service add to its appeal, and meat mavens maintain they'd "eat there nightly" if they could; N.B. there's live guitar Tuesday–Saturday.

Indigo ⚫Ⓜ *Asian Fusion*

23 | 23 | 21 | M

Chinatown | 1121 Nuuanu Ave. (Hotel St.) | 808-521-2900 | www.indigo-hawaii.com

"Wow your taste buds" with "irresistible" Asian fusion eats from chef Glenn Chu, who "blends unique flavors for a multicultural feast" at this "exotic" *Sex-and-the-City-meets-South-Pacific* "hipster" in Chinatown; it's a "favorite for the Downtown lunch crowd", and "trendy twenty- and thirtysomethings" seeking a "killer happy hour" can head to the attached Green Room lounge; it can get "noisy", but it's one of the most "provocative" settings around; P.S. "valet parking is recommended."

⚫ La Mer *French*

27 | 28 | 27 | VE

Waikiki | Halekulani Hotel | 2199 Kalia Rd. (Lewers St.) | 808-923-2311 | www.halekulani.com

At this "landmark" restaurant in Waikiki's Halekulani Hotel, the "breathtaking" oceanside location ("ask for a window seat") and the "impeccable" service are so "unforgettable" that surveyors have ranked it No. 1 for both Decor and Service in Honolulu; "each bite" of chef Yves Garnier's New French cuisine "with an island touch" is a "delectable" "taste of heaven", so even if you need to wear a jacket and the "cost rivals that of NYC's" top eateries, it's the "ultimate special date" choice.

Mekong Thai I *Thai*

24 | 14 | 19 | I

Ala Moana | 1295 S. Beretania St. (bet. Keeaumoku & Piikoi Sts.) | 808-591-8842

Mekong Thai II *Thai*

Ala Moana | 1726 S. King St. (McCully St.) | 808-941-6184

They may have "small, hole-in-the-wall" settings, but you can't miss with these twin Thai restaurants in Ala Moana, where the "intimate, homestyle" cuisine features "traditional" dishes ("try the evil jungle prince entree", created by founder Keo Sananikone, also owner of Keo's in Waikiki); though the service can seem "impersonal", the "reliable, straightforward flavors" and "good value" more than make up for it; N.B. the Beretania Street branch is BYO.

Michel's *French*

25 | 26 | 25 | E

Waikiki | Colony Surf Hotel | 2895 Kalakaua Ave. (Poni Moi Rd.) | 808-923-6552 | www.michelshawaii.com

It's "the place to go if you're in love" sigh surveyors who savor the "fantastic sunsets" and the "music of the surf caressing the shore" at this Classic French with "an island touch" in the Colony Surf Hotel at the foot of Diamond Head; it's "a bit dressy by Waikiki standards" (jackets for men are "requested but not required") and some say it "costs a bundle" – it's "only worth it if you have the view" – but others would happily return to feast on "sumptuous" standards like "steak Diane done tableside" and served by an "impeccable" staff.

Nick's Fishmarket *Seafood*

23 | 19 | 22 | E

Waikiki | Waikiki Gateway Hotel | 2070 Kalakaua Ave. (Olohanna St.) | 808-955-6333 | www.nicksfishmarket.com

A "Honolulu institution", this seafooder in the Waikiki Gateway Hotel still dazzles fans with its "always outstanding", "amazingly delicious" and "innovative" fresh fish presentations as well as its "romantic" curved booths and "efficient" service; critics complain that the decor "could use an injection of creativity" (it looks like "the '80s"), but "all in all, it's a grand experience."

NEW Nobu Waikiki *Japanese*

- | - | - | VE

Waikiki | Waikiki Parc Hotel | 2233 Helumoa Rd. (Lewers St.) | 808-237-6999 | www.noburestaurants.com

Celebrity chef Nobu Matsuhisa has brought his innovative international chain to a town known for its Asian restaurants, and Honolulu foodies are already flocking to the Waikiki Parc Hotel to sample Peruvian-accented Japanese fare that's as pricey as it is unique; it's set in a 7,500-sq.-ft. lobby space – complete with lounge, sushi bar and private dining room – that's been transformed by the Rockwell Group to include sophisticated Hawaiian and Asian touches.

Olive Tree Café ⊅ *Greek*

23 | 10 | 15 | I

Kahala | 4614 Kilauea Ave. (Pahoa Ave.) | 808-737-0303

For "fabulous", "authentic" Greek-Med cuisine, including "phenomenal fish souvlaki", head to this "popular neighborhood hangout" in Kahala, where counter service and a BYO policy keep the "prices low"; "parking and seating can be hard" and there's little decor, but it's "definitely worth" waiting amid "madhouse crowds" to eat at this "hidden treasure."

Orchids *American*

26 | 27 | 26 | E

Waikiki | Halekulani Hotel | 2199 Kalia Rd. (Lewers St.) | 808-923-2311 | www.halekulani.com

With "amazing breakfasts", a "fantastic Sunday brunch" and a "view over the water at sunset", this open-air, beachside American in the Halekulani Hotel (just downstairs from La Mer) is a "relaxing" choice; so "sip the most fabulous mai tai", feast on "superb" fare served by an "impeccable" staff, listen to the "lapping waves" and be "transported."

Pineapple Room *Hawaii Reg.*

24 | 18 | 21 | M

Ala Moana | Macy's, Ala Moana Shopping Ctr. | 1450 Ala Moana Blvd. (Atkinson Dr.) | 808-945-6573 | www.alanwongs.com

At this "little-known outpost" from "mega-talented" chef Alan Wong ("oddly located" in the Ala Moana Shopping Center Macy's and "a gift to the ladies who lunch"), the "master's touch" is discernible in the "excellent" Hawaii Regional fare, especially the "to-die-for Kahlua pig BLT", but the prices "will leave some padding in your wallet" compared with his eponymous King Street spot; still, sour sorts snap over "inconsistent service" and an underwhelming "view of the rooftop mall parking" lot; P.S. "reservations are a must."

☒ Roy's *Hawaiian* | 26 | 21 | 24 | E |

Hawaii Kai | 6600 Kalanianaole Hwy. (Keahole St.) | 808-396-7697 | www.roysrestaurant.com

This "original" Hawaii Kai "flagship" (of a 30-plus-location chain) "put Hawaiian fusion cuisine on the culinary map" and continues to thrill patrons with its "unpretentious, eye-appealing and always delicious" offerings and seemingly "choreographed" service; while some suggest dining in the "quieter" downstairs section, others say "come early", head upstairs and "watch the beautiful sunset."

Roy's Ko Olina *Hawaiian* | 26 | 23 | 25 | E |

Kapolei | Ko Olina Resort & Marina | 92-1220 Aliinui Dr. (Kamoana Pl.) | 808-676-7697 | www.roysrestaurant.com

"There's a reason Roy has become so ubiquitous" in the islands, the Mainland and abroad: "fabulous" Hawaiian fusion fare with "twists" and "creativity" that differ from location to location; for some, this Kapolei outpost is even "better than the [Honolulu-area] original" due to its "beautiful setting overlooking the Ko Olina Golf Course", its aloha "hospitality" and its "fabulous" fare (especially the signature macadamia-encrusted mahi mahi); so even if it's far away, most find it "well worth the drive"; N.B. also open for lunch.

Ruth's Chris Steak House *Steak* | 25 | 21 | 23 | E |

Ala Moana | 500 Ala Moana Blvd. (bet. Punchbowl & South Sts.) | 808-887-0800
NEW **Waikiki** | Waikiki Beach Walk | 226 Lewers St. (Helumoa Rd.) | 808-440-7910
www.ruthschris.com

"If you want a good steak" served "exactly how you like it", this chainster is "the place to go"; with dishes "generous enough for the local army", a "comfortable", "clubby" atmosphere on Restaurant Row and a "courteous" staff, it attracts locals as well as expense-accounters for a "very urban" yet "genteel" experience; N.B. a second location has opened in the Waikiki Beach Walk development.

Sansei *Japanese* | 24 | 18 | 21 | E |

Waikiki | Waikiki Beach Marriott | 2552 Kalakaua Ave. (Kapahulu Ave.) | 808-931-6286 | www.sanseihawaii.com

For "a bit of sushi heaven" in "the islands", head to this "innovative" Pacific Rim–Japanese in the Waikiki Beach Marriott, where everything from crispy Asian seafood ravioli to "fresh, fresh, fresh" sashimi is prepared by chef-owner D.K. Kodama and "his mom", who started the chain on Maui; the "cool, mod" joint gets crowded with "locals lining up for early-bird specials" and visitors digging into those "generous portions", and diners are advised to call ahead for information on happy-hour and late-night bargains.

Side Street Inn ❶ *Hawaii Reg.* | 23 | 7 | 15 | I |

Ala Moana | 1225 Hopaka St. (Piikoi St.) | 808-591-0253

Located in a "warehouse area" on the fringe of Ala Moana, this "friendly" "watering hole" is where the island's "top chefs go after a hard day's work" to grab some "local-style Hawaii" Regional fare including "great kalbi ribs", fried pork chops and "the best poke"; the "generous portions" are proffered at "cheap" prices, but if you're a tourist headed to this "party where everyone wants to be", you'll probably "be one of the only non-locals there."

3660 on the Rise M *Pacific Rim*

| 26 | 20 | 24 | E |

Kaimuki | 3660 Waialae Ave. (Wilhelmina Rise) | 808-737-1177 | www.3660.com

The "innovative" Pacific Rim cuisine of chef Russell Siu (a "master of food and wine") "amazes" diners at this Kaimuki "favorite" where the menu includes an "ahi katsu appetizer that will melt in your mouth", a "to-die-for bread pudding" and a "delicious" lychee martini brought to table by an "engaging", "informal" staff; there's "no view" and the interior "looks like a coffee shop" to some, but others counter "who cares?" – this one "rises" higher than most.

Houston

TOP FOOD RANKING

	Restaurant	Cuisine
28	Mark's	American
	Da Marco	Italian
27	Tony's	Continental/Italian
	Kanomwan	Thai
	China View	Chinese
	Pappas Bros.	Steak
26	Cafe Annie	Southwestern
	Vic & Anthony's	Steak
	Nielsen's Deli	Deli
	Japaneiro's	Japanese/S American
	Chez Nous	French
	Brennan's	Creole
	Hugo's	Mexican
	Lynn's Steak	Steak
	Fogo de Chão	Brazilian/Steak
	Jimmy Wilson's	Seafood
	Red Onion*	Pan-Latin/Seafood
	Café Rabelais	French
	Le Mistral	French
	Uptown Sushi	Japanese
25	Brenner's	Steak

Brennan's *Creole*   26 | 26 | 26 | E

Midtown | 3300 Smith St. (Stuart St.) | 713-522-9711 |
www.brennanshouston.com

"Truly a Houston classic" this "elegant" Midtowner from New Orleans' Brennan family brings together "impeccably prepared" Creole-Southwestern cuisine and "wines galore" in a "delightful" atmosphere well-suited for a "special occasion" or an "outstanding brunch" with live jazz; "gracious servers" and a "charming" patio add to the appeal of what supporters swear is "one of Houston's best"; N.B. jackets preferred.

Brenner's *Steak*   25 | 24 | 24 | E

Memorial | 10911 Katy Frwy. (bet. Brittmoore Rd. & Wilcrest Dr.) | 713-465-2901 | www.brennerssteakhouse.com

NEW **River Oaks** | 1 Birdsall St. (Memorial Dr.) | 713-868-4444 | www.brennersonthebayou.com

Longtime fans laud this "traditional", "high-end" Memorial steakhouse that's "held true" since 1936 (despite its acquisition by the Landry's empire) with "wonderfully aged" beef and "impeccable" service; prices may be high, but "inviting" decor with a working fireplace and a "pretty garden" make it a "memorable" pick for "special occasions"; N.B. scores may not reflect the newer River Oaks branch.

---

* Indicates a tie with restaurant above

☑ Cafe Annie ⓈSouthwestern   26 | 24 | 26 | E

Galleria | 1728 Post Oak Blvd. (San Felipe St.) | 713-840-1111 | www.cafe-annie.com

Robert del Grande "still has it" declare devotees of his "fabulous" Galleria-area destination where "businessmen" and "Chanel-clad ladies" sup on "exquisite" Southwestern cuisine ferried by "impeccable" servers in an "elegant" high-ceilinged dining room; though the less starry-eyed declare it "overpriced" and "overrated", most maintain that even with "occasional lapses", this is still among "the best in the city."

Café Rabelais ⓈFrench   26 | 20 | 22 | M

Rice Village | 2442 Times Blvd. (bet. Kelvin St. & Morningside Dr.) | 713-520-8841 | www.caferabelais.com

"Authentic" bistro cooking like "amazing mussels" and frites "to die for" "transport" diners to "Paris" at this "charming" Rice Village French that also pleases with "phenomenal wines" and a "knowledgeable" staff; "tables are tight, but the crowd is friendly" and prices a "great value, though they don't take reservations, so "get there early or expect to wait."

☑ Carrabba's Italian Grill Italian   22 | 19 | 22 | M

Champions | Champions Vill. | 5440 FM 1960 W. (Champion Forest Dr.) | 281-397-8255

Galleria | 1399 S. Voss Rd. (bet. San Felipe St. & Woodway Dr.) | 713-468-0868

Northwest Houston | 7540 Hwy. 6 N. (Longenbaugh Dr.) | 281-859-9700
Upper Kirby District | 3115 Kirby Dr. (Branard St.) | 713-522-3131
West Houston | 11339 Katy Frwy. (Wilcrest Dr.) | 713-464-6595
Webster | 502 W. Bay Area Blvd. (I-45) | 281-338-0574
Kingwood | 750 Kingwood Dr. (Chestnut Ridge Dr.) | 281-358-5580
Sugar Land | 2335 Hwy. 6 S. (Southwest Frwy.) | 281-980-4433
The Woodlands | 25665 North Frwy. (Rayford Rd.) | 281-367-9423
www.carrabbas.com

For over twenty years these "dependable" "fixtures" have been "beloved by families with small children" for "solid", "mid-range" Italian "without pretension" presented in "large portions"; insiders insist the Outback-controlled branches "can't compare" to the original "family-owned" outposts (Upper Kirby District and Galleria), though all locations remain "noisy" and "crowded."

Chez Nous ⓈFrench   26 | 21 | 26 | E

Humble | 217 S. Ave. G (Main St.) | 281-446-6717 | www.cheznousfrenchrestaurant.com

"A hidden treasure" that's "worth the drive to Humble" proclaim patrons of this "special occasion" destination set in a converted home serving "exceptional" "classic French cooking" featuring "fresh herbs and vegetables from their own garden"; the "charming" ambiance gets a boost from "top-notch" servers who lavish "personal attention" on diners, so even if a few longtimers lament it's "slipped just a bit", most maintain it's "still an all-time favorite"; N.B jacket suggested.

☑ China View Chinese   27 | 16 | 22 | I

West Houston | 11113½ Katy Frwy. (bet. Kirkwood Rd. & Wilcrest Dr.) | 713-464-2728 | www.chinaview.us

Helmed by "creative" and "caring" chef-owner Robin Luo, this West Houston "culinary pearl" "stands out" thanks to "exquisite" Chinese dishes that utilize local produce and seafood, and overcome the somewhat "dismal setting"; add in "very friendly service" and "bargain prices" and it's no wonder fans swear they "go there at least once a week."

Z Da Marco 🅂🅼 *Italian*   28 | 22 | 26 | E

Montrose | 1520 Westheimer Rd. (bet. Mandell & Windsor Sts.) | 713-807-8857 | www.damarcohouston.com

Aficionados "indulge" in "exemplary" Italian cuisine prepared from "the freshest ingredients" (including "superb pastas" "worth saving your carbs for") and sip wines from a "world-class" list at chef/co-owner Marco Wiles's pricey Montrose destination; its setting in a converted home cultivates a "cozy", "romantic" vibe, so even if "tables are too close together" and the "attentive" service sometimes feels "rushed", it still "stands out" as "one of Houston's finest."

Fogo de Chão *Brazilian/Steak*   26 | 22 | 26 | E

Briargrove | 8250 Westheimer Rd. (Dunvale Rd.) | 713-978-6500 | www.fogodechao.com

"Paradise for Atkins diet-lovers", this churrascaria chain imported from Brazil rolls out all-you-can-eat meats on skewers for folks seeking to "embrace their inner cave person"; the "meal-in-itself" salad bar is equally "tasty" and the drinks sure "pack a punch", but be careful and "pace yourself" to avoid the inevitable "protein swoon."

Hugo's *Mexican*   26 | 23 | 22 | M

Montrose | 1600 Westheimer Rd. (Mandell St.) | 713-524-7744 | www.hugosrestaurant.net

This stylish Montrose "class act" provides "gourmet, designer Mexican" that's both "innovative and traditional", making it "a great alternative" for chile-hounds "who want Latin cuisine but are tired of the old Tex-Mex"; "excellent handmade margaritas", a "great wine list", "cool setting" (though the noise-averse warn it has the "acoustics of an airplane hangar") and capable wait staff add to the allure; P.S. Sunday brunch is the "best-kept secret here."

Japaneiro's Sushi Bar &   26 | 20 | 22 | I
Latin Grill *Japanese/S American*

Sugar Land | Sugar Land Town Sq. | 2168 Texas Dr. (Hwy. 59) | 281-242-1121 | www.japaneiro.com

"It works!" exclaim initiates impressed by the "fusion of Japanese and Latin" at this colorful original on the Town Square in Sugar Land, where the "interesting" "balance of tastes" yields "excellent" eating and "lots to choose from" ("the only place to get plantains and sushi"); generous portions provide "value" for the quality, and "service is great as well."

Jimmy Wilson's   26 | 20 | 23 | M
Seafood & Chop House *Seafood*

NEW Briargrove | 5161 San Felipe St. (bet. Post Oak Blvd. & Sage Rd.) | 713-960-0333

Royal Oaks | 12109 Westheimer Rd. (Houston Center Blvd.) | 281-497-1110 | www.jimmywilsons.com

A rep for "excellent Cajun seafood" like the trademark gumbo precedes this Royal Oaks vet, home to "the freshest" fish and a menu "chock-full of seasonal delicacies" from the Gulf and beyond; with "friendly and efficient" service, it's "like a short trip to Louisiana", even if (or maybe because) the original site's rustic room "is a little tired"; N.B. the Briargrove location is newer and unrated.

☑ Kanomwan ⑤ Thai
27 | 7 | 11 | I

Neartown | 736½ Telephone Rd. (Dumble St.) | 713-923-4230

Despite an address change a couple of years back, the "same grumpy service" from a "curmudgeon of an owner" endures at this Neartown BYO stalwart (aka the 'Telephone Thai') where fans fervently proclaim the "addictive", "intensely flavored" Siamese eats "the best" in town "hands down"; the "lackluster room" is "nothing to look at", but at least a trip here "won't break the bank."

Le Mistral Ⓜ French
26 | 18 | 22 | E

West Houston | 1420 Eldridge Pkwy. (Briar Forest Dr.) | 832-379-8322 | www.lemistralhouston.com

"The Denis brothers bring St. Tropez to West Houston" at this "wonderful bistro", home to "fabulous" Provençal-inflected French fare proffered by "friendly" folks with "unassuming" style; Francophiles who make it a "favorite" acknowledge it's "a bit pricey, but worth it every time"; N.B. a post-Survey relocation puts the Decor score into question.

Lynn's Steakhouse ⑤ Steak
26 | 23 | 24 | E

West Houston | 955 Dairy Ashford St. (bet. I-10 & Memorial Dr.) | 281-870-0807 | www.lynnssteakhouse.com

Catering to "the expense account crowd", this "high-end" West Houston meatery rewards the "well-heeled" with "delectable" prime beef and "first-rate" seafood complemented by "superior service" and an "extensive wine list" boasting over 500 labels; the office-park exterior belies a "warm", "intimate setting" suitable for "that romantic dinner."

☑ Mark's American Cuisine American
28 | 26 | 27 | E

Montrose | 1658 Westheimer Rd. (bet. Dunlavy & Ralph Sts.) | 713-523-3800 | www.marks1658.com

"The old church still produces heavenly dishes" declare the faithful at this "upper-echelon" Montrose New American (voted Most Popular and No. 1 for Food in Houston) in a "beautifully converted" church, where "master chef" Mark Cox fuses the finest in "fresh ingredients" into "exquisite" seasonal fare that's "expensive but so worth it"; "attentive" but "not stuffy" service and a "vibrant", upscale setting "truly bring the meal to the next level", marking this one as "tops" for "special occasions."

Nielsen's Delicatessen Deli
26 | 4 | 18 | I

Galleria | 4500 Richmond Ave. (Mid Lane St.) | 713-963-8005
Spring | 26830 I-45 N. (Woodlands Pkwy.) | 281-363-3354 ⑤Ⓜ

After more than half a century, Nielsen ratings are still high for the "wonderful" deviled eggs, "great sandwiches" and "creamy potato salad" – all with that "famous" housemade mayonnaise – served at this "traditional" deli in the Galleria area; less of a hit is the no-frills, no-tips setting that suggests all effort goes into the food: "consider carryout" or delivery.

Pappas Bros. Steakhouse ⑤ Steak
27 | 24 | 25 | E

Galleria | 5839 Westheimer Rd. (Bering Dr.) | 713-780-7352 | www.pappasbros.com

"The Pappas family is doing it right" at this "standout" meatery in Houston, which keeps "packing them in" to its "sumptuous" quarters for a "phenomenal" combo of "awesome" beef, "killer wines" and "outstanding service" that's "worth every dollar" of the "very high" price tag; its "warm" atmosphere is "great for business dinners or a night out with the guys", so expect a strong showing of "men in suits."

☑ Perry's Steakhouse & Grille *Steak*   25 | 25 | 24 | E

Champions | 9730 Cypresswood Dr. (Cutten Rd.) | 281-970-5999
Memorial | 9827 Katy Frwy. (Memorial City Way) | 832-358-9000
Clear Lake | 487 Bay Area Blvd. (Rte. 3) | 281-286-8800
Sugar Land | Sugar Land Town Sq. | 2115 Town Square Pl. (Southwest Frwy.) | 281-565-2727
The Woodlands | 6700 Woodlands Pkwy. (Kuykendahl Rd.) | 281-362-0569
www.perrysrestaurants.com

"Superb for the suburbs", this locally based "chophouse chain" is a "classy but not stuffy" haven for those far from the city center that's "distinctive" for its "awesome meats" (including the "massive" "specialty" pork chop); the "sleek, stylish" space and "super service" make for a "top-notch" "night out", "especially on someone else's tab."

Red Onion Seafood y Mas ☒ *Pan-Latin/Seafood* 26 | 22 | 22 | M

Northwest Houston | 12041 Northwest Frwy. (43rd St.) | 713-957-2254 | www.caferedonion.com

"One of the most original" joints in town, Rafael Galindo's seafood specialist in Northwest Houston boasts an "innovative menu" that draws on Pan-Latin inspiration ("the seviche is fantastic!") with "consistently excellent" results; the "beautiful, upscale" decor exudes a stylishly "old-time" feel, with a pianist providing accompaniment on weekends.

☑ Tony's ☒ *Continental/Italian*   27 | 27 | 27 | E

Greenway Plaza Area | 3755 Richmond Ave. (Timmons Ln.) | 713-622-6778 | www.tonyshouston.com

An undisputed "Houston classic" installed in "knockout" Greenway Plaza quarters, this "world-class" tribute to "formal dining" "caters to the elite" with "the total package": "exceptional" Continental fare, the "toniest" service around (rated No. 1 in Houston) and "art-filled" surroundings that seem "ready for Vegas"; it's "expensive", but "you get what you pay for" and its "moneyed" clientele hardly objects if it's "a little stuffy."

Uptown Sushi ☒ *Japanese*   26 | 24 | 18 | E

Uptown | Uptown Park | 1131-14 Uptown Park Blvd. (Post Oak Blvd.) | 713-871-1200 | www.uptown-sushi.com

"Be sure to dress to impress" for the "upscale" "social scene" at this "trendy" Uptown Japanese, but "don't let its hipness throw you off", since it follows through with "top-quality" sushi in an "elegant space"; it's a key place to "see and be seen" and accordingly "pricey", even if the "party atmosphere" is slightly offset by "hit-or-miss" service.

Vic & Anthony's *Steak*   26 | 25 | 24 | E

Downtown | 1510 Texas Ave. (La Branch St.) | 713-228-1111 | www.vicandanthonys.com

It's "definitely pricey", but this "classic" Downtown steakhouse from "the Landry's empire" "ranks with the best", enticing a "power carnivore" crowd to its "opulent" digs with "huge" cuts of "fabulous" beef, an "amazing wine list" and "top-of-the-line" service; "in the shadow of" MinuteMaid Park, it's "perfect for the pre- or post-ball game" blowout.

Kansas City

TOP FOOD RANKING

	Restaurant	Cuisine
27	Bluestem	American
26	Oklahoma Joe's	BBQ
	Le Fou Frog	French
	Tatsu's	French
	40 Sardines	American
	Plaza III	Steak
	Room 39	American
	MelBee's	American
	American Restaurant	American
25	Danny Edwards'	BBQ
	Stroud's	American
	Fiorella's Jack Stack	BBQ
	Korma Sutra	Indian
	PotPie	French
	Café des Amis	French
	Starker's Reserve	American
	Ruth's Chris	Steak
	Bristol B&G	Seafood
	André's	Swiss
	Pachamama's	Eclectic
	Piropos	Argentinean/Steak

American Restaurant 🅢 *American*   `26` `24` `27` `E`

Crown Center | Crown Ctr. | 200 E. 25th St. (Grand Ave.), MO |
816-545-8000 | www.theamericankc.com

"Outstanding" chef Celina Tio produces "stellar" New American food
at this "formal" Crown Center stalwart where the menu is complemented by "fantastic" service and a deep wine list showcasing 1,500
selections; the "tired" decor "could use an upgrade", but the interior
setting is trumped anyway by the "amazing" city views.

André's Confiserie Suisse 🅢 *Swiss*   `25` `19` `22` `I`

Country Club Plaza | 5018 Main St. (bet. 50th & 51st Sts.), MO |
816-561-3440
Overland Park | 4929 W. 119th St. (Roe Ave.), KS | 913-498-3440
www.andreschocolates.com

A KC "treasure" for over 50 years, this Alpine-designed, Country Club
Plaza Swiss (and its more modern Overland Park offshoot) delivers "simply the best" pastries and "sublime" chocolates that easily justify the
"wait in line that's sometimes out the door"; both locations are lunch
only, but that doesn't dissuade fans from coming for the "tasty" savories.

🆉 Bluestem *American*   `27` `22` `24` `E`

Westport | 900 Westport Rd. (Roanoke Rd.), MO | 816-561-1101 |
www.bluestemkc.com

The "brilliant", "cutting-edge" dishes and their "remarkably" beautiful
presentations add up to "high art" at this Westport New American

(No. 1 for Food), a "nirvana" for gourmets that's guided by chef-owners Colby and Megan Garrelts, the latter the hand behind the "fabulous" desserts; it's a "big-city" experience where the urbane, "hip" space includes a lounge, the site of "delightful" libations and nicely priced fare.

Bristol Bar & Grill *Seafood*   25 | 23 | 24 | M

Leawood | Town Center Plaza | 5400 W. 119th St. (Nall Ave.), KS | 913-663-5777 | www.bristolseafoodgrill.com
You can "never go wrong" with the "fabulously" "fresh" fish at this Leawood seafooder whose products "compete" with what you'll find "hundreds of miles away" on the "East Coast"; plus, the staff "goes overboard" to ensure smooth sailing; P.S. the biscuits on their own are "worth" the journey.

Café des Amis Ⓜ *French*   25 | 21 | 25 | M

Parkville | 112½ Main St. (2nd St.), MO | 816-587-6767 | www.cafedesamiskc.com
Visitors "can't say enough" about this abundantly "charming" second-floor French in historic Parkville and its seriously "superb" Provençal selections that include "over-the-top" desserts that match the quality of the savories; the wooden deck is the "perfect place to dine" and helps confirm this cafe's winning status among supporters.

Danny Edwards'   25 | - | 19 | I
Famous Kansas City Barbecue Ⓢ *BBQ*

Downtown KCMO | 2900 Southwest Blvd. (W. 29th St.), MO | 816-283-0880
"Now, this is what I'm talking about" echoes the sentiment of 'cue pros who've tried this Downtown eatery "living up to its rep" thanks to the "best" burnt ends and other "tasty", "messy" chow; it's "what BBQ is meant to be", but just follow the smell – they're in new digs these days.

Ⓩ Fiorella's Jack Stack *BBQ*   25 | 21 | 22 | I

Crossroads | 101 W. 22nd St. (Wyandotte St.), MO | 816-472-7427
Country Club Plaza | 4747 Wyandotte St. (Ward Pkwy.), MO | 816-531-7427
Overland Park | 9520 Metcalf Ave. (95th St.), KS | 913-385-7427
Martin City | 13441 Holmes Rd. (135th St.), MO | 816-942-9141
www.jackstackbbq.com
"Don't even think of going to KC without eating here" say regulars of this relatively "fancy" (Most Popular) quartet that proves barbecue "doesn't have to be eaten in a dive", especially when the vittles are all "downright fabulous", from the "best" babybacks to "to-die-for" burnt ends; the "amazing" quality makes the sometimes "long waits" no big deal.

Ⓩ 40 Sardines *American*   26 | 22 | 24 | E

Overland Park | 11942 Roe Ave. (W. 119th St.), KS | 913-451-1040 | www.40sardines.com
"Clever", "fabulous" and "soulful" justly describe chef Debbie Gold's food at her "high-style", blue-hued Overland Park New American, a "peerless" performer whose "standards remain high", including service that "excels"; the restaurant "deserves all the credit it gets", and there's "value" here to boot, with "nicely priced" wines and a 'martini and panini' night on Wednesdays.

	FOOD	DECOR	SERVICE	COST

Korma Sutra Ⓜ Indian — 25 | 14 | 22 | I

Westport | 4113 Pennsylvania St. (Westport Rd.), MO | 816-931-7775
Overland Park | 7217 W. 110th St. (Metcalf Ave), KS | 913-345-8774
www.kckormasutra.com

The "modest" quarters may "not be fancy", but the food "awakens the taste buds" at these Overland Park and Westport Indians whose "earnest" servers tend to deliver "lots of tasty extra dishes"; the mood is "child friendly", and even kids will like the "fabulous" lunch buffet.

Ⓩ Le Fou Frog Ⓜ French — 26 | 19 | 22 | E

City Market | 400 E. Fifth St. (Oak St.), MO | 816-474-6060 |
www.lefoufrog.com

Serving up "a little slice of Paris" in the "rugged" City Market area, this "funky" French "doesn't look like much on the outside", but "marvelous" food and a perpetually changing chalkboard menu put folks at ease; the "incredible" early-bird specials make the "tight" quarters palatable.

Ⓩ Lidia's Italian — 23 | 26 | 23 | M

Crossroads | 101 W. 22nd St. (Baltimore Ave.), MO | 816-221-3722 |
www.lidiasitaly.com

TV- and NYC-celeb Lidia Bastianich is a "star" in KC too, "brightening the Italian scene" with her durable Crossroads restaurant (housed in a refurbed warehouse) that operates in "arguably the most beautiful" room in the city, thanks in part to the "gorgeous" chandeliers; the "gutsy", "high-quality" cooking is part of the toque's trademark, all made even better by "attentive" service.

Ⓩ McCormick & Schmick's Seafood — 23 | 24 | 23 | E

Country Club Plaza | 448 W. 47th St. (Pennsylvania Ave.), MO |
816-531-6800 | www.mccormickandschmicks.com

"Great" seafood in a "land-locked town" means lots of customers show up at this Country Club Plaza standby also prized for its extensive variety of "fresh" fish; sit under the stained-glass ceiling that covers most of the restaurant, or opt for the outdoor patio – either way, the "good" servers "work pretty hard at making you forget the fact" that it's a chain.

MelBee's Ⓩ American — 26 | 22 | 23 | E

Mission | 6120 Johnson Dr. (bet. Beverly Ave. & Horton St.), KS |
913-262-6121 | www.melbees.com

Allies quip "the best thing to happen to Mission" is this New American small-plates expert serving a "tasty", and "tastefully prepared", roster of fare; the "modern" decor frames all those "beautiful women and men dressed so hip they'd make Sinatra look like a hobo", another reason this restaurant dispels the notion that "not all the good places are in Midtown."

Ⓩ Oklahoma Joe's Barbecue & Catering Ⓩ BBQ — 26 | 12 | 18 | I

Olathe | 11950 S. Strang Line Rd. (119th St.), KS | 913-782-6858
Downtown KCKS | Shamrock Gas Station | 3002 W. 47th Ave. (Mission Rd.), KS | 913-722-3366
www.oklahomajoesbbq.com

No-nonsense types insist the "gas-station location is perfect" for enjoying "some of the world's best" pulled pork, "tender" ribs and other "amazing" low-cost cooking at this "great" barbecue joint in Roeland Park; if the Olathe spot's ambiance seems "less authentic", at least there's more space for gnawing.

Pachamama's Ⓜ *Eclectic*

| 25 | 25 | 23 | E |

Lawrence | 800 New Hampshire St. (W. 8th St.), KS | 785-841-0990 | www.pachamamas.com

"Inventive" preparations, "artfully presented" are the forte of this Eclectic that "makes you think you're not in Lawrence"; the consensus: it's "worth a trip from the KC metro area", even if only for its "excellent" wine list; P.S. for diners prone to small plates, the "beautifully appointed" bar is the way to go.

Piropos *Argentinean/Steak*

| 25 | 26 | 24 | E |

Kansas City, North | 4141 N. Mulberry Dr. (Briarcliff Pkwy.), MO | 816-741-3600 | www.piroposkc.com

To "escape the ordinary", look to this KC North Argentinean steakhouse, a purveyor of "absolutely satisfying", thoroughly "delicious" chops and such that "could even win over a vegetarian"; fans "wouldn't change a thing", and certainly not the "gorgeous" South American–style setting.

ⓏPlaza III The Steakhouse *Steak*

| 26 | 22 | 25 | E |

Country Club Plaza | Country Club Plaza | 4749 Pennsylvania Ave. (Ward Pkwy.), MO | 816-753-0000

Leawood | 5020 W. 137th St. (bet. Nall & Roe Aves.), KS | 913-239-8499 www.plazaiiisteakhouse.com

Packing "enough testosterone to make Chuck Norris blush" are these "quintessential" steakhouses that get props for "melt-in-your-mouth" meats, a "legendary" steak soup and even "sensational" desserts; "be prepared to pay", and for those who can swing with the tabs, "check out the jazz" on weekends.

PotPie ⓏⓂ *French*

| 25 | 18 | 21 | M |

Westport | 904 Westport Rd. (Roanoke Rd.), MO | 816-561-2702 | www.kcpotpie.com

You're as likely to see "someone with a tongue ring and pierced nose as you are to see someone in a suit and tie" at this homey, "funky" Westport French known for "delicious" homestyle cookery and a chalkboard menu that's updated regularly; modest prices and the "most friendly" service further guarantee "repeat" business.

Room 39 Ⓩ *American*

| 26 | 20 | 22 | M |

39th Street | 1719 W. 39th St. (bet. Bell & Genessee Sts.), MO | 816-753-3939 | www.rm39.com

A "favorite" for breakfast and lunch but also offering "marvelous", "clever twists on American originals" at dinner, this "funky", affordable address has become a "staple" on 39th Street; it's "highly recommended", as one can see from "all the chefs in town eating there come Saturday morning."

Ruth's Chris Steak House *Steak*

| 25 | 21 | 23 | E |

Country Club Plaza | 700 W. 47th St. (Jefferson St.), MO | 816-531-4800 | www.ruthschris.com

The "butter-drenched" steaks are reserved for those who "throw caution to the wind" at this Country Club Plaza outlet whose "reputation precedes it as one of the best steakhouse chains"; thanks to the "predictably wonderful" chops, backers say visits here are "worth" the "pricey" outcome.

Starker's Reserve ☒ *American* | 25 | 24 | 26 | E |

Country Club Plaza | 201 W. 47th St. (Wyandotte St.), MO | 816-753-3565 | www.starkersrestaurant.com

Get treated like "royalty" at this "romantic, secluded" "special-occasion" mainstay purveying chef-owner John McClure's "splendid" New American preparations that are "meticulously" executed and served; it's no secret that the restaurant is "favored" by oenophiles, who delight in the "incredible" 1,500-label wine list.

Stroud's *American* | 25 | 16 | 21 | I |

Kansas City, North | 5410 NE Oak Ridge Dr. (Vivion Rd.), MO | 816-454-9600 | www.stroudsrestaurant.com

"You haven't lived" till you've tried (and your "arteries have survived") the "legendary" fried chicken and gravy, "mouthwatering" pork chops and the "best" chicken fried steaks all dutifully doled out at this North KC American situated in a roomy 19th-century homestead amid a "farm" setting; it's the "classic comfort-food" experience par excellence, and fans insist the restaurant makes a "major contribution" to the city every time a dish is served.

☒ Tatsu's *French* | 26 | 19 | 24 | E |

Prairie Village | 4603 W. 90th St. (Roe Ave.), KS | 913-383-9801 | www.tatsus.com

"Sturdy", "reliably delicious" Classic French specialties (think Grand Marnier soufflés) set the tone for this "genteel" Prairie Village restaurant where meals are enhanced by "attentive" service; if you can abide the "staid", "granny's parlor" decor, you shouldn't have trouble enjoying this stalwart's "high standards."

Las Vegas

TOP FOOD RANKING

	Restaurant	Cuisine
28	L'Atelier de Joël Robuchon	French
	Joël Robuchon	French
	Rosemary's	American
	Nobu	Japanese
	Todd's Unique Dining	Eclectic
	Guy Savoy	French
27	Picasso	French
	Lotus of Siam	Thai
	Alex	French
	Tableau	American
	Michael Mina	Seafood
26	Del Frisco's	Steak
	André's	French
	B&B Ristorante	Italian
	Prime Steak	Steak
	Alizé	French
	Le Cirque	French
	Sterling Brunch	Eclectic
	SW Steak	Steak

Alex *French*　　　　27 | 28 | 27 | VE

Strip | Wynn Las Vegas | 3131 Las Vegas Blvd. S. (bet. Desert Inn & Spring Mountain Rds.) | 702-770-3463 | www.wynnlasvegas.com

"No detail is left undone" at "genius" chef Alex Stratta's "foodie fantasy come true" in the Wynn Las Vegas, where "achingly delicious" prix fixe meals of New French cuisine "hit their mark perfectly", "exceptional" servers "treat everyone like a high roller" and "even your purse gets a fancy chair"; from the first step "down the grand staircase" into the "opulent" room to the last "sublime" bite of dessert, it's a "luxurious" "over-the-top experience" that has some "big spender" types swearing that it's "worth repeating"; next time you're in town, just "skip the gambling and invest your money here."

Alizé *French*　　　　26 | 27 | 26 | VE

W of Strip | Palms Casino Hotel | 4321 W. Flamingo Rd. (Arville St.) | 702-942-7777 | www.alizelv.com

"Ooh-la-la – fine dining with magnificent views to boot" enthuse fans of this "sophisticated" André Rochat-owned French perched atop the Palms Hotel west of the Strip where the "phenomenal" dishes are best enjoyed when "day turns into night" and you can "watch the city come alive"; "impeccable" service from the "surprisingly unpretentious" staff and an "elegant" room that oozes with "romance" mean that most have no regrets about "offloading some winnings" here; N.B. jacket suggested, and no children under 10 please.

André's *French*

26 | 24 | 26 | VE

Downtown | 401 S. Sixth St. (bet. Bonneville St. & Bridger Ave.) | 702-385-5016 🗷
Strip | Monte Carlo Resort | 3770 Las Vegas Blvd. S. (bet. Harmon & Tropicana Aves.) | 702-798-7151
www.andrelv.com

"Old Las Vegas" comes alive at this Downtown "classic" from André Rochat serving "rich" French fare ("even the butter is sautéed in butter") in a venerable converted house with plenty of "charm"; the newer Strip outpost in the Monte Carlo offers the same "excellent" food but in more "elegant", "Louis XIV–style" quarters, while both pamper patrons with "impeccably polite service" that makes it all "worth the splurge."

☑ Aureole *American*

25 | 27 | 24 | VE

Strip | Mandalay Bay Resort | 3950 Las Vegas Blvd. S. (Mandalay Bay Rd.) | 702-632-7401 | www.charliepalmer.com

"It feels like walking into a dream" swoon surveyors "wowed" by chef Charlie Palmer's "NYC transplant" in Mandalay Bay where a "dramatic entranceway" opens into a "beautiful" room with a multistory wine tower famously attended to by "harnessed" "angels" who "elegantly ascend" to retrieve vintages from a "tremendous" collection; "first-class" New American cuisine "rises to new heights" as well in a "superb" prix fixe menu, while near "flawless" service "makes you feel like a million bucks"; in all, it's an experience of "sensory overload" that "more than satisfies", especially if "someone else is paying" the "insanely expensive" bill.

NEW B&B Ristorante *Italian*

26 | 24 | 24 | VE

Strip | Venetian Hotel | 3355 Las Vegas Blvd. S. (bet. Flamingo & Spring Mountain Rds.) | 702-266-9977 | www.bandbristorante.com

"Finally", "just what Vegas was missing" declare "foodies" "delighted" with Mario Batali's pricey new Venetian venture that mirrors the experience of NYC's Babbo with "phenomenal wines" and "ingenious" "twists on classic Italian dishes" like the "amazing" signature beef cheek ravioli; a "knowledgeable" staff and "intimate" digs decked out in dark woods also win raves, and if a few find "they still have a few kinks to work out", the majority is convinced this "exciting" arrival "will only get better."

☑ Bellagio Buffet *Eclectic*

24 | 19 | 19 | M

Strip | Bellagio Hotel | 3600 Las Vegas Blvd. S. (Flamingo Rd.) | 702-693-8255 | www.bellagio.com

"A certain diet destroyer" say the legions of surveyors who endure almost "constant lines" for what they call the "mac daddy" of all buffets, with a "vast" spread of Eclectic dishes from "Buffalo wings to wild boar", "bountiful quantities" of seafood, plus a "fantastic" brunch on Saturdays and Sundays where the champagne "flows like the Bellagio fountains themselves"; some contend it's more "expensive" than competitors, though defenders justify the "high" prices declaring "it's the only meal you need for the day."

☑ Bouchon *French*

25 | 24 | 24 | E

Strip | Venetian Hotel | 3355 Las Vegas Blvd. S. (bet. Flamingo & Spring Mountain Rds.) | 702-414-6200 | www.bouchonbistro.com

Thomas Keller's "relatively affordable" "outpost of gastronomy" in the Venetian is "absolutely true to his Yountville original", with "perfectly executed French bistro fare", from "heavenly breakfasts" ("light-as-a-feather waffles", a cheese Danish "to dream about") to "indescribably delicious" dinners; the "beautiful" Adam Tihany–designed dining area includes "relaxing" patio seating "overlooking a quiet, well-shaded pool" that "makes you forget where you are", so even if service is sometimes "a little lacking", patrons proclaim it all "thoroughly enjoyable" nonetheless.

Del Frisco's
Double Eagle Steak House *Steak*

| 26 | 23 | 25 | VE |

E of Strip | 3925 Paradise Rd. (Corporate Dr.) | 702-796-0063 | www.delfriscos.com

"A mix of locals and tourists" puts this east of the Strip chain beef bonanza "at the top of the list", saying "you can't go wrong" with its "divine" steaks, "extraordinary wines" and "remarkable" service, even if prices nearly "break the bank"; diners, however, take opposing sides on the mahogany wood and white-tablecloth decor, with some deeming it "classy", and others insisting it's "bland" and in need of an "update"; N.B. because of a change in Nevada's smoking law, the restaurant's cigar bar is no more.

☑ Delmonico Steakhouse *Steak*

| 26 | 23 | 25 | VE |

Strip | Venetian Hotel | 3355 Las Vegas Blvd. S. (bet. Flamingo & Spring Mountain Rds.) | 702-414-3737 | www.emerils.com

"Emeril has it all together here" gush groupies of celebrity chef Lagasse, whose "absolute hunk-o-meat perfection" in the Venetian pleases with "fabulous cuts" of beef (including a "primo" bone-in rib-eye), "wonderful Caesar salad" prepared tableside and an "amazing", "unending" wine list; in spite of a few "lapses", servers "take care of your every need", so the only complaint is the "monasterylike" atmosphere, which some say needs to be "kicked up a notch" – most would "prefer a little more grandeur", given the "high prices."

Guy Savoy Ⓜ *French*

| 28 | 26 | 27 | VE |

Strip | Caesars Palace | 3570 Las Vegas Blvd. S. (Flamingo Rd.) | 702-731-7731 | www.caesarspalace.com

"How do you say 'beyond perfect' *en français*?" ask acolytes of "genius" chef Guy Savoy, who has "outdone himself" with this "gastronomic adventure" in Caesars Palace, which some say is "better than the three-star Paris original", with "brilliantly presented" New French cuisine served à la carte or in an "exquisite" tasting menu plus a "terrific" wine list with 1,500 labels; also "memorable" is "impeccable", "unpretentious" service (ladies like the "purse perches") and a "stylish" setting done up in dark, rich woods, while "breathtaking prices" are commensurate with the "once-in-a-lifetime" experience; N.B. the Bubbles Bar inside the restaurant now offers a small-bites menu.

☑ Joël Robuchon *French*

| 28 | 27 | 28 | VE |

Strip | MGM Grand Hotel | 3799 Las Vegas Blvd. S. (Tropicana Ave.) | 702-891-7925 | www.mgmgrand.com

"Truly an experience for the ages" swoon surveyors "savoring each moment" of chef Joël Robuchon's "life-altering" New French in the MGM Grand, where the "exquisite" tasting menus "build to a crescendo of amazing intensity", rendering "all other [meals] a mere blur"; so don a jacket, "buckle in" and revel in the "elegant lavender and cream interior" and "pampering" treatment (earning it Las Vegas' No. 1 score for Service) – and if you're daunted by the "three-hour-plus" meal (not to mention the "stratospheric prices"), gastronomes advise "pace yourself, breathe deeply and keep looking at the dessert cart for motivation."

Z L'Atelier de Joël Robuchon *French*   28 | 24 | 26 | VE

Strip | MGM Grand Hotel | 3799 Las Vegas Blvd. S. (Tropicana Ave.) | 702-891-7358 | www.mgmgrand.com

This downscaled (but still "staggeringly" expensive) sister to Joël Robuchon in the MGM Grand is "a less stuffy way" for "hard-core foodies" to experience "the master's" "stunning" New French cuisine, which earns it the No. 1 Food score in Las Vegas thanks to "memorable" small plates best appreciated from the U-shaped bar, where "you can marvel at the action" in the open kitchen; refreshingly "unpretentious" service makes the black-and-red interior feel both "sleek" and "casual" at the same time, setting the scene for "one of the single best dining experiences in Vegas" – just bring your "sense of adventure."

Le Cirque *French*   26 | 27 | 26 | VE

Strip | Bellagio Hotel | 3600 Las Vegas Blvd. S. (Flamingo Rd.) | 702-693-8100 | www.bellagio.com

"A class act" "from start to finish", this "extravagant" NYC offshoot in the Bellagio is "delightful in every way" say those savoring "exceptional" repasts of New French cuisine, "smooth service" from waiters who "anticipate your every desire" and "spectacular views of the fountains" from the "playful" silk-tented dining room; in short, "it's simply one of the best" – so "bring a jacket" and a fat wallet; N.B. no kids under 12 allowed.

Lotus of Siam *Thai*   27 | 10 | 20 | M

E Side | Commercial Ctr. | 953 E. Sahara Ave. (bet. Maryland Pkwy. & Paradise Rd.) | 702-735-3033 | www.lotusofsiamlv.com

"Hitchhike if you have to", but "don't leave town" without a stop at this "local treasure" east of the Strip that intrepid eaters rank as the "best Thai restaurant in the country", with a "dazzling" "affordable" array of "complex" dishes including "exquisite" Northern-style "gems" like jackfruit curry that pair well with sips from an "excellent list of German Rieslings"; "friendly service" helps you forget all about the "strip-mall" setting and "nondescript" decor; N.B. no lunch on Saturday or Sunday.

Michael Mina *Seafood*   27 | 24 | 26 | VE

Strip | Bellagio Hotel | 3600 Las Vegas Blvd. S. (Flamingo Rd.) | 702-693-8255 | www.michaelmina.net

"Easily the best seafood on the Strip" rave regulars who savor the "divine scallops three ways", a lobster pot pie that's either "to die for" or "a reason to live", and other tastings that "tickle the senses" at chef/co-owner Michael Mina's "romantic", "beautiful and relaxing" Bellagio destination; a "superb" wine list and "marvelous" service help justify the "third mortgage required to fund the extravagance."

Z Nobu *Japanese*   28 | 23 | 24 | VE

E of Strip | Hard Rock Hotel | 4455 Paradise Rd. (bet. Flamingo Rd. & Harmon Ave.) | 702-693-5090 | www.noburestaurants.com

"Exceptional raw fish in the desert" attracts seekers of the "absolute freshest" "sushi and sashimi creations" as well as "amazing cooked dishes" ("love the miso cod"), all served by a "superb" staff at Nobu Matsuhisa's outpost in the Hard Rock Hotel east of the Strip; sure, "they blast music like eardrums are going out of style" and you can expect a "flabbergasting bill", but many advise "just say omakase", "watch the masters at work at the bar" and "enjoy the ride."

☑ Picasso *French*　　27 | 29 | 27 | VE

Strip | Bellagio Hotel | 3600 Las Vegas Blvd. S. (Flamingo Rd.) | 702-693-8255 | www.bellagio.com

"Perfection on a grand scale" comes via chef Julian Serrano's "lavish" New French palace in the Bellagio (voted tops for Decor as well as Most Popular in Las Vegas), where "high rollers" "live the luxe life" "surrounded by original Picassos" and an "abundance of fresh flowers" while tasting "transcendent" prix fixe meals paired with "fantastic" wines from an "extensive" European list; "polished" servers exhibit "pure finesse", making for a "sublime" experience that's sure to "break you out of your blue period" – at least until you get the check.

Prime Steakhouse *Steak*　　26 | 27 | 26 | VE

Strip | Bellagio Hotel | 3600 Las Vegas Blvd. S. (Flamingo Rd.) | 702-693-8255 | www.bellagio.com

"Now *this* is what it's like in the lap of luxury" purr proponents of Jean-Georges Vongerichten's "posh" 1930s-style chophouse in the Bellagio that's "straight out of a movie set", with velvet drapes and Baccarat chandeliers setting the scene for a "high-rolling" "celebrity crowd" sipping "well-poured drinks" and nibbling "perfectly cooked" steaks; from the "superb" service to the "hard-to-beat" views of the fountains outside, it's a "prime" contender for "one of the most elegant dining experiences" in town.

☑ Rosemary's *American*　　28 | 20 | 26 | E

W Side | West Sahara Promenade | 8125 W. Sahara Ave. (bet. Buffalo Dr. & Cimarron Rd.) | 702-869-2251 | www.rosemarysrestaurant.com

"A winner" that "hasn't lost its special touch", this West Sider proves "a tough act to follow" with chef-owners Michael and Wendy Jordan's "simply outstanding" New American cuisine showcasing "delicate flavors" and served à la carte or in an "excellent" $50 prix fixe meal available with "inspired" beer and wine pairings; "stellar" service makes the "pretty" (some say "dowdy") decor all the more "inviting", and though it's "quite a trip" from the Strip, most maintain they'd "go back in a heartbeat"; P.S. the "$28 three-course lunch may be the best deal in town."

Sterling Brunch ☒ *Eclectic*　　26 | 22 | 25 | VE

Strip | Bally's Las Vegas | 3645 Las Vegas Blvd. S. (Flamingo Rd.) | 702-967-7999 | www.ballyslasvegas.com

"Decadence" is the theme of Bally's "ritzy" Sunday brunch (9:30 AM–2:30 PM) featuring an "over-the-top" Eclectic spread with "abundant lobsters" and "caviar aplenty" and where you'll "never lack for champagne", thanks to waiters in "tuxes and white gloves" who keep the Perrier Jouët "flowing"; "reservations" are a must, and while it may be "expensive" ($65 for adults), some wallet-watchers insist it's a relative deal – at least "you won't need dinner"; N.B. reservations recommended.

SW Steakhouse *Steak*

`26` `26` `25` `VE`

Strip | Wynn Las Vegas | 3131 Las Vegas Blvd. S. (bet. Desert Inn & Spring Mountain Rds.) | 702-770-3325 | www.wynnlasvegas.com

"SW stands for 'swanky'" at this Wynn steakhouse "splurge" offering up "fabulous" food and bottles from a "dazzling wine list"; it may not be "as hip as other spots in town", but "incredible views" of the nightly fountain shows plus "expert" service keep it "crowded", just beware of occasional "waits, even with reservations"; N.B. the Food score may not fully reflect an October 2006 chef change.

Tableau *American*

`27` `25` `27` `VE`

Strip | Wynn Las Vegas | 3131 Las Vegas Blvd. S. (bet. Desert Inn & Spring Mountain Rds.) | 702-770-9966 | www.wynnlasvegas.com

"Exceptional breakfasts", "civilized lunches" and "delectable" dinners await at this French-influenced New American whose "exclusive" south tower location in the Wynn makes it feel like an "elegant" "private dining room", with poolside views and "flawless service" adding to the "appeal"; diehards decree that it "deserves more attention", though insiders insist the fact that it's "not so well known" is exactly what makes it "special."

☑ Todd's Unique Dining ⊠ *Eclectic*

`28` `16` `25` `E`

Henderson | 4350 E. Sunset Rd. (Green Valley Pkwy.) | 702-259-8633 | www.toddsunique.com

One of Henderson's "best-kept secrets", chef-owner Todd Clore's "valley favorite" "shines" with "serious", "sophisticated" seasonal Eclectic dishes plus a wine list with "phenomenal values" (and a "reasonable" $15 corkage, should you decide to bring your own); factor in "accommodating service" and enthusiasts appraise it's "as good as any on the Strip", but at "half the price"; even if the decor "could use sprucing up", everything else "just keeps getting better."

Los Angeles

TOP FOOD RANKING

	Restaurant	Cuisine
28	Mélisse	American/French
	Nobu Malibu	Japanese
	Asanebo	Japanese
27	Matsuhisa	Japanese
	Brandywine	Continental
	La Cachette	French
	Angelini Osteria	Italian
	Providence	American/Seafood
	Katsu-ya	Japanese
	Piccolo	Italian
	Derek's	Californian/French
	Tuscany	Italian
	Sona	French
	Leila's	Californian
	Water Grill	Seafood
	Hatfield's	American
	Spago	Californian
	Josie	American
	Sushi Nozawa	Japanese
	Babita	Mexican

Angelini Osteria Ⓜ *Italian*   27 | 17 | 23 | E

Beverly Boulevard | 7313 Beverly Blvd. (Poinsettia Pl.) | 323-297-0070 | www.angeliniosteria.com

"Incomparable feasts" crafted by "masterful" chef Gino Angelini "transport" guests at this "intimate" Beverly Boulevard Italian whose "rustic" dishes like pork chop *alla Milanese* "put you in pig heaven"; "tight seating" is part of the "bargain", but both "in-the-know locals and celebs" sit "cheek-by-jowl" as they savor "personal" service and "exquisite" wines to accompany the "superb" fare; P.S. "reserve early."

Ⓩ A.O.C. *Californian/French*   26 | 22 | 23 | E

Third Street | 8022 W. Third St. (bet. Crescent Heights Blvd. & Edinburgh Ave.) | 323-653-6359 | www.aocwinebar.com

Suzanne Goin's "small-plates heaven" (and sib to Lucques) presents "marvelous" Cal-French dishes and "spectacular wines and cheeses", ideal for "sharing with a group" and "perfect for dates" (romantic or "bacon-wrapped"); the "lovely" interior hosts "enough of a scene to entertain but not intimidate", and the "informed", "attentive" staff can convince you to "nosh all night", even if tabs do "add up quickly"; P.S. arrive early to "get a seat at the bar" if you don't have a reservation.

Ⓩ Asanebo Ⓜ *Japanese*   28 | 15 | 24 | E

Studio City | 11941 Ventura Blvd. (bet. Carpenter & Radford Aves.) | 818-760-3348

At this "superb find" on Studio City's "sushi row", Tetsuya Nakao slices up "incredible" sashimi in a "traditional Japanese" style that's "beautifully presented", though "sometimes not for the faint of heart" and never "for the faint of budget"; both insiders and initiates appreciate the "excellent" servers who "explain each dish", adding there's "no ambiance, but who cares?"

Babita Mexicuisine Ⓜ *Mexican* 　　27 | 14 | 21 | M

San Gabriel | 1823 S. San Gabriel Blvd. (Norwood Pl.) | 626-288-7265
"No burritos or taquitos here", this mecca for "haute Mexican cuisine" by chef Roberto Berrelleza delivers a "superior", "sensual" dining experience that converts call "the best reason to go to San Gabriel"; true, its 10-table space in a "humble building" is "far from ideal", but combined with the "warm family service", it provides an "extremely unpretentious" backdrop for the "awesome" food.

ⓩ Brandywine Ⓢ *Continental* 　　27 | 20 | 25 | E

Woodland Hills | 22757 Ventura Blvd. (Fallbrook Ave.) | 818-225-9114
For "amazing", albeit "rich", Continental cuisine encompassing foie gras, sweetbreads and flourless chocolate cake, Valleyites flock to this "teeny", "expensive" but "worth-every-penny" Woodland Hills "favorite" that's hard to find – "we drove by it three times" – but rewards diehards with "charming" live music and "top-notch" service; since the "special" lace-curtained booths are in high-demand, reviewers recommend "reserving well in advance."

ⓩ Café Bizou *Californian/French* 　　23 | 19 | 21 | M

Pasadena | 91 N. Raymond Ave. (Holly St.) | 626-792-9923
Sherman Oaks | 14016 Ventura Blvd. (bet. Costello & Murietta Aves.) | 818-788-3536
www.cafebizou.com
These "dependable", "all-occasion" Cal-French bistros in Pasadena and Sherman Oaks win kisses from the crowd for their "well-prepared" fare that's a "wonderful value" (especially with an "unbelievably low" $2 corkage fee); though the "no-attitude" staff is primarily "attentive", a few turn a cold shoulder after "long waits", "even with reservations."

🆕 Craft Ⓢ *American* 　　- | - | - | E

Century City | 10100 Constellation Blvd. (bet. Ave. of the Stars & Century Park E.) | 310-279-4180 | www.craftrestaurant.com
Top chef (and *Top Chef* judge) Tom Colicchio plants the first LA outpost of his popular NYC-bred New American right next to Century City's new Creative Artists HQ; featuring a glass-enclosed dining room, shiny glass-and-chrome bar and outdoor patio with cabanalike lounges, it's already being referred to as the 'CAA Commissary', so expect much moving and shaking over the plates of seasonal fare.

Derek's Ⓢ Ⓜ *Californian/French* 　　27 | 23 | 25 | E

Pasadena | 181 E. Glenarm St. (bet. Arroyo Pkwy. & Marengo Ave.) | 626-799-5252 | www.dereks.com
It's "a real find!" exclaim enthusiasts of Derek Dickenson's "exceptional" bistro "hidden" away in a Pasadena strip mall where the "inspired" menu of "adventurous and creative" Cal-French dishes "consistently delivers", as does the "fabulous wine list"; an "extremely knowledgeable" staff works the various dining rooms, which have a "high-end, but not stuffy" vibe; it may be "wildly expensive", but cognoscenti coo it's "worth every penny."

Hatfield's ⊠ *American* | 27 | 19 | 24 | E |

Beverly Boulevard | 7458 Beverly Blvd. (Gardner St.) | 323-935-2977 | www.hatfieldsrestaurant.com

"No feuds here" quip proponents of this "real McCoy" run by "gracious" married team Quinn and Karen Hatfield and set in a "sliver" of a space with "elegant", "modern" decor and a "beautiful" front patio; the "pitch-perfect" New American cuisine prepared from "impeccable" "farmer's market" ingredients "deserves all of its recent accolades" (and its high price), and if a few deem the "small portions" "a little precious", most "rave" this "darling" spot is shaping up to be "a real highlight" of the "burgeoning Beverly Boulevard" dining scene.

Josie *American* | 27 | 23 | 25 | E |

Santa Monica | 2424 Pico Blvd. (25th St.) | 310-581-9888 | www.josierestaurant.com

"Entirely pleasurable on all levels", this Santa Monica "favorite" "isn't trendy", but it's "pretty much perfect" say those praising chef Josie Le Balch's "sumptuous" New American fare that spotlights "fresh, local" ingredients and "excellent game"; "attentive service" and a "gorgeous" room with "romantic" fireside tables make it a "favorite haunt" for well-heeled locals, and if the "pricey" final tab intimidates some, insiders say "no-corkage Mondays" and Wednesday night's Farmers Market prix fixe are less expensive options.

Katsu-ya *Japanese* | 27 | 15 | 19 | M |

Encino | 16542 Ventura Blvd. (Hayvenhurst Ave.) | 818-788-2396
Studio City | 11680 Ventura Blvd. (Colfax Ave.) | 818-985-6976

"Sublime sushi" and "phenomenal", "nontraditional" "handrolls that are a work of art", plus the signature spicy tuna on crispy rice, keep these Japanese twins in Encino and Studio City "mobbed" with a "hip crowd" of "locals" and "stars" in spite of somewhat "sterile", "claustrophobic" digs; "prices can add up fast" and service is "rushed", but supporters swear the "flat-out terrific" fare "makes you forget" any shortcomings.

La Cachette *French* | 27 | 25 | 26 | VE |

Century City | 10506 Little Santa Monica Blvd. (Thayer Ave.) | 310-470-4992 | www.lacachetterestaurant.com

A "dignified", "gorgeous" light-filled "retreat in the middle of Century City" is how admirers view this "real treasure" and its "very talented" chef-owner Jean François Meteigner, who "removes most of the butter and cream", but none of the "flavor", from his "exquisite" seasonal New French creations; "spot-on" service can veer toward "stuffy", but that's no matter to the "posh" deep-pocket crowds who continue to celebrate it as "one of LA's finest" tickets – "it's outstanding in every way."

Leila's ⊠Ⓜ *Californian* | 27 | 20 | 24 | E |

Oak Park | RE/MAX Plaza | 706 Lindero Canyon Rd. (Kanan Rd.) | 818-707-6939 | www.leilasrestaurant.com

Supporters call this Oak Park Californian the "Spago of the suburbs" for chef Richie DeMane's "exquisite", "cleverly crafted" cuisine that's finished with "fantastic wine pairings"; though its "shop-front setting" and "minimalist" decor are a "major drawback" for some, the "quality service" makes for a "mellow", "intimate" meal, leading locals to cry "Leila's is ours! – stay away."

FOOD | DECOR | SERVICE | COST

☒ Matsuhisa *Japanese*   27 | 16 | 23 | VE
Beverly Hills | 129 N. La Cienega Blvd. (bet. Clifton Way & Wilshire Blvd.) | 310-659-9639 | www.nobumatsuhisa.com

"Place yourself in their hands and order omakase" advise those who've found sushi "nirvana" at Nobu Matsuhisa's "phenomenal" Beverly Hills original, which also excels with "exquisite" Peruvian-influenced Japanese cooking; space is so tight that "you might end up sitting in some famous person's lap", but the staff "makes everyone feel like a celebrity" according to grateful guests who find the "sublime" experience worth the "mighty" tab; N.B. his newest restaurant, Nobu Los Angeles, recently opened in the former L'Orangerie.

☒ Mélisse ☒ Ⓜ *American/French*   28 | 25 | 26 | VE
Santa Monica | 1104 Wilshire Blvd. (11th St.) | 310-395-0881 | www.melisse.com

"Incredible talent" Josiah Citrin earns this Santa Monica "temple" of French–New American dining the No. 1 Food score in LA for his "outstanding", "cutting-edge" dishes that strike a "balance between traditional and imaginative", matched with "always right-on" recommendations by sommelier Brian Kalliel; the "pristine" service and "sophisticated", "romantic" room ("love the purse stools") lend themselves to "three-hour" dinners that are "stratospherically" expensive but "stay in your memory as a beautiful experience."

☒ Nobu Malibu *Japanese*   28 | 21 | 24 | VE
Malibu | 3835 Cross Creek Rd. (PCH) | 310-317-9140 | www.nobumatsuhisa.com

"The food is off the charts" at Nobu Matsuhisa's "phenomenal" locale off PCH, presenting "superb" "sushi as art" as well as other "unbelievable" Japanese cuisine; "celebrities" and "Malibu mogul sightings" add a spark to the "traditional room" – "who cares if it's in a strip-mall?" – while the staff "ensures every need is fulfilled", leaving just the "samurai"-strength bill to give one pause.

Piccolo *Italian*   27 | 17 | 24 | E
Venice | 5 Dudley Ave. (Spdwy.) | 310-314-3222 | www.piccolovenice.com

"Just off the beach" in Venice, in what may be the "weirdest location for a fine-dining restaurant in LA", resides this "aptly named" "hole-in-the-wall" that "deserves its grand reputation" for fashioning "heavenly, inventive" Italian cuisine bursting with "big, authentic flavors" and coupled with an "impressive" (although "exceedingly expensive") wine list; "they don't take reservations", but "warm, helpful service" helps to allay the "hassle" of "waiting for a table."

Providence *American/Seafood*   27 | 24 | 26 | VE
Hollywood | 5955 Melrose Ave. (Cole Ave.) | 323-460-4170 | www.providencela.com

"Unstoppable" chef/co-owner Michael Cimarusti creates "absolutely sublime" New American seafood dishes ("of all stripes, colors and textures") at this "sensational" Hollywood "treasure chest" boasting a "memorable" tasting menu; the "seamless" staff "goes out of its way to serve you" amid a room that's "elegant", "subdued" and enlivened by aquatic touches, so while it demands a bit of "bling", gastronomes deem it "the Holy Grail" of LA dining experiences.

	FOOD	DECOR	SERVICE	COST

Sona 🗷Ⓜ French | 27 | 24 | 26 | VE

West Hollywood | 401 N. La Cienega Blvd. (bet. Beverly Blvd. & Melrose Ave.) | 310-659-7708 | www.sonarestaurant.com

"Outstanding in every way" swoon smitten surveyors of David Myers' West Hollywood boîte that "pushes the culinary envelope" with "exquisite" New French fare "prepared with imagination and care" and best appreciated via the "brilliant" tasting menu (either with wine pairings or "let the sommelier guide you" through the "biblical" list); the "beautifully appointed" room is "elegant and warm", while service is "top-notch" (if sometimes "overbearing"); all in all, it's "a strong contender for one of LA's best restaurants" – just be prepared for some "major sticker shock."

Ⓩ Spago Californian | 27 | 25 | 25 | VE

Beverly Hills | 176 N. Cañon Dr. (Wilshire Blvd.) | 310-385-0880 | www.wolfgangpuck.com

"Forget Gibraltar, this place is the rock of Los Angeles" sum up surveyors who award the Most Popular title to this "flashy", "irresistible" "legend" that's "well worth" the "big-ticket prices" for its "flawless" Californian cuisine from Lee Hefter and "cutting-edge" desserts from pastry chef Sherry Yard; owner Wolfgang Puck "can often be seen table hopping" in the "flamboyant" room that opens onto a "tree-filled patio" dotted with celebrities, while his "hard-to-fault" servers have been "trained by Beverly Hills' most high-maintenance clientele."

Sushi Nozawa 🗷 Japanese | 27 | 6 | 15 | E

Studio City | 11288 Ventura Blvd. (bet. Arch & Tropical Drs.) | 818-508-7017

"Master" chef-owner Kazunori Nozawa continues to "rule with an iron fist" at this "outstanding" Studio City "strip-mall" spot where the "famously nonexistent decor" is "part of the shtick", as is the somewhat "intimidating" man behind the counter who doles out "melt-in-your-mouth perfect" slabs of "buttery" fish on "warm rice" (but "no California rolls"); "purists" know to simply "order the omakase", "shut up" and "revel in the experience" – it's "worth the punishment" "at least once."

Tuscany Il Ristorante Italian | 27 | 22 | 24 | E

Westlake Village | Westlake Plaza | 968 S. Westlake Blvd. (Townsgate Rd.) | 805-495-2768 | www.tuscany-restaurant.com

Widely considered the "crème de la crème" for Westlake Village, this "outstanding" Italian kitchen presents creations that "taste as good as they look", including "fine specials" and a "good wine selection"; adding to the feel of "formal dining in a casual atmosphere" ("even better since the redesign") are "servers who genuinely care about making you happy", themselves overseen by "delightful owners."

Ⓩ Water Grill Seafood | 27 | 24 | 25 | E

Downtown | 544 S. Grand Ave. (bet. 5th & 6th Sts.) | 213-891-0900 | www.watergrill.com

A "mind-boggling assortment" of fish prepared in a "brilliantly" "imaginative manner" is what you'll find at this Downtown "favorite", which surveyors have once again deemed the "best damned seafood" spot in LA; a "terrific selection" of international wines adds to the "classy", "clubby" ambiance, as do the "sophisticated", "well-informed" servers, putting it "at the top" of the "short list" "for special occasions, business dinners" and other events that merit "ocean-deep pockets."

Miami

TOP FOOD RANKING

	Restaurant	Cuisine
28	Michy's	American/French
27	Palme d'Or	French
	Nobu Miami Beach	Japanese/Peruvian
	Romeo's Cafe	Italian
	Prime One Twelve	Seafood/Steak
	Pascal's on Ponce	French
26	Francesco	Peruvian
	Azul	Mediterranean
	Hiro's Yakko San	Japanese
	Cacao	Nuevo Latino
	Joe's Stone Crab	Seafood
	Tropical Chinese	Chinese
	Osteria del Teatro	Italian
	Chef Allen's	New World
	Oceanaire Seafood Room	Seafood
	Caffe Vialetto	Italian
	Quinn's	Seafood
	Escopazzo	Italian
	Capital Grille	Steak
	Matsuri	Japanese
25	Shibui	Japanese
	Ortanique	Caribbean/New World

Azul *Mediterranean* 26 | 27 | 25 | VE

Brickell Area | Mandarin Oriental Hotel | 500 Brickell Key Dr. (8th St.) | 305-913-8358 | www.mandarinoriental.com

"Creative, amazing food" – officially Mediterranean, but with "a touch of Asia, a touch of France and a touch of the U.S." thrown in – plus "excellent" wines and staffers who "know what you want before you do" make dining at the Mandarin Oriental an "orgasmic experience"; "you'll want to devour the view too", and the "as-chic-as-they-come" surroundings are "a great place to go spotting local celebrities"; some sigh that "prices rose after chef Michelle Bernstein left", but landing current toque Clay Conley "was quite a coup", and so overall this destination remains "one of Miami's top innovative restaurants."

Z Barton G...The Restaurant *American* 22 | 26 | 23 | VE

South Beach | 1427 West Ave. (14th Ct.) | Miami Beach | 305-672-8881 | www.bartong.com

"Good for celebrity spotting" and "for celebrations" too, it's always "showtime!" at SoBe's "DisneyWorld for foodies" where, amid a "beautiful garden" setting, "ridiculously huge"-sized – and huge-priced – New American dishes are "served in an unusual manner" (e.g. "popcorn shrimp in movie popcorn boxes"); if foes fear "this once-novel restaurant is becoming a novelty", with cuisine and staff "sacrificed to the humor, pomp and circumstance of the presentation", stalwarts swear "there may be places with better food, service or decor, but this puts all three together."

☑ Blue Door at Delano ● French 24 | 27 | 22 | VE

South Beach | Delano Hotel | 1685 Collins Ave. (17th St.) | Miami Beach | 305-674-6400 | www.chinagrillmgt.com

The "epitome of high-end SoBe decor", the Delano Hotel's "paradise in white" is a "fittingly swank location" for "checking out the rich and famous" as you consume "terrific" New French cuisine from *célébrité* chef Claude Troisgros, brought by "white-glove", if somewhat self-impressed, servers; skeptics sniff it's all "style over substance", but most deem the experience "worth it" – "even when they bring the check."

Cacao ☒ *Nuevo Latino* 26 | 23 | 24 | E

Coral Gables | 141 Giralda Ave. (bet. Galiano St. & Ponce de Leon Blvd.) | 305-445-1001 | www.cacaorestaurant.com

As its name suggests, "wonderful" chocolate desserts cap off Venezuelan chef-owner Edgar Leal's "gourmet riff on the best of Latin American fare"; "superb" service, "cosmopolitan" white/orange decor and a "wine cellar second to none" all enhance his "sophisticated" menu, and while some hesitate at the "high prices", few deny this is "a wonderful alternative to the tried-and-tired Coral Gables offerings."

Caffe Vialetto *Italian* 26 | 20 | 24 | E

Coral Gables | 4019 Le Jeune Rd. (bet. El Prado Blvd. & Malaga Ave.) | 305-446-5659

"A small restaurant, but a big restaurant taste and experience" gush groupies of this "simple storefront" in Coral Gables, where the Latin- and Caribbean-tinged Italian cuisine is both "excellent and consistent" and the staff "treats you like family"; the "jammed", "noisy" dining room is strictly small-time, though, as is the no-weekend-reservations policy, even if you do get "complimentary glasses of wine while you wait."

Capital Grille *Steak* 26 | 25 | 25 | E

Brickell Area | 444 Brickell Ave. (SE 5th St.) | 305-374-4500 | www.thecapitalgrille.com

"Dealmakers" and "Miami's who's who" bring their appetites and expense accounts to the Brickell Area's "mighty mecca of meat" where the "melt-in-your-mouth" steaks (including a "to-die-for" Kona-crusted sirloin), "clubby atmosphere" and service that is "beyond reproach" make it "ideal for business lunches or making good impressions"; "you may have to sell your first-born" to afford it, but converts claim "local steakhouses simply can't compete" with this DC chain link.

Chef Allen's *New World* 26 | 22 | 25 | VE

Aventura | 19088 NE 29th Ave. (bet. NE 191st St. & 28th Ave.) | 305-935-2900 | www.chefallens.com

Shining for over 20 years, "chef-owner Allen Susser is one of the brightest stars on the Southern Florida culinary scene" say fans of this "foodie paradise" that, despite its location in an Aventura strip mall, delivers "consistently superb", if "expensive", New World cuisine served by an "attentive, caring staff"; though a few feel the decor "could do with modernization" and sense "a sameness in every course", it definitely "remains a dependable high-end option."

Escopazzo ❶ *Italian*
26 | 19 | 23 | E

South Beach | 1311 Washington Ave. (bet. 13th & 14th Sts.) | Miami Beach | 305-674-9450 | www.escopazzo.com

"Real culinary genius" hides behind this "simple storefront" on SoBe, delivering "creative but classically inspired" Italian eats, an "exemplary" roster of wines and "conscientious service"; the "romantic" dining room contrasts with the decidedly "un-romantic street", but the "high-test clientele" doesn't mind that, nor the "incredibly expensive" tabs for a meal that "makes you feel like you're in the owners' home."

Francesco Ⓢ *Peruvian*
26 | 16 | 23 | E

Coral Gables | 325 Alcazar Ave. (bet. SW 42nd Ave. & Salzedo St.) | 305-446-1600 | www.francescorestaurant.com

"The best Peruvian north of Lima" say surveyors about this "quaint" Coral Gables eatery specializing in seafood that is "absolutely fresh and cooked perfectly", brought by "cordial" servers; and even if the decor's "nondescript" and the quarters "cramped", most deem it a "good value", given the "unique" fare and "unusual South American wines."

Hiro's Yakko San ❶ *Japanese*
26 | 12 | 20 | M

North Miami Beach | 17040-46 W. Dixie Hwy. (bet. 170th & 171st Sts.) | 305-947-0064

"A treasure hidden" in North Miami Beach, this "authentic Japanese" dishes up "superlative" cooked fare, including "innovative tapas" that pique the palates of "adventurous" diners who "like trying new and exotic foods"; it may be a "hole-in-the-wall" with "not-wonderful decor", but the "polite" staff, "great selection of sakes" and 2 AM closing time lead fish-o-philes to bubble "this is the real deal."

Ⓩ Joe's Stone Crab Ⓜ *Seafood*
26 | 19 | 23 | E

South Beach | 11 Washington Ave. (S. Pointe Dr.) | Miami Beach | 305-673-0365 | www.joesstonecrab.com

"Who doesn't love Joe's?" – no one, it seems, since this "South Beach classic", "a shrine to the stone crab", is voted Miami's Most Popular; the claws are simply "awesome", as are the "heavenly hash browns", and do "leave room for the best Key lime pie"; expect "excruciating" waits to get into the "cafeteria"-like room and, once inside, "astronomical" prices and "rushed" if "reponsive" service; even so, "you have to go once."

Matsuri Ⓜ *Japanese*
26 | 11 | 20 | M

South Miami | 5759 Bird Rd. (Red Rd.) | 305-663-1615

"Visiting Japanese businessmen", "celebs in-the-know" and "some of the top sushi chefs in town" flock to an "inauspicious" South Miami strip mall to scarf "the best and freshest sushi and sashimi in South Florida"; "religiously faithful" fans also savor the "surprisingly low prices"; P.S. a "desperately needed" decor redo was underway post-Survey.

Ⓩ Michy's Ⓜ *American/French*
28 | 19 | 25 | E

Upper East Side | 6927 Biscayne Blvd. (bet. NE 69th & 70th Sts.) | 305-759-2001

Chef "Michelle Bernstein stars" at this "cozy, intimate" Upper Eastsider where a "sophisticated menu for real foodies" – voted No. 1

for Food in Miami – lists a variety of tapas-style, New American-French dishes that "blend Latin, Southern, comfort food and just plain delicious flavors"; "warm, friendly" service is another plus, and though the "dodgy" neighborhood and "quirky" orange/blue decor "leave something to be desired", this place "would proudly hold its own with the best in New York."

☑ Nobu Miami Beach ● *Japanese/Peruvian* | 27 | 23 | 22 | VE |

South Beach | Shore Club | 1901 Collins Ave. (20th St.) | Miami Beach | 305-695-3232 | www.noburestaurants.com

"It's noisy, it's expensive, it's young, it's fabulous" – it's the "swanky" SoBe outpost of Nobu Matsuhisa's empire, with "the same incredible", "addictive" Japanese-Peruvian fare that features the "freshest, best-prepared sushi on the planet"; some say the staff, while "knowledgeable", is "more interested in being seen than in serving", and you better "be there exactly when it opens to avoid killer waits" (reservations for six or more only), but most hail this "shining star" (indeed, "stay long enough and you may see a star").

Oceanaire Seafood Room *Seafood* | 26 | 25 | 24 | VE |

Downtown | Mary Brickell Vill. | 900 S. Miami Ave. (10th St.) | 305-372-8862 | www.theoceanaire.com

"Part of a chain though it doesn't feel chain-y", this new, "elegant" fish house blows a "welcome breath of fresh air into Downtown", dishing up an "amazing variety of seafood" "served steakhouse-style" (e.g. separately priced sides) in a dining room "that looks like a cruise ship"; to be sure, it's "pricey" and the "friendly staff is maybe too friendly", but the "super-sized portions" and super-"fresh" fare make those of the piscine persuasion want to "go back again and again."

Ortanique on the Mile *Caribbean/New World* | 25 | 22 | 23 | E |

Coral Gables | 278 Miracle Mile (Salzedo St.) | 305-446-7710 | www.cindyhutsoncuisine.com

"Outstanding seafood" and "the best mojitos in Miami" are just two of the charms of this "chic" Coral Gables champion of Caribbean–New World cuisine, where the service remains "remarkable" from "decadent mains" through "fantastic desserts"; it may be "expensive as hell", with tables that are "too close for comfort" in a "loud" room, but that doesn't keep the place from always being "packed by 8:30, mostly with locals."

Osteria del Teatro ☒ *Italian* | 26 | 16 | 24 | E |

South Beach | 1443 Washington Ave. (Española Way) | Miami Beach | 305-538-7850

"There's no need to read the menu" at this "little bit of Italy in South Beach", but "you may want to take notes on the many specials" of "oh-so-simple, but oh-so-good" Northern Italian fare or risk "being overwhelmed with choices"; hungry throngs can overwhelm the "cramped" dining room, but servers who "anticipate your every need" help alleviate the pain of "paying dearly" for "food that reigns supreme."

☑ Palme d'Or ☒Ⓜ *French* | 27 | 26 | 26 | VE |

Coral Gables | Biltmore Hotel | 1200 Anastasia Ave. (Granada Blvd.) | 305-913-3201 | www.biltmorehotel.com

Francophiles fawn life "doesn't get better" than at this "luxurious", "sophisticated" Biltmore Hotel restaurant, a contemporary corner of the famed "shrine to turn-of-the-century Mediterranean architecture"; chef Philippe Ruiz's menu of New French small plates "brings new meaning to the word flavor", the wine list is "excellent" and the "formal, intelligent and well-trained personnel" are rated No. 1 for Service in Miami; the experience "doesn't come cheaply", but you'll "leave with a sense of well-being."

Pascal's on Ponce 🗷 *French* 27 | 18 | 24 | E

Coral Gables | 2611 Ponce de Leon Blvd. (bet. Almeria & Valencia Aves.) | 305-444-2024 | www.pascalmiami.com

The staff "treats you like VIPs" while the kitchen turns out "artistic", "classically inspired New French fare" at this "high-end bistro" run by "incredibly creative" chef Pascal Oudin; *"c'est magnifique!"* crows a contented Coral Gables crowd, whose "only gripe is that tables are oh-so-Parisian close."

☑ Prime One Twelve ● *Seafood/Steak* 27 | 23 | 23 | VE

South Beach | 112 Ocean Dr. (1st St.) | Miami Beach | 305-532-8112 | www.prime112.com

"The hottest restaurant south of the Mason-Dixon line" caters to celebrities from the "NBA to fashion to Hollywood and everyone in between" with "gargantuan" portions of "perfect seafood" and steaks that are "a religious experience"; "even with reservations, waits can be horrible" for a seat in the "crowded", "deafening" dining room, service swings from "surprisingly quick" to "standoffish" and critics crack it should be called "Crime One Twelve", given the "exceptionally expensive" tabs; nevertheless, this is "the ultimate SoBe" scene.

Quinn's Restaurant *Seafood* 26 | 23 | 24 | E

South Beach | Park Central Hotel | 640 Ocean Dr. (bet. 6th & 7th Sts.) | Miami Beach | 305-673-6400 | www.quinnsmiami.com

To "enjoy the alfresco atmosphere without all the crowds" on Ocean Drive – and get in some "great people-watching" as well – "request a seat on the patio" of chef-owner Gerry Quinn's "pretty" seafooder, home of "the highly touted bam bam shrimp"; advocates aver "everything about this place says 'winner'", from the "upbeat service" to the nightly guitarist.

☑ Romeo's Cafe 🗷Ⓜ *Italian* 27 | 18 | 26 | VE

Coral Way | 2257 SW 22nd St./Coral Way (bet. 22nd & 23rd Aves.) | 305-859-2228 | www.romeoscafe.com

For a "unique, romantic experience", get thee to this "jewel box" of a Northern Italian in Coral Way, where "there is no printed menu"; instead, namesake toque Romeo Majano "will visit your table to discern your likes and dislikes", then create an "incredible" multicourse meal; it's "like having your own personal chef", as well as your own "wonderful" staff for a "rich", elaborate and "expensive" evening – one that has "discerning diners" declaring "bravo Romeo!"

Shibui ● *Japanese* 25 | 19 | 22 | M

Kendall | 10141 SW 72nd St. (102nd Ave.) | 305-274-5578 | www.shibuimiami.com

"Uniformly enticing" "unique sushi" (plus a "huge" menu of cooked fare), "always great service" and a "relaxed atmosphere" mean you'd better "make reservations or it's going to be a long wait" at this

Kendall Japanese "favorite"; it may "need a decorator immediately" ("I swear the window treatments have been there since I first frequented the restaurant in 1981"), but it "makes up for this" with "the freshest fish" that "otherwise is only available at expensive places."

Tropical Chinese *Chinese*

FOOD	DECOR	SERVICE	COST
26	16	20	M

Westchester | Tropical Park Plaza | 7991 SW 40th St. (SW 79th Ave.) | 305-262-7576

"A nonstop gastronomic parade" of "incredible, inexpensive dim sum" is the "real attraction" of this "gourmet" Chinese where the "gruff" but "competent" waiters, "glassed-in kitchen" and "lazy Susans on large tables" make you "feel like you're in Hong Kong", even though you're really in an "out-of-the-way" Westchester strip mall; P.S. at night, "you must get the Peking duck – more than a dish, it's an art form."

New Orleans

TOP FOOD RANKING

	Restaurant	Cuisine
28	August	Continental/French
	Brigtsen's	Contemp. Louisiana
	Bayona	American
	Stella!	American
	Cuvée	Continental/Creole
27	La Provence	Creole/French
	Mosca's	Italian
	Vizard's*	Creole/Mediterranean
	Jacques-Imo's Café	Creole/Soul Food
	Clancy's	Creole
	Dakota, The	American/Contemp. Louisiana
	Galatoire's	Creole/French
	K-Paul's	Cajun
	Herbsaint	American/French
	Dick & Jenny's	Creole/Eclectic
26	Upperline	Contemp. Louisiana
	Dickie Brennan's	Steak
	Irene's Cuisine	Italian
	Lilette	French

Z August *Continental/French*   28 | 28 | 27 | E

Central Business Dist. | 301 Tchoupitoulas St. (Gravier St.) | 504-299-9777 | www.rest-august.com

"Spectacular" dishes blending "European style" with "a touch of the bayou" enchant guests at this "elegant" Central Business District Continental–New French, ranked No. 1 in New Orleans for Food and Service, where chef/co-owner John Besh crafts a "daring" menu that showcases local ingredients; the "drop-dead gorgeous" setting (curving brick walls, lustrous chandeliers), a "warm", "knowledgeable" staff and presentations "so beautiful you hesitate to mess up the plate" also impress, so if the tab's "pricey", you'll be "too blissed out to notice"; N.B. lunch is served on Fridays only.

Z Bayona *American*   28 | 25 | 26 | E

French Quarter | 430 Dauphine St. (bet. Conti & St. Louis Sts.) | 504-525-4455 | www.bayona.com

Admirers are adamant that it "doesn't get any better" than this French Quarter "favorite" where "masterful" celebrity chef-owner Susan Spicer serves up "original", "peerless" New American cuisine with "global influences" in a Creole-cottage setting that features a "gracious", slightly "formal" interior as well as a "lovely patio"; the prix fixe options for early-bird diners are "a deal", and the recently restored wine cellar houses an "amazing new" bottle selection.

---

* Indicates a tie with restaurant above

Z Brennan's *Creole* | 25 | 24 | 24 | E |

French Quarter | 417 Royal St. (bet. Conti & St. Louis Sts.) | 504-525-9711 | www.brennansneworleans.com

"One of those places that defines old New Orleans", this Creole origi- nator of "addictive bananas Foster" invites a "touristy" French Quarter crowd to "linger" over a "decadent" two-hour breakfast that costs big bucks "if you do it right"; "first-rate" dinners, "Southern hospitality", "pleasant" dining rooms (remodeled after Katrina) and a "beautiful courtyard" are pluses, and if opponents opine it's "overrated", more concur "you gotta go" "at least once"; N.B. closed Tuesday and Wednesday in the summer.

Z Brigtsen's ☒ Ⓜ *Contemp. Louisiana* | 28 | 22 | 27 | E |

Riverbend | 723 Dante St. (Maple St.) | 504-861-7610 | www.brigtsens.com

"Genius" chef/co-owner Frank Brigtsen provides a "true NOLA expe- rience" at this "charming Creole cottage" in Riverbend via "exquisite", "imaginative interpretations" of "Louisiana home cooking"; the blue-ribbon wine list, lively people-watching and a staff that "treats you like family" while displaying "excellent attention to detail" round out dinners that are more than "worth the cab ride" and the need to book early.

Clancy's ☒ *Creole* | 27 | 22 | 25 | E |

Uptown | 6100 Annunciation St. (Webster St.) | 504-895-1111

"Exquisite" dishes like "sublime smoked soft-shell crab" and "ooh-la-la" oysters with Brie tantalize a "tony", "table-hopping" "who's who" of "old New Orleans" at this "country club"–style Creole that some call the "Galatoire's of Uptown"; it can be "noisy and crowded" but "stands out as the quintessential locals' favorite", since it's "tucked away from all things touristy" and the "tuxedoed servers" have an "excellent rapport" with regulars; N.B. lunch is served Thursday and Friday.

Commander's Palace *Creole* | - | - | - | E |

Garden District | 1403 Washington Ave. (Coliseum St.) | 504-899-8221 | www.commanderspalace.com

Beautifully redecorated and more sumptuous than ever, with embroi- dered silk toile and leather banquettes, this grand old Garden District star (rated the city's Most Popular restaurant 1989–2005) reopened after a $6 million post-Katrina makeover; its sophisticated Creole menu reflects the inventiveness of chef Tory McPhail, and its polished service shows the guidance of a new generation of Brennan owner- ship: cousins Lally Brennan and Ti Martin; N.B. jackets recommended.

Z Cuvée ☒ *Continental/Creole* | 28 | 26 | 26 | E |

Central Business Dist. | St. James Hotel | 322 Magazine St. (bet. Gravier & Natchez Sts.) | 504-587-9001 | www.restaurantcuvee.com

Even in "the darkest days" just after Katrina, this "shining light" in the CBD – a sibling of The Dakota – maintained "exceptional" stan- dards, starting with chef Bob Iacovone's "outstanding", "creative" Continental-Creole cuisine with rich touches (e.g. "last meal"– worthy duck confit); the "wonderful" "French-focused wine list", "polished service" and "warm, dark decor" also help make it a "special-occasion" "gem."

Dakota, The 🅉 *American/Contemp. Louisiana* | 27 | 23 | 25 | E |

Covington | 629 N. Hwy. 190 (¼ mi. north of I-12) | 985-892-3712 | www.thedakotarestaurant.com

"Excellent game", "fabulous crab and Brie soup" and other "decadent, delicious" New American–Contemporary Louisiana dishes inspire diners to call this Covington classic the "most accomplished restaurant on the North Shore"; factor in "awesome wines", "exceptional service" and a setting enriched by deep colors and "great art on the walls", and most agree it's "worth the drive across the Causeway."

Dick & Jenny's 🅉🅼 *Creole/Eclectic* | 27 | 21 | 24 | M |

Uptown | 4501 Tchoupitoulas St. (Jena St.) | 504-894-9880 | www.dickandjennys.com

Following what many call a "seamless" change of owners post-Katrina, this clapboard-cottage bistro on a "working-class" Uptown block remains "beloved" thanks to its "sumptuous", "soulful" and affordable Creole-Eclectic "comfort food"; with the same "friendly" servers and "laid-back", "folk-art" atmosphere, it continues to be a draw for fans who roll with the no-reserving policy by "relaxing on the patio rockers."

Dickie Brennan's Steakhouse *Steak* | 26 | 25 | 25 | E |

French Quarter | 716 Iberville St. (bet. Bourbon & Royal Sts.) | 504-522-2467 | www.dickiebrennanssteakhouse.com

"Astounding steaks" "so tender they practically melt on the plate" wrangle French Quarter frequenters to this "beef eater's paradise" from the Brennan clan; the menu comes through with "all the extras" plus a "superior" wine selection to boot, and the "clubby", "masculine" wood-paneled rooms, "well-trained" staff and hefty price tag are exactly what you'd expect "when you need that meat."

🆉 Emeril's *Contemp. Louisiana* | 25 | 24 | 25 | E |

Warehouse District | 800 Tchoupitoulas St. (Julia St.) | 504-528-9393 | www.emerils.com

"Don't let the celebrity-chef status hold you back" say a bevy of "bam!" believers who laud this Lagasse flagship in the Warehouse District for "robustly flavored", "earthy" eats that "capture the essence of New Orleans–style haute cuisine"; its "crisp" service, "sleek" looks and high energy ("the chef's bar is what I call 'dinner and a show'") please most, though some knock it as a "tourist mecca" that needs to kick the noise level and cost "down a notch."

🆉 Galatoire's 🅼 *Creole/French* | 27 | 26 | 27 | E |

French Quarter | 209 Bourbon St. (Iberville St.) | 504-525-2021 | www.galatoires.com

"You could see Blanche DuBois sipping a Sazerac" at this "old-line", "almost cultish" French Quarter centenarian – the city's Most Popular restaurant – where "bigwigs" and "ladies in hats" find "gastronomic heaven" in a "classic" Creole-French cornucopia of "unbelievable seafood"; it's a "'dress up and live large' kinda place", so snag a table in the tiled downstairs ("where the action is"), "get to know your waiter" and don't be surprised if a leisurely lunch "turns into dinner", especially on Fridays; N.B. jackets required after 5 PM and on Sundays.

	FOOD	DECOR	SERVICE	COST

Herbsaint ☒ *American/French* — 27 | 22 | 25 | E

Warehouse District | 701 St. Charles Ave. (Girod St.) | 504-524-4114 | www.herbsaint.com

In "top form" post-Katrina, the kitchen at this Warehouse District "winner" turns out "stellar" New American–New French fare with a "Southern twist" and a touch of "whimsy", thanks to "truly talented" chef/co-owner Donald Link; energized by "enticing" cocktails, a "wonderful wine list" and "smart service", its "chic" dining room is both "casual" and "electric" – in sum, "another home run" from co-owner Susan Spicer.

Irene's Cuisine ☒ *Italian* — 26 | 22 | 23 | E

French Quarter | 539 St. Philip St. (bet. Chartres & Decatur Sts.) | 504-529-8811

"Locals love" this "dark", "romantic" dinner-only trattoria that tourists seem to "find with their noses" as the scent of "delectable" Southern Italian food wafts from its French Quarter digs; inside, "cozy, quirky" dining rooms, a "delightful staff" and a "great piano bar" keep spirits soaring – but since limited reservations can mean "painful" waits, you'd best show up early, add your name to the list and "take the opportunity" to explore the area.

Jacques-Imo's Café ☒ *Creole/Soul Food* — 27 | 21 | 22 | M

Carrollton | 8324 Oak St. (bet. Cambronne & Dante Sts.) | 504-861-0886 | www.jacquesimoscafe.com

Fans of Jack Leonardi's "big-flavored", "down-home" Creole soul cooking at this dinner-only Carrollton "dive" insist you'll be "sighing in bliss and loosening your pants" before you can say "alligator cheesecake" (a "must-try"); sure, many bemoan "insanely long" waits that can run over an hour, but most still consider this "funky", "boisterous" "Tulane students' favorite" "a blast" that "could only exist in New Orleans."

K-Paul's Louisiana Kitchen ☒ *Cajun* — 27 | 21 | 24 | E

French Quarter | 416 Chartres St. (bet. Conti & St. Louis Sts.) | 504-596-2530 | www.kpauls.com

"Not the cliché you'd expect", the French Quarter birthplace of blackened redfish (now prepared with drumfish instead) maintains high standards thanks to "flavor virtuoso" Paul Prudhomme, exec chef Paul Miller and their "complex, sophisticated interpretations" of "robustly" spiced Cajun food; "long waits" are often a prelude to the "hot and pricey" dinners, but "spirited" service and a "charming" vibe help pass the time.

La Provence ☑ *Creole/French* — 27 | 26 | 26 | E

Lacombe | 25020 Hwy. 190 (bet. Bremermann & Raymond Rds.) | 985-626-7662 | www.laprovencerestaurant.com

John Besh (August) has purchased and revived this unexpected, Creole-accented "bit of Provence" in rural Lacombe, where his culinary mentor, the late "treasured" toque Chris Kerageorgiou, turned out "superb" French fare for over three decades; while the "welcoming" service remains the same, recent renovations should heighten the already "romantic" ambiance (think "lovely hearth fires"), and the fresh arrival of chef René Bajeaux (ex René Bistrot) is further cause for rejoicing; N.B. closed Monday and Tuesday.

FOOD | DECOR | SERVICE | COST

Lilette ⛤Ⓜ *French*
26 | 23 | 23 | E

Uptown | 3637 Magazine St. (Antonine St.) | 504-895-1636 |
www.liletterestaurant.com

For an "intimate dinner" or a "sybaritic lunch", this "top-tier" French bistro impresses Uptowners with "inventive combinations" of "fresh seasonal ingredients" from "brilliant" chef-owner John Harris; "chic" yet "relaxed", it draws "young professionals" and other locals who "love the booths" and the "cool bar", all tended by a "friendly", "unrushed" staff.

Mosca's ⛤Ⓜ⌖ *Italian*
27 | 12 | 20 | M

Avondale | 4137 Hwy. 90 W. (bet. Butler Dr. & Live Oak Blvd.) | 504-436-9942

"I'd do dishes to eat here!" exclaim enthusiasts about this hallowed "old roadhouse" in Avondale, where the "garlic-powered" menu of "inspired" Italian like chicken à la grande and oysters Mosca is served "family-style" to a crowd that always includes a few fascinating "characters"; insiders advise "call first to get directions", "bring at least six people so you can get everything on the menu" and always "take cash."

Ⓩ NOLA *Contemp. Louisiana*
26 | 23 | 24 | E

French Quarter | 534 St. Louis St. (bet. Chartres & Decatur Sts.) |
504-522-6652 | www.emerils.com

"Delicious Creole-inspired" Contemporary Louisiana cuisine "served with style" draws the masses to Emeril Lagasse's "alternative" French Quarter outpost, which many find "hipper" and "more casual" than his namesake venue; most agree it's a "good value" and "runs like a clock", though the "touristy" crowd ups the "noise to stratospheric levels."

Ⓩ Stella! *American*
28 | 25 | 26 | E

French Quarter | Hôtel Provincial | 1032 Chartres St. (bet. St. Philip & Ursuline Sts.) | 504-587-0091 | www.restaurantstella.com

At this "intimate" hotel dining room in the Quarter, "ambitious" chef-owner Scott Boswell crafts an "innovative" New American menu of "superlative" "experimental Creole fare" and "surprising flavor combinations" that are "worth the exclamation point"; if some cry "expensive", those who cherish a "memorable" meal are "shouting 'Stella!' all night."

Upperline Ⓜ *Contemp. Louisiana*
26 | 24 | 25 | E

Uptown | 1413 Upperline St. (bet. Pitt & Prytania Sts.) | 504-891-9822 |
www.upperline.com

"Wonderful chef" Ken Smith and "consummate hostess" JoAnn Clevenger have "kept the torch lit" at this "quirky" Uptowner that offers "splendid", "inventive" Contemporary Louisiana fare and an optional "excellent" seven-course 'Taste of New Orleans' menu; it's all served by a "cordial" staff and set in a lofty 1877 house featuring four rooms decorated with objects and paintings from Clevenger's personal collection.

Vizard's ⛤Ⓜ *Creole/Mediterranean*
27 | - | 25 | E

Uptown | 5015 Magazine St. (Robert St.) | 504-529-9912 |
www.vizardsontheavenue.com

"Imaginative" hometown chef-owner Kevin Vizard is currently in transition, taking his "spellbinding" Creole-Med cuisine from the Garden District to the former Alberta space Uptown (set to open February 2008); his "pleasant" staff is coming along too, and most of the warm-toned room in an ivy-covered building will remain the same, with the addition of New Orleans–accented art by Vizard's sister, Beth Lambert.

New York City

TOP FOOD RANKING

	Restaurant	Cuisine
28	Daniel	French
	Sushi Yasuda	Japanese
	Le Bernardin	French/Seafood
	Per Se	American/French
	Peter Luger	Steak
	Jean Georges	French
	Bouley	French
27	Chanterelle	French
	Sushi Seki	Japanese
	L'Atelier de Joël Robuchon	French
	Nobu	Japanese
	Gotham B&G	American
	Café Boulud	French
	Gramercy Tavern	American
	Di Fara	Pizza
	La Grenouille	French
	Babbo	Italian
	Saul	American
	Annisa	American
	Il Mulino	Italian
	Aureole	American
	Masa/Bar Masa	Japanese

NEW Adour *French*

`- | - | - | VE`

E 50s | St. Regis Hotel | 2 E. 55th St. (bet. 5th & Madison Aves.) | 212-710-2277 | www.adour-stregis.com

Alain Ducasse comes to New York – again – with this tony, *vin*-focused arrival in the landmark St. Regis space that was Lespinasse, updated by David Rockwell to feature a luminous glass scrim-wrapped dining room bedecked with numerous wine 'armoires' and a gold-flecked mural meant to evoke the namesake river in France; Ducasse alum Tony Esnault's *très-haute* New French cuisine emphasizes locally sourced ingredients and is designed to marry well with the impressive selection of vintages, all of which is presided over by a polished but approachable staff; N.B. there are several semi-private tasting rooms and a diminutive 'interactive' front bar.

Annisa *American*

`27 | 22 | 26 | VE`

G Village | 13 Barrow St. (bet. 7th Ave. S. & W. 4th St.) | 212-741-6699 | www.annisarestaurant.com

"Top-tier chef" Anita Lo's Greenwich Village oasis woos patrons with its roster of "refined, beautiful" New American cuisine, "impeccable service" and "stylish" "white-curtained" decor that all together add up to "magical" meals; such "superior" experiences don't come cheap, but for a relative bargain "go for the tasting menu" at $88.

Aureole ⧈ *American* | 27 | 25 | 26 | VE |

E 60s | 34 E. 61st St. (bet. Madison & Park Aves.) | 212-319-1660 | www.charliepalmer.com

Excelling "in all categories", Charlie Palmer's "flower-filled" East Side "celebratory dining spot" continues to delight with "outstanding" prix fixe–only New American fare and "phenomenal service" that add up to a "royal experience" surely "worth the cost"; N.B. à la carte ordering is an option at lunch, when there's also a "bargain" $38 set menu.

⧈ Babbo ● *Italian* | 27 | 23 | 25 | VE |

G Village | 110 Waverly Pl. (bet. MacDougal St. & 6th Ave.) | 212-777-0303 | www.babbonyc.com

"When it's this good" "it's not hype" is still the consensus as Mario Batali and Joe Bastianich celebrate the 10th anniversary of their "fabulously popular" Village flagship that's voted NYC's No. 1 Italian; given its "mind-blowing" cuisine, "epic wine list", "superlative" service and "cozy" carriage house setting, you'd better "keep their reservation number on redial"; sure, it's "expensive", but it's "worth every *centesimo*."

Bouley ● *French* | 28 | 26 | 27 | VE |

TriBeCa | 120 W. Broadway (Duane St.) | 212-964-2525 | www.davidbouley.com

David Bouley's TriBeCa "mecca" "never ceases to amaze", carrying "class" to an "exemplary level" with "stunning" New French cuisine and "dazzling" but "unstuffy service"; the "opulent" space's "vaulted ceilings" and "soothing" lighting impart a "sense of contentment" that "memories are made of"; and no, it's "not cheap"; N.B. watch for a 2008 move to gorgeous new digs down the block.

Café Boulud *French* | 27 | 23 | 26 | VE |

E 70s | Surrey Hotel | 20 E. 76th St. (bet. 5th & Madison Aves.) | 212-772-2600 | www.danielnyc.com

Dining is "bliss" at "Daniel's Uptown sibling", where the "superb experiences" are "less formal" and less costly (if still "not cheap") than at the flagship; a "chic" UES clientele "savors each bite" of its "innovative" French fare served in "simple, elegant" environs by "pampering" pro staffers; P.S. lunch is a particularly "good buy."

Chanterelle *French* | 27 | 26 | 27 | VE |

TriBeCa | 2 Harrison St. (Hudson St.) | 212-966-6960 | www.chanterellenyc.com

"Damn near perfect", David and Karen Waltuck's TriBeCa French "benchmark" keeps "getting better with age", providing a "regal dining experience" across "all categories"; "every bite of every course is heavenly", while the "elegant", "understated" interior is perfect for "special occasions" with "spot-on", "balletic" service to match; it's "oh so pricey", but "worth every dollar" to most; N.B. dinner is prix fixe only, but ordering à la carte is an option at Thursday-Saturday lunch.

⧈ Daniel ⧈ *French* | 28 | 28 | 28 | VE |

E 60s | 60 E. 65th St. (bet. Madison & Park Aves.) | 212-288-0033 | www.danielnyc.com

An "unparalleled dining experience" awaits at Daniel Boulud's "impeccable" UES namesake, the "standard" for "luxe" prix fixe–only New French fare and rated NYC's No. 1 for Food; add an "amazing" wine list, "breathtaking" decor and "flawless", "white-glove service" and it's easy to see why this is at the "top of the NY dining food chain"; yes, the tab equals a "mortgage payment", but "if you're going to splurge", splurge on "perfection"; N.B. you can order à la carte in the lounge; jackets required.

Di Fara ✍ Pizza
27 | 4 | 7 | I

Midwood | 1424 Ave. J (bet. 14th & 15th Sts.) | Brooklyn | 718-258-1367
It "looks like hell", waits can be "timed with a calendar", but at "old-school artisan" Dominic De Marco's circa-1963 Midwood "mecca", the "heavenly" pizzas are "all they're cracked up to be" – i.e. No. 1 in NYC.

Gotham Bar & Grill American
27 | 25 | 26 | VE

G Village | 12 E. 12th St. (bet. 5th Ave. & University Pl.) | 212-620-4020 | www.gothambarandgrill.com
At this Village culinary "temple", "grand master" Alfred Portale continues to "excite" enthusiasts with his "soigné" "skyscrapers" of "spectacular" New American fare, while staffers "grant your wishes before you even know what to ask for" in a room that's "urbane" but "never pretentious"; to a few it "feels dated", but the majority declares this "quintessential NYC" experience still "vibrant after all these years."

☑ Gramercy Tavern American
27 | 25 | 27 | VE

Flatiron | 42 E. 20th St. (bet. B'way & Park Ave. S.) | 212-477-0777 | www.gramercytavern.com
Supporters of this "superb-in-all-respects" Flatiron New American hail the new chef – Michael Anthony, formerly of Blue Hill at Stone Barns – and salute his "spellbinding" market-centric cuisine, matched with an "extraordinary wine list"; the flower-filled, "rustic-yet-refined" main room "puts diners at ease", as does the "quicksilver" staff that's "on top of everything without being on top of you"; prix fixe–only tabs are "costly" and reservations "tough" ("getting into Harvard is easier"), but there's always the "lower-priced", "drop-in" front tavern.

Il Mulino ●☑ Italian
27 | 18 | 24 | VE

G Village | 86 W. Third St. (bet. Sullivan & Thompson Sts.) | 212-673-3783 | www.ilmulinonewyork.com
"Age has not diminished" the "one-of-a-kind" experience at this "outstanding", "crowded" Village Italian "classic", where nearly "every dish is a masterpiece" and the "white-glove" service has patrons feeling "like royalty"; while some insist "it's the best meal you'll ever have", it's also among "the hardest to book and the hardest to pay for" – to improve your chances in both respects, go for lunch.

☑ Jean Georges ☒ French
28 | 26 | 27 | VE

W 60s | Trump Int'l Hotel | 1 Central Park W. (bet. 60th & 61st Sts.) | 212-299-3900 | www.jean-georges.com
"From start to finish", expect "profound dining experiences" at Jean-Georges Vongerichten's "stunning", jackets-required New French "temple to gastronomy" at Columbus Circle, where the regularly changing, prix fixe–only menus based on fresh seasonal ingredients are probably the "most creative" in town; add "flawless" formal service (supervised by the chef's brother, Philippe), "elegant", recently redone rooms overlooking Central Park and alfresco seating, and it's no wonder it's voted one of the city's most popular places; P.S. for "NYC's best bargain", the Nougatine Room offers "ethereal" $24 prix fixe lunches.

La Grenouille ⏻Ⓜ *French*

27 | 28 | 27 | VE

E 50s | 3 E. 52nd St. (bet. 5th & Madison Aves.) | 212-752-1495 | www.la-grenouille.com

NY's "last great haute French", the Masson family's "timeless" Midtowner is "superlative" in every way, boasting "done-to-perfection" cuisine, "impeccable service" and an "enchanting" room filled with "flowers galore" (even the "diners exude class"); yes, you may need to "raid your piggy bank" to foot the prix fixe–only bill at this *"magnifique* grande dame", but it's "worth the splash"; N.B. jackets required.

L'Atelier de Joël Robuchon *French*

27 | 24 | 26 | VE

E 50s | Four Seasons Hotel | 57 E. 57th St. (bet. Madison & Park Aves.) | 212-350-6658 | www.fourseasons.com

From the "brilliant" Robuchon comes this "consolidation of French technique and Japanese style", where "decadent" dishes in "tapas-style" portions come with a "perfectly designed wine list" and "impeccable service"; although there are comfortable tables, "counter seating is the way to go" in the "minimalist", "casually elegant" space, as the "theater of the open kitchen" is almost as "memorable" as the "eye-popping prices."

❷ Le Bernardin ⏻ *French/Seafood*

28 | 27 | 28 | VE

W 50s | 155 W. 51st St. (bet. 6th & 7th Aves.) | 212-554-1515 | www.le-bernardin.com

All the "accolades are well deserved" at Maguy LeCoze's Midtown French "phenomenon" where "piscatorial fantasy" meets "culinary perfection" via chef Eric Ripert's "beyond sublime" seafood, abetted by "smooth-as-silk service" and a "quietly elegant" setting; to get around the "sky-high", prix fixe–only prices, try the $64 lunch, or go for broke and chalk it up as a "must-do experience"; N.B. jackets required.

Masa ⏻ *Japanese*

27 | 24 | 26 | VE

W 60s | Time Warner Ctr. | 10 Columbus Circle, 4th fl. (60th St. at B'way)

Bar Masa ☾⏻ *Japanese*

W 60s | Time Warner Ctr. | 10 Columbus Circle, 4th fl. (60th St. at B'way) 212-823-9800 | www.masanyc.com

At this Zen-like Time Warner Center Japanese, you can enjoy star chef Masayoshi Takayama's "exquisite" omakase – an "unforgettable" "parade of perfection" for an "astronomical" $400 prix fixe that some consider a deal when set against the cost of floor seats for the Knicks; the more "unassuming" Bar Masa next door is "not cheap", but still a "bargain compared with its big brother."

Nobu *Japanese*

27 | 23 | 23 | VE

TriBeCa | 105 Hudson St. (Franklin St.) | 212-219-0500

Nobu, Next Door ☾ *Japanese*

TriBeCa | 105 Hudson St. (bet. Franklin & N. Moore Sts.) | 212-334-4445 www.noburestaurants.com

"Exquisite", "palate-awakening" Japanese-Peruvian delicacies gratify gourmets at this ever-"buzzing" TriBeCan that hosts a "who's who" crowd right out of an "episode of *Entourage*"; constants include "informative" service and "one big bill" at meal's end, but "getting a table is a problem – unless you're Cameron Diaz"; its more "casual" Next Door sibling is "less expensive" and "every bit as delicious", "without the reservation fuss", since it only takes walk-ins.

Z Per Se *American/French*

| 28 | 28 | 28 | VE |

W 60s | Time Warner Ctr. | 10 Columbus Circle, 5th fl. (60th St. at B'way) | 212-823-9335 | www.perseny.com

Like a "four-hour stroll through culinary paradise", Thomas Keller's French–New American offers "epic dining" in a "Zen-like space" featuring "drop-dead views" of Central Park and Columbus Circle; "telepathic service" (voted No. 1 in our NYC Survey) adds to the overall "magic", so even if the reservations process can be "grueling" and the prix fixe–only tariffs "stratospheric", this "once-in-a-blue-moon treat" is "everything it's cracked up to be" – "Per-Fect!"; N.B. jackets required.

Z Peter Luger Steak House ⊄ *Steak*

| 28 | 14 | 20 | VE |

Williamsburg | 178 Broadway (Driggs Ave.) | Brooklyn | 718-387-7400 | www.peterluger.com

The "holy grail of steakhouses", this Williamsburg "landmark" (NYC's No. 1 chop shop for the 24th year running) makes carnivores "salivate just hearing the name", which is synonymous with the "ultimate" in "succulent" beef, particularly those "buttery, perfectly marbled porterhouses"; "don't look for coddling" from the "brutally efficient" staff – just "consider them an amusement", like the "old-world" *brauhaus* atmospherics and that "outdated cash-only" policy.

Saul *American*

| 27 | 19 | 24 | E |

Boerum Hill | 140 Smith St. (bet. Bergen & Dean Sts.) | Brooklyn | 718-935-9844 | www.saulrestaurant.com

Helmed by chef-owner Saul Bolton, this Boerum Hill New American "deserves all the raves" for its "sophisticated" yet "unpretentious" seasonal menu; a "remarkably helpful" staff, "civilized" setting and fair pricing add up to a "top-flight" experience.

Sushi Seki ●⊠ *Japanese*

| 27 | 13 | 21 | VE |

E 60s | 1143 First Ave. (bet. 62nd & 63rd Sts.) | 212-371-0238

"Put your trust in chef Seki" and he'll lead the way to "omakase heaven" at this "cult-ish" UES Japanese where the "faultless" sushi easily out-"sparkles" the dull decor; even better, you can "keep it coming" (while "spending a small fortune") until 3 AM.

Z Sushi Yasuda ⊠ *Japanese*

| 28 | 22 | 24 | VE |

E 40s | 204 E. 43rd St. (bet. 2nd & 3rd Aves.) | 212-972-1001 | www.sushiyasuda.com

Sushi verges on the "spiritual" at this Grand Central–area "pinnacle" voted NYC's No. 1 Japanese, where chef Naomichi Yasuda provides raw fish "bliss" via "celestial" morsels that "span the seven seas" ("try a snorkel if you want it fresher"); service is "knowledgeable", the decor "simple" but elegant and the vibe "calm" – at least until the bill arrives.

Z Union Square Cafe *American*

| 26 | 22 | 26 | E |

Union Sq | 21 E. 16th St. (bet. 5th Ave. & Union Sq. W.) | 212-243-4020 | www.unionsquarecafe.com

Voted Most Popular in this Survey, Danny Meyer's New American off Union Square "proves its reputation every time", thanks to Michael Romano's "artfully executed" cuisine, a choice of "well-appointed" spaces and "friendly" service that "never wavers"; true, a reservation can be "problematic", but the walk-in bar area is always available to experience this "definition of comfortable NY dining."

Orlando

	FOOD	DECOR	SERVICE	COST

TOP FOOD RANKING

	Restaurant	Cuisine
27	Le Coq au Vin	French
	Victoria & Albert's	American
	Chatham's Place	Continental
	Del Frisco's	Steak
	Taquitos Jalisco	Mexican
26	Primo	Italian
	Norman's	New World
	California Grill	Californian
	Amura	Japanese
25	K Restaurant	Eclectic
	Jiko	African
	Ruth's Chris	Steak
	Seasons 52	American
	Thai House	Thai
	Roy's	Hawaiian
	Enzo's	Italian
	Antonio's La Fiamma	Italian
	Vito's Chop House	Steak
24	Boma	African
	Palm	Steak

Amura *Japanese* | 26 | 20 | 19 | M |

Bay Hill/Dr. Phillips | Plaza Venezia | 7786 W. Sand Lake Rd. (bet. Della Dr. & Dr. Phillips Blvd.) | 407-370-0007
Downtown Orlando | 55 W. Church St. (bet. S. Garland & S. Orange Aves.) | 407-316-8500
Lake Mary | Colonial Town Ctr. | 950 Market Promenade Plaza (Townpark Ave.) | 407-936-6001
www.amura.com

"Sushi lovers will be delighted" by this "trendy" trio's "King Kong portions" of "super-fresh seafood" and "inventive rolls" "with an edge" selected from a "seemingly endless list of options"; a few frown on service that "could be quicker", but most find them "funky, vibrant" and "aglow with ambiance"; N.B. the locations in Dr. Phillips and Lake Mary also offer teppanyaki.

Antonio's La Fiamma Ristorante *Italian* | 25 | 22 | 23 | E |

Maitland | 611 S. Orlando Ave. (Maitland Ave.) | 407-645-1035
Antonio's Sand Lake 🅱 *Italian*
Bay Hill/Dr. Phillips | The Fountains | 7559 W. Sand Lake Rd. (bet. Dr. Phillips Blvd. & Turkey Lake Rd.) | 407-363-9191
www.antoniosonline.com

For what some claim is the "best Italian food outside of Italy", head to this "popular" Maitland mainstay owned by local legend Greg Gentile, where "wonderful, authentic", "zesty dishes like mama made" are accompanied by a "can't-beat" wine list; "though sometimes noisy", it has a "lovely atmosphere" courtesy of servers who "treat you like a

family member" and a dining room with "romantic lake views";
N.B. the Sand Lake Road location opened post-Survey.

Boma – Flavors of Africa *African*

| 24 | 24 | 22 | M |

Animal Kingdom Area | Disney's Animal Kingdom Lodge | 2901 Osceola Pkwy. (Sherbert Rd.) | Lake Buena Vista | 407-938-4722 | www.disneyworld.com

"Take a safari and never leave your table" at this "unique" buffet in Disney's Animal Kingdom Lodge, where "an excellent spread" mingles "exotic African preparations" for "adventurous palates" with "common but well-prepared American dishes" for kids and "picky eaters"; the "amazing variety of flavors" extends to "mouthwatering desserts" and a small but "fantastic South African wine list", all served in a themed setting that's "done remarkably well, without being campy"; N.B. no lunch.

☑ California Grill *Californian*

| 26 | 25 | 24 | E |

Magic Kingdom Area | Disney's Contemporary Resort | 4600 N. World Dr., 15th fl. (Contemporary Resort Access Rd.) | Lake Buena Vista | 407-939-3463 | www.disneyworld.com

Located on the 15th floor of Disney's Contemporary Resort, the Orlando area's Most Popular restaurant is an "unparalleled" "retreat", from its "inventive" if "expensive" Californian menu and "exemplary staff" to its "upscale" ambiance and a "wine list that's second to none"; but "make your reservations ahead of time" and "request a window seat" in order to catch the "spectacular" view of the nightly "fireworks exploding over the Magic Kingdom."

☑ Chatham's Place *Continental*

| 27 | 19 | 26 | E |

Bay Hill/Dr. Phillips | 7575 Dr. Phillips Blvd. (Sand Lake Rd.) | 407-345-2992 | www.chathamsplace.com

At this "heavenly" "local favorite" in Dr. Phillips, "a serious kitchen" spins out "pricey but excellent" and "creative" Florida-tinged Continental cuisine that's served by "attentive and gracious" "professionals"; it's located "out of the way" "in an office building", but its supporters find it a "small but special" option offering an "intimate", "old-world ambiance" complete with "romantic" nightly guitar music.

☑ Del Frisco's Prime Steak & Lobster ☒ *Steak*

| 27 | 18 | 25 | E |

Winter Park | 729 Lee Rd. (I-4) | 407-645-4443 | www.delfriscosorlando.com

"Don't change a thing!" cry carnivores captivated by this Winter Park chophouse "for a man to love", where what some believe is "the best steak at any restaurant, in any city, at any price" (plus "lobsters better than in Maine") is served in "huge portions" by an "excellent", "old-school" staff; a "very good wine list", nightly live music and "typical", "dark-wood and leather" decor round out the "expense-account" experience.

☑ Emeril's Orlando *Contemp. Louisiana*

| 24 | 22 | 23 | E |

Universal Orlando | Universal Studios CityWalk | 6000 Universal Blvd. (Vineland Rd.) | 407-224-2424 | www.emerils.com

This culinary "island of adventure" in Universal Studios CityWalk provides a "sophisticated break from the theme parks" via Emeril Lagasse's "delicious", "memorable" Contemporary Louisiana cuisine – "close your eyes and you're in NOLA" – plus "friendly service" and "great wines"; it's "pricey", however, and can get "packed" with "tourists" "in tank tops and shorts", leading some to suggest "a novel idea: a dress code"; P.S. "make reservations in advance."

Enzo's Restaurant on the Lake ⑤Ⓜ *Italian* | 25 | 22 | 22 | E |

Longwood | 1130 S. Hwy. 17-92 (Wildmere Ave.) | 407-834-9872 | www.enzos.com

"A big-city-quality restaurant in a small suburb", this "Italian delight" in Longwood "has been cranking out first-rate meals forever", from an "amazing antipasti table" to "authentic", "fresh, flavorful, fabulous" classics that are "worth the splurge" – "you can taste the love in the handmade pasta"; it's the "perfect blend of true hospitality" and "lovely" lakeside setting, and it has a "buzz" that "keeps 'em coming back"; N.B. lunch is served on Fridays only.

Jiko – The Cooking Place *African* | 25 | 25 | 25 | E |

Animal Kingdom Area | Disney's Animal Kingdom Lodge | 2901 Osceola Pkwy. (Hwy. 192) | Lake Buena Vista | 407-938-4733 | www.disneyworld.com

"Let your taste buds be adventurous" counsel safari-seekers who trek to this "sleek", "serene" spot in Disney's Animal Kingdom Lodge for "sumptuous", "African-inspired cuisine" featuring sub-Saharan spices on foods from an array of cultures; the "exotic tastes" are complemented by "tantalizing" South African wines and "helpful" service.

K Restaurant Wine Bar ⑤ *Eclectic* | 25 | 20 | 22 | E |

College Park | 2401 Edgewater Dr. (Vassar St.) | 407-872-2332 | www.krestaurantwinebar.com

Owned by "talented" chef Kevin Fonzo, this "bustling" "culinary prize" in Orlando's College Park delivers "to-die-for" "food art" in the form of a "pricey", "ever-changing menu" chock-full of "scrumdiddlyumptious" Eclectic eats that are served by a "charming, down-to-earth staff"; it also boasts a "solid wine list" and "yummy desserts", and the "pleasant", "casual" setting is enhanced by local artwork, leading many to give this K an "A++."

Ⓩ Le Coq au Vin Ⓜ *French* | 27 | 19 | 25 | E |

South Orlando | 4800 S. Orange Ave. (Holden Ave.) | 407-851-6980 | www.lecoqauvinrestaurant.com

"Julia Child would be proud" of this "longtime favorite" "hidden" away in an unlikely South Orlando locale, because this "petite" "farm-style French" is the area's No. 1 for Food "year after year" courtesy of chef-owner Louis Perrotte's "unpretentious yet spectacular" seasonal dinner menu; "quaint", "country-style decor", "professional service" and "decent prices" all make it "a pleasure to eat" here, leading patrons to plead: "shhh! don't tell anyone"; P.S. there are now half-portions, meaning you'll "have room for the spectacular soufflé."

Norman's *New World* | 26 | 26 | 26 | VE |

South Orlando | Ritz-Carlton Orlando, Grande Lakes | 4012 Central Florida Pkwy. (John Young Pkwy.) | 407-393-4333 | www.normans.com

"South Florida's best chef rocks Orlando!" declare devotees "in love with New World cuisine" thanks to the Ritz-Carlton's "superb" dinner destination from chef-owner Norman Van Aken, whose original Coral Gables eatery closed in June 2007; the tasting menu is "the way to go" and "worth the price" (four courses for $80), while a "gorgeous room" and "terrific service" make for "elegant dining on all levels"; in short, "on a scale of one to five, it's a 10!"

Palm *Steak*   24 | 21 | 24 | E

Universal Orlando | Hard Rock Hotel | 5800 Universal Blvd. (Vineland St.) | 407-503-7256 | www.thepalm.com

"An oasis of attentive service", this chophouse in Universal's Hard Rock Hotel "is where you go for beef if you're on the attractions side of Orlando", offering "enormous portions" of "always consistent" steaks and lobster, plus desserts for which you'll want to "save room"; dissenters deem it "middle of the pack", but most declare that this "satisfying" chain link is "as good as the ones in NYC without the attitude", i.e. "don't expect power brokers."

Primo *Italian*   26 | 26 | 24 | E

South Orlando | JW Marriott Orlando Grande Lakes | 4040 Central Florida Pkwy. (John Young Pkwy.) | 407-393-4444 | www.grandelakes.com

At this "primo experience" in South Orlando's JW Marriott Grande Lakes, "foodies will not be disappointed" by the "glorious" Italian "surprises" from "amazing" Maine-based maestro Melissa Kelly, whose menu includes organic touches and "fresh, local produce (often from the chef's own garden)"; the same "exquisite care given" to the "intriguing pastas" and seafood can also be seen in the "attentive service" and "casual but elegant setting."

Roy's *Hawaiian*   25 | 23 | 22 | E

Bay Hill/Dr. Phillips | Plaza Venezia | 7760 W. Sand Lake Rd. (Dr. Phillips Blvd.) | 407-352-4844 | www.roysrestaurant.com

Roy Yamaguchi "is king of Hawaiian [fusion] cooking, even in Orlando" aver admirers of the chefs and this chain outpost in Dr. Phillips that "will stun you" with its "creative preparations" of "exotic", "swooningly delicious" "twists on seafood" and "aloha hospitality"; the "busy", "happening scene makes it a winner" for some, although sensitive sorts insist "the acoustics could use a bit of tuning . . . down."

Ruth's Chris Steak House *Steak*   25 | 22 | 24 | E

Bay Hill/Dr. Phillips | 7501 W. Sand Lake Rd. (Turkey Lake Rd.) | 407-226-3900

Lake Mary | 80 Colonial Center Pkwy. (Village Oak Ln.) | 407-804-8220

Winter Park | Winter Park Village | 610 N. Orlando Ave. (Webster Ave.) | 407-622-2444

www.ruthschris.com

"Bring a big appetite and a bigger wallet" to these "class acts" that offer "the juiciest cuts of beef", tableside service and "quiet, subdued" decor; while a few feel they've "seen one, seen 'em all", most think these steakhouse "havens" "have got it down to a science", although they view the Sand Lake Road venue as "vulnerable to Mouseketeers in flip-flops"; N.B. Lake Mary and Winter Park both serve lunch on Fridays.

☑ Seasons 52 *American*

25 | 26 | 25 | M

Altamonte Springs | The Altamonte Mall | 463 E. Altamonte Dr.
(Palm Springs Dr.) | 407-767-1252
Bay Hill/Dr. Phillips | Plaza Venezia | 7700 W. Sand Lake Rd. (bet. Della Dr. &
Dr. Phillips Blvd.) | 407-354-5212
www.seasons52.com

"You'll feel positively angelic as you devour" the "light, flavorful" seasonal cuisine at these "sophisticated yet comfortable" "formula restaurants that finally get the equation right": "creative", "guilt-free" New American entrees "each under 475 calories" that are complemented by a "wonderful wine list", topped off with "amazing", "shot glass–sized desserts" and served by a "well-trained staff"; but since both the Dr. Phillips and Altamonte Springs locations are "always packed", "good luck getting in (or even near) them."

☑ Taquitos Jalisco *Mexican*

27 | 17 | 22 | I

MetroWest | MetroWest Village Shopping Ctr. | 2419 S. Hiawassee Rd.
(Westpointe Blvd.) | 407-296-0626
Winter Garden | Tri-City Shopping Ctr. | 1041 S. Dillard St. (W. Colonial Dr.) |
407-654-0363

At these twin "family restaurants" in MetroWest and Winter Garden, you'll "feel like you're on vacation in Mexico" as you down *delicioso* south-of-the-border eats that are "consistent, authentic" and served with "big smiles"; live mariachi bands play Thursday–Sunday at both locations, so "sip a cold Corona" (or a "great margarita") and enjoy the "comfortable decor", "fun" ambiance and low tabs.

Thai House ☒ *Thai*

25 | 15 | 22 | I

East Orlando | 2117 E. Colonial Dr. (N. Hillside Ave.) | 407-898-0820 |
thaihouseoforlando.com

Satisfied surveyors "can't wait to get back" to this "consistent" east-of-Downtown "favorite" for "delicious" Thai food made with the "freshest ingredients"; despite unassuming decor, this "not-to-be-missed restaurant" "exceeds expectations by far", right down to the "professional" service and "downright cheap" charges.

☑ Victoria & Albert's *American*

27 | 27 | 27 | VE

Magic Kingdom Area | Disney's Grand Floridian Resort |
4401 Grand Floridian Way (bet. Maple Rd. & W. Seven Seas Dr.) |
Lake Buena Vista | 407-939-3463 | www.disneyworld.com

Rated No. 1 for Decor and Service in the Orlando area, this jacket-required "oasis of civility" in Disney's Grand Floridian Resort "really does [try] to spoil you", offering "pricey" six-course New American meals from "culinary god" Scott Hunnel that can be "exquisitely matched" with wines or enjoyed at the "coveted chef's table" (reservable six months in advance); if a few find it "overhyped", more consider it a "once-in-a-lifetime experience" complete with nightly harp music and "superb service" from a Victorian-garbed staff; N.B. children under the age of ten are no longer allowed.

Vito's Chop House *Steak*

25 | 21 | 24 | E

International Drive | 8633 International Dr. (bet. Austrian Row &
Via Mercado) | 407-354-2467 | www.vitoschophouse.com

An old-timer "in the heart of tourist land" near the convention center, this Italian-style chophouse "blows away the other big-name" beef purveyors by "doing the classics well", offering "succulent" aged steaks and seafood plus an "amazingly long", "nicely priced" wine list to "make any connoisseur quiver"; although a handful of surveyors suggest it's "solid, but not overly memorable", meat mavens maintain that "attentive", "professional" service and a "cozy" setting are just two more reasons that "Vito's has it all."

Z Wolfgang Puck Café *Californian* | 21 | 19 | 18 | M |

Downtown Disney Area | 1482 E. Buena Vista Dr. (Hotel Plaza Blvd.) | Lake Buena Vista | 407-938-9653 | www.wolfgangpuckorlando.com

If you "want variety and quality", "the Puck stops here" praise pals of this Downtown Disney Californian, a "bright, breezy" culinary oasis encompassing a "fun downstairs" cafe and sushi bar, a "more refined" upstairs dining room ("i.e. a thousand fewer kids"), plus a quick-service section; still, opponents point to "long lines", "shaky service" and a "noisy atmosphere" as proof that Wolfgang's "well-known name is pretty much all he brought to this place."

Palm Beach

Ⓩ Abe & Louie's *Steak*   25 | 24 | 23 | E

Boca Raton | 2200 W. Glades Rd. (Renaissance Way) | 561-447-0024 | www.bbrginc.com

"Attractive" and "old school" (though it opened in 2005), this Boston-based steakhouse beckons "Boca's rich and beautiful" with "yum-o" filets, "superlative service" and "a fine wine list"; but the "decibel level is like the Florida turnpike", and even with "huge portions", "prices are crazy", so it's "worth paying the sharing charge" or "skipping the dinner scene" altogether (some feel it's "best for lunch or brunch", anyway).

Bluefin Sushi *Japanese/Thai*   25 | 18 | 20 | M

Boca Raton | 861 Yamato Rd. (Congress Ave.) | 561-981-8986 | www.bluefinsushi.com

"Who needs to go to Nobu?" when "outstanding sushi" (including a "lobster bomb that's da bomb"), plus "solid Thai" fare, is on hand at this "small", "off-the-beaten-path" Boca spot; it's "almost impossible to get a table in season" however, and "ambiance is sadly lacking", so some say it's "not for fine dining – strictly eating."

Bronze Ⓩ *American*   25 | 15 | 21 | M

Juno Beach | Plaza La Mer | 805 Donald Ross Rd. (bet. Ellison Wilson Rd. & U.S. 1) | 561-803-7701

"More than a wine bar" (though they do have "an A+" by-the-glass list), this Juno New American "sleeper" serves "fantastic food", "beautifully presented" by "servers who are attentive, but don't hover"; the "hip", bronze art-bedecked decor is not for all, especially the "strange seating"; nevertheless, nervous fans implore "don't tell the world about this wonderful little place"; P.S. "in a land of giant portions", "being able to order a half of most entrees is a nice feature."

☒ Café Boulud *French*   26 | 27 | 25 | VE

Palm Beach | Brazilian Court Hotel | 301 Australian Ave. (Hibiscus Ave.) | 561-655-6060 | www.danielnyc.com
Almost "as good as its NYC sister" declare devotees of Daniel Boulud's Brazilian Court Hotel bistro, a "beautifully serene" site with the "best courtyard dining room on Fantasy Island"; the food is a "French event" – "delicious and beautiful" – and service is "smooth as old silk", particularly the "pleasant" sommeliers; a "very 'old money' PB atmosphere" prevails, but many say "it's a pleasure to see men wearing jackets", and even those who "had to hock some jewelry" to pay the "astronomical prices" proclaim "it's worth it."

Cafe Chardonnay *American*   26 | 22 | 24 | E

Palm Beach Gardens | Garden Square Shoppes | 4533 PGA Blvd. (Military Trail) | 561-627-2662 | www.cafechardonnay.com
"Don't be put off by the shopping center" locale of this Palm Beach Gardens New American – still a "standout" after 21 years – where a "dynamite wine list" ("by the glass too!") and "well-trained staff" complement the "creative", "consistently excellent" food in a "beautiful setting"; it's "like New York in Florida" – read: "crowded in season" – so "reservations in advance are a must."

Café L'Europe *Continental*   25 | 26 | 24 | VE

Palm Beach | 331 S. County Rd. (bet. Australian & Brazilian Aves.) | 561-655-4020 | www.cafeleurope.com
"The wealth of Palm Beach dines here" at the town's "most glamorous and well-decorated" place; "an oasis of flowers" sets the scene for "divine, luscious" Continental cuisine that "balances between old standbys and creative new dishes", backed by an "extensive" wine list and "genteel" service; the sensitive sense a "somewhat haughty" attitude toward non-regulars, but "if your budget can handle it", "this is the place to splurge"; P.S. for a "better deal", try the "late week lunch" prix fixe.

Captain Charlie's Reef Grill *Seafood*   25 | 11 | 20 | M

Juno Beach | 12846 U.S. 1 (bet. Juno Isles Blvd. & Packwood Rd.) | 561-624-9924
"Wonderful", "inexpensive" seafood with a "Caribbean flair" makes this "relaxed" Juno Beach strip-mall spot a "must-visit"; there's "no decor or ambiance, but who cares" when there are "generous appetizers" to "make a meal of" and an "unbelievable wine list for the money."

☒ Chez Jean-Pierre Bistro ☒ *French*   27 | 22 | 25 | VE

Palm Beach | 132 N. County Rd. (bet. Sunrise & Sunset Aves.) | 561-833-1171
"Simply the best in PB" (with the No. 1 Food rating to prove it), this "family-owned and -run jewel" of a Classic French furnishes a "fantasy dining experience" for the flush, with "fun", diversely decorated rooms and "professional" but "not stuffy" service to complement chef Jean-Pierre Leverrier's "fahbulous" fare; "reservations can be difficult, but persevere – you won't regret it."

NEW Chops Lobster Bar *Seafood/Steak* | 26 | 27 | 24 | VE |

Boca Raton | Royal Palm Pl. | 101 Plaza Real (SE Mizner Blvd.) | 561-395-2675 | www.chopslobsterbar.com

"Brand new in Boca", this "beautiful" bi-parte "addition from Atlanta" has surveyors licking their chops over the "incredible steaks" – even "the smallest are huge" – and "to-die-for fried lobster" fetched from the "cool open kitchen" by an "obliging staff"; yes, you better "bring bags of bucks" and be braced for a highly "noisy" scene, but "fortunately the food is so good, conversation is not necessary."

11 Maple Street M *American* | 26 | 24 | 25 | E |

Jensen Beach | 3224 NE Maple Ave. (11th Ave.) | 772-334-7714

"Drive an hour if you have to" for the "sublime dining experience" of this veteran in Jensen Beach ("MapQuest it if you're not familiar with the area"); converts "can't get enough" of chef-owner Mike Perrin's "towering edible constructions" – "imaginative" New American fare offered in a "charming Old Florida" "antiques-adorned house", along with an "amazing rare wine list and amazing servers too (a rarity!)."

Z Four Seasons – The Restaurant M *Floridian* | 27 | 27 | 27 | VE |

Palm Beach | Four Seasons Resort | 2800 S. Ocean Blvd. (Lake Ave.) | 561-533-3750 | www.fourseasons.com

Exuding "the quality wannabes should strive for", this "beautiful oasis" perched oceanside boasts "the best service" in Palm Beach (voted No. 1) from a staff that'll "spoil you rotten", "even matching the napkins to your outfit"; while Hubert Des Marais, "the original chef, has left" (not fully reflected in the Food score), the kitchen is still turning out "imaginative" Floridian favorites "layered with so many exquisite flavors" that, "even if you go broke, you must eat here once in your lifetime – this is heaven!"

Kathy's Gazebo Café S *Continental* | 26 | 22 | 24 | E |

Boca Raton | 4199 N. Federal Hwy. (Spanish River Blvd.) | 561-395-6033 | www.kathysgazebo.com

"Jackets are not required, but everyone wears one" at this "romantic" "classic" Continental in Boca, where an "older crowd" delights in "Dover sole as it should be" and "old-fashioned European service"; it all may be "too traditional" for trendsetters, especially given the "tight quarters", but most enjoy this "elegant" experience.

Z Kee Grill *Seafood* | 24 | 21 | 21 | E |

Juno Beach | 14010 U.S. 1 (Donald Ross Rd.) | 561-776-1167
Boca Raton | 17940 N. Military Trail (bet. Champion Blvd. & Clint Moore Rd.) | 561-995-5044

Though they're technically surf 'n' turfers, the "seafood is king" at this pair voted Most Popular in Palm Beach County; true, there's "too long a wait for a table" – reservations are taken only at the Boca branch – and some protest "your plate's cleared before the fork hits the china", but most focus on the "always-fresh fish", "awesome spinach side" and bamboo-walled "Florida atmosphere", declaring this duo "a class act."

Z L'Escalier S M *French* | 27 | 28 | 26 | VE |

Palm Beach | The Breakers | 1 S. County Rd. (Breakers Row) | 561-655-6611 | www.thebreakers.com

The "breathtaking", "grand atmosphere of The Breakers is the setting" for the "finest" "flawlessly executed" French cuisine and "excellent wines", backed by "solicitous but discreet service"; "elegant" and "extraordinary", it's "expensive" of course – but also a "unique experience", so "bring out the jewels and sell some to eat here" at this historic hotel haven.

🔡 Little Moirs Food Shack 🖩 Seafood   27 | 12 | 22 | M

Jupiter | Jupiter Sq. | 103 U.S. 1 (E. Indiantown Rd.) | 561-741-3626

"It's all about the food" at this "kooky", "ultracasual" pescatorial place, since the decor's pure beach "shack-y", the wine "severely lacking, as is the plastic stemware" and the "fast service" ensures "no lingering" at table (though you "wait . . . and wait . . . and wait" to get in); but oh, those "so-fresh" and "fantastic" fish choices with "unusual" coatings ("sweet potato is my favorite") – they cause even the intially skeptical to say "don't walk, run" to this Jupiter joint.

🔡 Marcello's La Sirena 🖩 Italian   27 | 19 | 23 | E

West Palm Beach | 6316 S. Dixie Hwy. (Forest Hill Blvd.) | 561-585-3128 | www.lasirenaonline.com

An "old-timer" "off the beaten path" in West Palm Beach, this Italian has a "chef-owner who can cook with the country's best" and backs up his *cucina* with a "great cellar of fine wines" from around the globe; the service is "refined", and heeding pleas "to spruce the place up a little", they've repainted lately (not reflected in the Decor score).

Morton's, The Steakhouse Steak   24 | 21 | 23 | VE

West Palm Beach | Phillips Point Office Bldg. | 777 S. Flagler Dr. (Lakeview Ave.) | 561-835-9664

Boca Raton | Boca Ctr. | 5050 Town Center Circle (Military Trail) | 561-392-7724

www.mortons.com

"Prime steak from a prime steakhouse" keeps the carnivores contented at these Boca and West Palm Beach branches of "one of the great chains"; the "gentleman's club atmosphere" is "comfortable", if a bit "gloomy", and the service "solid", though "they could do without the show-and-tell presentation (I know what a steak looks like)"; overall, though, it "never disappoints" – especially "on an expense account."

🔡 New York Prime Steak   25 | 21 | 21 | VE

Boca Raton | 2350 Executive Center Dr. NW (Glades Rd.) | 561-998-3881 | www.newyorkprime.com

Expect "prime food" at "prime prices" at this "loud" "very Boca" meatery where "many celebs" and other "with-it" types nosh on the "top-quality" fillets after quaffing a few at the "old-world Euro bar"; if the bellicose beef there's "attitude everywhere" and you "have to wait even with a reservation", advocates argue it's "annoying but worth it."

Paradiso Italian   24 | 21 | 23 | E

Lake Worth | 625 Lucerne Ave. (bet. K & L Sts.) | 561-547-2500 | www.paradisolakeworth.com

A "trip to Italy [lies] behind these doors" declare disciples of this Downtown Lake Worth eatery, whose "amazing" *cucina* "would pass muster in NYC or Roma", as would the "old-fashioned, cater-to-your-needs staff"; less paradiso-cal, however, are the "way expensive" tabs, which – depending on your bank account – may or may not be "worth it."

FOOD | DECOR. | SERVICE | COST

Ruth's Chris Steak House *Steak*

25 | 21 | 23 | E

North Palm Beach | 661 U.S. 1 (Lighthouse Dr.) | 561-863-0660
Boca Raton | 225 NE Mizner Blvd. (NE 2nd St.) | 888-722-4361
www.ruthschris.com

The secret to the "awesome steaks" at these links in the "trusted" chain is the "butter and hot plates" they're served on, unleashing a "sizzling buttery deliciousness" that's complemented by "New Orleans-style sides and appetizers"; so, carnivores, "dress up", bring "big cash" and let the "highly competent staff" serve you within the "masculine ambiance" – "it's the ultimate gift to yourself."

Sushi Jo's *Japanese*

25 | 17 | 21 | M

West Palm Beach | 319 Belvedere Rd. (S. Olive Ave.) | 561-868-7893
Boynton Beach | Ocean Plaza | 640 E. Ocean Ave. (SE 6th Ct.) | 561-737-0606
www.sushijo.com

"Go for the food, stay for the hip scene" at this West Palm and Boynton Beach duo where "top-notch" "insanely fresh" sushi and a "fantastic selection of cold sake" are served in a "dim" "lounge-type atmosphere"; raw fish fans rave this is "not your typical 'clinical' Japanese restaurant", even if the "hip music" can be "too loud" and the prices – "well, just don't look."

32 East *American*

25 | 19 | 22 | E

Delray Beach | 32 E. Atlantic Ave. (bet. SE 1st & Swinton Aves.) | 561-276-7868 | www.32east.com

Offering a "scene-o-rama" with "sexy atmosphere", this Delray Beach New American is where "the who's who of Palm Beach County hang", sampling "market-fresh cuisine" from "wildly creative chef" Nick Morfogen, who "changes the menu at whim" (and "depending on what he finds" that day); while "knowledgeable", the staff can be "distracted – perhaps by the eardrum-splitting volume of the room" – but when this "cosmopolitan" place "is on, it's all the way."

Trattoria Romana *Italian*

25 | 17 | 20 | E

Boca Raton | 499 E. Palmetto Park Rd. (NE 5th Ave.) | 561-393-6715

"They take care of the regulars" at this "dependable" "old-time Italian" where the "spare-nothing" menu includes a "humongous veal chop" and "b-i-ggg" drinks; there's "not much atmosphere" and it gets quite "loud" (tip: the back room "has a lot less noise"), but believers bellow "*buonissimo!*" for this East Boca bit of The Boot.

Philadelphia

TOP FOOD RANKING

	Restaurant	Cuisine
28	Fountain	Continental/French
	Le Bar Lyonnais	French
	Birchrunville Store	French/Italian
	Le Bec-Fin	French
	Vetri	Italian
27	Lacroix/Rittenhouse	French
	Gilmore's	French
	Morimoto	Japanese
	Savona	French/Italian
	Amada	Spanish
	Buddakan	Asian
	Bluefin	Japanese
26	Paloma	French/Mexican
	Gayle	American
	Mainland Inn	American
	Striped Bass	Seafood
	Blue Sage	Vegetarian
	La Bonne Auberge	French
	Swann Lounge	American/French
	Alison/Blue Bell	American
	Totaro's	Eclectic

Alison at Blue Bell ⊠Ⓜ⊜ *American*   26 | 16 | 22 | E
Blue Bell | 721 Skippack Pike (Penllyn-Blue Bell Pike) | 215-641-2660 |
www.alisonatbluebell.com
There's "no need to schlep to Center City", since "skilled" chef-owner
Alison Barshak is "on top of every detail" at her cash-only New
American in the Montco 'burbs; her fan club calls it a "foodie's delight" with "innovative", "Manhattan-quality" eats served in a "warm",
"simple" space – just "get used to sitting in your neighbor's lap".

Amada *Spanish*   27 | 25 | 23 | E
Old City | 217 Chestnut St. (bet. 2nd & 3rd Sts.) | 215-625-2450 |
www.amadarestaurant.com
Spanish-loving surveyors dip into their bag of superlatives over Jose
Garces' Old City venue, where "magical" justly describes the tapas
that are accompanied by "fantastic" sangria, "phenomenal" flamenco
dancers (some nights) and "attentive" service; it's the "best thing to
happen to Philadelphia in a long time", but it's advisable to go early
before the "noise" rises "above the pain threshold."

⊠ Birchrunville
Store Cafe ⊠Ⓜ⊜ *French/Italian*   28 | 23 | 26 | E
Birchrunville | 1403 Hollow Rd. (Flowing Springs Rd.) | 610-827-9002 |
www.birchrunvillestorecafe.com
Bring cash along with your GPS to Francis Trzeciak's "remote", "bare-
bones" BYO in an old Chester County "country" store; diehards know

to "reserve" a spot "well in advance" for the "sophisticated" Franco-Italian cuisine prepared with "thought and care", "romantic" atmosphere and servers so "gracious" you "want them as your friends"; N.B. closed Sunday–Tuesday.

Bluefin ⊠ *Japanese* · · · · · · · · · · · · · · 27 | 14 | 20 | M

Plymouth Meeting | 1017 Germantown Pike (Virginia Rd.) | 610-277-3917 | www.sushibluefin.com

Sushi-philes swear "if you aren't going to Morimoto", this "tiny" Japanese BYO in a "slightly dated" Plymouth Meeting strip center is an "excellent" alternative, where the "phenomenal", "amazingly fresh" fare includes rolls that are a "treat for the eyes and taste buds"; a "pleasant" staff helps make up for the "modest" decor.

Blue Sage Vegetarian Grille ⊠Ⓜ *Vegetarian* 26 | 14 | 22 | M

Southampton | 772 Second St. Pike (Street Rd.) | 215-942-8888 | www.bluesagegrille.com

Come "prepared to wait" – even with "reservations" – for the "ridiculously good" fare at Mike and Holly Jackson's "tiny", Bucks strip-mall vegetarian BYO, where fans forget about "mock" ingredients, "substitutes" and meat, since what they taste is an "amazing creativity with veggies"; who cares if the setting "isn't fancy-schmancy" when "huge" portions can supply you with a "tantalizing" meal the next day?

⧅ Brasserie Perrier *French* · · · · · 26 | 24 | 24 | E

Center City West | 1619 Walnut St. (bet. 16th & 17th Sts.) | 215-568-3000 | www.brasserieperrier.com

Philly's "established boomer crowd" keeps "coming back" to Le Bec-Fin's nearby, "scaled-down" Center City brother "for the rest of us", an art deco–designed destination where Georges Perrier and Chris Scarduzio join forces to deliver "divine" New French cuisine; though the fare's "not cheap", a "professional" staff helps – overall, this one "hits all the right notes"; insider's dish: check out the bar area before "a night on the town."

⧅ Buddakan *Asian* · · · · · · · · · 27 | 27 | 23 | E

Old City | 325 Chestnut St. (bet. 3rd & 4th Sts.) | 215-574-9440 | www.buddakan.com

If you want to "impress someone" who's "hard to impress", join the "wait list" for Stephen Starr's "swank", "theatrical" Asian in Old City, a fave of "fashionistas" and "celebs"; it's Philly's Most Popular restaurant thanks to "memorable", "groundbreaking" food served by "solicitous" servers and a "gorgeous" setting that "makes you feel beautiful, even if you think you're not"; as far as scoring a reservation in prime time, try rubbing the "giant" Buddha's belly.

⧅ Fountain Restaurant *Continental/French* 28 | 28 | 29 | VE

Center City West | Four Seasons Hotel | 1 Logan Sq.
(Benjamin Franklin Pkwy.) | 215-963-1500 | www.fourseasons.com

"As good as it gets" sizes up the Philly Survey's winner of the triple crown (No. 1 for Food, Decor and Service) in the Four Seasons Hotel; Philly's "elite" "live it up" and find "a treat for all the senses" in an "opulent" setting that showcases Martin Hamann's "divine" New French-Continental cuisine and "formal", yet "low-key" service that gives you the "royal treatment" ("they could serve me Cheerios and I'd think it was the best meal I ever had"); yes, the "shockingly high" tabs may be hard to absorb, but they're easily justified, especially for "expense-account" or "special-occasion" visits; N.B. jacket required.

Gayle ⬛Ⓜ *American* | 26 | 19 | 24 | E |

South St. | 617 S. Third St. (bet. Bainbridge & South Sts.) | 215-922-3850 | www.gaylephiladelphia.com

"Go and be adventurous" at former Le Bec-Fin executive chef Daniel Stern's "little" New American off South Street, a "casual" though still upscale venue blowing away fans with "knowledgeable" service and "well-executed", "complex" fare that deftly combines the "experimental" and "classic"; N.B. it's à la carte Tuesdays, Wednesdays and Thursdays, but prix fixe only Fridays and Saturdays.

Gilmore's ⬛Ⓜ *French* | 27 | 23 | 27 | E |

West Chester | 133 E. Gay St. (bet. Matlack & Walnut Sts.) | 610-431-2800 | www.gilmoresrestaurant.com

Peter Gilmore (an alum of Le Bec-Fin) "amazes" with his Classic French West Chester BYO widely regarded as the "Le Bec of the 'burbs" for its "fantastic" "special-occasion" cuisine served by an "attitude-free" staff; at 35 seats, scoring a reservation in the snug, "intimate" quarters means either many redials or divine intervention.

La Bonne Auberge Ⓜ *French* | 26 | 27 | 26 | VE |

New Hope | Village 2 Apartment Complex | 1 Rittenhouse Circle (River Rd.) | 215-862-2462 | www.bonneauberge.com

An auberge to remember is Gerard Caronello's "formal", "precious" French serving up a "romantic" ambiance, "super" food and "super" service to "special-occasion" seekers; the 18th-century farmhouse setting (within a New Hope apartment complex) evokes the French "countryside", though "stratospheric" prices bring everyone back to reality; N.B. dinner only, Thursday–Sunday.

☒ Lacroix at The Rittenhouse *French* | 27 | 27 | 27 | VE |

Center City West | Rittenhouse Hotel | 210 W. Rittenhouse Sq. (bet. Locust & Walnut Sts.) | 215-790-2533 | www.lacroixrestaurant.com

For a taste of what "the gods on Olympus eat", there's no better example than Jean-Marie Lacroix's "dreamy" New French extravaganza in the Rittenhouse Hotel; count on "culinary mastery", with a menu devised of three-, four- and five-course "artfully presented" small plates, a "modern", "tranquil" room overlooking the Square and "sublime" service; true, you'll have to dip heavily into your piggy bank, but it's sure to impress; N.B. post-Survey, Lacroix has yielded the reins to new executive chef Matt Levin; jacket and tie preferred.

☒ Le Bar Lyonnais ⬛ *French* | 28 | 23 | 25 | E |

Center City West | 1523 Walnut St. (bet. 15th & 16th Sts.) | 215-567-1000 | www.lebecfin.com

"Philly" Georges Perrier's "hidden" Center City "gem" beneath Le Bec-Fin continues to impress gourmets who crave an "intimate" meal with "spectacular" French bistro food and "fantastic" service but can't fork over a "whole paycheck" at the mother ship upstairs; it's even better when you can visit the bar at peak times and gaze at the "impressive examples of plastic surgery."

	FOOD	DECOR	SERVICE	COST

⬛ Le Bec-Fin ⬛ *French* — 28 | 27 | 27 | VE

Center City West | 1523 Walnut St. (bet. 15th & 16th Sts.) | 215-567-1000 |
www.lebecfin.com

Still "the pinnacle" of Philly restaurants is Georges Perrier's "big-bucks" haute Center City French institution that "bows to no other" in its class and is a "must-see", "must-experience" "masterpiece"; indeed, the "magnificent" food (including the "unbelievable" dessert cart), ornate, "beautiful Parisian" setting and "perfect" service from a "fleet" of waiters all leave you as "breathless" as the "sticker-shock"-inducing bill, but it's all worth the admission to "one of the best ever"; N.B. jacket recommended at dinner.

Mainland Inn *American* — 26 | 23 | 25 | E

Mainland | 17 Main St. (Sumneytown Pike) | 215-256-8500 |
www.themainlandinn.com

"Understated" is another name for this central Montco "secret" decorated in "18th-century Americana" that "lives up to its rep" as "one of the best" in the 'burbs with "sublime" New American food and service that make you "forget about traveling to Center City"; insiders advise if you want to make an impression on someone, check out the $21.95 Sunday brunch.

Morimoto *Japanese* — 27 | 27 | 25 | VE

Washington Square | 723 Chestnut St. (bet. 7th & 8th Sts.) | 215-413-9070 |
www.morimotorestaurant.com

Even with 'Iron Chef' Masaharu Morimoto spending time in the new namesake NYC offshoot, Stephen Starr's "trendy" "neo"-Japanese "masterpiece" in Center City is still a "must visit" for "sublime", "Tokyo-quality" sushi and "exciting" fusion fare in a "surreal" and "seriously sexy" setting complete with "changing mood lights"; "flawless" service is part of an overall experience that feels like "winning the lottery", so it's advised to "splurge" to take advantage of what will be a "memorable" meal ("you won't be sorry, even when you get the bill").

Paloma ⬛Ⓜ *French/Mexican* — 26 | 18 | 25 | E

Northeast Philly | 6516 Castor Ave. (bet. Hellerman St. & Magee Ave.) |
215-533-0356 | www.palomafinedining.com

In a "food-starved", "down-at-the-heels" Northeast Philly area resides this "haute" French-Mexican "standout" wowing those who've been to its "relaxing" space for Adan Saavedra's "artistic" presentations backed by "reasonably" priced wines and "excellent" service; for some who're thinking twice about making the trip, consider that food "doesn't get any better than this."

Rae *American* — - | - | - | VE

University City | Cira Ctr. | 2929 Arch St. (30th St.) | 215-922-3839 |
www.raerestaurant.com

Gayle chef-owner Daniel Stern's New American in a gorgeous, ultramodern setting next to Amtrak's 30th Street Station is on track to become the season's glitziest (and most expensive) newcomer; from the open kitchen comes classic meat and fish preparations as well as more adventurous entrees; N.B. vino fans are already booking the six-seat wine room.

Savona *French/Italian*

27 | 26 | 25 | VE

Gulph Mills | 100 Old Gulph Rd. (Rte. 320) | 610-520-1200 |
www.savonarestaurant.com

For a "special occasion" (like "winning the lottery") Main Liners "heartily recommend" this "formal" yet "convivial" "winner" in Gulph Mills for Andrew Masciangelo's "glorious" French-Italian menu, an "incredible" 1,000-label wine list and "romantic" Riviera-style setting; "mind-reading" servers tend to a well-heeled crowd so enthralled they thought they "owned the place."

Striped Bass *Seafood*

26 | 26 | 24 | VE

Center City West | 1500 Walnut St. (15th St.) | 215-732-4444 |
www.stripedbassrestaurant.com

A "Starr's shining" on this "reincarnated" Center City seafooder, Stephen Starr's "grand" yet "sexy", high-ceilinged "triumph" where the "extraordinary creativity" shows in every one of the "cleverly presented", "intensely flavorful" dishes supported by "crisp" service; it's no surprise then that the room swarms with a "contented", "beautiful" crowd that willingly pays "top dollar" for the experience.

Swann Lounge ● *American/French*

26 | 27 | 27 | E

Center City West | Four Seasons Hotel | 1 Logan Sq.
(Benjamin Franklin Pkwy.) | 215-963-1500 | www.fourseasons.com

"All the best for a little less" than the Fountain, and "less formal" (but still a picture of "luxury"), this New American–New French at the Four Seasons offers "spectacular" food, whether in the cafe, at the "great" bar, at the "amazing" brunch and buffets or during afternoon tea; P.S. some should go here for a "primer" on service, for "every restaurant should treat its customers this well."

Totaro's ⊠ *Eclectic*

26 | 13 | 22 | E

Conshohocken | 729 E. Hector St. (bet. Righter & Walnut Sts.) |
610-828-9341 | www.totaros.com

"Who woulda thunk" something so "plain" on the outside could produce such "great" food? is the first question you'll ask yourself after a meal at this "intimate" Conshy Italian-influenced Eclectic, where "wild game of all sorts" pops up on the "adventurous" menu; insiders know to "head for the happy hour" at the bar, but also advise "don't let the decor fool you – this place isn't cheap."

☑ Vetri ⊠ *Italian*

28 | 22 | 27 | VE

Avenue of the Arts | 1312 Spruce St. (bet. Broad & 13th Sts.) | 215-732-3478 |
www.vetriristorante.com

"I thought I'd died and gone to Italy" is a common refrain when speaking of "genius" chef Marc Vetri's "rustic" 35-seat Italian in an Avenue of the Arts brownstone; "become the guest who doesn't want to leave" after you sample "wondrous" fare that's the "essence of pleasure", served without "pomp" by the "expert" staff; you'll need to use "speed-dial" on your phone to land a reservation, and sure, it's "costly", but then again, it's a "great use for a home-equity loan", since it may be the "best restaurant of its kind in America."

Phoenix/Scottsdale

TOP FOOD RANKING

	Restaurant	Cuisine
28	Pizzeria Bianco	Pizza
	Sea Saw	Japanese
27	Binkley's	American
	Barrio Cafe	Mexican
	T. Cook's	Mediterranean
	Mary Elaine's	French
	Mastro's City Hall	Steak
26	Mastro's Steak	Steak
	Cyclo	Vietnamese
	Vincent's on Camelback	French
	Eddie V's	Seafood/Steak
25	Roaring Fork	American
	Los Sombreros	Mexican
	Rancho Pinot	American
	Atlas Bistro	Eclectic
	Fleming's Prime	Steak
	La Grande	Pizza
	elements	American
	deseo	Nuevo Latino
	Tarbell's	American
	Ruth's Chris	Steak
24	Roy's	Hawaiian

Atlas Bistro 🖂Ⓜ *Eclectic*   25 | 15 | 24 | M

Scottsdale | Wilshire Plaza | 2515 N. Scottsdale Rd. (E. Wilshire Dr.) | 480-990-2433

Though it's "small" and "nondescript", this South Scottsdale Eclectic unites gourmets and over-the-moon oenophiles in "paradise"; the restaurant itself is BYO (with a $10 corkage fee), but patrons can pair the "excellent" Southwestern-inspired dishes with one of over 2,000 "extraordinary wine selections", all sourced from "the adjacent wine store."

Ⓩ Barrio Cafe Ⓜ *Mexican*   27 | 17 | 22 | M

Phoenix | 2814 N. 16th St. (Thomas Rd.) | 602-636-0240 | www.barriocafe.com

"Come early or late" or "bet on a wait" at this "small", "popular" no-reservations "gem" in Phoenix dishing out "exciting" renditions of southern Mexican cuisine; it draw crowds unafraid to venture "beyond the burrito", and if the "amazing guacamole" (prepared tableside at dinner) and "scrumptious churros" aren't enough, you can take the edge off by sipping "sangria with a hit of Jack Daniels."

Ⓩ Binkley's Restaurant Ⓜ *American*   27 | 20 | 25 | E

Cave Creek | 6920 E. Cave Creek Rd. (½ mile west of Tom Darlington Dr.) | 480-437-1072 | www.binkleysrestaurant.com

"Fresh", "fabulous" and "fastidiously prepared" New American cuisine comes to Cave Creek thanks to the "Gary Danko of the desert", "rising culinary star" Kevin Binkley (ex French Laundry in Napa and Inn at Little Washington in VA), who revises the menu daily, inventing "splendid tasting menus" to sate the appetites of "serious foodies"; it's all set in a "sophisticated", "art-filled" space that's managed by wife, partner and maitre d' Ann Binkley; N.B. closed Sundays from May till September.

Cyclo 🅂 Ⓜ *Vietnamese* — 26 | 15 | 20 | I

Chandler | 1919 W. Chandler Blvd. (Dobson Rd.) | 480-963-4490 | www.cycloaz.com

Expect "plenty of sass" and "charm" from "fashionable" proprietor/menu designer/server Justina Duong, who "makes everyone feel like a lifelong friend" at her "casual" BYO Vietnamese in a Chandler strip mall; since the "amazing" food is as "fresh" and "lovely" as its creator, this "small" "piece of Saigon" is always "worth the wait."

deseo *Nuevo Latino* — 25 | 25 | 23 | E

North Scottsdale | Westin Kierland Resort & Spa | 6902 E. Greenway Pkwy. (bet. Scottsdale Rd. & 64th St.) | Scottsdale | 480-624-1030 | www.kierlandresort.com

Consulting chef Douglas Rodriguez "does it again" at this "stunning" Nuevo Latino in the Westin Kierland, where the "best-ever" ceviche and "awesome mojitos" are the overture to an "outstanding" meal guaranteed to be a "departure from the usual"; "sit at the bar and enjoy the show" from the open kitchen, and remember to save room for desserts like the chocolate cigar with cappuccino gelato – they're "works of art."

Eddie V's Edgewater Grille *Seafood/Steak* — 26 | 25 | 24 | E

North Scottsdale | 20715 N. Pima Rd. (E. Thompson Peak Pkwy.) | Scottsdale | 480-538-8468 | www.eddiev.com

Find some surf on desert turf at this "large", "clubby" eatery in North Scottsdale serving "fresh", "fantastic" plus "excellent" steaks and chops for red-meat mavens; budget-seekers baited by the "amazing 50-cent oysters" and select half-price happy-hour appetizers forsake the "vibrant dining room" for the "happening" jazz lounge.

elements *American* — 25 | 27 | 24 | E

Paradise Valley | Sanctuary on Camelback Mountain | 5700 E. McDonald Dr. (bet. Scottsdale Rd. & Tatum Blvd.) | 480-607-2300 | www.elementsrestaurant.com

"Request a window table at sunset" and treat yourself to a "breathtaking view" at this "stunning", "romantic" New American tucked away on the northern slope of Camelback Mountain; the "spectacular architecture" and "contemporary", "Zen-like" decor echo the Asian-influenced menu, which offers "divine", "healthy" cuisine in "artful", "minimalist" presentations; all things considered, it's a "perfect" choice for a "special occasion."

Fleming's Prime Steakhouse *Steak* — 25 | 23 | 24 | E

Chandler | 905 N. 54th St. (West Ray Rd.) | 480-940-1900
Scottsdale | 20753 N. Pima Rd., Bldg. R (Thompson Peak Pkwy.) | 480-538-8000
Scottsdale | 6333 N. Scottsdale Rd. (E. Citrus Way) | 480-596-8265
www.flemingssteakhouse.com

These "typically clubby", "upscale" chophouses (owned by the Outback chain) serve "incredibly consistent" cuts that "taste as good as they are big", along with "fabulous" sides; given the "impressive", "high-quality" fare, "superb" wine list and "friendly" staff, backers believe this trio tops "the rest of the competition."

La Grande Orange Grocery & Pizzeria *Pizza* `25` `19` `19` `I`
Phoenix | 4410 N. 40th St. (Campbell Ave.) | 602-840-7777 | www.lagrandeorangepizzeria.com
The "coolest eatery in Phoenix" is this "arty", "upscale" combo purveying baked goods, cheeses and wines on one side, while the adjacent pizzeria offers "delicious" pies and "mesmerizing toppings" on the other; though patrons have to "fight for a table" ("the waits seem interminable"), the food's "worth it" – and "takeout is a perfect option."

Los Sombreros Ⓜ *Mexican* `25` `19` `20` `M`
Scottsdale | 2534 N. Scottsdale Rd. (E. Wilshire Dr.) | 480-994-1799 | www.lossombreros.com
Turning out "authentic" yet "original" (and "absolutely amazing") takes on regional Mexican cuisine, this South Scottsdale eatery is the secret that many residents just "hate to share"; diners dub it the "best of its kind" in Arizona, which may explain why you'll find the "cozy" digs "packed" on any given day – so try to score a spot on the "fabulous" patio instead.

Ⓩ Mary Elaine's Ⓜ *French* `27` `28` `27` `VE`
Scottsdale | The Phoenician | 6000 E. Camelback Rd. (N. 60th St.) | 480-423-2530 | www.thephoenician.com
Setting the standard for a "special-occasion" experience, this "elegant", "ultrafancy" dining room at The Phoenician features "exquisite" New French cuisine complemented by an "extraordinary" wine list and "heavenly" city views; the "unparalleled" service "anticipates every desire", so even though you'll need to dress up – jackets are suggested – and bring "buckets of cash", it's "more than worth it"; N.B. a new lounge with nightly jazz offers a more casual alternative.

Mastro's City Hall Steakhouse *Steak* `27` `24` `25` `E`
(fka Drinkwater's City Hall Steakhouse)
Scottsdale | 6991 E. Camelback Rd. (Goldwater Blvd.) | 480-941-4700 | www.mastrosoceanclub.com
Soak up the "dark", "sexy" atmosphere at this Scottsdale beefery crowned "king of AZ's steakhouses" for "unbeatable" chops that are as "juicy" as the scene – think "great martinis", live music and a "terrific bar area" where a "spunky" crowd dances off the "huge portions" of meat; in short, "if you have to go somewhere, make this the place."

Ⓩ Mastro's Steakhouse *Steak* `26` `24` `24` `E`
North Scottsdale | La Mirada | 8852 E. Pinnacle Peak Rd. (N. Pima Rd.) | Scottsdale | 480-585-9500 | www.mastrosoceanclub.com
Meat mavens give this North Scottsdale "paradise" an "A+" for serving up "mouthwatering" steaks along with "excellent sides" plus a "seafood tower that's not to be missed"; scene-seekers say the "lively" piano bar ("eye candy" included) amps up both the "East Coast vibe" and the "noise levels", so even though "high rollers" concede it's "expensive", the majority just can't help "loving it."

	FOOD	DECOR	SERVICE	COST

☑ P.F. Chang's China Bistro *Chinese* | 21 | 20 | 20 | M |

Chandler | Chandler Fashion Ctr. | 3255 W. Chandler Blvd.
(bet. Chandler Village Dr. & Rte. 101) | 480-899-0472
Fashion Square | The Waterfront | 7135 E. Camelback Rd. (Scottsdale Rd.) |
Scottsdale | 480-949-2610
Mesa | 6610 E. Superstition Springs Blvd. (Power Rd.) |
480-218-4900
Peoria | 16170 N. 83rd Ave. (E. Alameda St.) | 623-412-3335
Scottsdale | Kierland Commons | 7132 E. Greenway Pkwy.
(N. Scottsdale Rd.) | 480-367-2999
Tempe | 740 S. Mill Ave. (E. University Dr.) | 480-731-4600
www.pfchangs.com

"Wear comfortable shoes" to help cushion the invariably "unbearable waits" at these "busy" outposts of a national chain; while purists pan the provisions as "Americanized Chinese", partisans praise the "dependably delicious" fare, singling out the "fabulous lettuce wraps."

☑ Pizzeria Bianco ☒Ⓜ *Pizza* | 28 | 20 | 21 | I |

Phoenix | Heritage Sq. | 623 E. Adams St. (N. 7th St.) | 602-258-8300 |
www.pizzeriabianco.com

"Believe the hype": chef/co-owner Chris Bianco's "adorable" "pizza temple" cops the No. 1 rating for Food in the Phoenix area for "outstanding" pies ("they make life worth living") deemed "the best in the country"; expect "mind-numbing waits", but insiders suggest stopping for a pre-meal drink at the adjacent Bar Bianco; N.B. no lunch.

Rancho Pinot ☒Ⓜ *American* | 25 | 20 | 24 | E |

Scottsdale | Lincoln Vill. | 6208 N. Scottsdale Rd. (E. Lincoln Dr.) |
480-367-8030 | www.ranchopinot.com

"Creative" "comfort food" abetted by a "comfortable", "rustic" ranch setting turns this "low-key" New American into an "all-around winner"; it's located in a Scottsdale strip mall, but chef Chrysa Kaufman's "excellent" cooking and partner Tom Kaufman's "fantastic wine list" have supporters saying "you owe it to yourself" to eat here.

Roaring Fork *American* | 25 | 24 | 24 | E |

Scottsdale | Finova Bldg. | 4800 N. Scottsdale Rd. (Chaparral Rd.) |
480-947-0795 | www.roaringfork.com

Locals "love" this Scottsdale "favorite" that elevates American "cowboy cooking" to the level of "fine dining"; that it's also known as a "happy-hour" "hangout" (its "legendary" "big-ass burgers" and "great" huckleberry margaritas are the order of the day) helps to corral even more fans into its "Western"-decorated digs; N.B. the departure of chef Robert McGrath may outdate the above Food score.

☑ Roy's *Hawaiian* | 24 | 22 | 22 | E |

Chandler | 7151 W. Ray Rd. (bet. N. 54th & 55th Sts.) | 480-705-7697
Phoenix | JW Marriott Desert Ridge Resort & Spa | 5350 E. Marriott Dr.
(bet. Deer Valley Rd. & Tatum Blvd.) | 480-419-7697
Scottsdale | Scottsdale Seville | 7001 N. Scottsdale Rd. (Indian Bend Rd.) |
480-905-1155
www.roysrestaurant.com

"Magical", "cutting-edge" Hawaiian fusion fare lands in the desert at these "gorgeous" links in Roy Yamaguchi's international chain; though some find they "don't compare" to the original island locations, most swim with the tide, insisting the "beautifully prepared fish" and down-right "sinful desserts" "meet the highest standards."

Ruth's Chris Steak House Steak

| 25 | 21 | 23 | E |

Phoenix | 2201 E. Camelback Rd. (N. 22nd St.) | 602-957-9600
Scottsdale | Scottsdale Seville | 7001 N. Scottsdale Rd. (E. Indian Bend Rd.) | 480-991-5988
www.ruthschris.com

A "refuge for carnivores", this "dependable" duo belonging to a national steakhouse chain serves "incredible", butter-bathed beef in portions fit for a "T. rex"; though there's no way around the "heavy dose of cholesterol" or the "high prices", the majority unites behind these standbys, saying they're "absolutely the best" around.

☑ Sea Saw Japanese

| 28 | 18 | 25 | E |

Old Town | 7133 E. Stetson Dr. (E. 6th Ave.) | Scottsdale | 480-481-9463 | www.seasaw.net

"Take out a loan" if necessary before visiting this spartan, 28-seat "foodie destination" in Old Town Scottsdale, where "astonishing" Japanese tapas and "unsurpassed sushi" (courtesy of "genius" chef Nobuo Fukuda) are prepared in "ways you never thought possible"; an "incredible" 2,800-plus-label wine list and the "best sake selection in town" also help put it into the "inspirational" category.

Tarbell's American

| 25 | 21 | 24 | E |

Phoenix | Camelback East Shops | 3213 E. Camelback Rd. (N. 32nd St.) | 602-955-8100 | www.tarbells.com

Still "buzzing" after more than a decade, this Phoenix eatery offers "satisfying" American cooking in a setting that manages to be both "trendy" and "comfortable"; with owner Mark Tarbell's "superb" wine list (including "wide-ranging" by-the-glass options) and a staff that "goes out of its way" to please, most aren't surprised that it remains "a winner."

☑ T. Cook's Mediterranean

| 27 | 28 | 26 | E |

Phoenix | Royal Palms Resort and Spa | 5200 E. Camelback Rd. (bet. N. Arcadia Dr. & N. 56th St.) | 602-808-0766 | www.royalpalmshotel.com

"All around", it "doesn't get better" than this "romantic" retreat in the Royal Palms – the Most Popular restaurant in the Phoenix/Scottsdale area – that "blows away" admirers with its "beautiful hacienda-style" setting (voted No. 1 for Decor) and "luxurious" atmosphere; it's also impossible to overlook the "marvelous" Mediterranean creations and the "professional staff", making a trip here "a must for out-of-town guests" and "lots of locals" alike.

Vincent's on Camelback ☒ French

| 26 | 22 | 24 | E |

Phoenix | 3930 E. Camelback Rd. (N. 40th St.) | 602-224-0225 | www.vincentsoncamelback.com

Considered a "classic" by its fans, this "elegant" Camelback Corridor stalwart still "charms" via Vincent Guerithault's "terrific", "innovative" Gallic interpretation of Southwestern fare and "elegant" country French decor; if it's "tired" to a few, this piece of "gastronomic heaven" in the desert remains "at the top" for most.

San Diego

TOP FOOD RANKING

	Restaurant	Cuisine
28	Sushi Ota	Japanese
	WineSellar & Brasserie	French
27	El Bizcocho	French
	Karen Krasne's	French/Italian
	Pamplemousse Grille	American/French
	Market Restaurant	American
	Tapenade	French
	A.R. Valentien	Californian
26	Primavera	Italian
	Morton's	Seafood/Steak
	Mille Fleurs	French
	Donovan's Steak	Steak
	NINE-TEN	Eclectic
	Rama	Thai
	George's California Modern	Californian
	Arterra	American
	Cavaillon	French
	Le Fontainebleau	French
	Fleming's Steak	Steak

Arterra *American* | 26 | 20 | 23 | E
Del Mar | San Diego Marriott Del Mar | 11966 El Camino Real
(Carmel Valley Rd.) | 858-369-6032 | www.arterrarestaurant.com
"You'll never believe you're in" the Marriott Del Mar when you "treat"
yourself to this destination's "inventive", "foodie-quality" New American
cuisine imbued with "contrasting flavors" that "never fail to work"; a
"rockin' wine selection" and "professional" staffers add to the "wonderful experience" – in fact, the "New Age decor" and "odd hotel setting" are
"the only weaknesses"; N.B. the post-Survey departure of chef Brian
Pekarcik may affect the Food score.

A.R. Valentien *Californian* | 27 | 27 | 26 | E
La Jolla | The Lodge at Torrey Pines | 11480 N. Torrey Pines Rd. (Callan Rd.) |
858-777-6635 | www.lodgetorreypines.com
"Exquisite Craftsman-style architecture", a study in gleaming woods and
stained-glass fixtures, amid the "ethereal surroundings" of the Torrey
Pines golf course and the Pacific "amazes" the "high rollers" at this "fantastical experience" in La Jolla, voted No. 1 for Decor in SD; just as "unforgettable" is chef Jeff Jackson's "amazing", "innovative" Californian
cuisine, using "farm-fresh local produce" and "presented with creative
flair" by "impeccable" servers; P.S. "sitting outside is paradise."

Cavaillon *French* | 26 | 21 | 24 | E
Santaluz | 14701 Via Bettona (Camino Del Sur) | 858-433-0483 |
www.cavaillonrestaurant.com
"Three cheers" for chef-owner Philippe Verpiand's "grand slam", a
"charming" French "oasis" in Santaluz that can be "hard to find" but

"worth the search" for "decadent" "tastes of Provence" "so expertly prepared", "you'll think you've died and gone to heaven"; the "noisy setting" and "minuscule table separation" "may be authentic", but it sometimes "makes conversation impossible", in which case you may have better luck on the "pleasant patio."

Donovan's Steak & Chop House 🖾 *Steak* | 26 | 23 | 25 | E |

Golden Triangle | 4340 La Jolla Village Dr. (Genesee Ave.) | 858-450-6666 | www.donovanssteakhouse.com

"You simply can't go wrong" with any "hunk of mouthwatering beef" you order at this Golden Triangle "steakhouse extraordinaire", be it an "outstanding bone-in rib-eye", a "spectacular filet mignon" or an "off-the-charts New York strip", all of which comes with "luscious sides" ("unlike others" of this ilk); in a manner befitting the "refined, wood-paneled" "gentleman's club–like" environs, the "superb" servers remain "unruffled" even when the "rather large" tabs (especially from the "overpriced wine list") draw protests.

🖾 El Bizcocho *French* | 27 | 26 | 27 | VE |

Rancho Bernardo | Rancho Bernardo Inn | 17550 Bernardo Oaks Dr. (Francisco Dr.) | 858-675-8550 | www.ranchobernardoinn.com

"Firing on all cylinders", this Rancho Bernardo Inn "delight" zooms to the "top of the line" by utilizing "surprising flavor combinations" and "complex techniques" to create "challenging", "spectacular" French cuisine worthy of the "beyond-description" 1,600-label wine cellar; "discreet" yet "responsive" servers and an "elegant" setting add to the "special-occasion" feel, so "bring the diamond ring to propose to your sweetie" (or hock it beforehand to pay for it all); P.S. let's hope the post-Survey departure of "young, world-tested" chef Gavin Kaysen doesn't affect the Food score.

Fleming's Prime Steakhouse & Wine Bar *Steak* | 26 | 23 | 24 | E |

Gaslamp Quarter | 380 K St. (4th Ave.) | 619-237-1155
Golden Triangle | Aventine Shopping Ctr. | 8970 University Center Ln. (Lebon Dr.) | 858-535-0078
www.flemingssteakhouse.com

This "upscale chain" in the Gaslamp offers "just what you want in a steakhouse": "dark wood, white linens, the scent of money" and, of course, "tasty, juicy" beef with "clever side dishes"; indeed, everything from "reliably smooth service" to the "tremendous list" of "100 wines by the glass" is "a cut above", keeping it permanently "on the 'refer to friends' list"; P.S. the Golden Triangle entry is equally "excellent."

George's California Modern *Californian* | 26 | 25 | 25 | E |

La Jolla | 1250 Prospect St. (bet. Cave St. & Ivanhoe Ave.) | 858-454-4244 | www.georgesatthecove.com

"By George, it's still superb!" – this "revamped" incarnation of the La Jolla "classic" features chef Trey Foshee's "brilliantly" "edgy", "light", "delectable Californian" cuisine, boasting "the freshest ingredients" and "elegant flavor pairings" (even before the first bite, "the dishes come alive" as the "warm" servers explain them); the "contemporary" new decor (an "abundance of glass and steel") "ranks high" but will always place second to the "spectacular sunsets" "over the ocean" – and though "you pay for the privilege", it's "worth the pretty penny."

	FOOD	DECOR	SERVICE	COST

⊠ George's Ocean Terrace *Californian*

La Jolla | 1250 Prospect St. (bet. Cave St. & Ivanhoe Ave.) | 858-454-4244 | www.georgesatthecove.com

24 | 24 | 23 | E

Feel like you're "sitting on top of the world" as you take in "wine, sunshine" and "incomparable ocean views" at this rooftop "tradition" "overlooking La Jolla Cove", the "perennial favorite for tourists and locals alike" voted San Diego's Most Popular restaurant; a "more casual", "less expensive version of George's California Modern downstairs", it offers the "same great quality", "inventive", "artistic" Californian fare for "languid lunches" or dinners; P.S. a post-Survey refresh of the decor probably won't affect the score as long as those "gorgeous sunsets" remain.

⊠ Karen Krasne's Extraordinary Desserts *Dessert*

Bankers Hill | 2929 Fifth Ave. (bet. Palm & Quince Sts.) | 619-294-2132

27 | 21 | 17 | I

⊠ Karen Krasne's Little Italy *French/Italian*

Little Italy | 1430 Union St. (bet. W. Ash & W. Beech Sts.) | 619-294-7001 www.extraordinarydesserts.com

"You'll moan in ecstasy" when tasting the "decadent" "über-desserts" at this "cozy cottage" in Bankers Hill and its Little Italy offshoot, which also offers a "savory menu" of "light" French and Italian "small plates", a "wide selection of wines" and a "techno-modern" design that's of definite "architectural interest"; everything at both is so "artfully crafted", you may forgive counter help that can be "lackadaisical" and somewhat "snobby" – that is, if they don't "ignore you."

Le Fontainebleau *French*

Downtown | Westgate Hotel | 1055 Second Ave. (B'way) | 619-557-3655 | www.westgatehotel.com

26 | 25 | 27 | E

"Take a step back into the past" at this "prestigious" dining room in Downtown's Westgate Hotel, where a "proper and responsive" staff – voted No. 1 for Service in San Diego – makes "you feel like royalty" as it presents "gourmet", "visually exciting" (and "expensive") French meals; "elegant chandeliers", "ornate plastering" and "live piano music" create an environment "as beautiful as any palace" – indeed, it's all so "very formal", your fellow diners warn they "don't want to see you there in jeans!"

Market Restaurant & Bar *American*

Del Mar | 3702 Via de la Valle (El Camino Real) | 858-523-0007 | www.marketdelmar.com

27 | 21 | 23 | E

"Well-trained" "creative" "genius" Carl Schroeder "raises the bar" at this Del Mar "star" with his "daily changing menu" of New American dishes "so fresh and carefully thought out", they yield an "absolutely mouthwatering", "near-perfect mix of flavors and textures"; persimmon walls and chocolate leather banquettes figure heavily into decor that's "hip but not tragically so", and while the floor staff is "well-trained" and "helpful", some report "rude" front-of-housers.

Mille Fleurs *French*

Rancho Santa Fe | Country Squire Courtyard | 6009 Paseo Delicias (Avenida de Acacias) | 858-756-3085 | www.millefleurs.com

26 | 25 | 26 | VE

You can just "smell the money around you" at this "world-class" exercise in "investment dining" where the "glitterati of Rancho Santa Fe" revel in chef Martin Woesle's "sublime" New French fare that's "fresh and exciting without being too off-the wall"; the "impeccably presented" dishes are then conveyed by "utterly professional" servers through the "lovely", "formal" space, which has been "enhanced" by a "recent remodel."

Morton's The Steakhouse *Seafood/Steak*   26 | 22 | 24 | E

Downtown | 285 J St. (3rd Ave.) | 619-696-3369 | www.mortons.com
"A guy's steakhouse that women love" too, this Downtown spot may be a "typical" representation of the chain, but it's "nonetheless great" for "piping-hot, juicy and tender" beef paired with "fine trimmings", served in "wow" sizes and "outrageously priced" (don't forget about the lobster, it "will thrill you as well"); though many diners deem the "waiters bringing the trays" of raw meat "out for you to admire" "just plain idiotic", said servers are "fun and nice."

NINE-TEN *Eclectic*   26 | 22 | 24 | E

La Jolla | Grande Colonial | 910 Prospect St. (Girard Ave.) | 858-964-5400 | www.nine-ten.com

"Flavors that make your palate dance" are the stock-in-trade of chef Jason Knibb's "beautifully plated" Eclectic dishes made with "organic produce" "straight from the market" at this "stylish little" "champ" in La Jolla's Grande Colonial Hotel ("try the innovative Mercy of the Chef" tasting menu – "you won't know what hit you!"); it may be "a little spendy", but it's "worth the splurge" when you factor in "impeccable wines", "incredible desserts" and "engaging" service.

ⓩ Pamplemousse Grille *American/French*   27 | 22 | 25 | E

Solana Beach | 514 Via de la Valle (I-5) | 858-792-9090 | www.pgrille.com
"If you win big at the racetrack" "across the street", "blow it" at this "elegant" Solana Beach "special-occasion" "splurge" where chef Jeffrey Strauss provides "dinner and a show" by first whipping up "amazing" American-French fare that displays "a great flair for the unusual", then "floating through the dining room" to "entertain guests" with his "amusing", "schmoozing" ways; P.S. lunch is served Friday only, and "what a way to end the week" it is!

ⓩ Prado at Balboa Park *American*   22 | 26 | 22 | M

Balboa Park | House of Hospitality | 1549 El Prado (Plaza de Panama) | 619-557-9441 | www.pradobalboa.com

"Top off a day" in "famously gorgeous" Balboa Park with this "special treat": "gracious" American dining in a "magical" "paradise", a vision of "pure loveliness" embodied by a "beautiful garden" and a "cool" "blown glass"–bedecked interior; the "divine dishes" "dazzle the eye and palate", while "silky smooth service" makes it a "great place to bring out-of-town guests" or the object of your affection.

Primavera Ristorante *Italian*   26 | 21 | 25 | E

Coronado | 932 Orange Ave. (bet. 9th & 10th Sts.) | 619-435-0454 | www.primavera1st.com

It may be "under the radar", but this "tiny jewel" "in the heart of Coronado" "flies high", as "mouthwatering" Northern Italian cuisine "for the discerning palate" is served by "superb" servers; also "top-notch" is a wine list that's sufficiently "proper" for such an "intimate", "old-fashioned" "high-class" setting.

Rama *Thai*

26 | 25 | 21 | M

Gaslamp Quarter | 327 Fourth Ave. (bet. J & K Sts.) | 619-501-8424 | www.ramarestaurant.com

"Metropolitan elegance" meets "pure fantasy" at this "stunningly" "evocative" Gaslamp Thai emporium, where "filmy curtains" create "semiprivate spaces ideal for romantic interludes", and a "lovely water wall" further "arouses desires"; the "consistently delicious" cuisine exhibits "fresh ingredients" and "wonderful nuances", while service is mostly "helpful and friendly" – just as long as you have a reservation (call for one "several days to a few weeks in advance").

☑ Roppongi *Asian Fusion*

25 | 22 | 21 | E

La Jolla | 875 Prospect St. (Fay Ave.) | 858-551-5252 | www.roppongiusa.com

"Amazing Asian-fusion" small plates are "creatively crafted" and "presented as if every one were headed for the cover of *Gourmet* magazine" at this La Jolla "winner"; it's "elegant without being stuffy" inside, while the "beautiful outdoor fire-pit seating" gets the "stylish crowd" to engage in "excessive frivolity" (abetted by "a full selection of sake" no doubt); P.S. your "best bets" are the "half-price (yes, *half-price*) tapas and sushi 4–6 PM daily", so "order up a storm and share with friends."

☑ Sammy's Woodfired Pizza *Pizza*

21 | 15 | 18 | I

Del Mar | Del Mar Highlands | 12925 El Camino Real (Del Mar Heights Rd.) | 858-259-6600
Downtown | 770 Fourth Ave. (F St.) | 619-230-8888
Golden Triangle | Costa Verde Ctr. | 8650 Genesee Ave. (bet. La Jolla Village & Nobel Drs.) | 858-404-9898
La Jolla | 702 Pearl St. (Draper Ave.) | 858-456-5222
Mission Valley | Mission Valley Mall | 1620 Camino de la Reina (Mission Center Rd.) | 619-298-8222
Carlsbad | 5970 Avenida Encinas (Palomar Airport Rd.) | 760-438-1212
Scripps Ranch | 10785 Scripps Poway Pkwy. (Springs Canyon Rd.) | 858-695-0900
www.sammyspizza.com

"Savvy restaurateur" Sammy Ladeki's homegrown chain is a "San Diego favorite" for "fresh and tasty" "West Coast pizza" with "innovative toppings" ("arugula and pear is a true wonder"), "massive", "addictive salads" and "yummy messy sundaes" for dessert ("be sure to scrape the glass, that's where all the caramel is!"); the staff of "surfers" sometimes "moves at a snail's pace", and with "a lot of kids" eating, they're "a bit on the noisy side", but the pies "never disappoint."

☑ Sushi Ota *Japanese*

28 | 12 | 19 | E

Pacific Beach | 4529 Mission Bay Dr. (Bunker Hill St.) | 858-270-5670

As "amazing" "as any place on the planet", this "pearl in a trashcan" conjures not only the "absolute best Japanese" in Pacific Beach but the No. 1 Food in San Diego courtesy of "genius" chef Yukito Ota and his "expert panel of sushi doctors" who assemble "silky" "treats" "so fresh, they almost evaporate on your tongue" ("sit at the bar" and let them "guide you"); its "oddball" setting in a strip mall is "lame", and you "need to book way too far in advance", but "ignore everything but the taste" and "you'll have an experience you'll never forget."

	FOOD	DECOR	SERVICE	COST

Tapenade *French* ⎸ 27 ⎸ 21 ⎸ 25 ⎸ E ⎸

La Jolla | 7612 Fay Ave. (bet. Kline & Pearl Sts.) | 858-551-7500 | www.tapenaderestaurant.com

"You're in for a great experience" when you venture "off-the-beaten" La Jolla path to this "close-to-ideal" New French "destination" where diners "trust" chef Jean-Michel Diot's "obvious commitment to quality ingredients" in creating "inventive" dishes that display "harmonious flavors and a counterplay of textures" (they're "well-matched" by "extraordinary wines" too); it may be "a little stark" for being so "expensive", but it's "quiet and intimate", and "cordial" servers make sure everyone "goes home happy."

Z WineSellar & Brasserie ⑤Ⓜ *French* ⎸ 28 ⎸ 20 ⎸ 27 ⎸ E ⎸

Golden Triangle | 9550 Waples St. (off Mira Mesa Blvd.) | 858-450-9557 | www.winesellar.com

It's "hard to find" in a "random" Golden Triangle "industrial zone", but this "tiny" "dream restaurant" is "well worth the hunt" for "imaginatively prepared", "beautifully presented" French fare; the "staggering" selection from the *vin* "warehouse" below is available upstairs at "minimal markups", the corkage fees are zero to "nominal" and the "phenomenal", "informed" servers "recommend delicious pairings", all of which makes it "a must" for "wine dummies" and "oenophiles" alike.

San Francisco Bay Area

TOP FOOD RANKING

	Restaurant	Cuisine
29	Gary Danko	American
	French Laundry	American/French
28	Cyrus	French
	Erna's Elderberry	Californian/French
	Fleur de Lys	Californian/French
	Sushi Ran	Japanese
	Kaygetsu	Japanese
	Michael Mina	American
27	Chez Panisse	Californian/Mediterranean
	Le Papillon	French
	Ritz-Carlton	French
	Chez Panisse Café	Californian/Mediterranean
	La Folie	French
	Acquerello	Italian
	Chapeau!	French
	Masa's	French
	Rivoli	Californian/Mediterranean
	Boulevard	American
	Farmhouse Inn	Californian
26	Aqua	Californian/French
	Quince	French/Italian
	Redd Restaurant	Californian

Acquerello 🕼 Ⓜ *Italian*   27 | 24 | 27 | VE

Polk Gulch | 1722 Sacramento St. (bet. Polk St. & Van Ness Ave.) |
San Francisco | 415-567-5432 | www.acquerello.com

One of SF's "rare quiet", "formal" Italian restaurants with "old-world
sophistication", this "intimate" Polk Gulch "foodie delight" ("no noisy
young 'uns here") set in a converted church is "the absolutely perfect
setting" for a "fantastic celebratory experience"; "raid your piggy
bank", order the chef's "sublime" wine-inclusive tasting menu ("each
table gets their own decanter") and "ride it all the way", letting the
"remarkable staff cater to your every need"; N.B. a recent remodel
may not be reflected in the Decor score.

Aqua *Californian/French*   26 | 25 | 25 | VE

Downtown | 252 California St. (bet. Battery & Front Sts.) | San Francisco |
415-956-9662 | www.aqua-sf.com

"Posh", "packed" to the gills and "still swimming strong" under chef
Laurent Manrique's stewardship, this Downtown "power-lunch institution" remains a "shrine to seafood", wowing fans with "fantastic" Cal-
French "flavor combinations" (and "terrestrial options" like foie gras);
"wine and dine your client or stuffy in-laws" with "inventive, unexpected" fare and "incredible wines" "artfully presented" by a "superlative" staff in a "chic" setting accented with "gorgeous flower
arrangements fit for the glamorous" VIP crowd; there are "no à la carte
options", but "if you have to look at the prices . . . well you know the rest."

☑ **Boulevard** *American*

27 | 25 | 25 | E

Embarcadero | Audiffred Bldg. | 1 Mission St. (Steuart St.) | San Francisco | 415-543-6084 | www.boulevardrestaurant.com

This "sizzling" belle epoque brasserie on the Embarcadero with "breathtaking views of the Bay" may be a "wallet flattener", but remains the "consummate" "go-as-you-are" San Francisco hot spot delivering "unforgettable food" "without the 'tude"; "suits", "tourists and locals" "sit elbow to elbow" soaking up the "party" vibe and Nancy Oakes' French-influenced New American fare that's "inventive without being fussy", while the "sensational" staff "goes above and beyond the call of duty" and "never fails to provide the perfect" wine match.

Chapeau! Ⓜ *French*

27 | 18 | 26 | E

Outer Richmond | 1408 Clement St. (15th Ave.) | San Francisco | 415-750-9787

"Budget-minded foodies" "make the trek" to this "quaint" – alright, "cramped" – bistro so "religiously", they "should move" to the Outer Richmond, because the "extraordinary" French cuisine is "better than restaurants [that charge] twice the price" (the "early-bird prix fixe is a steal"); the pièce de résistance is Philippe Gardelle, the "charming" chef-owner who "personally greets everyone" as well as "seats, cuts meats and pecks cheeks", transforming every meal into "a special experience"; N.B. an ongoing renovation may impact the Decor score.

Chez Panisse Ⓢ *Californian/Mediterranean*

27 | 23 | 26 | VE

Berkeley | 1517 Shattuck Ave. (bet. Cedar & Vine Sts.) | 510-548-5525 | www.chezpanisse.com

"Don't know whether to dine or bow" quip "those lucky enough" to savor the "sublime simplicity" of Berkeley "pioneer" Alice Waters' Cal-Med "culinary delights" that "celebrate what's at the peak of the season"; expect "no frills" at this "modest" Craftsman-style "mother ship", "just thrills, naturally" – "every foodie must go to complete their Bingo card" and "partake" of the "divine" daily prix fixe menu that spotlights the "clear, crisp" "essence" of local ingredients; the "combinations make you sigh with delight", the staff is "enthusiastic" and the wine list is a "knockout" – it's "all it's cracked up to be."

Chez Panisse Café Ⓢ *Californian/Mediterranean*

27 | 22 | 25 | E

Berkeley | 1517 Shattuck Ave. (bet. Cedar & Vine Sts.) | 510-548-5049 | www.chezpanisse.com

A "near mystical experience" exclaim budget-conscious Berkeleyites who sample the "pure flavors" of "Alice Waters' culinary frontier" "without spending half the month's rent" at this "wonderfully relaxed" "Paradise Lite" cafe above the "legendary" original and staffed with "attentive", not "smothering" servers; she may be "the Queen" but the organic, sustainable ingredients are "king", resulting in "dreamy pizzas" and "delectable", "straightforward" à la carte Cal-Med dishes that "reflect both the seasons and the incredible abundance" of local purveyors.

☑ **Cyrus** *French*

28 | 27 | 28 | VE

Healdsburg | Les Mars Hotel | 29 North St. (Healdsburg Ave.) | 707-433-3311 | www.cyrusrestaurant.com

"Who needs Napa?" quip fans "blown away" by this "pull-out-the-stops" lair of "luxury", a "gorgeous" "budget-breaker" in Healdsburg's

Les Mars Hotel; "no detail is overlooked", from the "caviar cart, where the pricey eggs are weighed on a scale with a real gold bullion", to the "decadent" New French "mix-and-match" prix fixe menus "beautifully presented" by staffers that move like a "well-choreographed ballet"; there are no "absurd reservation hoops" to jump through, plus "everyone is treated" "like the leader of a small country" – what a "memorable experience."

ⓩ Erna's Elderberry House *Californian/French* | 28 | 26 | 28 | VE |

Oakhurst | Château du Sureau | 48688 Victoria Ln. (Hwy. 41) | 559-683-6800 | www.elderberryhouse.com

Yosemite-bound adventurers "strike gourmet gold just south of the Gold Country" at this "quaint Europe-in-America setting" on the grounds of the Château du Sureau hotel in Oakhurst, basically the "middle of nowhere"; "what an amazing" "symphony" of flavors – every "breathtakingly beautiful" Californian-French dish on the prix fixe menus is "different and unexpected" – and coupled with "fine" wine pairings and "attentive service" that's rated No. 1 in this Survey, it's a "delightful dining experience" that will "put you in a high state."

Farmhouse Inn & Restaurant *Californian* | 27 | 25 | 25 | E |

Forestville | Farmhouse Inn | 7871 River Rd. (bet. Trenton & Wohler Rds.) | 707-887-3300 | www.farmhouseinn.com

"Put on your best duds", grab "your most significant other" and "hop over" to this "charming" "old" clapboard farmhouse in "lovely" Forestville hidden "away from the Napa crowds" for the "fabulous" signature rabbit dish; add in a "cheese course that would tempt a Frenchman" and other "wonderfully prepared" Californian fare made with bounty from the family ranch and an "extensive wine list", all "served with a deft hand", and it's plain to see why this "sparkling gem" is on a par with the "biggies."

ⓩ Fleur de Lys 🅢 *Californian/French* | 28 | 27 | 26 | VE |

Nob Hill | 777 Sutter St. (bet. Jones & Taylor Sts.) | San Francisco | 415-673-7779 | www.fleurdelyssf.com

"Can you improve on fabulous?" ask the starstruck who spend a "magical evening of luxury" at Nob Hill's "ultraromantic" Cal–New French "oasis of calm and civility", where "even the menu is pretty", the decor is *très* "Moulin Rouge" and the "bright servers suggest, deliver and describe" the "culinary delights"; longtime chef Hubert Keller keeps everything "fresh and exciting", crafting "decadent" prix fixe options (including an "exquisite" vegetarian choice) with "whimsical touches"; *oui*, prices are "princely", but the "outstanding" wine list alone "seduces you back."

ⓩ French Laundry, The *American/French* | 29 | 26 | 28 | VE |

Yountville | 6640 Washington St. (Creek St.) | 707-944-2380 | www.frenchlaundry.com

"Thomas Keller's magnum opus" in Yountville may be "famous for being famous, but consider yourself royalty if you land a table" at this "haute" French–New American "gastronomic experience" that's "expensive" enough "for three-lifetimes" and "fantastic" enough to "halt all conversation"; "foodies with four hours on their hands" know the drill: "stroll through the gardens", then let the "gracious", "mind-reading" staff handle the "spot-on wine pairings" and "prepare for orbit" as each "wildly imaginative" course in the tasting menus arrives; P.S. it's "better than ever" with new chef de cuisine Corey Lee onboard.

☑ Gary Danko _American_

| 29 | 26 | 28 | VE |

Fisherman's Wharf | 800 N. Point St. (Hyde St.) | San Francisco | 415-749-2060 | www.garydanko.com

"Gary Swanko" "fully merits its superb reputation" gush "flush" "foodies" who vote the "celebrity" chef-owner's "sleek" New American "temple of gastronomy" in Fisherman's Wharf No. 1 in the SF Survey for Food and Popularity; it's an "epicurean extravaganza", from the glass of champagne when you sit down to the "impeccable" "build-your-own" "haute" tasting menus and "perfect wine pairings" you'll "talk about for weeks, months and years" to the "simply amazing cheese course"; add in a "surprisingly unstuffy", "synchronized" staff that "treats customers like VIPs" and it's little wonder devotees declare it's the "epitome of fine dining, San Francisco-style."

Kaygetsu Ⓜ _Japanese_

| 28 | 18 | 25 | VE |

Menlo Park | Sharon Heights Shopping Ctr. | 325 Sharon Park Dr. (Sand Hill Rd.) | 650-234-1084 | www.kaygetsu.com

"You'll be hard-pressed to find Japanese food made with more care and flair" without "getting on a jet to Tokyo" attest admirers who say get thee to this "spartan" yet "transcendent" "power dining spot for VCs" in a Menlo Park strip mall; the fish is "über-fresh" and the seasonal kaiseki dinners are "extraordinary", from the "beautiful presentation" that's like "art on a plate" to the "melt-in-your-mouth creations" that taste like "heaven"; the "drawback: you must offer your paycheck to the sushi gods" ("genius chef"/owner Toshi), but it's "worth every penny."

La Folie Ⓢ _French_

| 27 | 23 | 26 | VE |

Russian Hill | 2316 Polk St. (bet. Green & Union Sts.) | San Francisco | 415-776-5577 | www.lafolie.com

Oui, "'twould be a folly to miss" this "haute French" "culinary experience" on Russian Hill where "masterful chef" "Monsieur Passot cooks his heart out" crafting "perfection on a plate" à la carte dishes and "artfully displayed" prix fixe menus "well worth the special-occasion prices"; it's _"magnifique_ in every way", from the "amazing wine" list and "grand", "intimate environment" to the "dazzling" staff that exudes a "touch of Gallic humor"; P.S. if the "elbow-to-elbow seating" in the main room "crimps your privacy", the back room provides "an elegant alternative."

Le Papillon _French_

| 27 | 24 | 27 | VE |

San Jose | 410 Saratoga Ave. (Kiely Blvd.) | 408-296-3730 | www.lepapillon.com

Escape the "hustle and bustle of Silicon Valley" at this "hidden gem" in San Jose that feels like a "little bit of France"; the "classy" environment means you can "speak quietly to your tablemates" – it's enough to make you "stand and cheer", the staff that's "second to none" extends the "elegant treatment" and the "over-the-top", "outstanding" wine-and-food pairings on the New French tasting menu offer "interesting twists" that "leave you floating like the proverbial butterfly."

Masa's 🖼🅜 *French*

27 | 24 | 26 | VE

Downtown | Hotel Vintage Ct. | 648 Bush St. (bet. Powell & Stockton Sts.) | San Francisco | 415-989-7154 | www.masasrestaurant.com

Bring "your quiet voice" and "a few credit cards" to Downtown's "high-end bastion" of "old-boy network" fine dining that's "settled into a rhythm" since chef "Gregory Short was poached from French Laundry" to oversee the "haute" New French tasting menus; the "taupe everything" digs are "understated", but the *gastronomique* "theatrics" are definitely not "for a simple steak-and-potatoes eater", while the "wine list is thicker than the Bible"; in short, it's "worth" donning a "loaner blazer" and the "Brobdingnagian prices."

🆉 Michael Mina *American*

28 | 24 | 27 | VE

Downtown | Westin St. Francis | 335 Powell St. (bet. Geary & Post Sts.) | San Francisco | 415-397-9222 | www.michaelmina.net

"Mmmmichael Mmmmmmina's" Downtown "hi-style, hi-concept, hi-priced" temple to "food wizardry" (where "everything comes in three different preparations") is a "triple treat" attest "foodies" who enjoy the "sublime experience of being coveted, cosseted and pampered"; the "delectable" New American tasting menus and "mind-boggling" wine list are served in a "stunning" setting, plus you can order "classics" à la carte at the bar – what a "marvelous" way to "spend all your money"; if some shout "you need a semaphore to talk" over the Westin lobby din, others retort "there's a lovely energy, but it's never raucous."

Quince *French/Italian*

26 | 23 | 25 | VE

Pacific Heights | 1701 Octavia St. (bet. Bush & Pine Sts.) | San Francisco | 415-775-8500 | www.quincerestaurant.com

A "definite 'must' on the foodie circuit" when you want a "dining extravaganza" but don't "want to eat in a theater", this "quinti-sensual", "fancy with a curlicue 'f'" Pac Heights "delight" is "like being in a fine home with a private waiter and chef"; the "dazzling", "one-of-a-kind" New French–Italian creations are fashioned from "pure", "pedigreed ingredients" ("handmade" "luscious pastas" "should be mandatory"), while the "excellent" staff is "beyond reproach"; if a few wince that it's "a bit prissy", for most it's "lovely in all respects."

Redd Restaurant *Californian*

26 | 22 | 23 | VE

Yountville | 6480 Washington St. (California Dr.) | 707-944-2222 | www.reddnapavalley.com

"We're always 'reddy' for our next visit" to chef Richard Reddington's "astonishingly good", "much-heralded" Californian "gem" in "glorious", "foodie-filled Yountville"; "prices soar", but so do the "dazzling" à la carte and tasting menus "starring" "fabulous" ingredients "gathered from local farms" and served by an "attentive" staff in "modern, minimalist" digs with a "pretty patio" ("think Finland meets Amish Country") that dispense with that "tired rustic-wine-country cliché"; N.B. the bar has its own "unique menu."

Ritz-Carlton Dining Room 🖼🅜 *French*

27 | 26 | 28 | VE

Nob Hill | Ritz-Carlton Hotel | 600 Stockton St. (bet. California & Pine Sts.) | San Francisco | 415-773-6198 | www.ritzcarltondiningroom.com

"For that special occasion when a little formality (some would call it stuffiness) is called for" ("tux optional"), Ritz it up at this "pampering"

Nob Hill dining room; you can almost "hear an orchestra warming up" before embarking on chef Ron Siegel's prix fixe or tasting menu and wine pairings showcasing "unimaginable", "untraditional" New French creations "with Japanese touches"; it's akin to an operatic "performance", "from the first amuse"-bouche down to the "candy cart", with "lots of 'eye-closing' moments" in between.

Rivoli *Californian/Mediterranean* | 27 | 23 | 25 | E |

Berkeley | 1539 Solano Ave. (bet. Neilson St. & Peralta Ave.) | 510-526-2542 | www.rivolirestaurant.com

We "can't stop ooohing and aaahing" about Wendy and Roscoe's "lovely, tranquil" Berkeley "treasure" exclaim hometown "foodies" and "even the fussiest oenophiles"; the "imaginative" and "soul-satisfying" Californian-Mediterranean cuisine is "comparable to anyplace in the City", plus it's all ferried to table by a staff that "seems to have PhDs in the art of making a meal enjoyable"; yes, you can expect "snug quarters", nevertheless it's still a "real treat" to look out at the "illuminated garden" filled with "a wildlife menagerie snacking" on their own food.

⊠ Slanted Door, The *Vietnamese* | 26 | 22 | 21 | E |

Embarcadero | 1 Ferry Bldg. (Market St.) | San Francisco | 415-861-8032 | www.slanteddoor.com

"Local celebs", "adventurous" tourists and Missionites who visited the old site "back in the day" all "fight for a table" at Charles Phan's "straight-up" "phantastic" Vietnamese "empire", a "jam-packed" waterfront-wonder deemed the "crown jewel" of the Embarcadero's Ferry Building; the "industrial" digs are as "noisy as a Hanoi street corner" and not everyone's cup of "blossoming tea", but the "high-end" Saigon specialties served "speedily" and enhanced by "insightful" wine pairings "shine brighter than the Bay Bridge" outside the "expansive windows"; N.B. for takeout pop into Out the Door next door.

Sushi Ran *Japanese* | 28 | 20 | 22 | E |

Sausalito | 107 Caledonia St. (bet. Pine & Turney Sts.) | 415-332-3620 | www.sushiran.com

"If there's a better" place to shed your "disposable income" than Sausalito's fin-fare "mecca" that "takes Japanese food to a totally different solar system", "I haven't found it" report gaga "gaijins" and "true aficionados"; whether you "splurge" on rolls that "rival sushi temples in Tokyo" or "innovative", "top-notch cooked entrees", "every meal here" ends with "a sigh of profound pleasure"; P.S. it's "hard to hook a reservation", but remember the adjacent "sake bar has blossomed with its own identity."

Seattle

TOP FOOD RANKING

	Restaurant	Cuisine
29	Herbfarm, The	Pacific NW
28	Mistral	American/French
	Rover's	French
	Cafe Juanita	Italian
	Sitka & Spruce	Eclectic
	Armandino's	Italian/Sandwiches
27	Paseo	Caribbean
	Kisaku Sushi	Japanese
	Inn at Langley	Pacific NW
	Nishino	Japanese
	Szechuan Chef*	Chinese
	Canlis	Pacific NW
	Phoenecia at Alki	Mediterranean
	Maneki	Japanese
	Restaurant Zoë	American
	Lark	American
	Le Gourmand	French
	Monsoon	Vietnamese
	Shiro's Sushi	Japanese
	Il Terrazzo Carmine	Italian

Armandino's Salumi ⑤Ⓜ *Italian/Sandwiches* | 28 | 11 | 20 | I |

Pioneer Square | 309 Third Ave. S. (bet. Jackson & Main Sts.) | 206-621-8772 | www.salumicuredmeats.com

"Unforgettable" "handmade" Italian sandwiches and salamis draw kudos to this Pioneer Square "hawg heaven" where Armandino Batali (Mario's dad) cranks out "amazing" "homemade" cured meats in the back; the cafe is "shoebox"-sized, the mood "fun" and the lines "out the door" as both regular folk and "food luminaries" make the pilgrimage.

Ⓩ Cafe Juanita *Italian* | 28 | 22 | 26 | E |

Kirkland | 9702 NE 120th Pl. (97th St.) | 425-823-1505 | www.cafejuanita.com

Chef Holly Smith's Northern Italian fare is "consistently" "stunning" thanks to her "creative" touch with "impeccably" fresh local ingredients say the suppers who've "battled traffic" to get to this "foodie" go-to in a Kirkland rambler redo; its "deep" wine list has "lots" of *Italiano* "hard-to-finds", and "informed" servers add to the abundant "sense of competence and bonhomie" – so while "not cheap", it is "worth every penny."

Ⓩ Canlis ⑤ *Pacific NW* | 27 | 27 | 27 | VE |

Lake Union | 2576 Aurora Ave. N. (Halladay St., south of Aurora Bridge) | 206-283-3313 | www.canlis.com

"Spoil yourself" royally at this old-schooler that's been the city's "gold-standard" "special-event restaurant" for more than 50 years;

---

* Indicates a tie with restaurant above

the "world-class" Pacific NW food and wine are matched by "million-dollar" Lake Union views from a "chic", and some say "formal", mid-century modern room, and by the "gracious" "how-did-they-know" service that borders on magic; so leave your worries at home, but don't forget to "bring your platinum card."

Z Dahlia Lounge *Pacific NW*

25 | 24 | 23 | E

Downtown | 2001 Fourth Ave. (Virginia St.) | 206-682-4142 | www.tomdouglas.com

Tom Douglas' pricey flagship may be "not as exciting as it once was", but it remains an über-popular "perennial favorite" proffering "delightful" Pacific NW cuisine that riffs on Asian flavors, capped off by the "world's best coconut cream pie" (available to go at Douglas' bakery next door); there's "lots of space" between tables in the "whimsical", "gorgeous" Downtown room, so settle in for a "comfortable sit-down meal" served by a "thoughtful" staff.

Z Herbfarm, The M *Pacific NW*

29 | 26 | 28 | VE

Woodinville | 14590 NE 145th St. (Woodinville-Redmond Rd.) | 425-485-5300 | www.theherbfarm.com

A "once-in-a-lifetime dining experience", the "sublime" cuisine at this "over-the-top" "oasis" – ranked No. 1 for Food and Service – features "vibrant herbs" in a nine-course Pacific NW prix fixe menu (plus paired wines) that changes nightly, delivered by an "impeccable" staff; a "quick tour" of the garden is de rigueur before settling into the "lush" dining room in Woodinville's wine belt, and the bill, while "huge", covers four or five hours of "exquisite" eating; N.B. a new chef took the reins post-Survey.

Il Terrazzo Carmine Z *Italian*

27 | 25 | 26 | E

Pioneer Square | 411 First Ave. S. (bet. Jackson & King Sts.) | 206-467-7797 | www.ilterrazzocarmine.com

"Veal is spoken fluently" at Carmine Smeraldo's "gold standard" Italian, a "classic and classy" Pioneer Square "institution" that's always packed with "politicians" and "power-lunchers" seeking "superb" traditional cuisine; "tucked away" in an office building's courtyard, its "lovely" Tuscan dining room calms the spirit, as does the "flawless" service; all in all, expect to have a "lush, sexy and unsurpassed" experience.

Inn at Langley M *Pacific NW*

27 | 23 | 22 | VE

Langley | Inn at Langley | 400 First St. (Anthes Ave.) | 360-221-3033 | www.innatlangley.com

Not just a meal, an "experience" awaits Seattleites who ferry to this Whidbey Island inn for Matt Costello's "exquisite" and expensive six-course prix fixe that focuses on "fresh, honest" Pacific NW market finds; in the "intimate" kitchen/dining room, gourmands get a gander of the chatty chef at work and may end up so sated that they'll want to "stay the night"; N.B. open only Thursday–Sunday in the summer, and Friday–Sunday the rest of the year.

Kisaku Sushi *Japanese*

27 | 20 | 23 | M

Green Lake | 2101 N. 55th St. (Meridian Ave.) | 206-545-9050 | www.kisaku.com

"You cannot go wrong" when you "let the chef" choose your food at this Green Lake Japanese that sates with a "startling array" of "exceedingly fresh", "creative sushi"; serene decor and "reasonable prices" make this a "favorite", affordable haunt for locals who'd rather keep it their "secret."

Lark ▣ American
27 | 23 | 25 | E

Capitol Hill | 926 12th Ave. (bet. E. Marion & Spring Sts.) | 206-323-5275 | www.larkseattle.com

Sybarites swoon over chef John Sundstrom's "bonanza" of New American small plates prepared with "stellar" "organic" ingredients – and a healthy dose of "love"; some say the "simple" "farmhouse" setting on Capitol Hill can be "uncomfortable" and quibble over tabs that are "too pricey by the ounce", but all agree on the "engaging", "gracious" service; N.B. no reserving means that there's often a line, which patrons wait out at the owners' bar next door.

Le Gourmand ▣▣ French
27 | 22 | 26 | E

Ballard | 425 NW Market St. (6th Ave.) | 206-784-3463

At Bruce and Sara Naftaly's "lovely" French bistro, "fresh herbs grown in the backyard garden" meet traditional Gallic preps that are "extraordinary" even as "you feel your arteries clog"; the "slightly funky, yet charming" Ballard dining room features hand-painted murals and down-filled silk pillows, and the service is "impeccable without being stuffy", making for a "just plain superb" experience.

Maneki ▣ Japanese
27 | 17 | 21 | M

International District | 304 Sixth Ave. S. (bet. Jackson & Main Sts.) | 206-622-2631

The "oldest" Japanese restaurant in Seattle, this "authentic" hideaway tucked into an ID hillside offers "homestyle" "comfort food" alongside what fans consider the "best deal" for "top-quality sushi" in the city, plus a large sake selection; the vintage decor is sweet, but the secret's out, so "you need a reservation, even on Tuesday night."

▣ Metropolitan Grill Steak
26 | 22 | 25 | E

Downtown | 820 Second Ave. (Marion St.) | 206-624-3287 | www.themetropolitangrill.com

This "old-fashioned" Downtown "power scene" is a "perennial favorite" thanks to its "absolutely outstanding" aged steaks (which could "make a cardiologist weep") and "colossal" lobsters; the "manly" 1940s-style dining room has a "classic" feel and the service is "near perfect", so most don't fret the "pricey" tabs – just "loosen your wallet" or "bring the corporate card", since it's "worth every penny and then some."

▣ Mistral ▣▣ American/French
28 | 21 | 26 | VE

Belltown | 113 Blanchard St. (bet. 1st & 2nd Aves.) | 206-770-7799 | www.mistralseattle.com

A "must-stop for any serious gourmet", chef-owner William Belickis' "magical" New American–New French "haute cuisine" haven "could be tops in any city in the country, if not the world"; "decadent" tasting menus provide a "symphony of tastes" set against a "sparse but romantic" Belltown room and service that's "impeccable" – as for the final check, well, "baby, is it a stunner!"

	FOOD	DECOR	SERVICE	COST

Monsoon *Vietnamese* · 27 · 19 · 21 · M

Capitol Hill | 615 19th Ave. E. (bet. Mercer & Roy Sts.) | 206-325-2111 | www.monsoonseattle.com

"Oohs and aahs" erupt from satisfied suppers at Eric and Sophie Banh's "upscale" Capitol Hill Vietnamese venue where the "delight-ful", "complex flavors" "never disappoint"; a "superb" European and American wine list (including some cult pours) wins raves from raters who are split over the "small", "minimalist" room ("beautiful" vs. "feels like the company cafeteria") and sometimes "inattentive" ser-vice, though all advise "don't hesitate to eat here."

Nishino *Japanese* · 27 · 21 · 24 · E

Madison Park | 3130 E. Madison St. (Lake Washington Blvd.) | 206-322-5800 | www.nishinorestaurant.com

For a "nirvanic" experience, sushistas and Seattle movers-and-shakers "let the chefs go crazy" in concocting "fabulous" "omakase" dinners at this "refined, if expensive" Madison Park Japanese; if it seems like "Nobu for half the price", that's because owner Tatsu Nishino is a Nobu Matsuhisa protégé, so it's little surprise that this "spectacular" spot is "the real deal."

Paseo 🆇Ⓜ⇄ *Caribbean* · 27 · 7 · 13 · I

Fremont | 4225 Fremont Ave. N. (bet. 42nd & 43rd Sts.) | 206-545-7440

The "aroma will draw you in" to this "funky" Fremont "shack" proffer-ing "generous" portions of "killer" Cuban sandwiches and Caribbean on the "cheap"; a "cramped" interior includes only a few seats (at the counter, where service is "friendly"), so it's best if you "don't plan on eating in" and opt for takeout; N.B. cash only, no liquor.

Phoenecia at Alki Ⓜ *Mediterranean* · 27 · 16 · 26 · M

West Seattle | 2716 Alki Ave. SW (bet. 60th & 61st Aves.) | 206-935-6550

"Relax, ignore the menu" and let owner Hussein Khazaal "make some-thing very special just for you" at this "hidden" Med "treasure" that turns out "awesome" seafood, "spicy" chicken and "charred flat-breads"; though it can "get expensive", the trade-off is a "great loca-tion" on West Seattle's Alki Beach with "wonderful" Elliott Bay views.

🆉 Restaurant Zoë *American* · 27 · 22 · 25 · E

Belltown | 2137 Second Ave. (Blanchard St.) | 206-256-2060 | www.restaurantzoe.com

There are "no zzzzzzs" at this zesty restaurant joke reviewers, since it's got a "cool beyond cool" Belltown vibe that's "bustling and fun", and the "flawless" New American cuisine boasts "knock-your-socks-off flavors" from "local, fresh ingredients"; "seating is tight" in the slightly "sterile" space, but "personable" "service makes up for it", as do the bar's "delicious" "twists on classic" cocktails.

🆉 Rover's 🆇Ⓜ *French* · 28 · 24 · 27 · VE

Madison Valley | 2808 E. Madison St. (28th Ave.) | 206-325-7442 | www.rovers-seattle.com

Thierry Rautureau's "unparalleled" New French degustation menus (including five- and eight-course options, plus a "stellar" vegetarian version) make this "elegant", "world-class" Madison Valley farm-house a "haven" for appreciative locals and loads of visiting celebri-ties; service that "defines perfection" rounds out the "breathtakingly

	FOOD	DECOR	SERVICE	COST

expensive" "experience"; N.B. à la carte options and Friday lunches can soften the wallet impact.

Shiro's Sushi *Japanese* | 27 | 15 | 21 | E |

Belltown | 2401 Second Ave. (Battery St.) | 206-443-9844 | www.shiros.com

In a "town filled with sushi joints", this "much-touted", "bustling" Belltowner is among "the best", since Kyoto expat Shiro Kashiba cuts "nothing but the freshest" fish (his "knife work is exceptional"), much of it "local"; a $30 tasting menu is a bargain, though sushistas recommend getting the "spendy" "omakase" for maximum "dazzle"; P.S. "no reservations" mean "be prepared to wait."

☒ Sitka & Spruce ⓜ *Eclectic* | 28 | 14 | 18 | M |

Eastlake | 2238 Eastlake Ave. E. (bet. Boston & E. Lynn Sts.) | 206-324-0662 | www.sitkaandspruce.com

This "funky" "strip-mall" storefront in Eastlake is an "unbelievable surprise", turning out "plate-lickingly delicious" food courtesy of chef-owner Matt Dillon, whose "inventive" Eclectic menu features "local" ingredients "you've never tasted" before; the "tiny", "cramped" room "fills up fast", so expect "aggravatingly long waits", plus "shared tables" and service that "could use some polish" – none of which bothers the "haute"-minded foodies who flock here.

Szechuan Chef *Chinese* | 27 | 15 | 18 | I |

Bellevue | Kelsey Creek Ctr. | 15015 Main St. (148th Ave.) | 425-746-9008

"So hot but worth the sweat" pant admirers of the "huge selection" of "fantastic", "fiery" Sichuan fare at this "always wonderful" Chinese "hole-in-the-wall"; it's "easy to miss" in a Bellevue "strip mall", so follow your nose toward the "aroma of deliciousness", and expect the "friendly" service to get the food out "fast."

☒ Wild Ginger *Pacific Rim* | 25 | 23 | 22 | E |

Downtown | 1401 Third Ave. (Union St.) | 206-623-4450 | www.wildginger.net

It's "come a long way" since its start on Western Avenue 18 years ago say the legions who "love" this still-"buzzy", "beautiful" 350-seat Pacific Rim "hot spot" that's once again Seattle's Most Popular restaurant thanks to anthropologist-turned-restaurateur Rick Yoder's "sumptuous" menu of Asian curries, satays and spicy lahksa soups served by an "accommodating" staff; its Downtown digs are "noisy", "crowded" and "over-the-top" decry objectors, yet diners still can't get enough of it, so the lion's share of voters urge even "if you have to wait for a table, do it."

St. Louis

TOP FOOD RANKING

Restaurant	Cuisine
28 Sidney St. Cafe	American
Paul Manno's	Italian
27 Tony's	Italian
Trattoria Marcella	Italian
Niche	American
Al's Restaurant	Seafood/Steak
Dominic's	Italian
Pomme	American/French
26 Crossing, The	American
Annie Gunn's	American
Atlas	French/Italian
Nippon Tei	Asian Fusion
Grill at the Ritz-Carlton	American
Giovanni's	Italian
LoRusso's Cucina	Italian
Chez Leon	French
25 Harvest	American
American Place	American
Cardwell's at the Plaza	American
Pho Grand	Vietnamese
1111 Mississippi	Californian/Italian
Monarch	Eclectic
Anthony's	American

Al's Restaurant 🅂🅼 *Seafood/Steak*   27 | 18 | 26 | E

Downtown | 1200 N. First St. (Biddle St.) | 314-421-6399 |
www.alsrestaurant.net

Although longtime owner Al Baroni has passed away, this "true
St. Louis landmark" ("since 1925") remains "a trip back in time",
an Italian-style chophouse featuring "fabulous steaks, veal" and
seafood that are "worth" both "the dress code" (jackets required
in fall and winter) and the "expense-account" prices; sure, the
"tired but nostalgic" Downtown digs "could use some dusting", but
given the "fantastic" food and service, most folks "don't even
remember the decor."

American Place, An 🅂🅼 *American*   25 | 27 | 23 | E

Downtown | 822 Washington Ave. (bet. 8th & 9th Sts.) | 314-418-5800 |
www.aapstl.com

Rated No. 1 for Decor in St. Louis, this Downtown Traditional
American located "in the former lobby of a historic hotel" boasts a
space whose soaring, 40-ft. ceilings, "marble columns and rich colors"
are "so beautiful, you'll want to eat" the setting, although diners
may wish to nibble instead on chef-owner Larry Forgione's "even
more delicious" dishes; hearty eaters pout about "portions too small
for the prices", but admirers insist this "special-occasion place is
worth the money."

	FOOD	DECOR	SERVICE	COST

☑ Annie Gunn's ▥ *American* | 26 | 21 | 23 | E |

Chesterfield | 16806 Chesterfield Airport Rd. (Baxter Rd.) | 636-532-7684 | www.anniegunns.com

One of "the best West County has to offer" is this Traditional American that's "worth the trip" to Chesterfield for "superb steaks" and "top-notch seafood" from chef "Lou Rook, the genius in the kitchen"; it's "pricey, but you get what you pay for" – "terrific service", a "casual atmosphere" and a "fantastic wine list" – although a few warn that it's also "crowded", making reservations "a must"; P.S. don't forget to "fill up your car with goodies" from the attached Smoke House Market.

Anthony's ▣ *American* | 25 | 21 | 24 | M |

Downtown | 10 S. Broadway (Market St.) | 314-231-7007 | www.tonysstlouis.com

"Exactly what you'd expect from a place run by [one of] St. Louis' premier restaurants", this "pared-down version of Tony's" "across the hall" is "a secret for Downtown workers" who head here for "divine" American food ("the best hamburger in St. Louis") "without all the fuss"; the tiny, "casual", chrome-and-glass "value" is also near to Busch Stadium, making it "fun" "before a game" or "after the Cardinals win!"

Atlas Restaurant ▣▥ *French/Italian* | 26 | 20 | 25 | M |

Midtown | 5513 Pershing Ave. (bet. De Baliviere Ave. & Union Blvd.) | 314-367-6800 | www.atlasrestaurantstl.com

Regulars "hope nobody ever finds out about" Midtown's "true Paris bistro without the jet lag", where the "honest, uncontrived, classic" French and Italian dishes are both "toe-curlingly good" and "a great value"; the seasonal fare (plus a "nice late-night dessert and coffee menu") is enhanced by "warm", "attentive owners", a "thoughtful" staff and a "simple", recently "redesigned interior that's wonderful" and "much more roomy."

Cardwell's at the Plaza *American* | 25 | 22 | 22 | M |

Frontenac | 94 Plaza Frontenac (Clayton Rd. & Lindbergh Blvd.) | 314-997-8885 | www.cardwellsattheplaza.com

"Don't let the mall location fool you": this Plaza Frontenac New American offers "some of St. Louis' finest cooking" in the form of an "exceptionally delicious", "daily changing menu" with "something for everyone", including "amazing vegetarian dishes"; so "dress up" and "stop in after a day of shopping", because given the "beautiful", "well-heeled crowd", there's "no better place to people-watch"; P.S. there's also a "relaxing outdoor area."

Chez Leon ▥ *French* | 26 | 24 | 24 | E |

Central West End | 4580 Laclede Ave. (Euclid Ave.) | 314-361-1589 | www.chezleon.com

"There's something about it that makes me happy" smile supporters of this "authentic" Central West End bistro where a "skillfully executed menu" is paired with "faithfully French decor" that's "so charming, you feel like you're in Paris"; the "lively, inviting atmosphere" comes complete with "fantastic service", sidewalk seating and a pianist on Fridays and Sundays, so "order the Grand Marnier soufflé" and "settle in for the evening"; P.S. the prix fixe menu is a "great value."

	FOOD	DECOR	SERVICE	COST

Crossing, The ⊠ *American* | 26 | 20 | 24 | E |

Clayton | 7823 Forsyth Blvd. (Central Ave.) | 314-721-7375 |
www.thecrossingstl.com

Chef-owner Jim Fiala delivers one of "the finest dining experiences in St. Louis" at this Clayton New American offering a "continually updated" selection of "innovative, delicious" dishes "with French and Italian influences" ("the tasting menu with wine flights is the way to go"); "unmemorable decor" gives nitpickers pause, but most agree it's an "intimate", "charming environment" with "seamless" "service to match", hence fans "never come away with anything but a giant smile."

Dominic's ⊠ *Italian* | 27 | 23 | 26 | E |

The Hill | 5101 Wilson Ave. (Hereford St.) | 314-771-1632

"Old-world charm meets fine Italian cuisine" at this "all-around wonderful", family-owned "classic" that's "a must on the Hill" for its "outstanding, authentic" fare and "extremely attentive", "personal tableside service"; entering the "dimly lit, romantic" space is "like stepping back in time", and its "elegant", "classy" decor makes it a "favorite" "for special occasions and business dinners."

⊅ 1111 Mississippi ⊠ *Californian/Italian* | 25 | 25 | 23 | M |

Lafayette Square | 1111 Mississippi Ave. (Chouteau Ave.) | 314-241-9999 |
www.1111-m.com

"A cornerstone in the Lafayette Square revival", this "trendy" spot located in a "renovated warehouse" offers an "interesting menu" of Tuscan-Californian cuisine, keeping "an emphasis on fresh provisions", "variety and quality" but "without pretension"; the "multilevel interior" can get "noisy, but who cares" counter fans who focus instead on the "meticulous service", "superbly cultivated wine list" and patio seating; P.S. the "gooey butter cake is a must-try!"

Giovanni's on the Hill ⊠ *Italian* | 26 | 22 | 25 | E |

The Hill | 5201 Shaw Ave. (Marconi Ave.) | 314-772-5958 |
www.giovannisonthehill.com

"Take a special someone" to this "remarkable" "institution" on the Hill that "deserves its reputation as one of the finest restaurants" in the area due to its "truly exceptional", "classic" Italian cuisine, "top-quality service" from a "tuxedoed" staff and "decor that reminds you of a palace"; it's an "excellent choice for a romantic night on the town" – the "place to get engaged!" – but as much as the "food will amaze you, so will the bill."

Grill at the Ritz-Carlton, The *American* | 26 | 26 | 27 | E |

Clayton | Ritz-Carlton Hotel | 100 Carondelet Plaza (Hanley Rd.) |
314-863-6300 | www.ritz-carlton.com

"It's a Ritz, and it lives up to expectations" enthuse admirers of this hotel dining "oasis" voted No. 1 for Service in the St. Louis area, where a "downright incredible" staff that's "second to none" "makes you feel important" as you indulge in "utterly sublime", "inventive" New American food; the "quiet", "beautiful" setting is "perfect for a special evening" or "business lunch", and while "the price will leave you shocked", it's "worth it."

Harvest ▣ American
25 | 23 | 24 | E

Richmond Heights | 1059 S. Big Bend Blvd. (Clayton Rd.) | 314-645-3522 | www.harveststlouis.com

This "fabulous" Richmond Heights restaurant is "worth checking out every few months" for some of "the most creative cooking in St. Louis" courtesy of a "seasonally changing menu" that "incorporates regional, market-ready ingredients" into "adventurous takes on [New] American cuisine"; the "cozy", "rustic atmosphere" and "wonderful service" are "exceeded only by the wine list", although a few sweet tooths find "the bread pudding alone" reason enough to go.

LoRusso's Cucina ▣ Italian
26 | 20 | 24 | M

The Hill | 3121 Watson Rd. (Arsenal St.) | 314-647-6222 | www.lorussos.com

"The snob appeal is low and the food appeal is high" at this "excellent" veteran Italian on "the edge of the Hill", where chef-owner "Rich LoRusso wins over a loyal clientele with his delicious" "menu that's authentic but still manages to feel fresh" via a "range of standard pastas and innovative dishes"; a recently expanded space now matches the "ample portions", while "excellent service", a "welcoming" ambiance and a "decent wine list" add up to "a well-rounded experience."

Monarch ❶▣ Eclectic
25 | 25 | 23 | E

Maplewood | 7401 Manchester Rd. (Sutton Ave.) | 314-644-3995 | www.monarchrestaurant.com

"After just a few years", this Maplewood "delight" has emerged as "one of St. Louis' top restaurants" thanks to chef-"magician" Brian Hale's "adventurous" Eclectic cuisine; the "delicious" dishes are "anchored by a killer wine list" and served by "a staff that makes anyone feel special" in three "dramatic" spaces: a "gorgeous" dining room with "stunning prints of butterfly wings" on the walls, a more "casual bistro" and a "wonderful wine bar"; nevertheless, a few fret about "inconsistent food" and "hefty prices."

❷ Niche ▣ American
27 | 25 | 24 | M

Benton Park | 1831 Sidney St. (I-55) | 314-773-7755 | www.nichestlouis.com

"Bringing great food and an enjoyable ambiance together", this "welcome newcomer" in Benton Park offers a "short" "but top-notch" menu of "flawless", "cutting-edge" New American cuisine in a "sleek, modern" setting that "makes you feel chic"; meanwhile, "outstanding service" and a "fabulous value" of a three-course $30 prix fixe meal "make it a delight on every visit"; N.B. a late-night dessert and wine menu is served until 1:30 AM on Fridays and Saturdays.

Nippon Tei ▣ Asian Fusion
26 | 21 | 20 | M

Ballwin | 14025 Manchester Rd. (Weidmann Rd.) | 636-386-8999

Delivering "some of the best sushi in town" ("the fish is the freshest, or it's not served"), this Japanese–Asian fusion in suburban Ballwin also draws praise for its "excellent" entrees, including tableside sukiyaki and shabu-shabu; "don't be fooled by the strip-mall location" – it's actually "very elegant" – but do "take your time and enjoy" the "artistic presentations" and "well-trained" service; P.S. "make sure you have reservations", as it can "get crowded."

	FOOD	DECOR	SERVICE	COST

⚡ Paul Manno's ⬛ *Italian*   28 | 18 | 24 | M

Chesterfield | 75 Forum Shopping Ctr. (Woods Mill Rd.) |
314-878-1274

"Skip the Hill" and head to this veteran Italian "hidden" in a
Chesterfield strip mall, where the "marvelous", "authentic"
Sicilian fare is "just like mama used to make, because mama is still
in the kitchen"; an "attentive staff" provides "impeccable service",
while owner Paul Manno "loves to make his customers happy";
but a "small" dining room means you "sometimes have to
wait" and then "eat elbow-to-elbow" – so do yourself a favor and
"don't tell anyone."

Pho Grand   *Vietnamese*   25 | 17 | 21 | I

South City | 3195 S. Grand Blvd. (Wyoming St.) | 314-664-7435 |
www.phogrand.com

Providing that "rare experience where you actually get much more
than what you pay for", this South Grand Boulevard Vietnamese is de-
clared "best in class" for its "huge menu" of "exceptional", "fresh",
"well-prepared food" at "downright economical" prices; the "tantalizing" dishes are served by a "welcoming", "efficient staff" that helps to
distract from "nothing-special decor."

Pomme ⬛Ⓜ *American/French*   27 | 22 | 25 | E

Clayton | 40 N. Central Ave. (bet. Forsyth Blvd. & Maryland Ave.) |
314-727-4141 | www.pommerestaurant.com

For "inventive cuisine that's always satisfying" and "executed with
care", take a detour to this "intimate" Clayton venue where chef-
owner Bryan Carr delivers "big flavor" via "fresh, innovative, seasonal"
New French–New American cuisine that "uses only the best ingredients"; it's "great for a date or quiet dinner", with a "comfortable atmosphere" that's enhanced by "attentive service" and a "thoughtful wine
list"; nevertheless, a handful harrumph about portions that are "modest given the prices."

⚡ Sidney Street Cafe ⬛Ⓜ *American*   28 | 23 | 26 | E

Benton Park | 2000 Sidney St. (Salena St.) | 314-771-5777 |
www.sidneystreetcafe.com

Rated No. 1 for Food and Popularity in St. Louis, this Benton Park
"standard for others to follow" is a "perennial favorite" proffering a
"superb", "inventive" array of "universally wonderful" New American
cuisine; the "friendly", "knowledgeable" servers recite "from chalkboard menus" "with appetizing flair", while the "inviting" and "romantic atmosphere" proves "perfect for business, dates or special
occasions"; nevertheless, "for such fine dining", regulars recommend
"calling weeks in advance for a reservation."

⚡ Tony's ⬛ *Italian*   27 | 24 | 27 | E

Downtown | 410 Market St. (B'way St.) | 314-231-7007 |
www.tonysstlouis.com

It's "still the best special-occasion restaurant in St. Louis" sigh
supporters of this Downtown "treasure" that "lives up to its reputation" via "impeccable" Italian cuisine and "professional servers"
who "anticipate your every need"; an "elegant ambiance" and "attention to detail" make this "a class act" for most, although modernists

maintain it can be "a bit old-fashioned" (jackets are required) and cite "high prices."

⚡ **Trattoria Marcella** ⚠️Ⓜ️ *Italian*   27 | 20 | 25 | M

South City | 3600 Watson Rd. (Pernod Ave.) | 314-352-7706 | www.trattoriamarcella.com

"Sometimes the labor of love that goes into a restaurant is so palpable you can taste it in the food" fawn fans of this "vibrant", "convivial" South Side Italian where "always remarkable", "reasonably priced" fare ("risotto to dream about") is served by a "friendly, gracious staff"; "now that they've expanded, you can get a seat" in the still-"cramped" space, although a nostalgic few feel it "lost a little of its ambiance" in the process.

Washington, DC

TOP FOOD RANKING

	Restaurant	Cuisine
29	Inn at Little Washington	American
28	Makoto	Japanese
	Citronelle	French
	Marcel's	Belgian/French
27	Eve	American
	2941 Restaurant	American
	Ray's The Steaks	Steak
	L'Auberge Chez François	French
	Obelisk	Italian
	Le Paradou	French
	Prime Rib	Steak
	Seasons	American
26	CityZen	American
	Kinkead's	Seafood
	Palena	American
	Tosca	Italian
	Thai Square	Thai

NEW Café du Parc French

`-` `-` `-` `M`

Downtown | Willard InterContinental Washington | 1401 Pennsylvania Ave. NW (bet. 14th & 15th Sts.) | 202-942-7000 | www.cafeduparc.com

The White House is just a bonbon's toss away from the Willard InterContinental's handsome double-decker French bistro, where the menus were designed by one of France's top toques, consulting chef Antoine Westermann; its cafe tables, overlooking Pennsylvania Avenue's Pershing Park, are an ideal perch for people-watching.

Z Citronelle French

`28` `25` `26` `VE`

(aka Michel Richard's Citronelle)

Georgetown | Latham Hotel | 3000 M St. NW (30th St.) | 202-625-2150 | www.citronelledc.com

Georgetown's "Washington monument" for "visiting dignitaries" is chef-owner Michel Richard's "extraordinary" New French, where "sterling ingredients, a sure hand and a dollop of whimsy" (try the "breakfast" dessert, a "masterwork of trompe l'oeil") make it "the best DC has to offer"; get a table near the see-in kitchen to watch the "fun", then relax in the "lovely" modern space and be "spoiled" by an "impeccable" staff; P.S. the lofty prices match the "high caliber", but both the bar/lounge and terrace offer a more casual menu.

CityZen ⊠Ⓜ American

`26` `26` `25` `VE`

SW | Mandarin Oriental | 1330 Maryland Ave. SW (12th St. SW) | 202-787-6006 | www.cityzenrestaurant.com

For "New York chic" in a "government town" head to this New American "extravaganza" in the "plush" Mandarin Oriental in SW; its "sleek" look, with an open kitchen, a wall of flames in the bar and lots of steel, leather

FOOD	DECOR	SERVICE	COST

and wood, suits the "fashionable" enthusiasts of its "glorious" tasting menus, "attractive wine list" and "creative" details like the "fantastic mini–Parker House rolls"; add in a "personable" staff and you might want to remember this "flawless operation" "for birthdays and anniversaries."

ⓩ Eve, Restaurant Ⓢ *American*

| 27 | 24 | 25 | VE |

Old Town | 110 S. Pitt St. (bet. King & Prince Sts.) | Alexandria, VA | 703-706-0450 | www.restauranteve.com

"Save the superlatives" for this Old Town Alexandria New American "foodie paradise", where Irish-born chef-owner Cathal Armstrong's "creative insights into flavors" transform "interesting ingredients" (tripe as well as foie gras) into "mind-blowing" meals with "memorable" matches of wine; "knowledgeable" staffers "treat you like VIPs", and you can choose among its "romantic bistro", "happening bar" or tasting room where the "beautiful dance of waiters" is "worth every penny"; since "none of the faces of Eve disappoint", she's a "tough" reservation.

Farrah Olivia Ⓜ *American*

| - | - | - | E |

Old Town | 600 Franklin St. (S. Washington St.) | Alexandria, VA | 703-778-2233 | www.farraholiviarestaurant.com

This elegant Old Town Alexandria destination provides a white-tablecloth setting for distinctive New American cuisine that features influences from France and from chef-owner Morou Ouattara's native Ivory Coast; coconut-shell rings that hang from the ceiling enliven the sophisticated, neutral-toned room.

ⓩ Inn at Little Washington *American*

| 29 | 28 | 28 | VE |

Washington | The Inn at Little Washington | 309 Middle St. (Main St.), VA | 540-675-3800 | www.theinnatlittlewashington.com

"Heaven on earth" is found in the VA countryside at this "romantic" "mecca of fine dining" that scores a triple: a No. 1 rating for Food, Decor and Service; its loyalists find a "gourmand's paradise" that features the "best" New American cuisine, a setting that's a "treat for the eyes" and "choreographed" "masterful service" that makes you "feel coddled from the moment" you pull in; everything from the "exquisite" amuse-bouche to the "hilarious" "cow-shaped mooing cheese cart" "exceeds expectations" – but, of course, "perfection doesn't come cheap."

ⓩ Jaleo *Spanish*

| 23 | 20 | 19 | M |

Penn Quarter | 480 Seventh St. NW (E St.) | 202-628-7949 ⓓ
Bethesda | 7271 Woodmont Ave. (Elm St.), MD | 301-913-0003
Crystal City | 2250A Crystal Dr. (23rd St. S.) | Arlington, VA | 703-413-8181
www.jaleo.com

Invite your amigos to "nibble the evening away" on "tantalizing", "imaginative" yet "authentic" Spanish tapas with "never-ending sangria to wash it all down" at this trio of "crowd-pleasers"; they're a "loud", "chaotic" "fiesta", and they're among the "few places where 'small plate' does not equal 'large bill'"; P.S. beware of "long waits", as they take only a limited number of reservations.

ⓩ Kinkead's *Seafood*

| 26 | 21 | 24 | E |

Foggy Bottom | 2000 Pennsylvania Ave. NW (I St.) | 202-296-7700 | www.kinkead.com

"The perfect catch" for "seafood-inside-the-Beltway power dining", Bob Kinkead's Foggy Bottom "classic", rated the DC Survey's Most Popular, "easily holds its own with newer pretenders to the throne", serving "glistening" fin fare "inventively prepared" in quarters filled with "celebs and politicos"; it has a "can't-miss location" – a "short walk from the White House" and an "easy trip" to the Kennedy Center – and while the service is generally "meticulous", it's probably "best in the company of a VIP."

L'Auberge Chez François Ⓜ French | 27 | 26 | 27 | VE |

Great Falls | 332 Springvale Rd. (Beach Mill Rd.), VA | 703-759-3800 | www.laubergechezfrancois.com

"Special occasions" are made "memorable" at this "universally beloved" "rustic" Alsatian in a "magical" country setting in Great Falls that takes you to "pastoral" France; the "excellent" French fare is served by a staff that makes you "feel loved and taken care of" whether you're enjoying the "fireplace warmth" in winter or the garden "on a lovely summer night", so overall many find it a "top value."

Le Paradou Ⓩ French | 27 | 25 | 24 | VE |

Penn Quarter | 678 Indiana Ave. NW (bet. 6th & 7th Sts.) | 202-347-6780 | www.leparadou.net

"Brilliant" chef Yannick Cam "has done it again" at this "unique and exquisite" New French Penn Quarter eatery that's risen to DC's "top echelon"; the "out-of-this-world" tasting menu can be paired with bottles from an "amazing wine bible" in a "sublime setting", presided over by "professional" (if sometimes "haughty") help; devotees are surprised it's "easy to get into", but that's probably because a meal here could cost "more than your mortgage payment"; N.B. prix fixe lunch and dinner options make its luxury more affordable.

Ⓩ Makoto Ⓜ Japanese | 28 | 21 | 27 | E |

Palisades | 4822 MacArthur Blvd. NW (U St.) | 202-298-6866

"Take off your shoes" and time travel "back to the 19th century" when you enter this "shoebox"-size Palisades eatery, reminiscent of a Kyoto "ryokan" (rustic inn) that feels "more Japanese than today's Japan"; its highlights include "exquisite", "authentic" omakase meals that are "almost too pretty to eat" and "witty sushi chefs" who create "a wonderful meal at the bar"; it's just the "uncomfortable" box seats that annoy.

Ⓩ Marcel's Belgian/French | 28 | 24 | 27 | VE |

West End | 2401 Pennsylvania Ave. NW (24th St.) | 202-296-1166 | www.marcelsdc.com

"A class act" from the "exquisitely prepared" Belgian-French fare to the "first-rate" staff to the "door-to-door" sedan service to the Kennedy Center, this West End fine-dining venue oozes ambiance; chef-owner Robert Wiedmaier's cooking, including a "wonderful" pre-theater prix fixe, "makes your heart sing" (and the cash register ring) with selections like the "best boudin blanc (sausage) in the city"; but lovers beware, when it gets "loud" it's "not the place for intimacy."

Obelisk Ⓩ Ⓜ Italian | 27 | 20 | 25 | VE |

Dupont Circle | 2029 P St. NW (bet. 20th & 21st Sts.) | 202-872-1180

"Fanatic" chef-owner Peter Pastan "keeps you focused on the finest Italian in the city" at his "intimate" Dupont Circle space; connoisseurs swear his daily changing prix fixe menu "could pass a blind taste test" with Italy's "best", and the "unique" dishes are "prepared and served by people who clearly respect food" and want to "take very good care

	FOOD	DECOR	SERVICE	COST

of you"; just remember to reserve "well in advance" if you want to "spend an evening with your true love" in this 30-seat room.

Palena ☒Ⓜ️ *American* | 26 | 22 | 22 | E |

Cleveland Park | 3529 Connecticut Ave. NW (bet. Ordway & Porter Sts.) | 202-537-9250 | www.palenarestaurant.com

Have "a night to remember" with "all-around excellence in food, wine and service" at this "casual" Cleveland Park New American, "whether supping in the bar"/cafe or dining in the "quieter and more romantic" formal space in back; "if you can get reservations", you'll be amazed at chef-owner Frank Ruta's "superbly prepared" "twists on classics" and his "ambitious" "attention to detail" from the "house-cured" charcuterie to the "produce from his garden."

Prime Rib ☒ *Steak* | 27 | 24 | 26 | E |

Golden Triangle | 2020 K St. NW (bet. 20th & 21st Sts.) | 202-466-8811 | www.theprimerib.com

"Swanky and all dressed up", this black-lacquered "old-fashioned supper club" in Golden Triangle is the quintessential spot to celebrate anniversaries or "close a big deal" over "massive cuts of buttery, beefy, masculine prime rib", the "most succulent" crab and "perfect" martinis brought by "impeccable" tuxedoed waiters; it's still a "powerhouse scene" where "high-profile politicians" "wine and dine", but even sentimentalists say the leopard-print rug can "be retired to a '70s time capsule."

Ray's The Steaks *Steak* | 27 | 10 | 22 | E |

Courthouse | Colonial Vill. | 1725 Wilson Blvd. (bet. Quinn & Rhodes Sts.) | Arlington, VA | 703-841-7297

Chef-owner/butcher Mike 'Ray' Landrum is "a genius with a side of cow" – and the "no-frills ambiance" at his "bare-bones" meatery in an Arlington strip mall near the Courthouse metro "keeps the price down" for "some of the best red meat you'll eat anywhere", "cooked to perfection" and complemented by a "thoughtful, gently priced wine list"; still, "come early", as they don't take reservations; N.B. expect a move to more spacious quarters in Clarendon by the end of 2008.

Seasons *American* | 27 | 25 | 27 | E |

Georgetown | Four Seasons Hotel | 2800 Pennsylvania Ave. NW (28th St.) | 202-944-2000 | www.fourseasons.com

The Georgetown Four Seasons' "high standards pay off" at its New American restaurant where the "out-of-this-world" fare, "quiet ambiance, terrific service and tables spaced so that you're not afraid to tell the person you're with what you're thinking" draw a "diplomatic and senior policy crowd"; it's "*the* business hotel in DC", so "having breakfast anywhere else before you've been elected (or after you've been impeached) is just plain silly", plus there's a "mind-boggling" weekend brunch.

ⓩ TenPenh ☒ *Pan-Asian* | 24 | 24 | 23 | E |

Downtown | 1001 Pennsylvania Ave. NW (10th St.) | 202-393-4500 | www.tenpenh.com

"Everyone looks beautiful" at this Downtowner, and "the food is just as pretty": a "killer menu of tongue-tingling favorites" from chef Jeff Tunks "pushes the Pan-Asian envelope without straying into truly rebellious territory", and the "dramatic, colorful atmosphere" is as "stylish" as its crowd; even though pensive types pout it "gets really loud" and the "tables are too close together", seasoned vets say the "biggest problem will be getting past the appetizers" – they're the "winners."

Thai Square *Thai*　　26 | 10 | 18 | I

Arlington | 3217 Columbia Pike (S. Highland St.), VA | 703-685-7040 | www.thaisquarerestaurant.com

"Hot means hot for a change" at this "authentic" Arlington "hole-in-the-wall" "where Thais go for Thai food"; it "doesn't put on airs, decorwise" – the "space is cramped" and service can be "surly" – but "in terms of pricing and quality" "no other place can match" the "exciting blend of texture and flavors" in the "simply wonderful" dishes.

Tosca ☒ *Italian*　　26 | 23 | 25 | E

Penn Quarter | 1112 F St. NW (bet. 11th & 12th Sts.) | 202-367-1990 | www.toscadc.com

Celebrated for "inventive modern interpretations of Northern Italian", this "understated and elegant" Penn Quarterite is set in a "serene, monochromatic" space that's usually "buzzing with 'heavy hitters'"; it "always lives up" to "expectations of the highest quality in food and service" with "amazing dishes and beautiful presentations", but it can be a "somewhat expensive date" unless you opt for the "absolute steal" $35 pre-theater three-course dinner.

2941 Restaurant *American*　　27 | 28 | 25 | VE

Falls Church | 2941 Fairview Park Dr. (off I-495), VA | 703-270-1500 | www.2941.com

"Manhattan meets the Beltway in this surprisingly sophisticated suburban enclave" set in a Falls Church office park, where "wonderful" French-inflected New American is served in "gorgeous" tall-windowed dining rooms overlooking koi ponds and waterfalls; chef-owner Jonathan Krinn "architects flavors masterfully", pairs them "excellently" with wines and has them served by a "gracious, pampering" staff; but with all those "generous" end-of-meal goodies (chocolates, cotton candy), you'll wonder "does 2941 refer to the bill or the calories from the extra desserts?"

NEW Westend Bistro by Eric Ripert *American*　　– | – | – | M

West End | Ritz-Carlton Hotel | 1190 22nd St. NW (M St.) | 202-974-4900 | www.westendbistrodc.com

At this signature eatery in The Ritz-Carlton, sleek environs glowing with gold leaf and seductive lighting set the stage for Eric Ripert's (of NYC's acclaimed Le Bernardin) take on classic French and American fare prepared by Le Bernardin's former sous-chef Leonardo Marino; while there's no tablecloth formality here, there are several secluded booths for private conversations – after all, this is DC.

☒ Zaytinya ● *Mediterranean/Mideastern*　　25 | 25 | 20 | M

Penn Quarter | Pepco Bldg. | 701 Ninth St. NW (G St.) | 202-638-0800 | www.zaytinya.com

"Stunning, sleek white walls provide a dramatic background for a buzzing crowd" at this "fabulous" "fast-paced" Penn Quarter "meze heaven" where an "epic menu" of Med–Middle Eastern (Turkish, Greek and Lebanese) "unique" small plates encourages "sharing", and a "knowledgeable staff keeps it from being overwhelming"; its "divine" "big-city atmosphere" (one of the "best-looking restaurants in town"), "excellent" prices and limited reservations can make "tables hard to come by."

ALPHABETICAL PAGE INDEX

CITY ABBREVIATIONS

AMS	Amsterdam	MAD	Madrid
AT	Atlanta	MI	Miami
ATH	Athens	MIL	Milan
BA	Baltimore	MON	Montréal
BAR	Barcelona	MOS	Moscow
BEI	Beijing	MUN	Munich
BER	Berlin	NO	New Orleans
BO	Boston	NY	New York City
BRU	Brussels	OR	Orlando
BUD	Budapest	OSA	Osaka
CH	Chicago	PAR	Paris
COP	Copenhagen	PB	Palm Beach
DC	Washington, DC	PH	Philadelphia
DEN	Denver Area	PRA	Prague
DF	Dallas/Ft. Worth	PS	Phoenix/Scottsdale
DUB	Dublin	ROM	Rome
FLO	Florence	SD	San Diego
FRA	Frankfurt	SE	Seattle
GEN	Geneva	SF	San Francisco Area
HAM	Hamburg	SHA	Shanghai
HK	Hong Kong	SL	St. Louis
HO	Honolulu	STO	Stockholm
HS	Houston	TOK	Tokyo
IST	Istanbul	TOR	Toronto
KC	Kansas City	VAN	Vancouver
LA	Los Angeles	VEN	Venice
LIS	Lisbon	VIE	Vienna
LON	London	WAR	Warsaw
LV	Las Vegas	ZUR	Zurich

Z indicates places with the highest ratings, popularity and importance.

subscribe to ZAGAT.com

subscribe to ZAGAT.com

subscribe to ZAGAT.com

subscribe to ZAGAT.com

Wine Vintage Chart

This chart, based on our 0 to 30 scale, is designed to help you select wine. The ratings (by **Howard Stravitz,** a law professor at the University of South Carolina) reflect the vintage quality and the wine's readiness to drink. We exclude the 1991–1993 vintages because they are not that good. A dash indicates the wine is either past its peak or too young to rate. Loire ratings are for dry white wines.

Whites

	88	89	90	94	95	96	97	98	99	00	01	02	03	04	05	06
French:																
Alsace	-	25	25	24	23	23	22	25	23	25	27	25	22	24	25	-
Burgundy	-	23	22	-	28	27	24	22	26	25	24	27	23	27	26	24
Loire Valley	-	-	-	-	-	-	-	-	-	24	25	26	23	24	27	24
Champagne	24	26	29	-	26	27	24	23	24	24	22	26	-	-	-	-
Sauternes	29	25	28	-	21	23	25	23	24	24	28	25	26	21	26	23
California:																
Chardonnay	-	-	-	-	-	-	-	-	24	23	26	26	25	27	29	25
Sauvignon Blanc	-	-	-	-	-	-	-	-	-	-	27	28	26	27	26	27
Austrian:																
Grüner Velt./ Riesling	-	-	-	-	25	21	26	26	25	22	23	25	26	25	26	-
German:	25	26	27	24	23	26	25	26	23	21	29	27	24	26	28	-

Reds

	88	89	90	94	95	96	97	98	99	00	01	02	03	04	05	06
French:																
Bordeaux	23	25	29	22	26	25	23	25	24	29	26	24	25	24	27	25
Burgundy	-	24	26	-	26	27	25	22	27	22	24	27	25	25	27	25
Rhône	26	28	28	24	26	22	25	27	26	27	26	-	25	24	25	-
Beaujolais	-	-	-	-	-	-	-	-	-	24	-	23	25	22	28	26
California:																
Cab./Merlot	-	-	28	29	27	25	28	23	26	22	27	26	25	24	24	23
Pinot Noir	-	-	-	-	-	-	24	23	24	23	27	28	26	25	24	-
Zinfandel	-	-	-	-	-	-	-	-	-	-	25	23	27	24	23	-
Oregon:																
Pinot Noir	-	-	-	-	-	-	-	-	-	-	27	25	26	27	-	
Italian:																
Tuscany	-	-	25	22	24	20	29	24	27	24	27	20	25	25	22	24
Piedmont	-	27	27	-	23	26	27	26	25	28	27	20	24	25	26	-
Spanish:																
Rioja	-	-	-	26	26	24	25	22	25	24	27	20	24	25	26	24
Ribera del Duero/Priorat	-	-	-	26	26	27	25	24	25	24	27	20	24	26	26	24
Australian:																
Shiraz/Cab.	-	-	-	24	26	23	26	28	24	24	27	27	25	26	24	-
Chilean:	-	-	-	-	-	-	24	-	25	23	26	24	25	24	26	-